LAND
OF THE
LUSTROUS
6

HARUKO ICHIKAWA

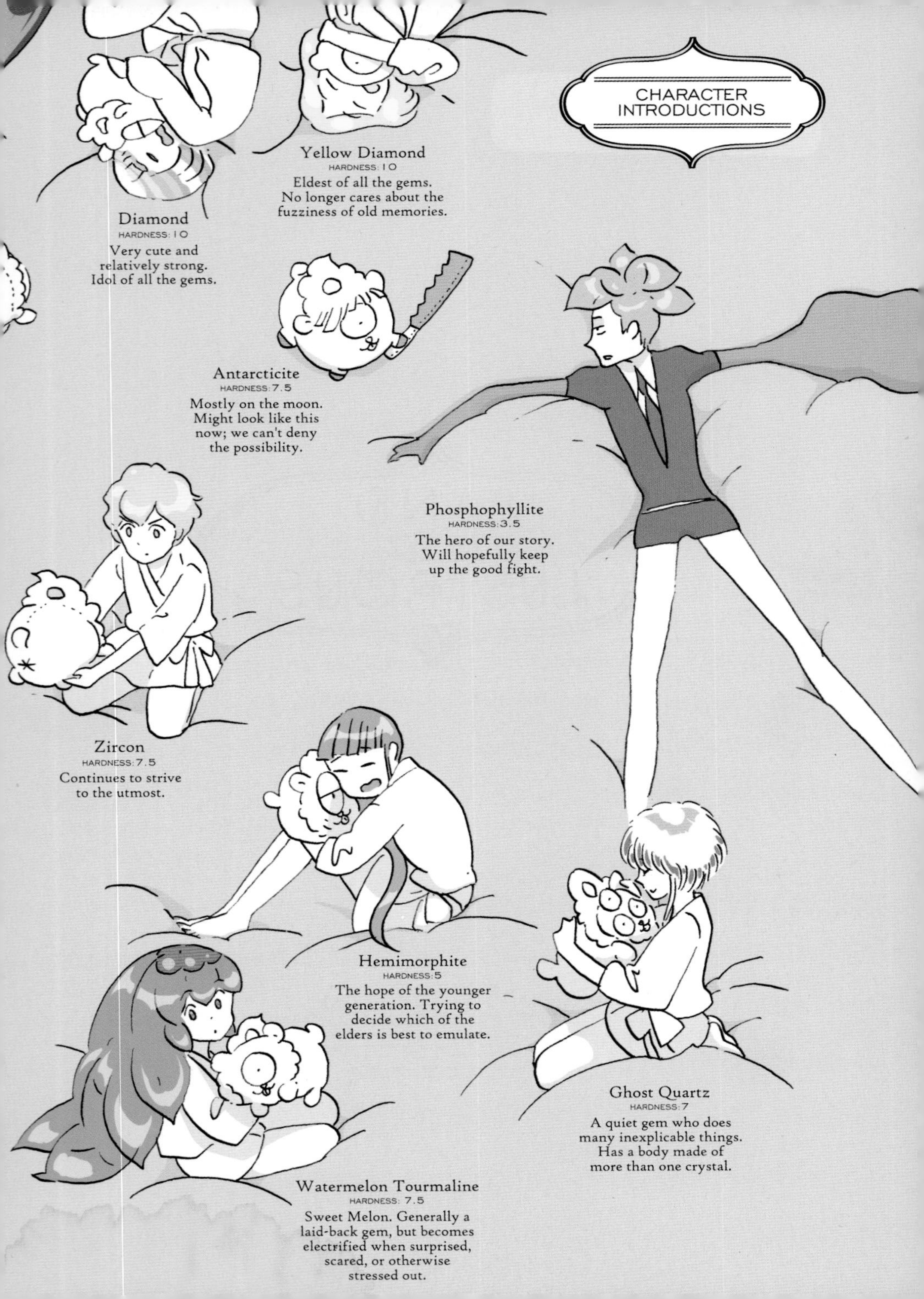
CHARACTER INTRODUCTIONS
Yellow Diamond
HARDNESS: 10
Eldest of all the gems. No longer cares about the fuzziness of old memories.
Diamond
HARDNESS: 10
Very cute and relatively strong. Idol of all the gems.
Antarcticite
HARDNESS: 7.5
Mostly on the moon. Might look like this now; we can't deny the possibility.
Phosphophyllite
HARDNESS: 3.5
The hero of our story. Will hopefully keep up the good fight.
Zircon
HARDNESS: 7.5
Continues to strive to the utmost.
Hemimorphite
HARDNESS: 5
The hope of the younger generation. Trying to decide which of the elders is best to emulate.
Ghost Quartz
HARDNESS: 7
A quiet gem who does many inexplicable things. Has a body made of more than one crystal.
Watermelon Tourmaline
HARDNESS: 7.5
Sweet Melon. Generally a laid-back gem, but becomes electrified when surprised, scared, or otherwise stressed out.

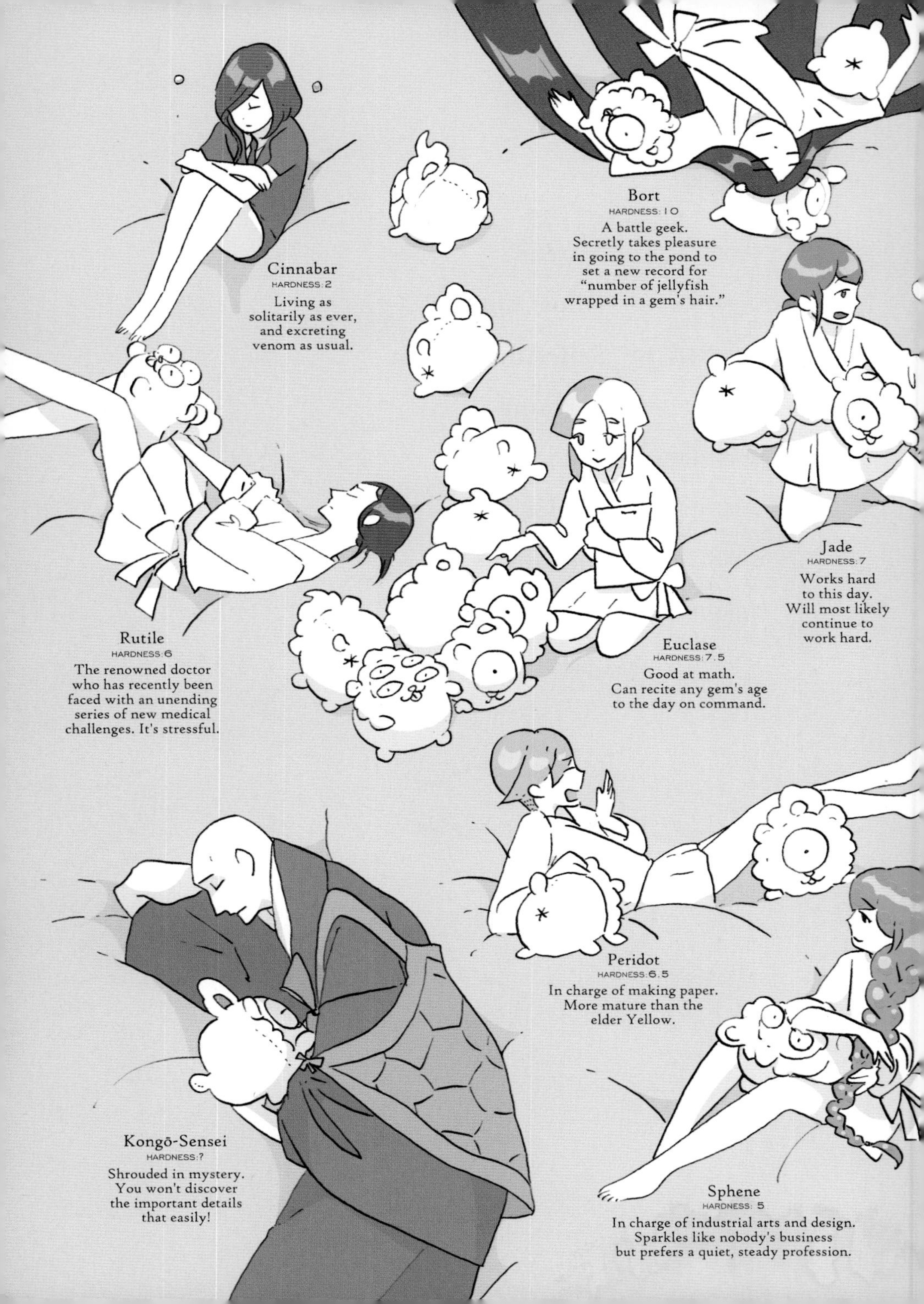
Bort
HARDNESS: 10
A battle geek. Secretly takes pleasure in going to the pond to set a new record for "number of jellyfish wrapped in a gem's hair."
Cinnabar
HARDNESS: 2
Living as solitarily as ever, and excreting venom as usual.
Jade
HARDNESS: 7
Works hard to this day. Will most likely continue to work hard.
Euclase
HARDNESS: 7.5
Good at math. Can recite any gem's age to the day on command.
Rutile
HARDNESS: 6
The renowned doctor who has recently been faced with an unending series of new medical challenges. It's stressful.
Peridot
HARDNESS: 6.5
In charge of making paper. More mature than the elder Yellow.
Sphene
HARDNESS: 5
In charge of industrial arts and design. Sparkles like nobody's business but prefers a quiet, steady profession.
Kongō-Sensei
HARDNESS: ?
Shrouded in mystery. You won't discover the important details that easily!

CONTENTS

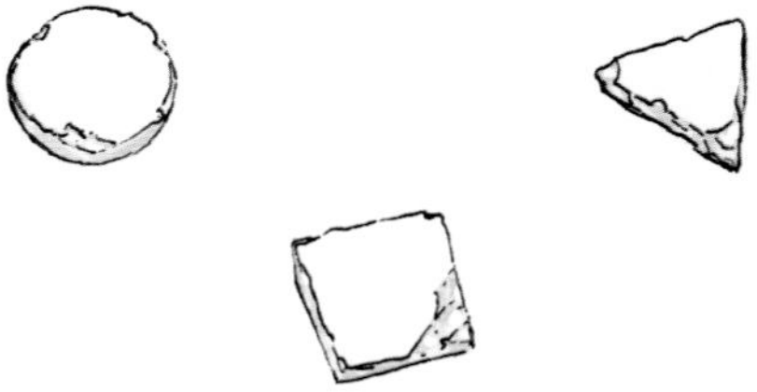

CHAPTER 37: Instead

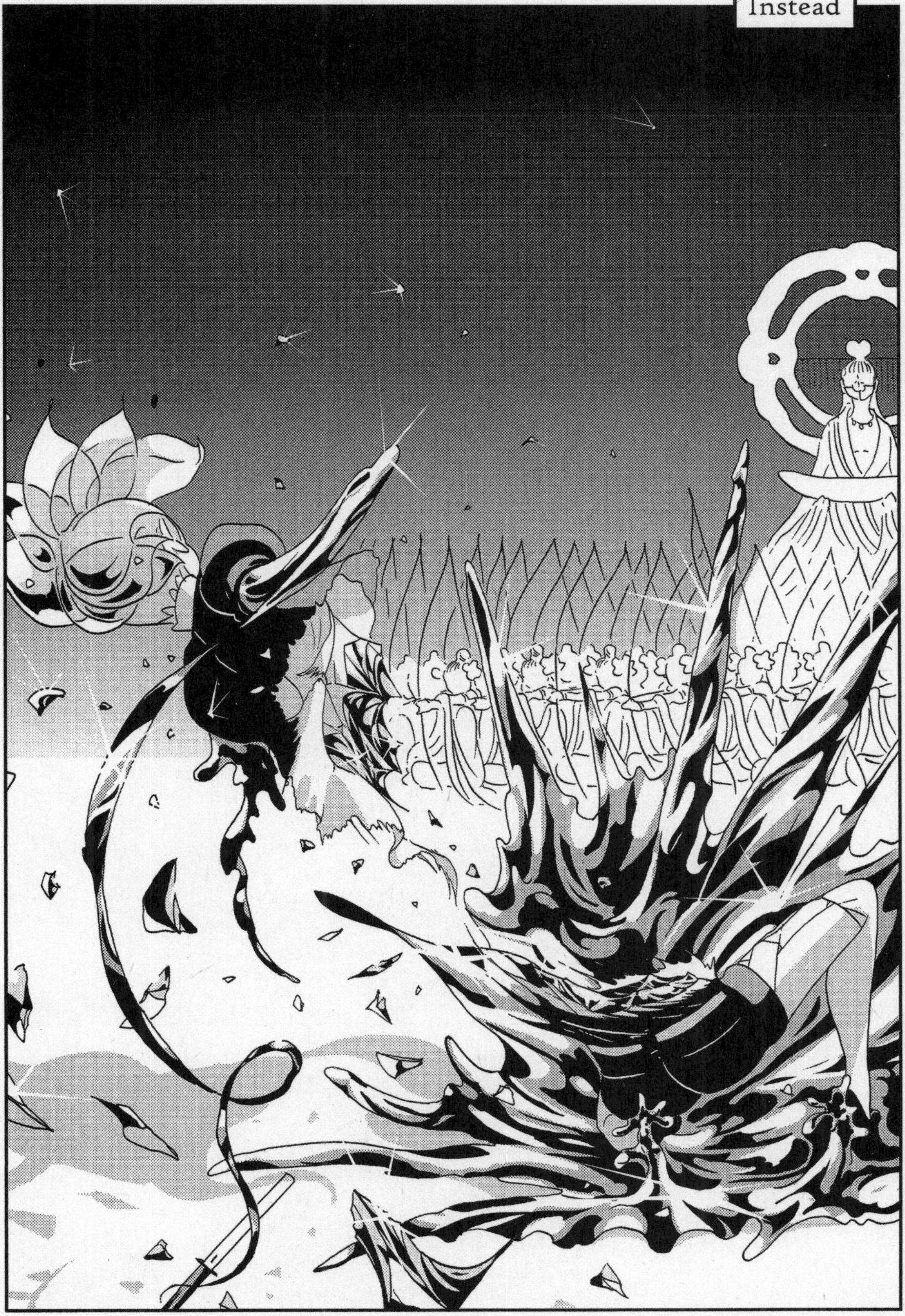

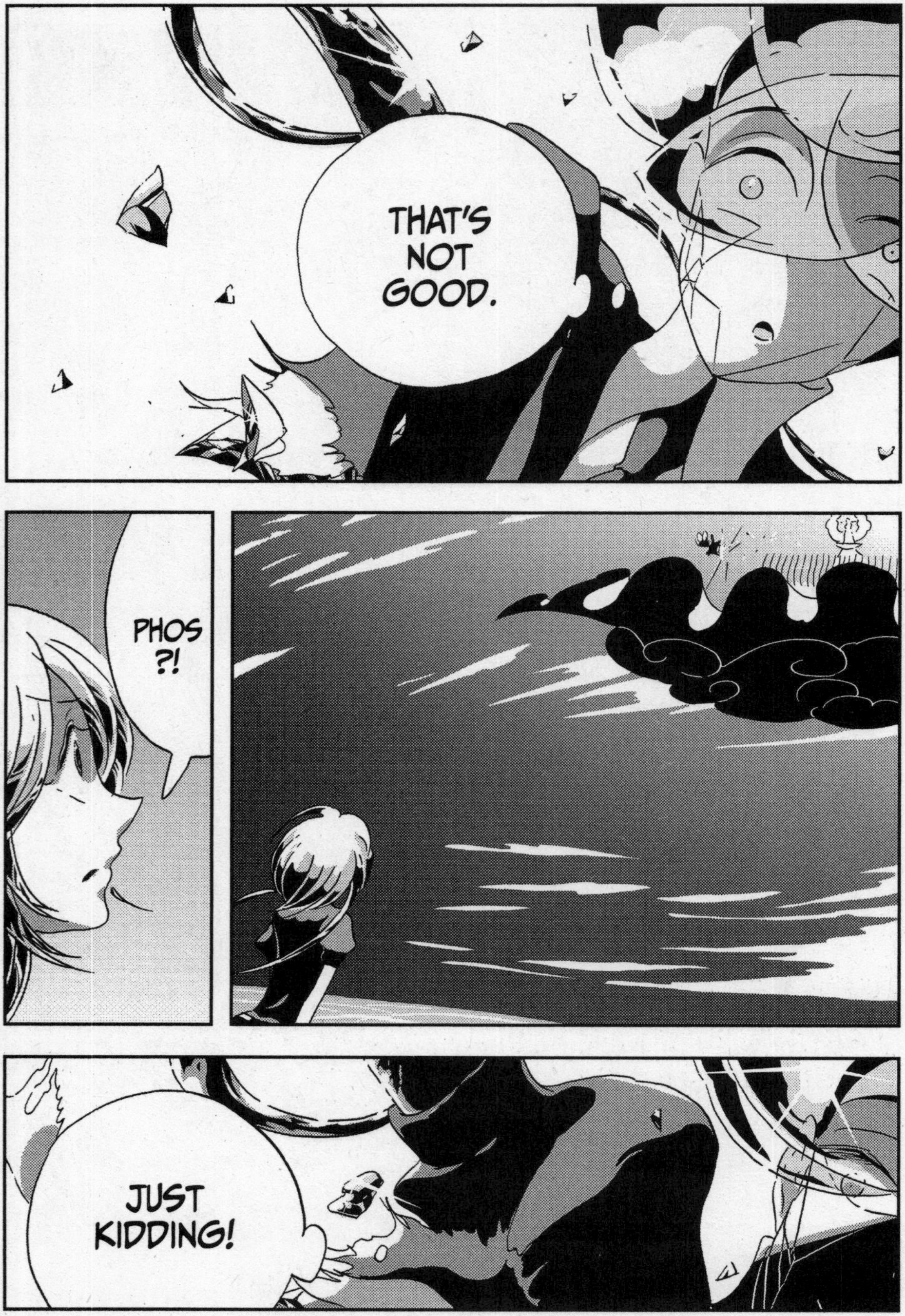
THAT'S NOT GOOD.
PHOS ?!
JUST KIDDING!

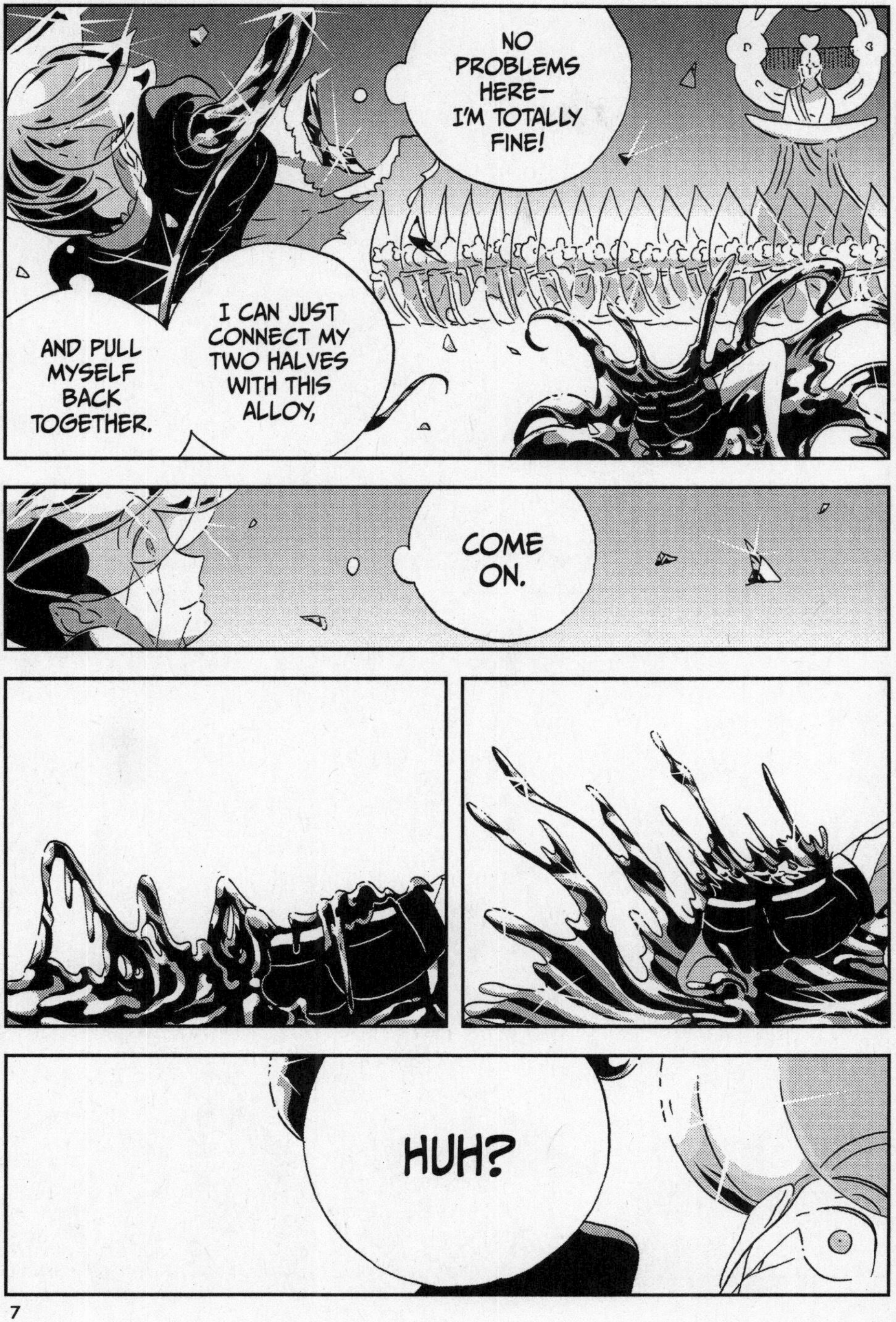

NO PROBLEMS HERE— I'M TOTALLY FINE!
I CAN JUST CONNECT MY TWO HALVES WITH THIS ALLOY,
AND PULL MYSELF BACK TOGETHER.
COME ON.
HUH?

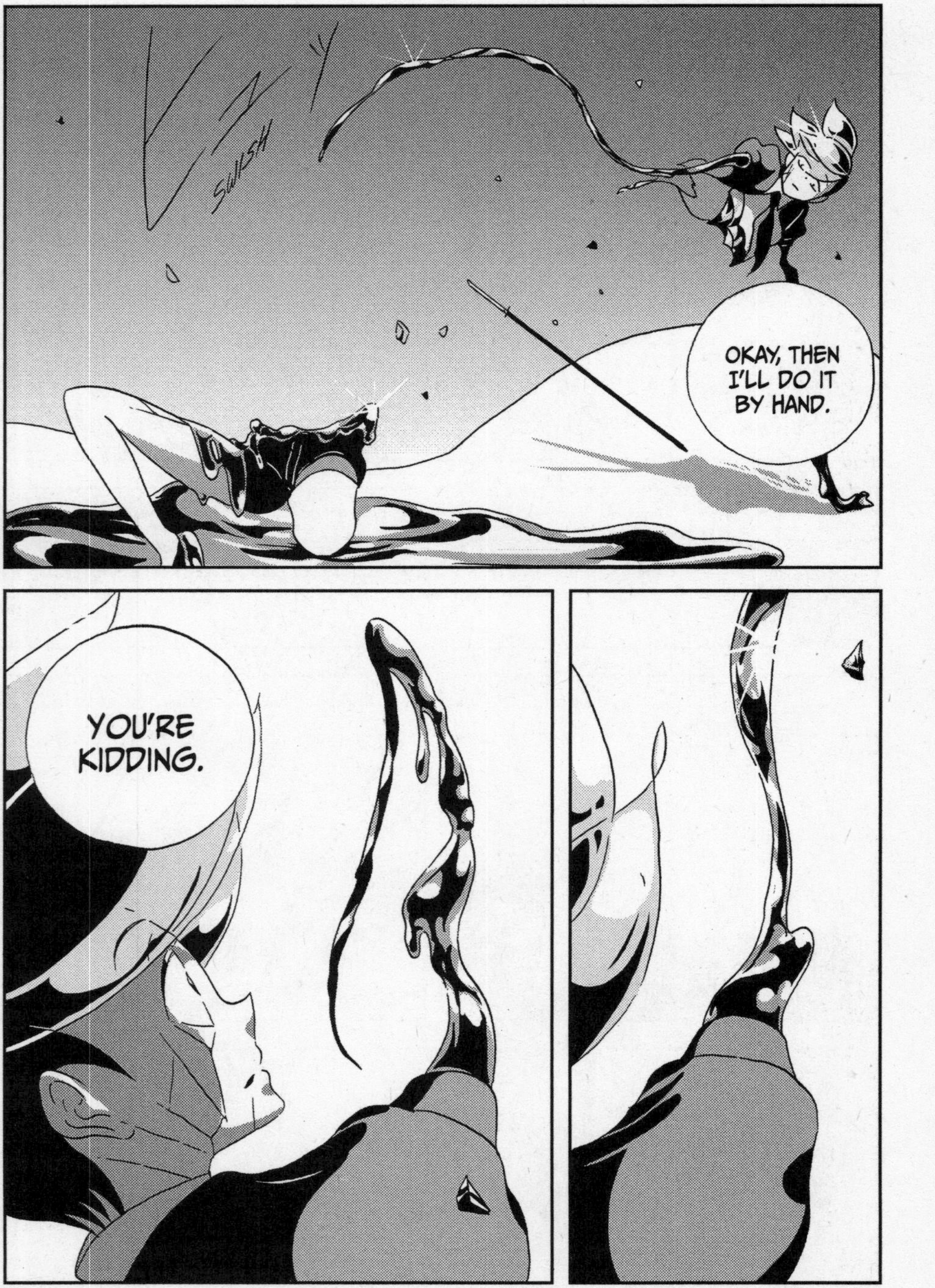
SWISH
OKAY, THEN I'LL DO IT BY HAND.
YOU'RE KIDDING.

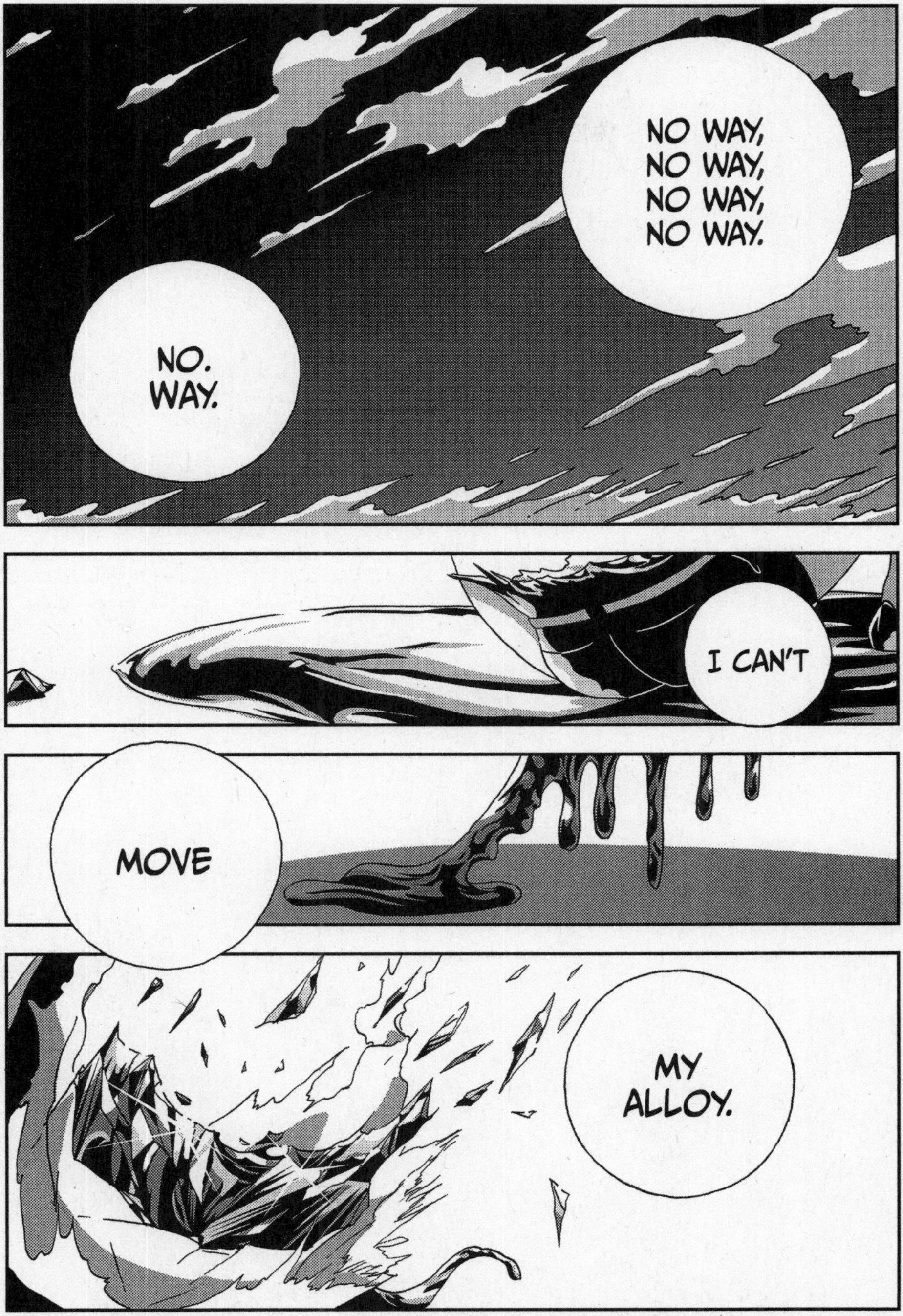
NO WAY, NO WAY, NO WAY, NO WAY.
NO. WAY.
I CAN'T
MOVE
MY ALLOY.

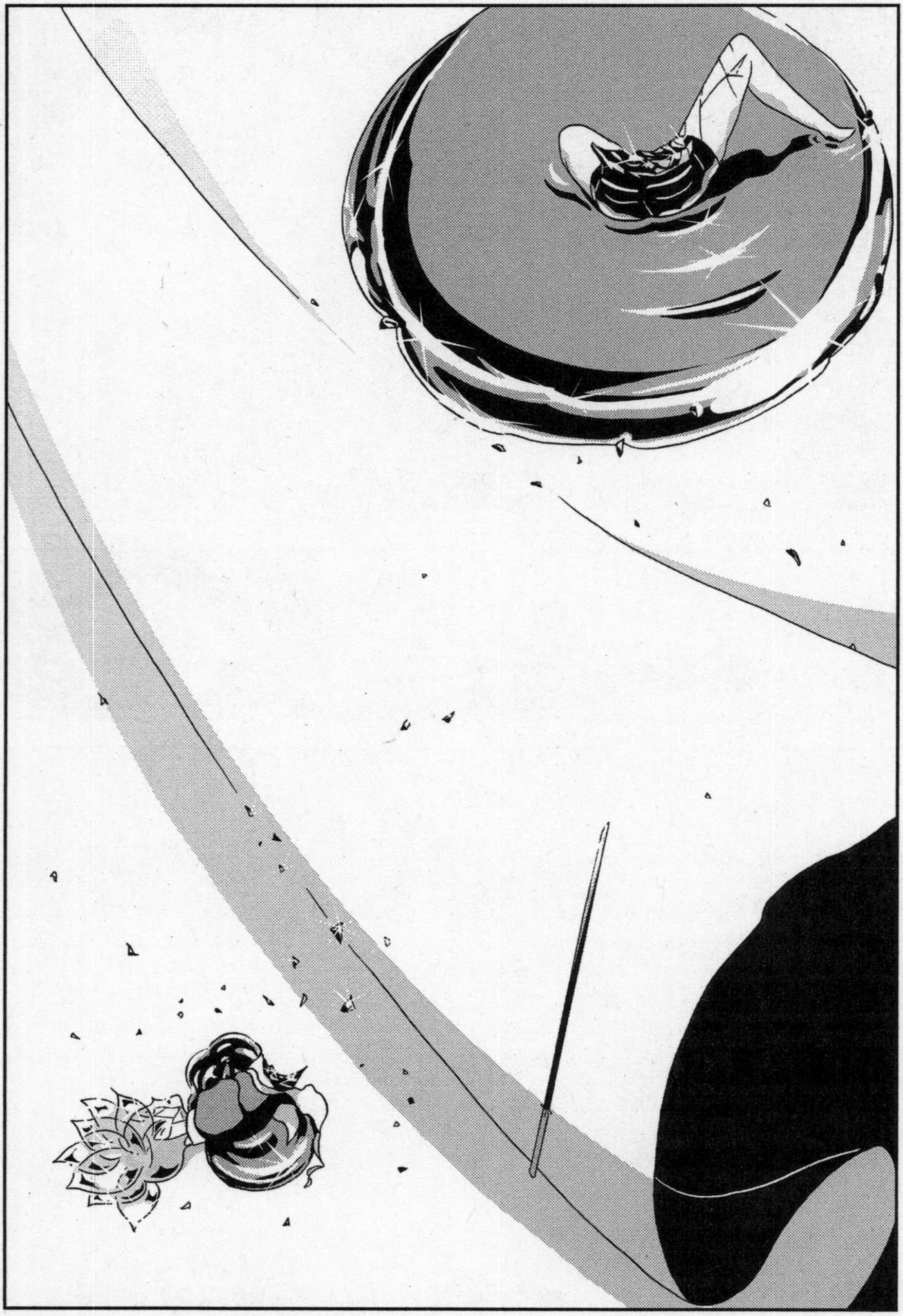

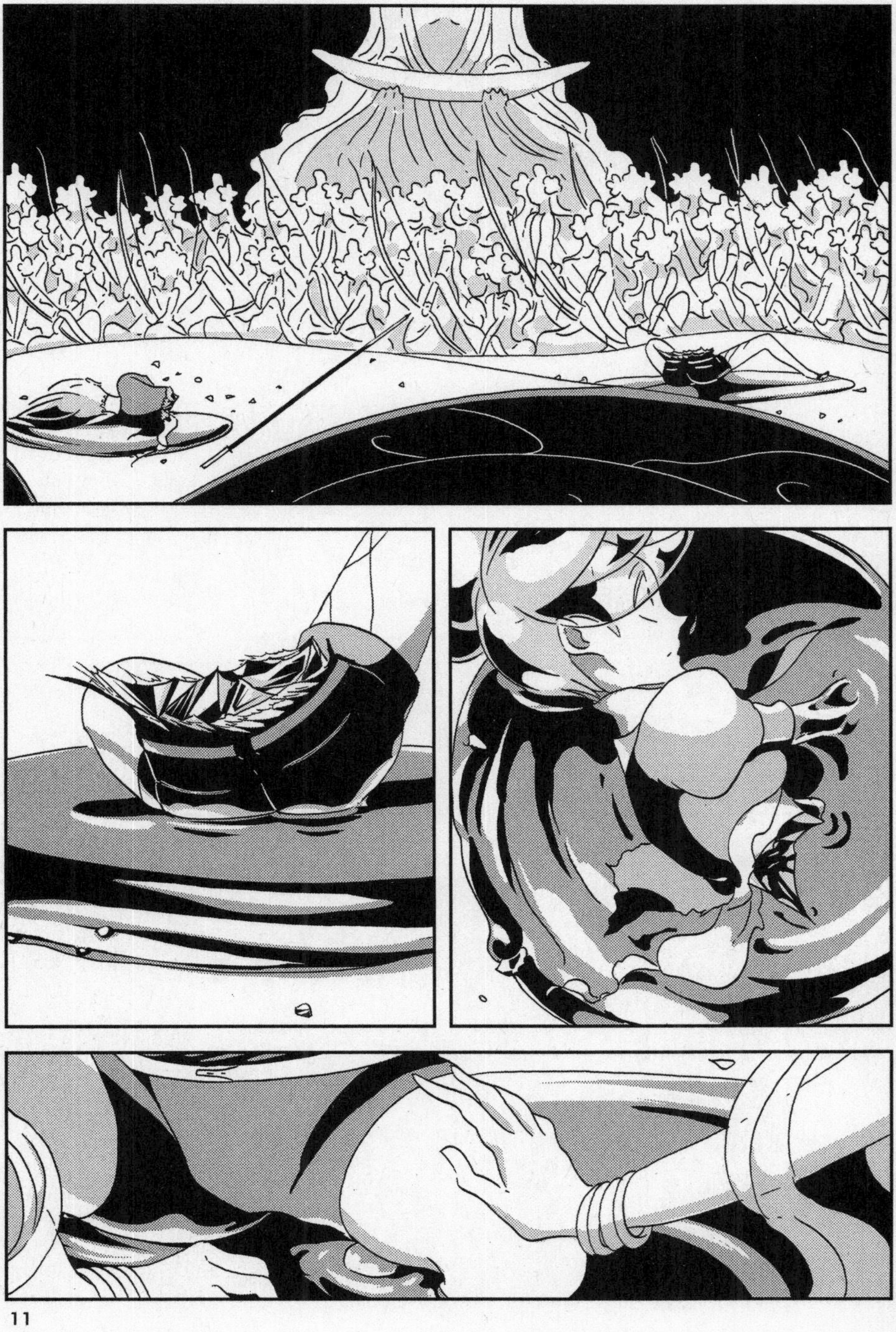

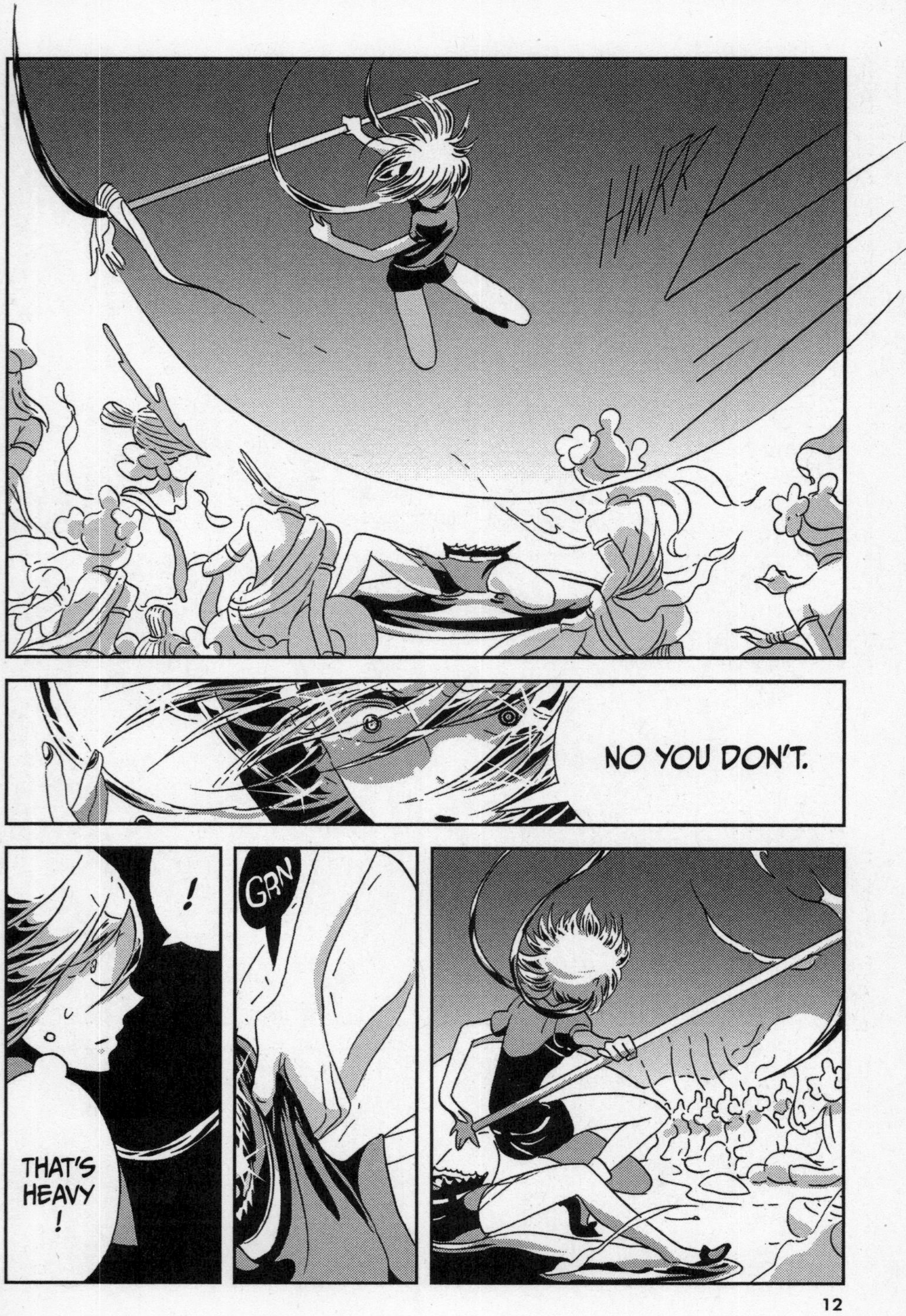
HWRR
NO YOU DON'T.
GRN
!
THAT'S HEAVY !

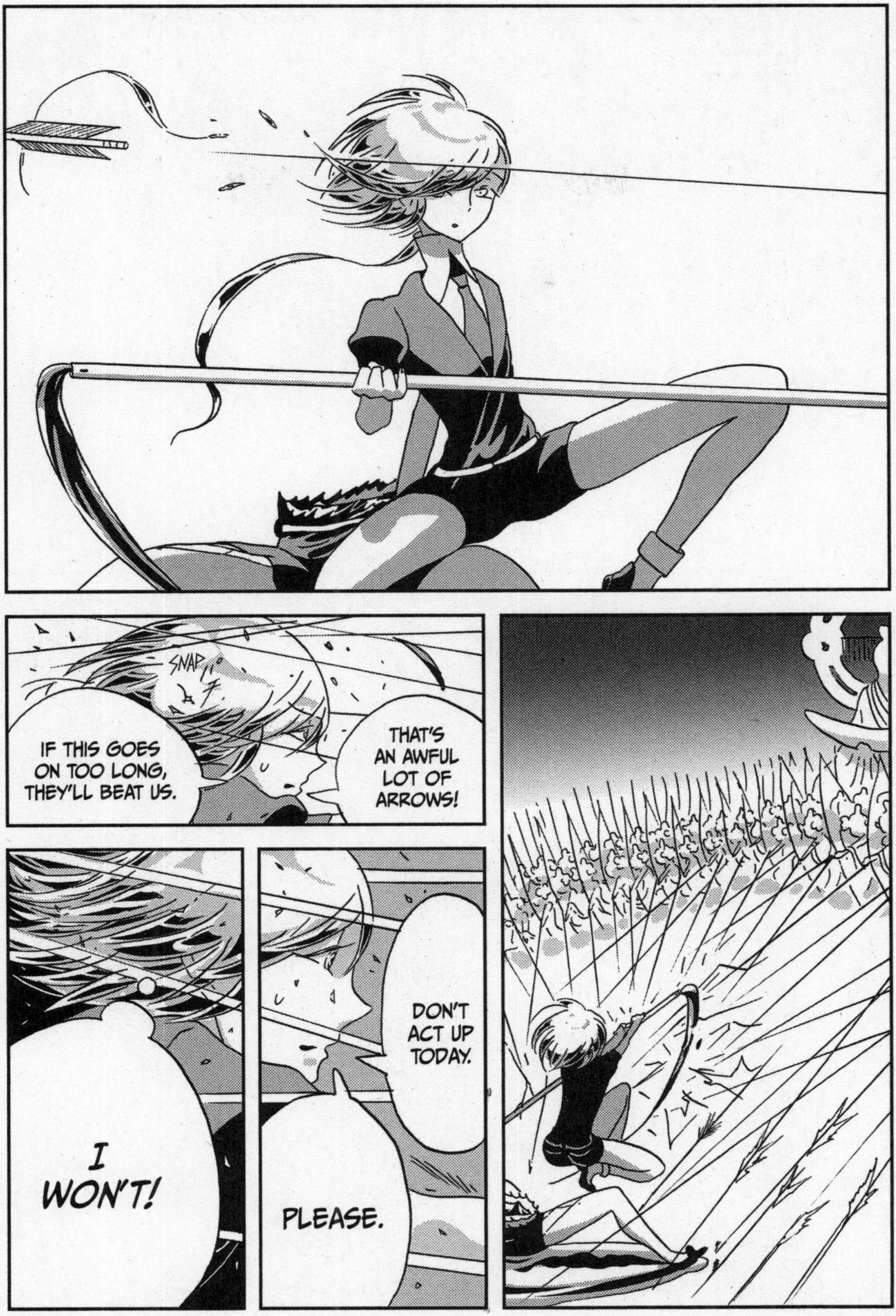
THAT'S AN AWFUL LOT OF ARROWS!
SNAP
IF THIS GOES ON TOO LONG, THEY'LL BEAT US.
DON'T ACT UP TODAY.
PLEASE.
I WON'T!

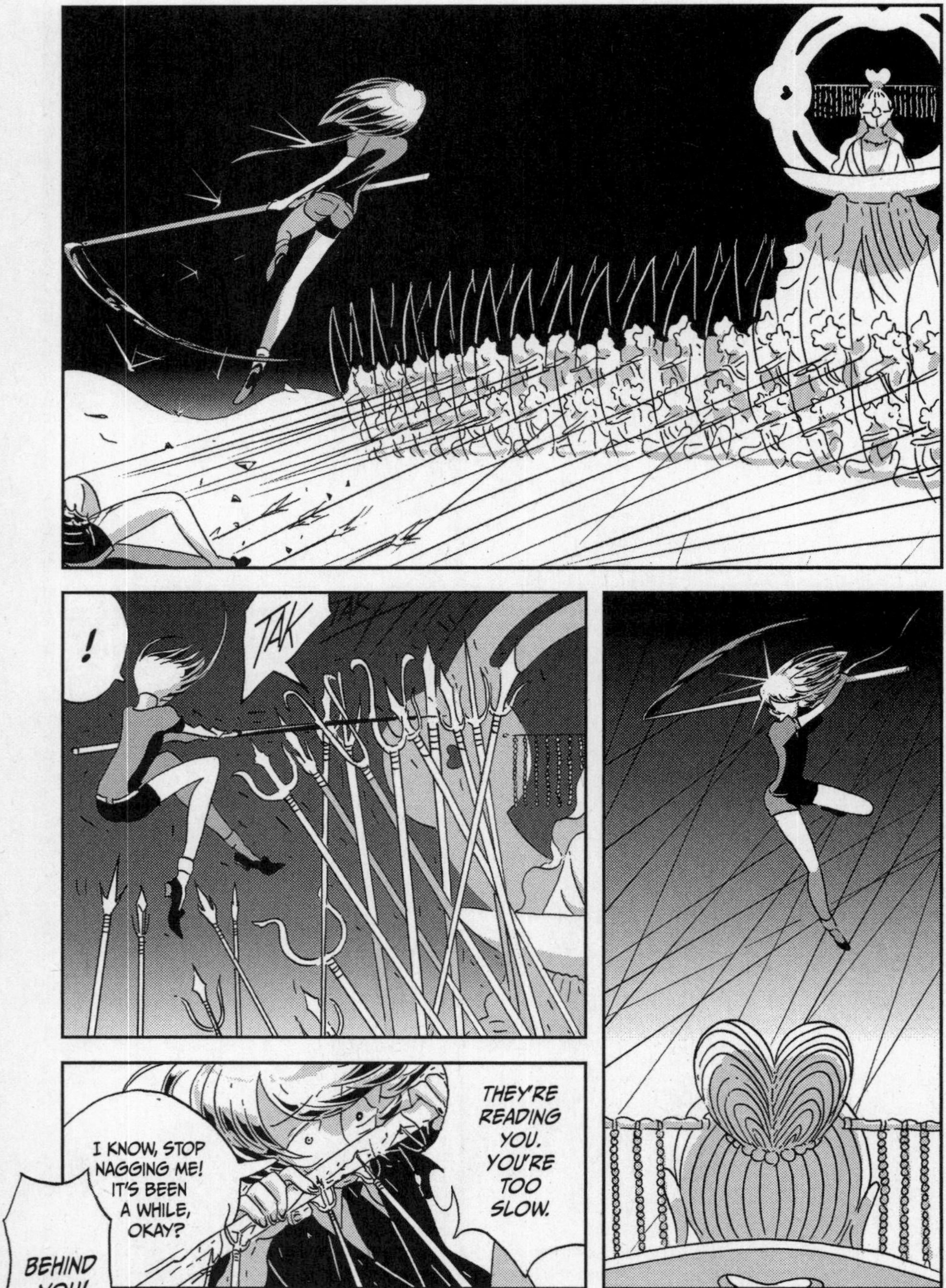
TAK
TAK
!
THEY'RE READING YOU. YOU'RE TOO SLOW.
I KNOW, STOP NAGGING ME! IT'S BEEN A WHILE, OKAY?
BEHIND YOU!

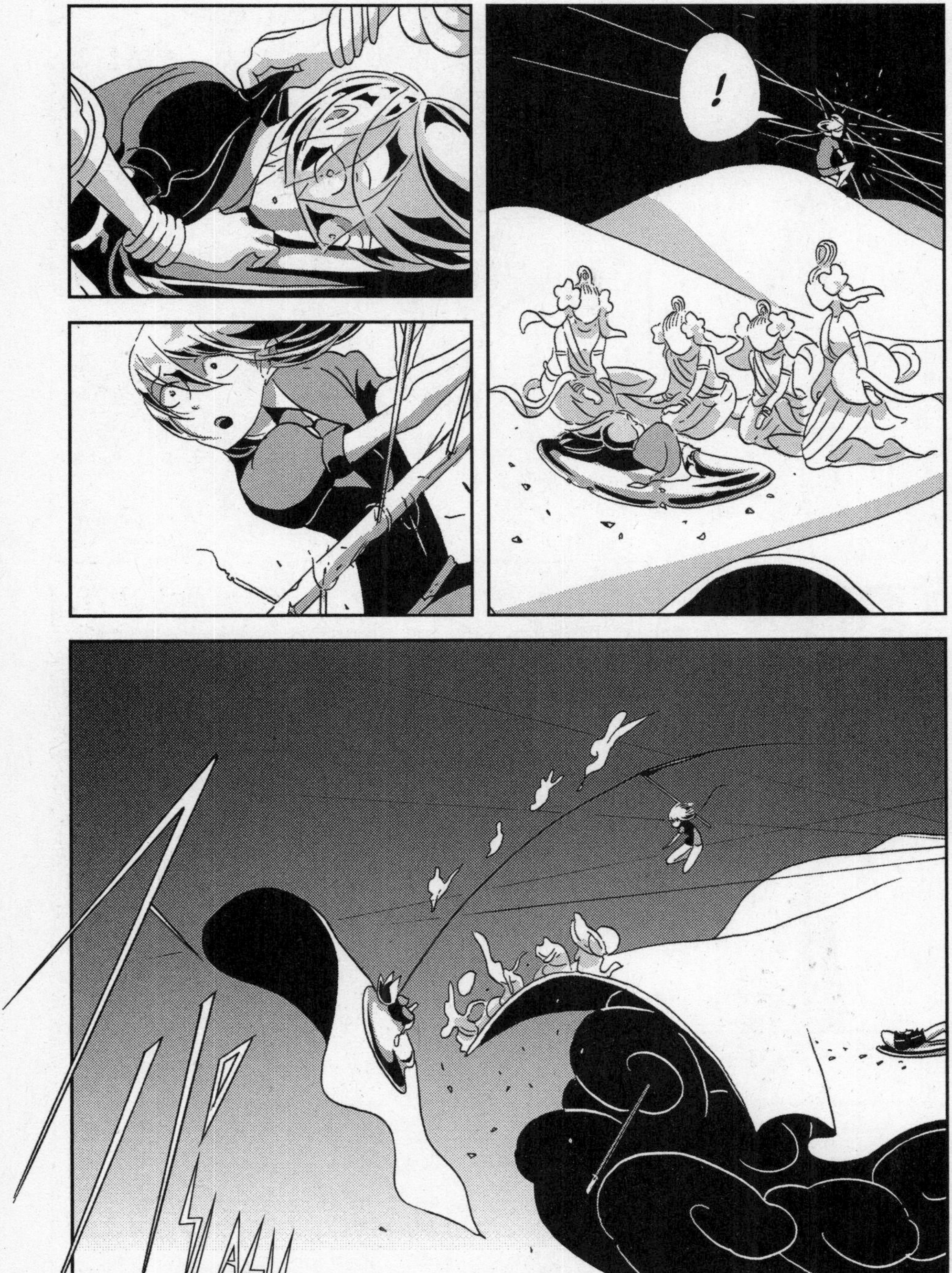
!
SLASH

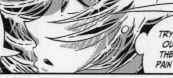

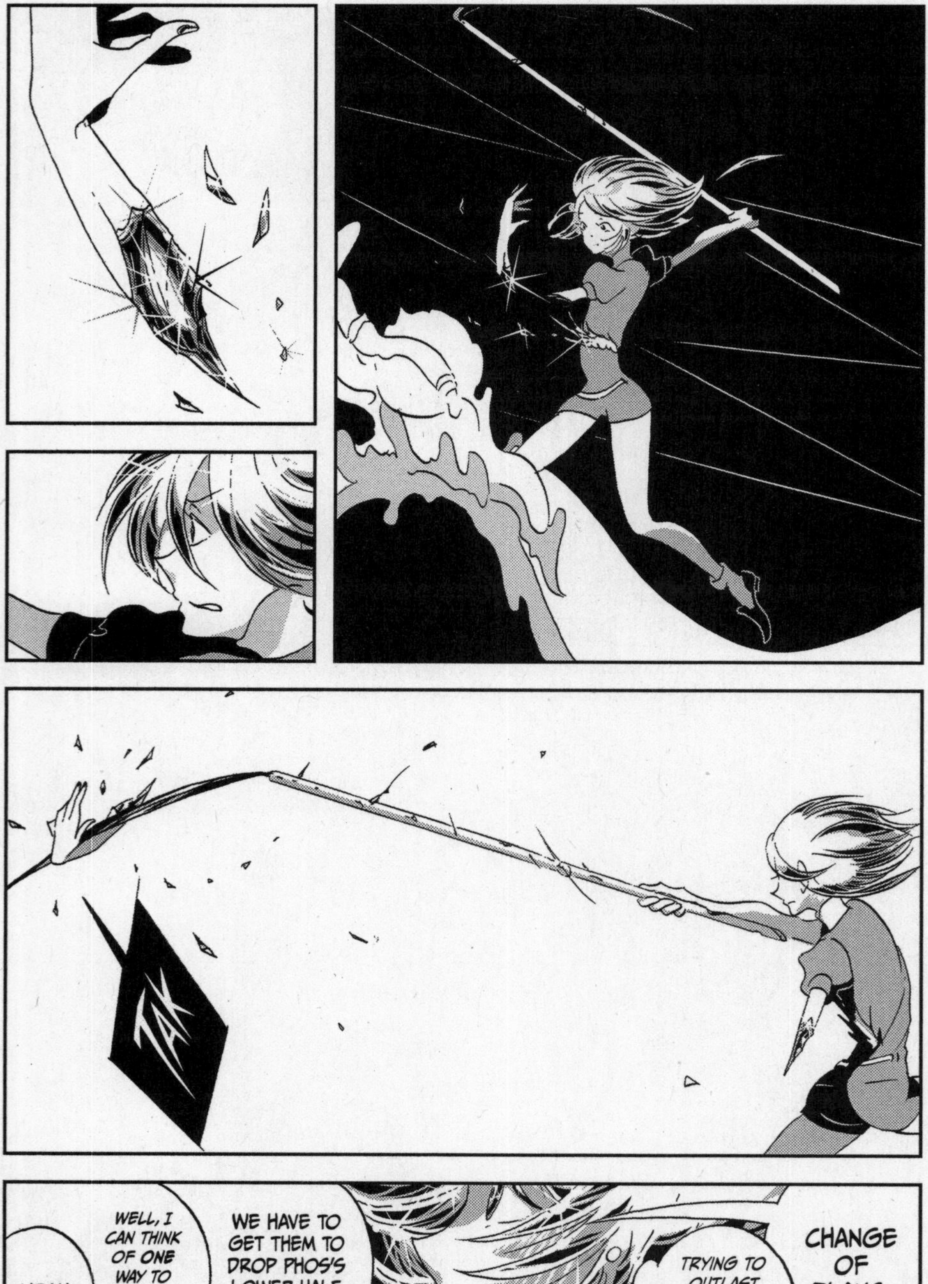
TAK
CHANGE OF PLANS.
TRYING TO OUTLAST THEM, EH? PAIN IN THE...
WE HAVE TO GET THEM TO DROP PHOS'S LOWER HALF FIRST.
WELL, I CAN THINK OF ONE WAY TO DISTRACT THEM.
YEAH.

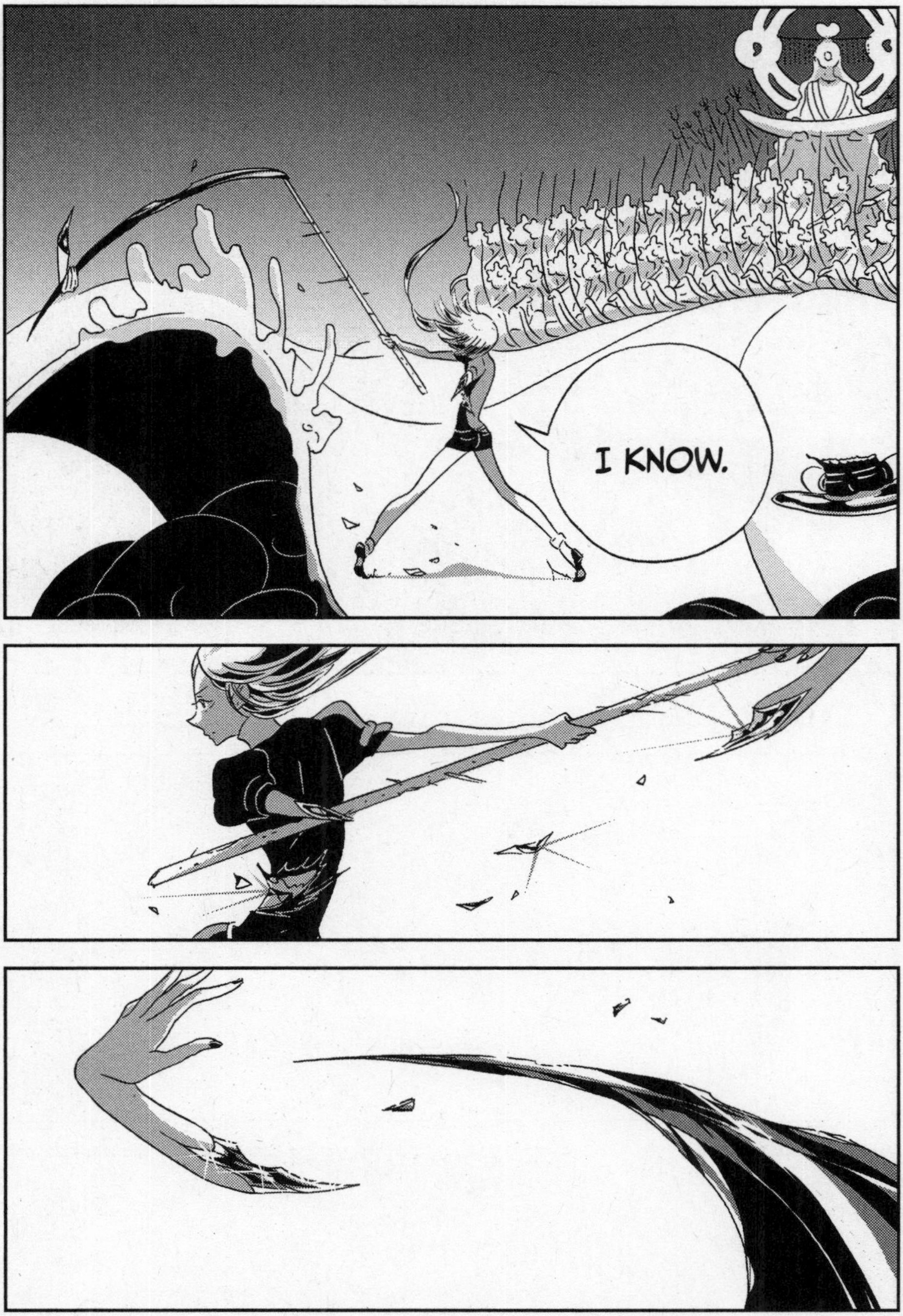
I KNOW.

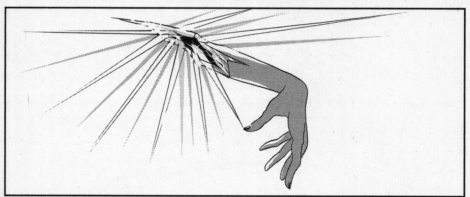

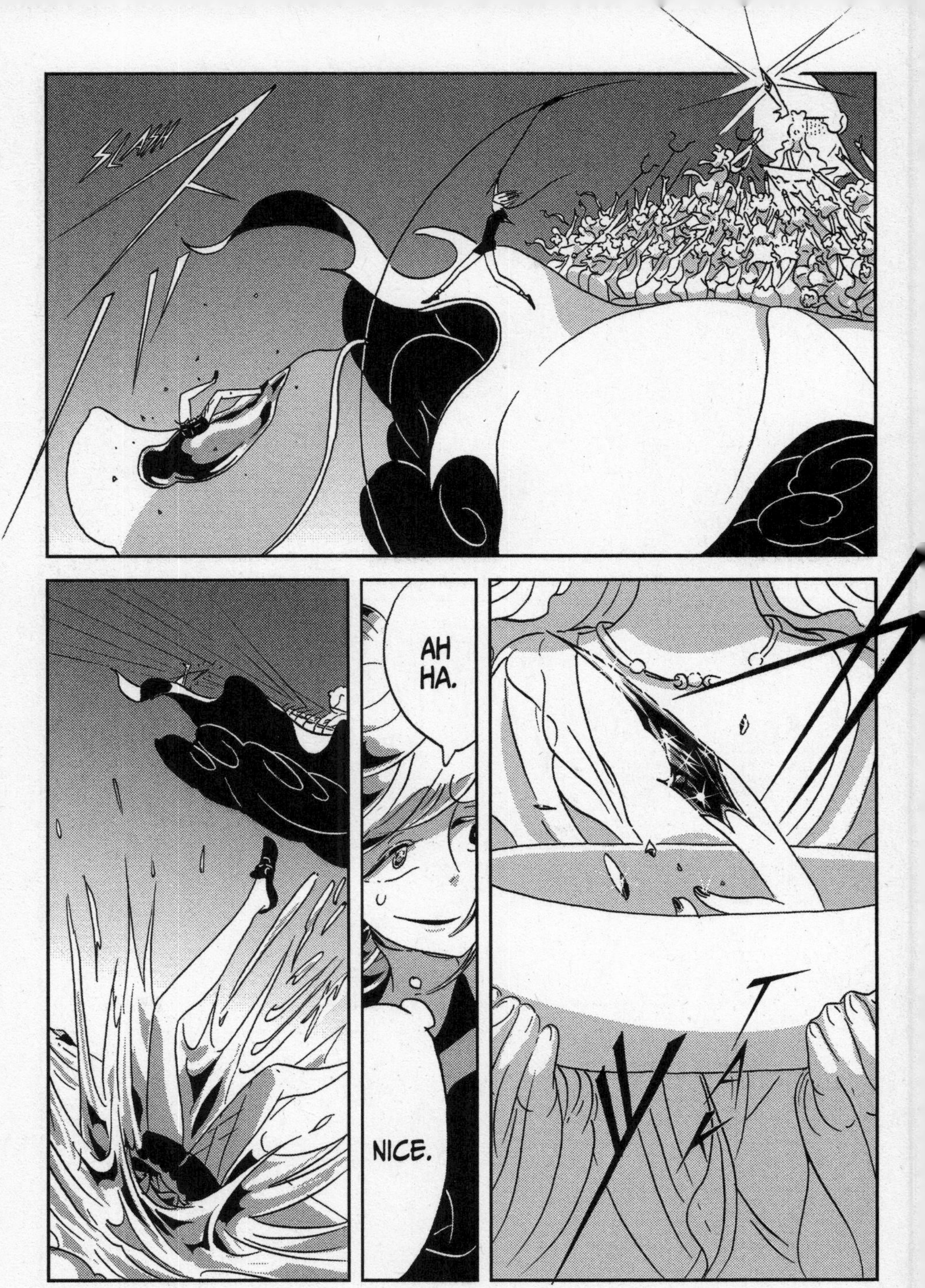
SLASH
AH HA.
NICE.

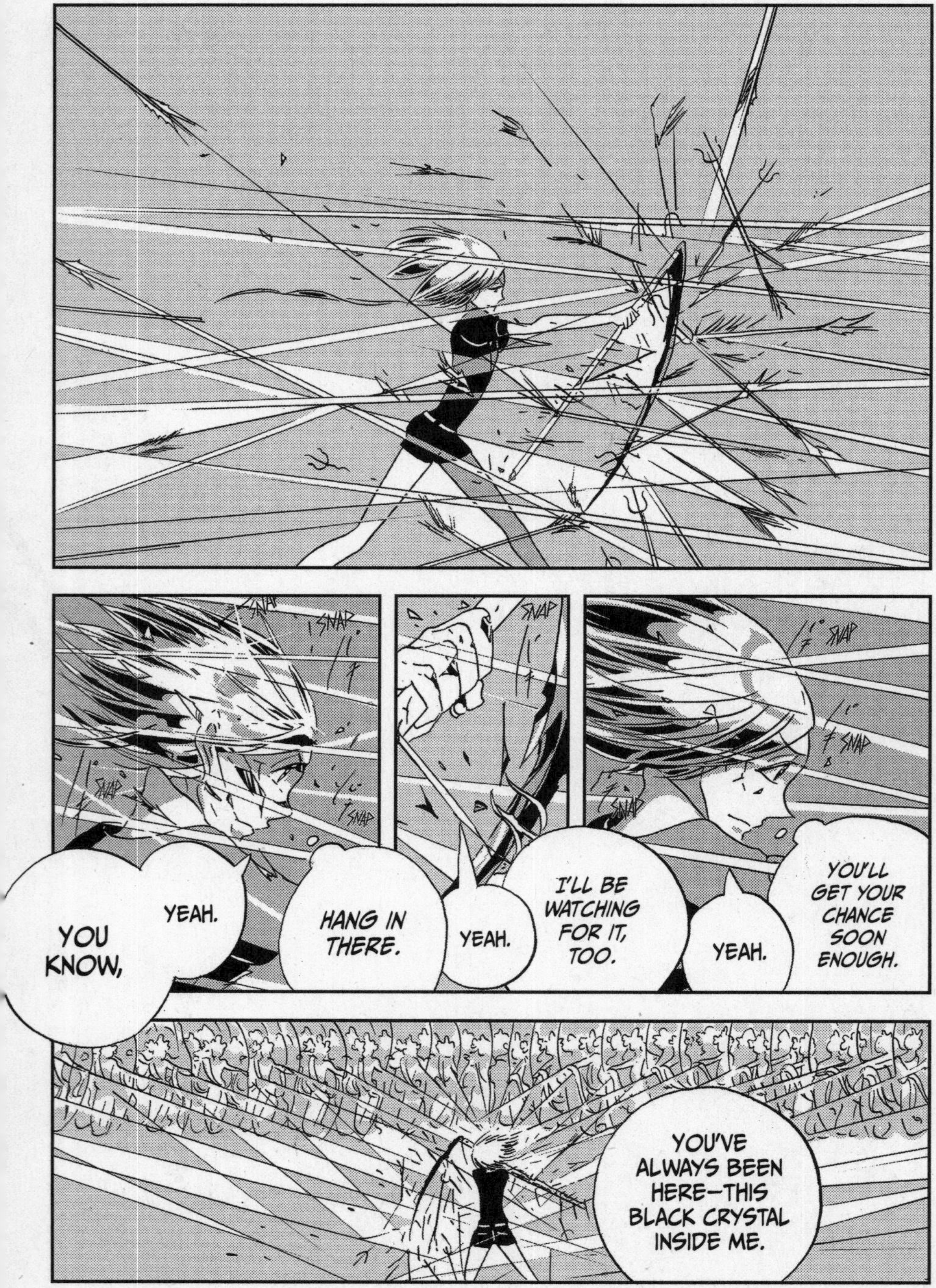
SNAP
SNAP
SNAP
YOU'LL GET YOUR CHANCE SOON ENOUGH.
YEAH.
SNAP
I'LL BE WATCHING FOR IT, TOO.
YEAH.
SNAP
SNAP
SNAP
SNAP
HANG IN THERE.
YEAH.
YOU KNOW,
YOU'VE ALWAYS BEEN HERE—THIS BLACK CRYSTAL INSIDE ME.

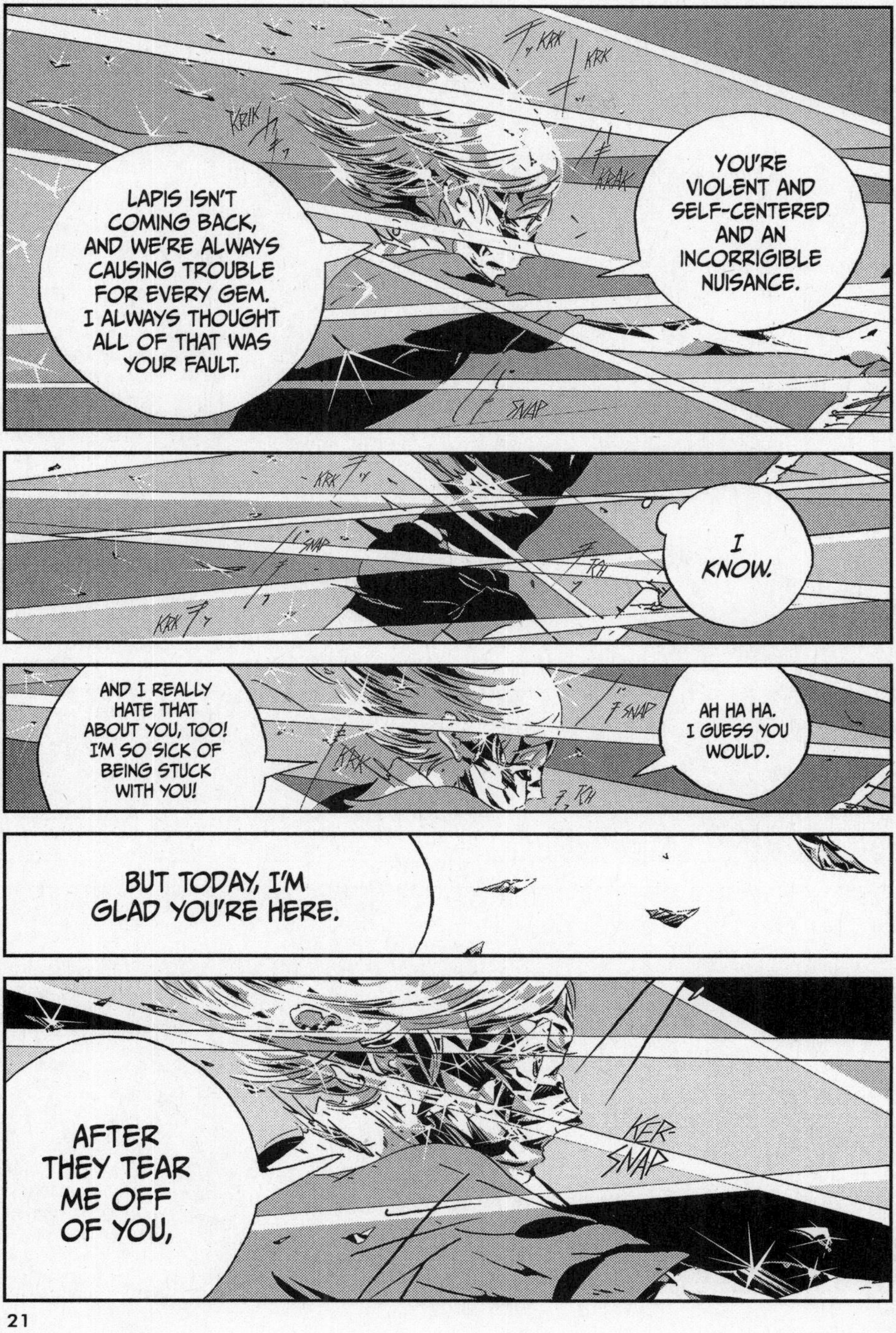

KRK
KRX
KRAK
YOU'RE VIOLENT AND SELF-CENTERED AND AN INCORRIGIBLE NUISANCE.
KRIK
LAPIS ISN'T COMING BACK, AND WE'RE ALWAYS CAUSING TROUBLE FOR EVERY GEM. I ALWAYS THOUGHT ALL OF THAT WAS YOUR FAULT.
SNAP
I KNOW.
KRK
SNAP
KRK
AH HA HA. I GUESS YOU WOULD.
SNAP
KRK
AND I REALLY HATE THAT ABOUT YOU, TOO! I'M SO SICK OF BEING STUCK WITH YOU!
BUT TODAY, I'M GLAD YOU'RE HERE.
KER-SNAP
AFTER THEY TEAR ME OFF OF YOU,

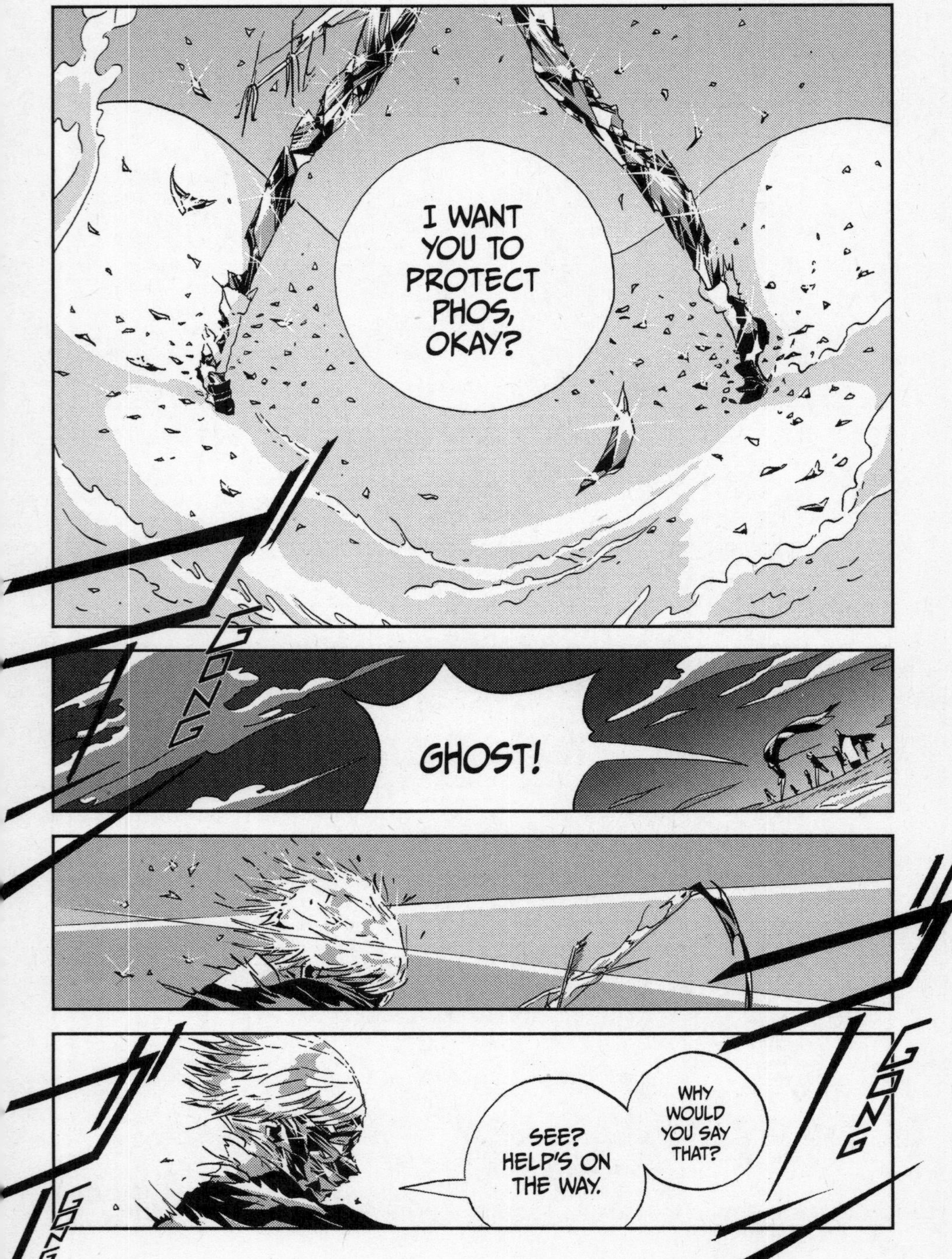
I WANT YOU TO PROTECT PHOS, OKAY?
GONG
GHOST!
GONG
WHY WOULD YOU SAY THAT?
SEE? HELP'S ON THE WAY.
GONG

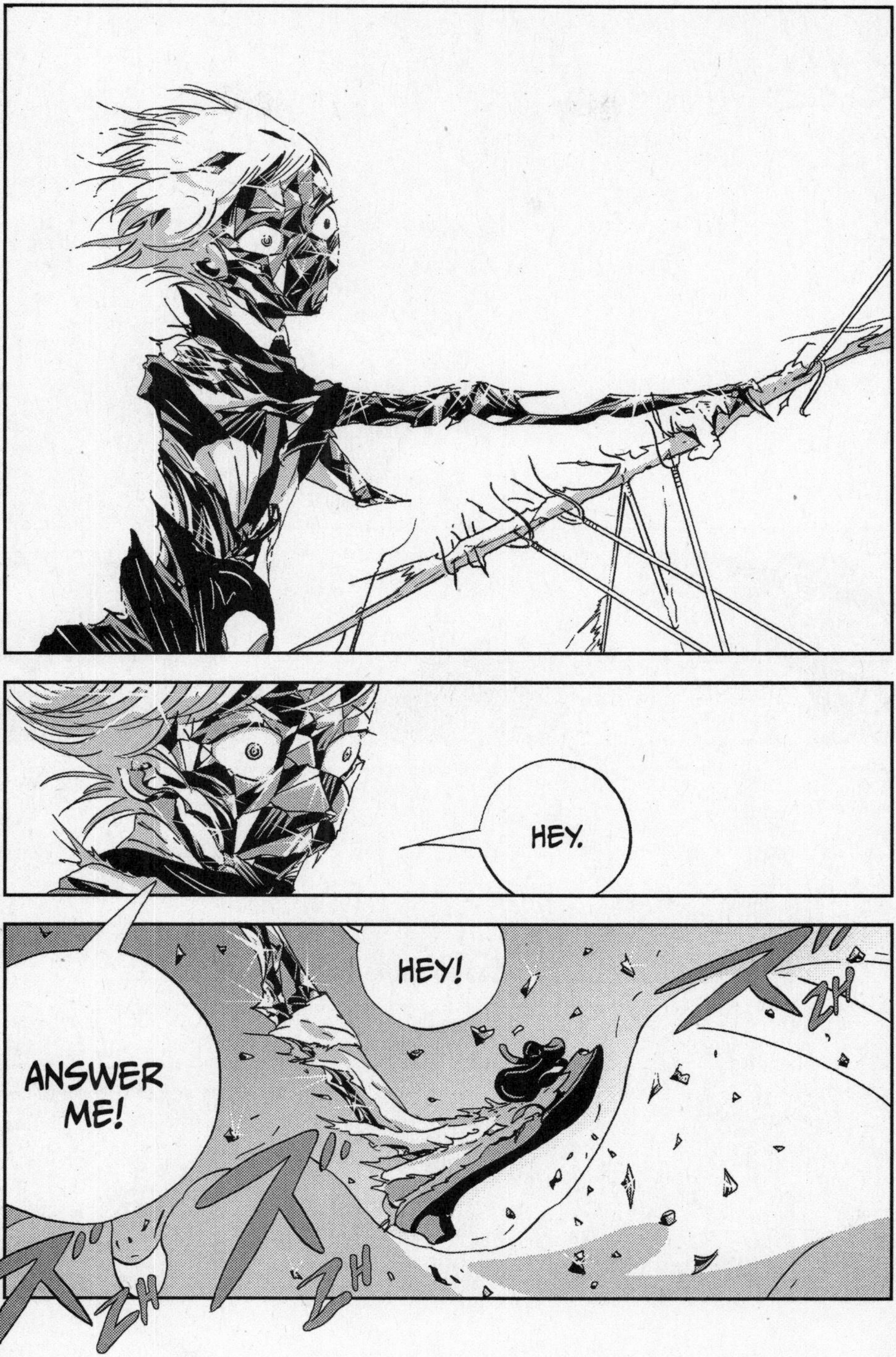
HEY.
ZH
HEY!
ANSWER ME!
ZH
ZH

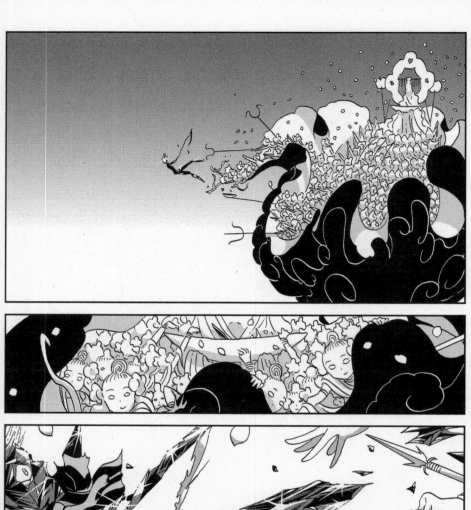

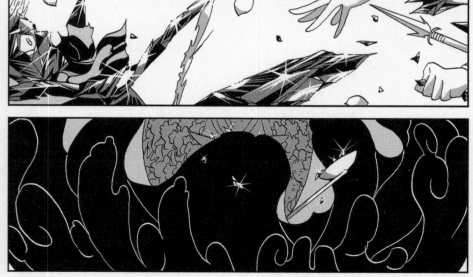

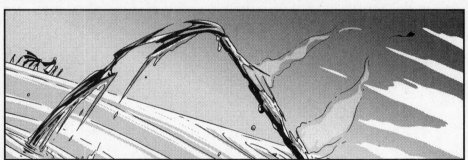

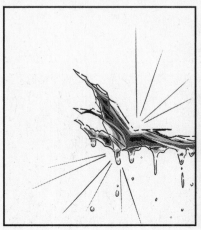

ZSHH

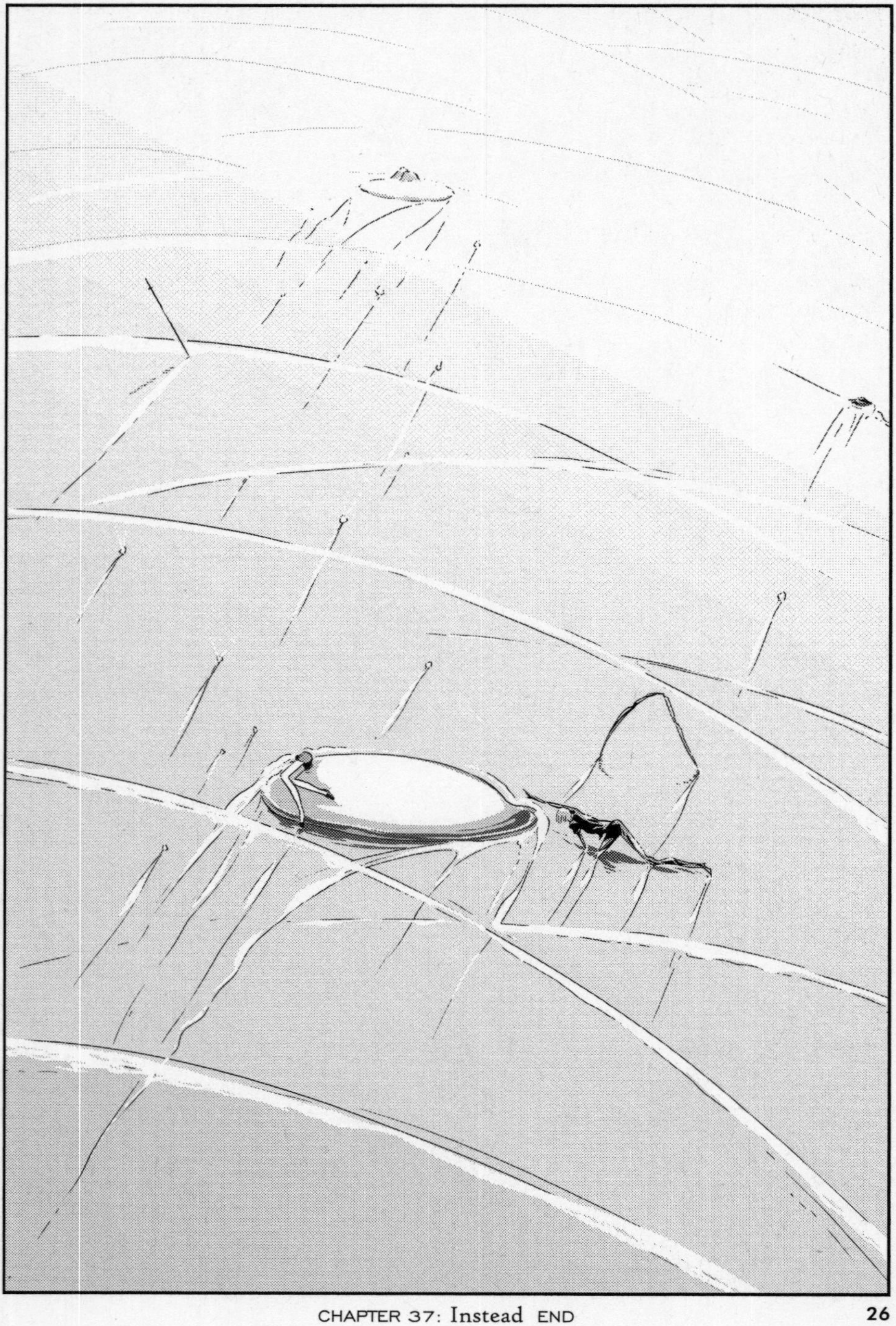

CHAPTER 37: Instead END

CHAPTER 38: Ghost Quartz

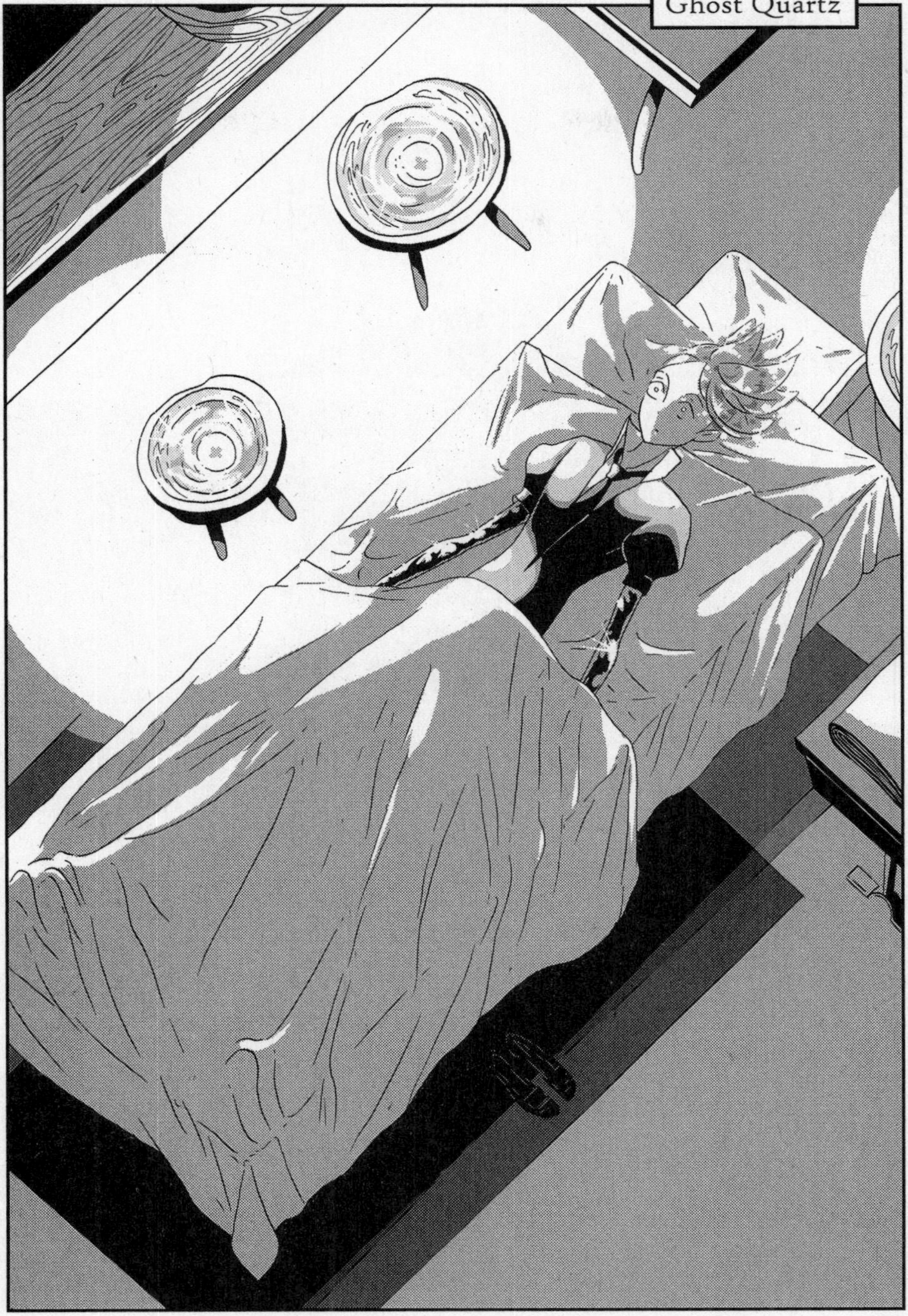

CLATTER

FWOOSH

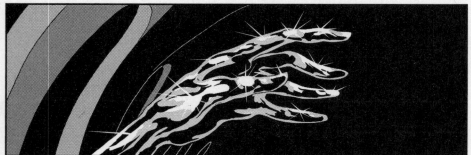

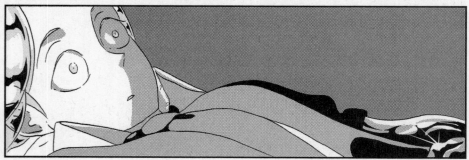

WHERE'S GHOST?

WHAT A RELIEF... GHOST IS OKAY.

OH, GOOD.

...

...

WITH SENSEI.

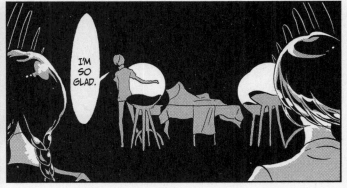

I'M SO GLAD.

29

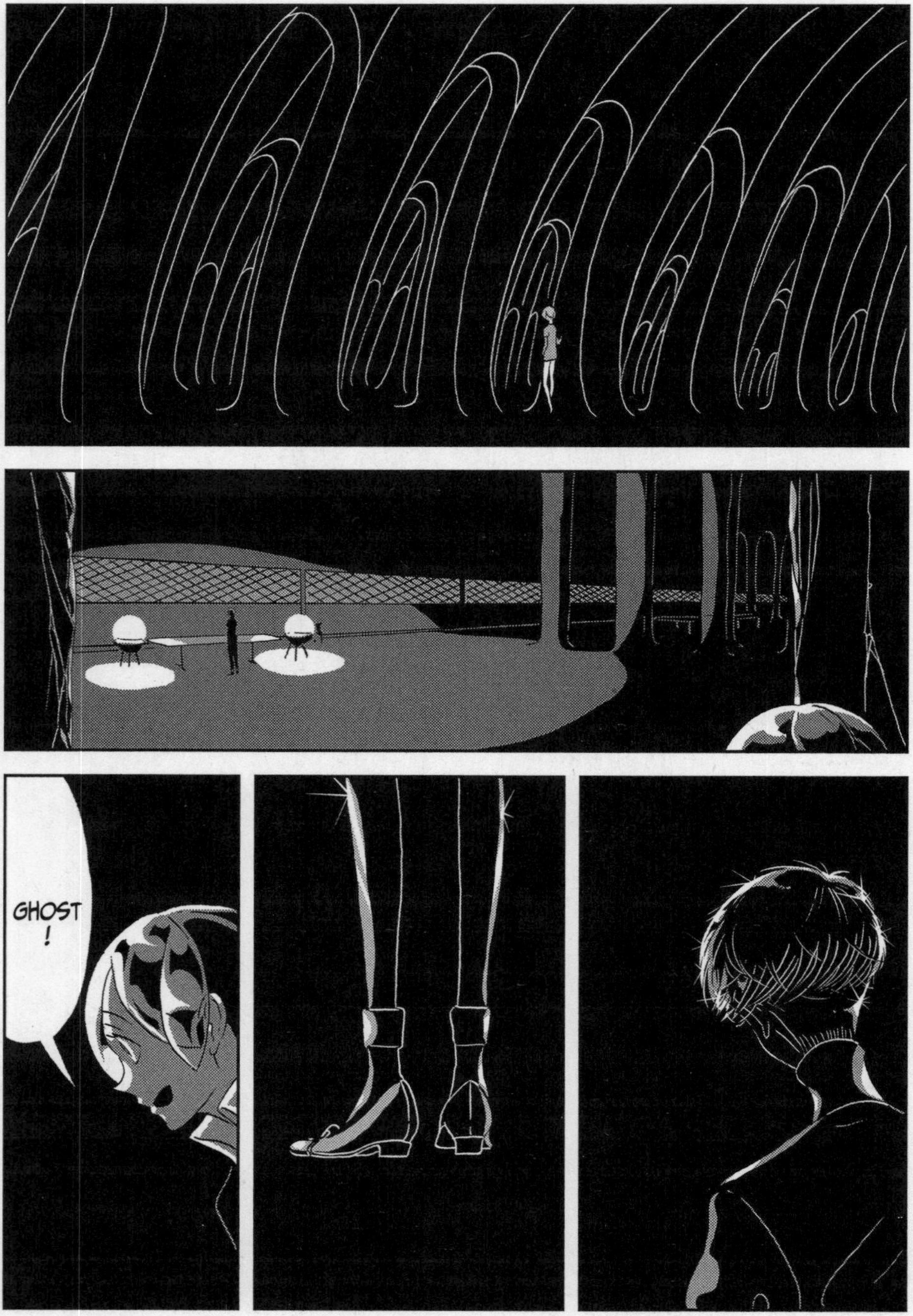
GHOST
!

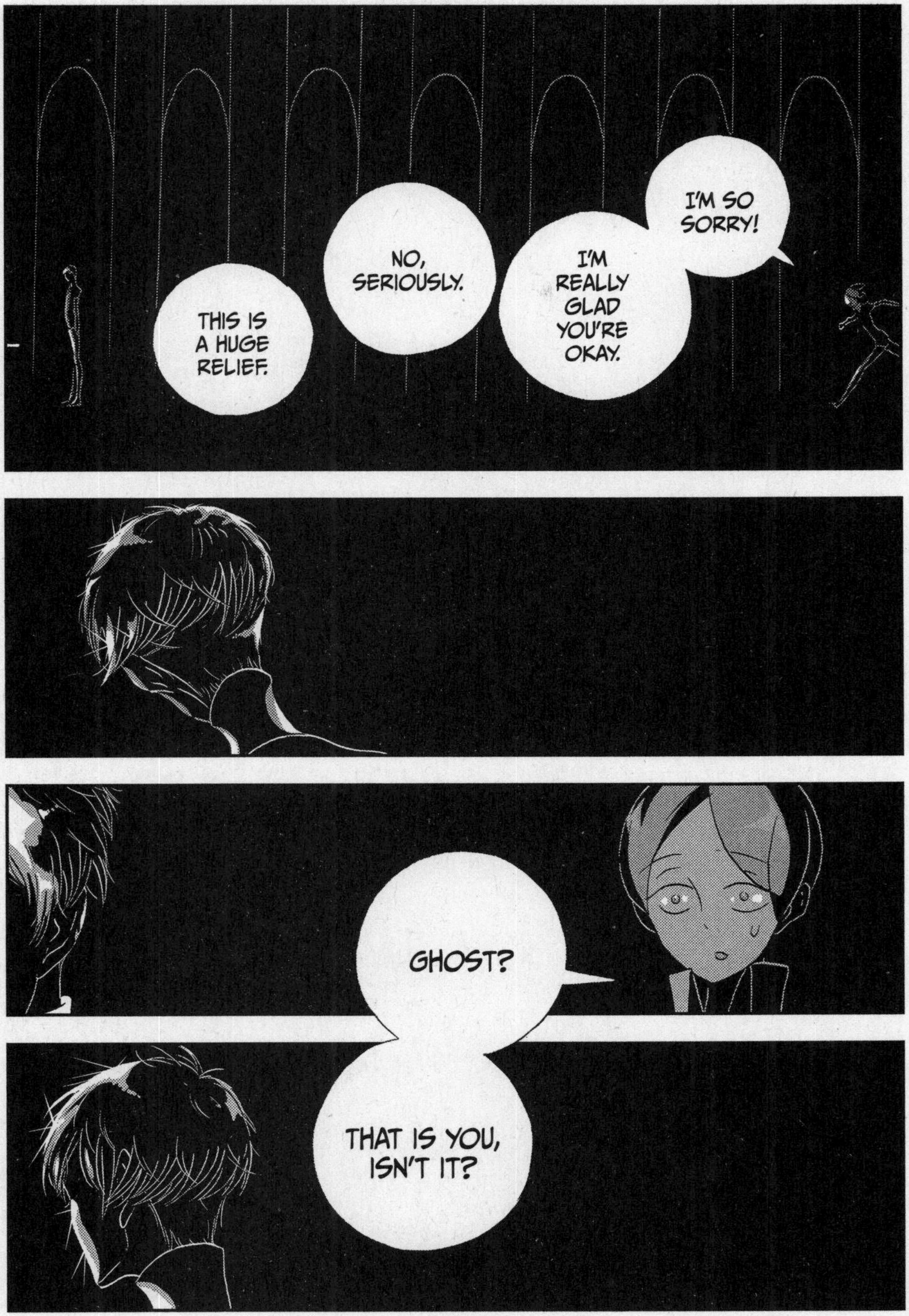
I'M SO SORRY!
I'M REALLY GLAD YOU'RE OKAY.
NO, SERIOUSLY.
THIS IS A HUGE RELIEF.
GHOST?
THAT IS YOU, ISN'T IT?

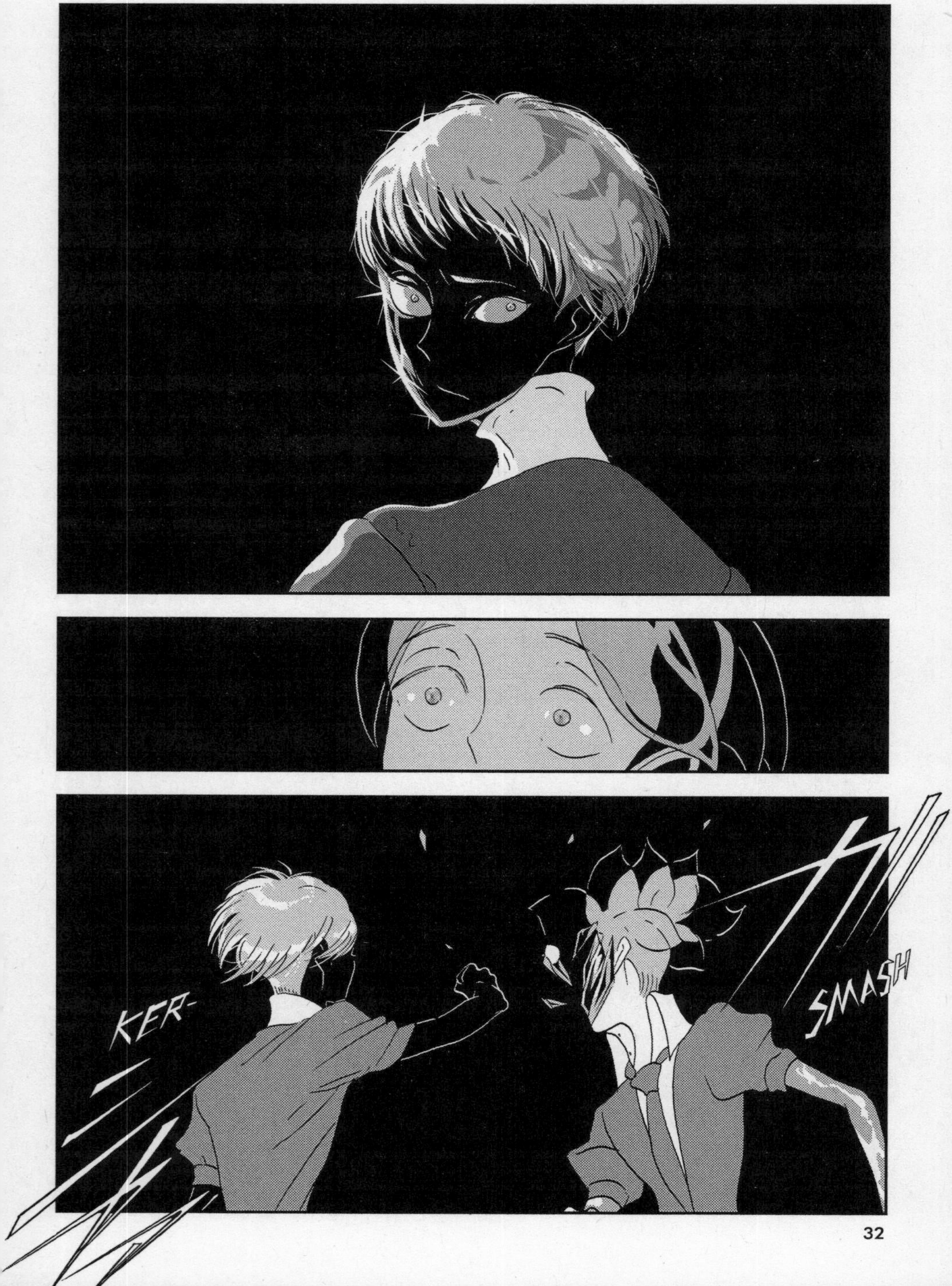
KER-
SMASH

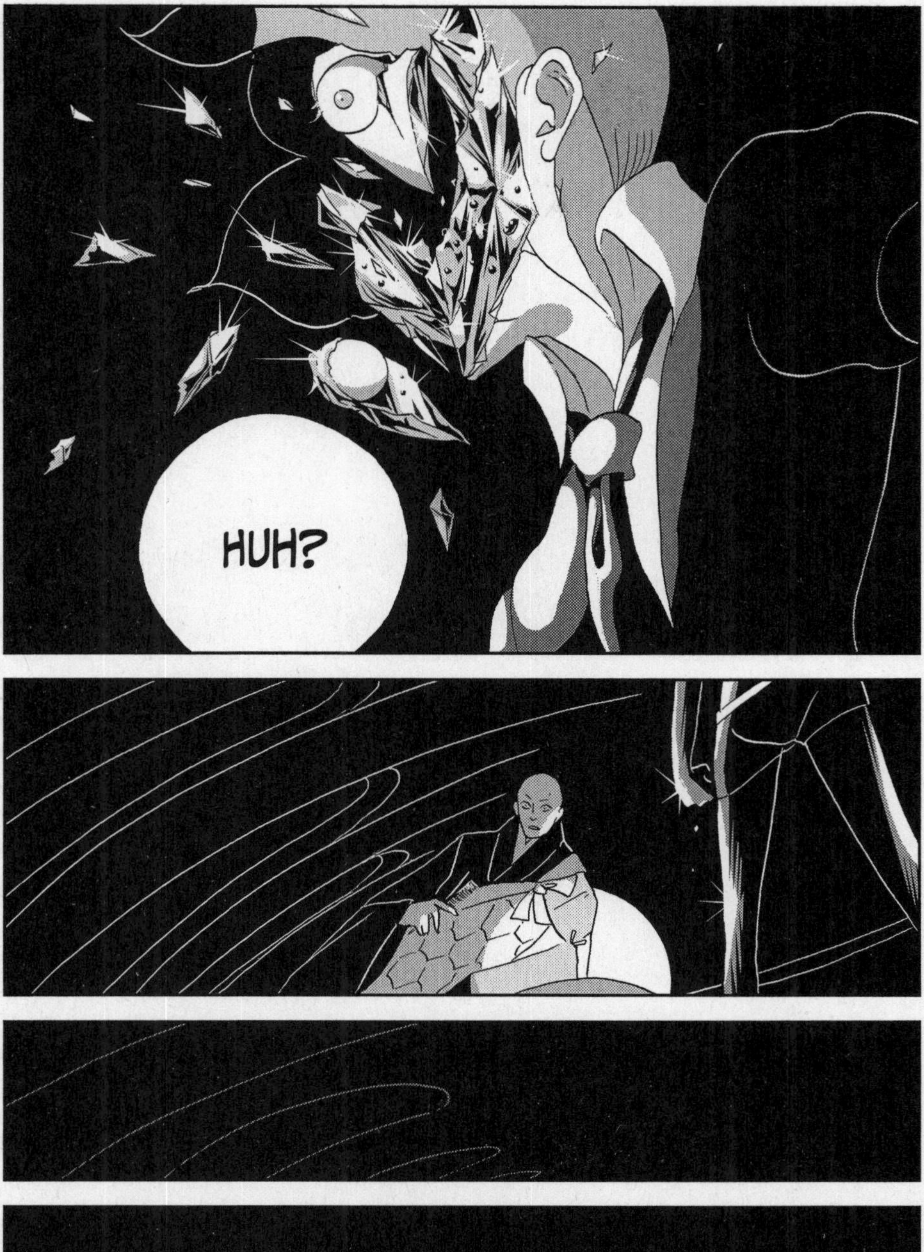
HUH?

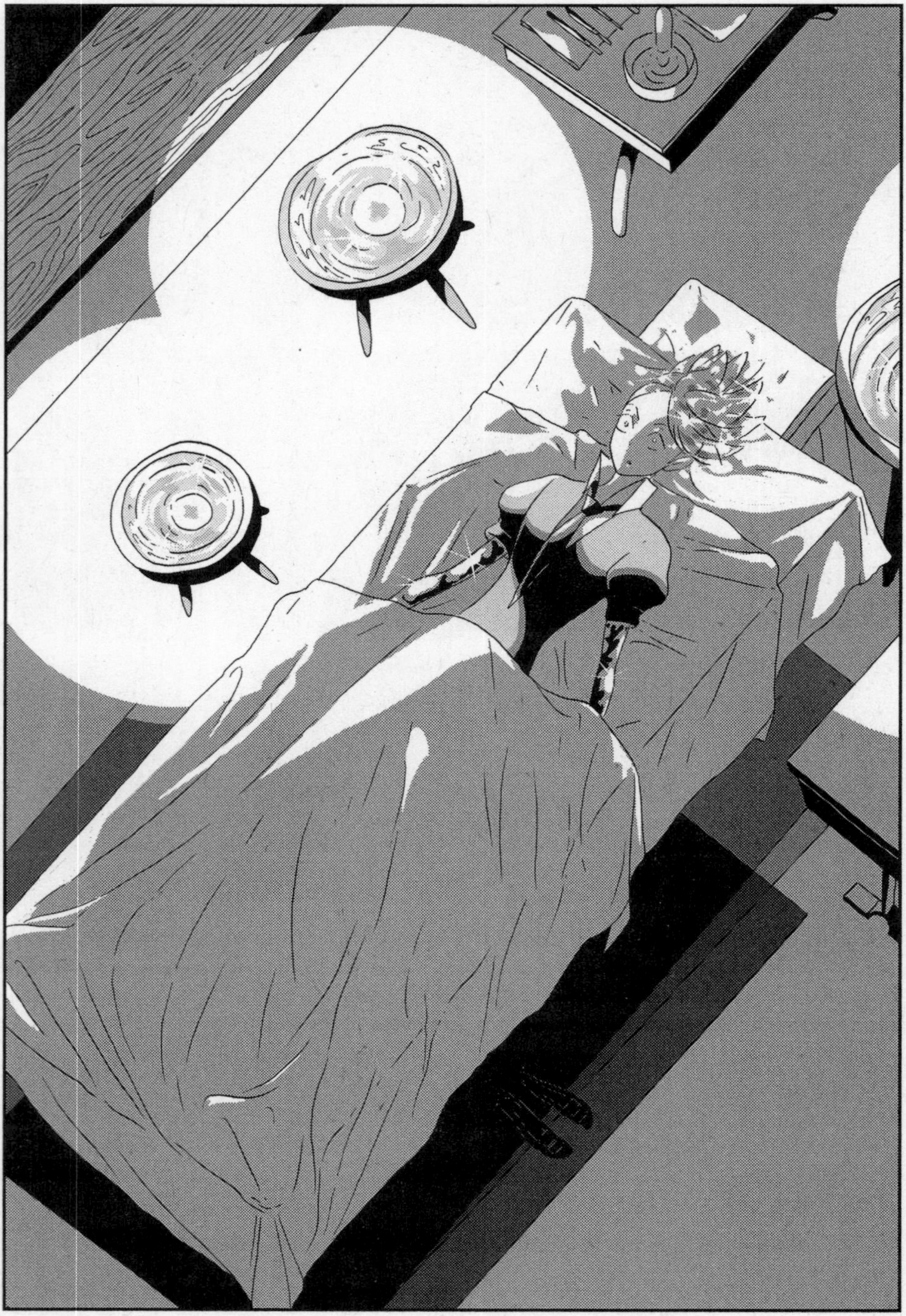

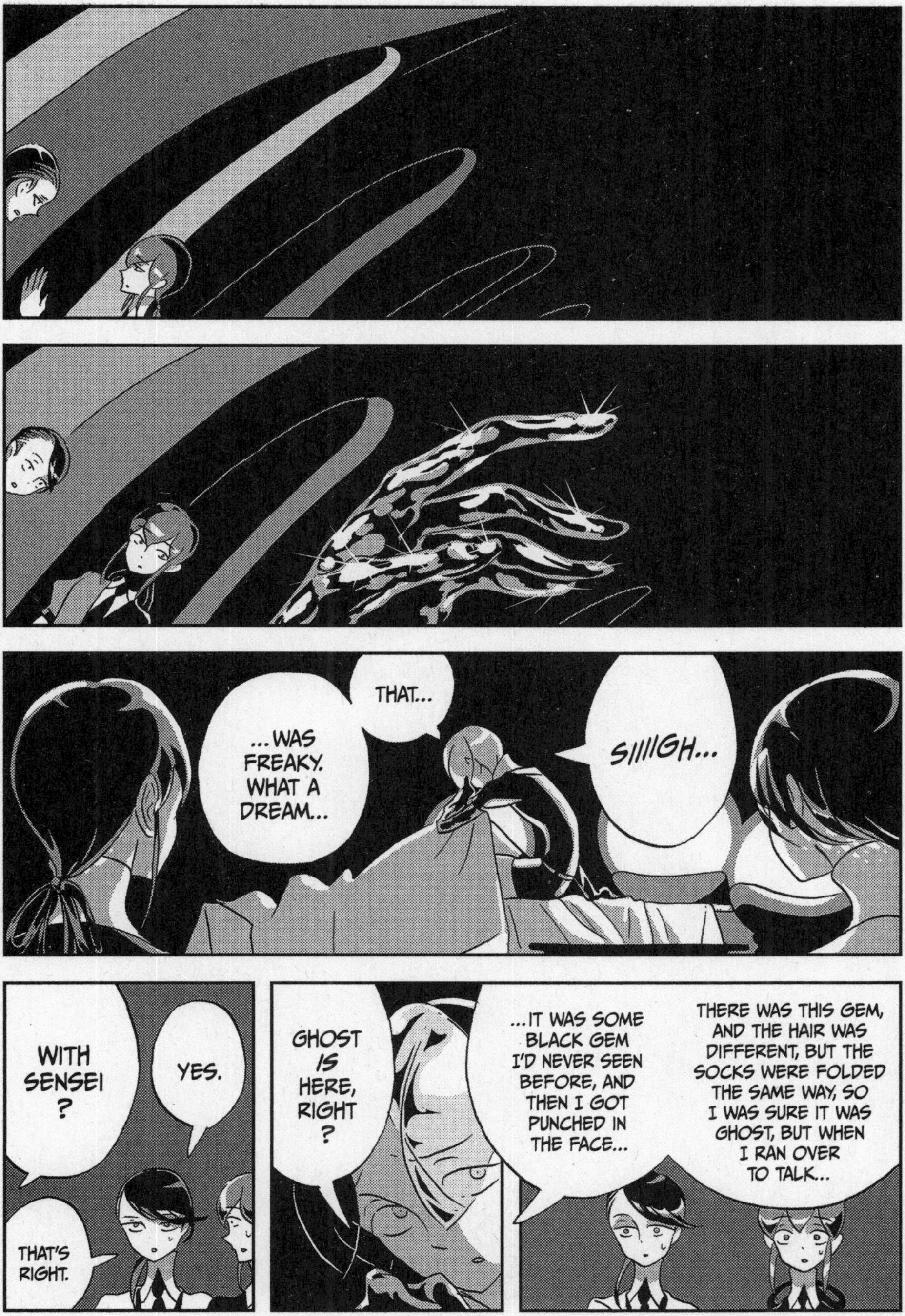
SIIIIGH...
THAT...
...WAS FREAKY. WHAT A DREAM...
THERE WAS THIS GEM, AND THE HAIR WAS DIFFERENT, BUT THE SOCKS WERE FOLDED THE SAME WAY, SO I WAS SURE IT WAS GHOST, BUT WHEN I RAN OVER TO TALK...
...IT WAS SOME BLACK GEM I'D NEVER SEEN BEFORE, AND THEN I GOT PUNCHED IN THE FACE...
GHOST *IS* HERE, RIGHT?
YES.
WITH SENSEI?
THAT'S RIGHT.

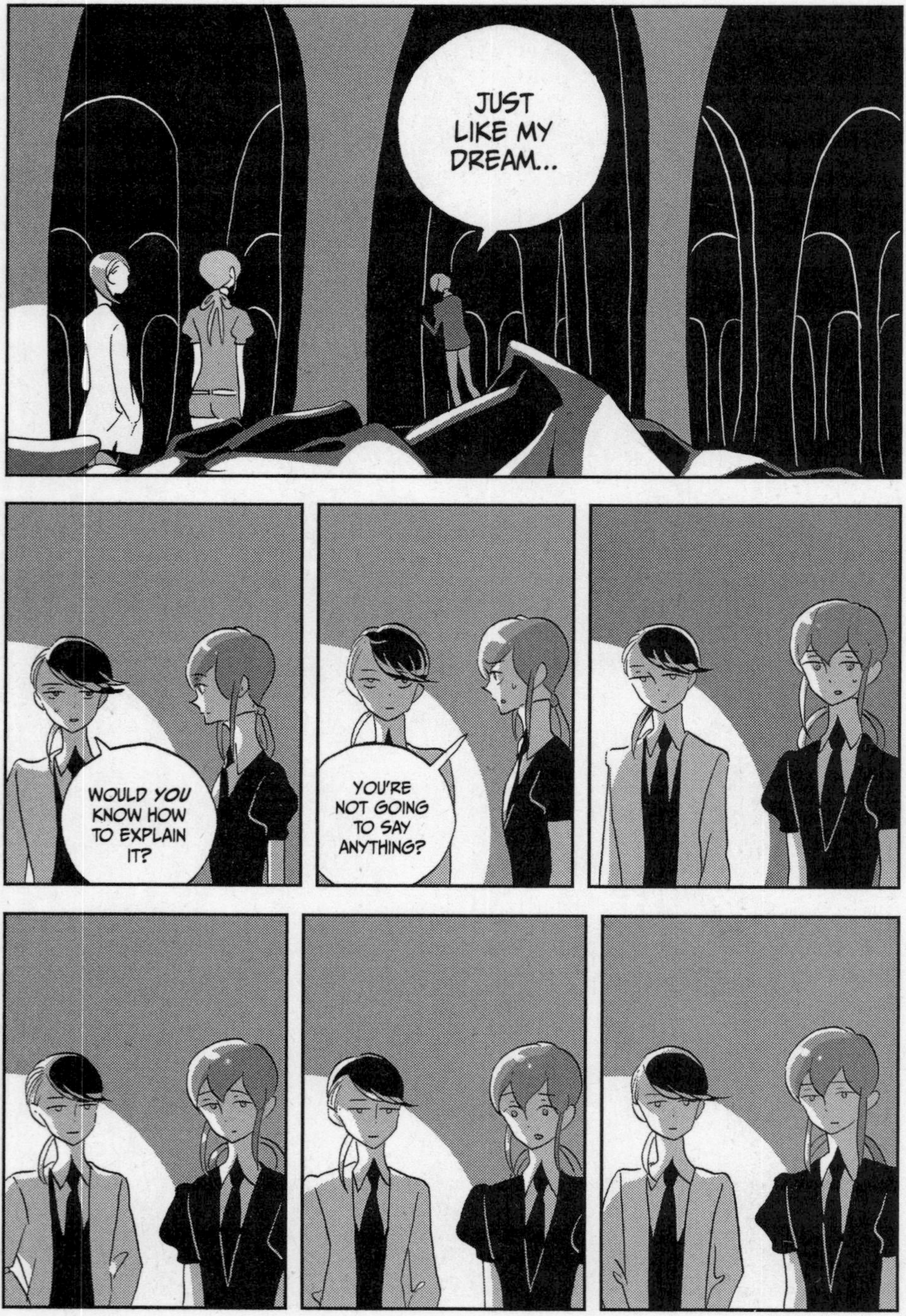
JUST LIKE MY DREAM...
YOU'RE NOT GOING TO SAY ANYTHING?
WOULD *YOU* KNOW HOW TO EXPLAIN IT?

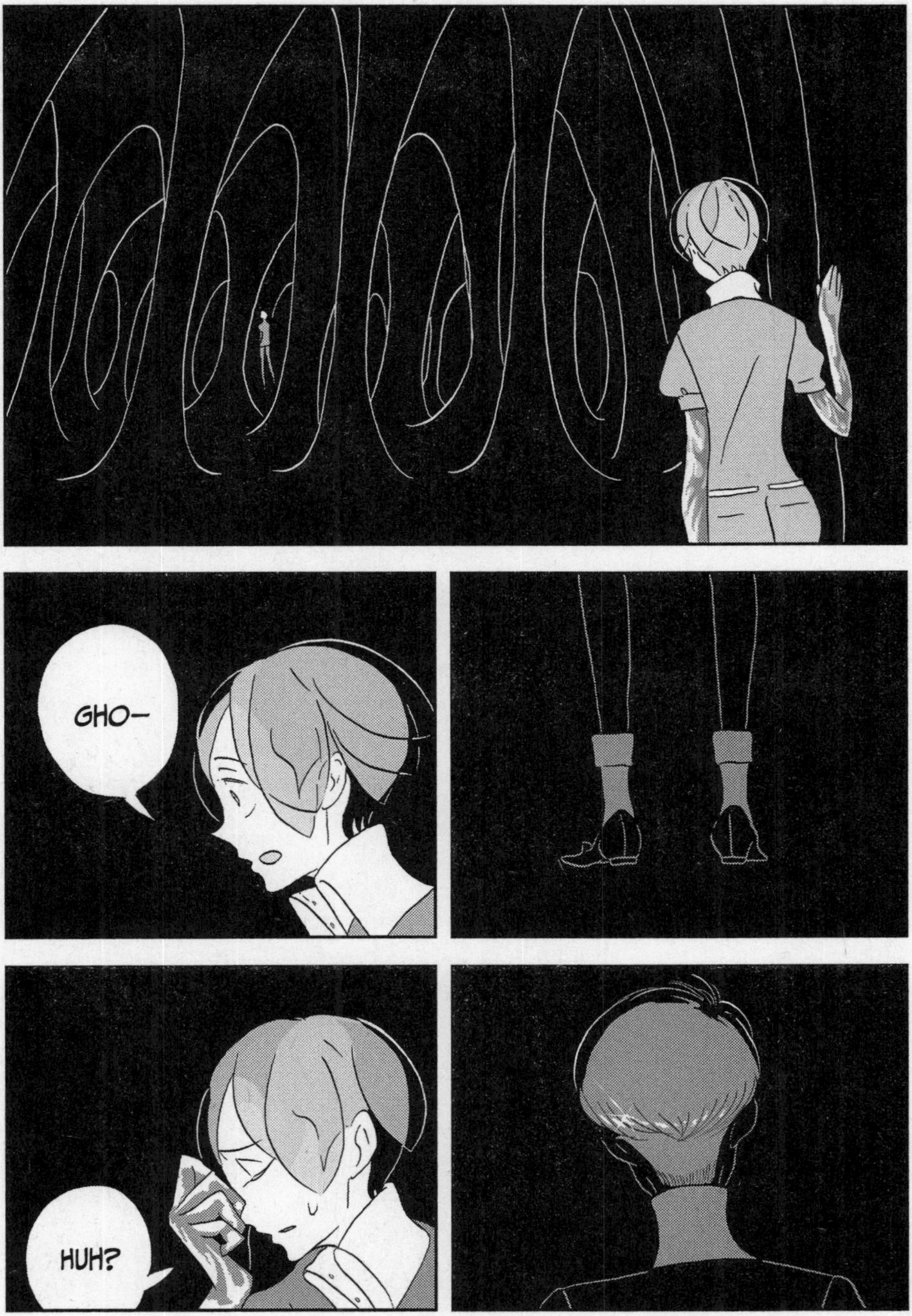
GHO-
HUH?

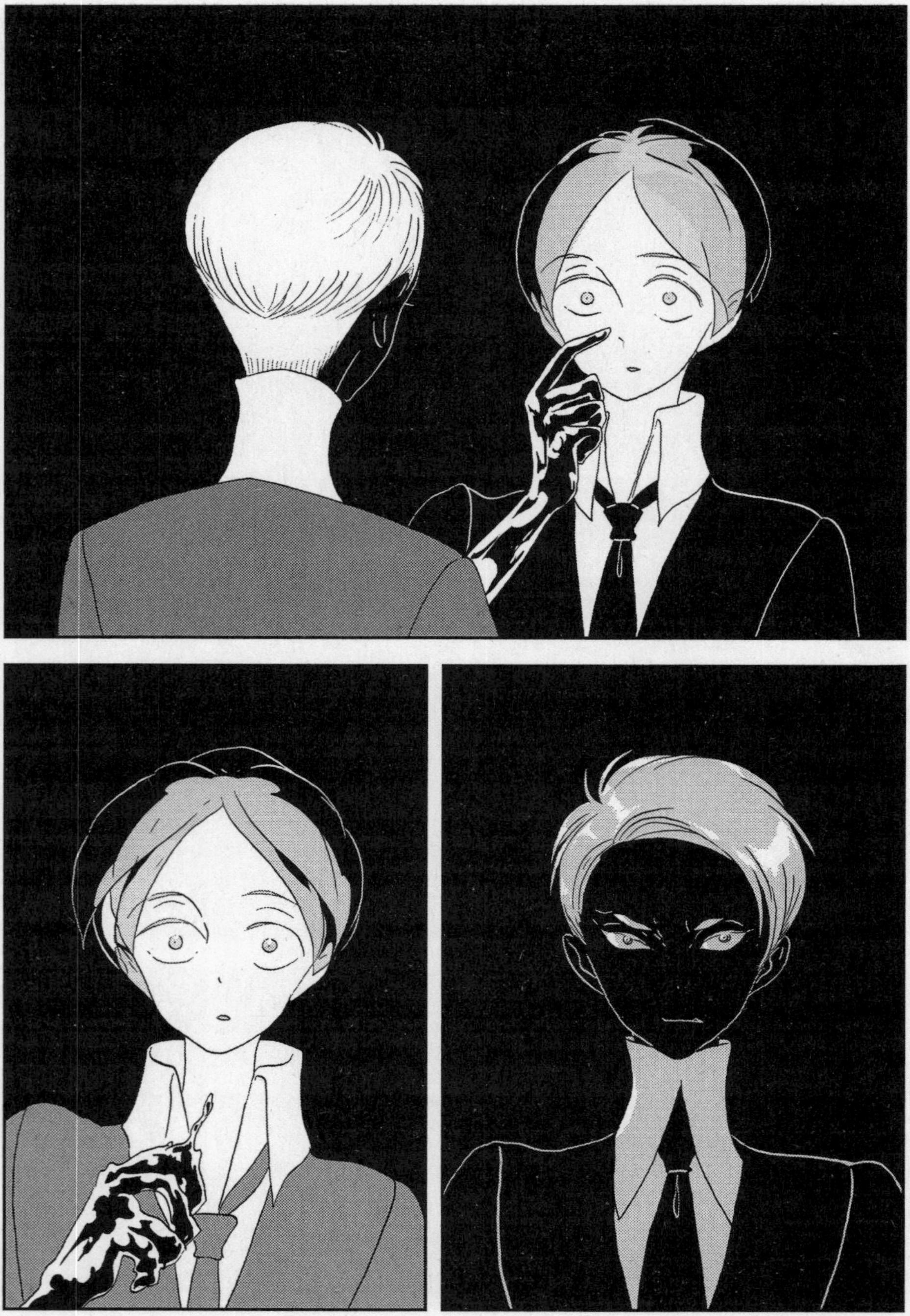

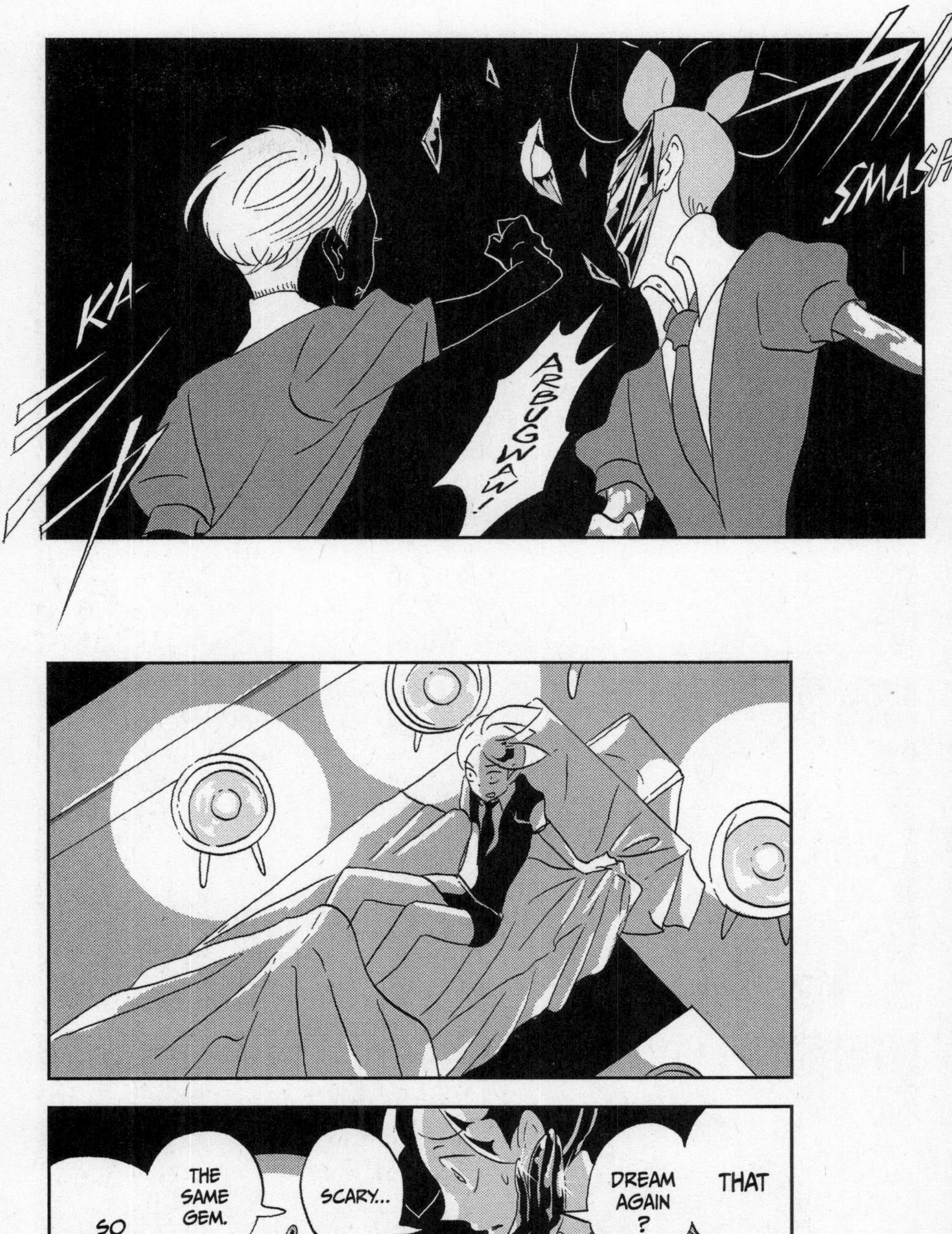
SMASH
ARBUGWAW!
KA-
THAT
DREAM AGAIN ?
SCARY...
THE SAME GEM.
SO CREEPY ...

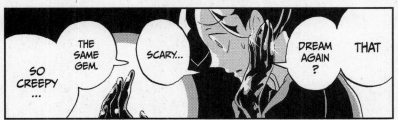

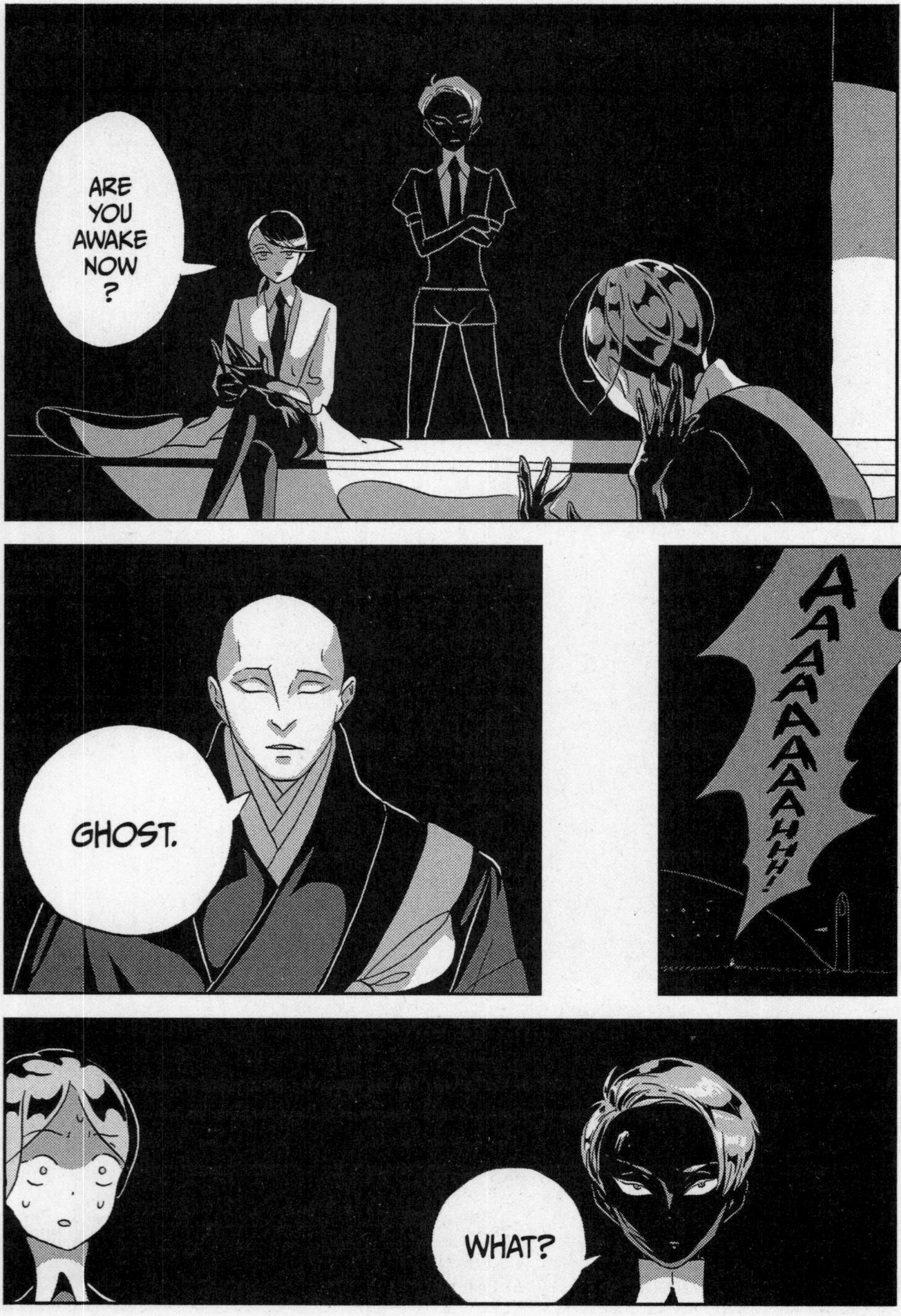
ARE YOU AWAKE NOW?
AAAAAAAAHHH!
GHOST.
WHAT?

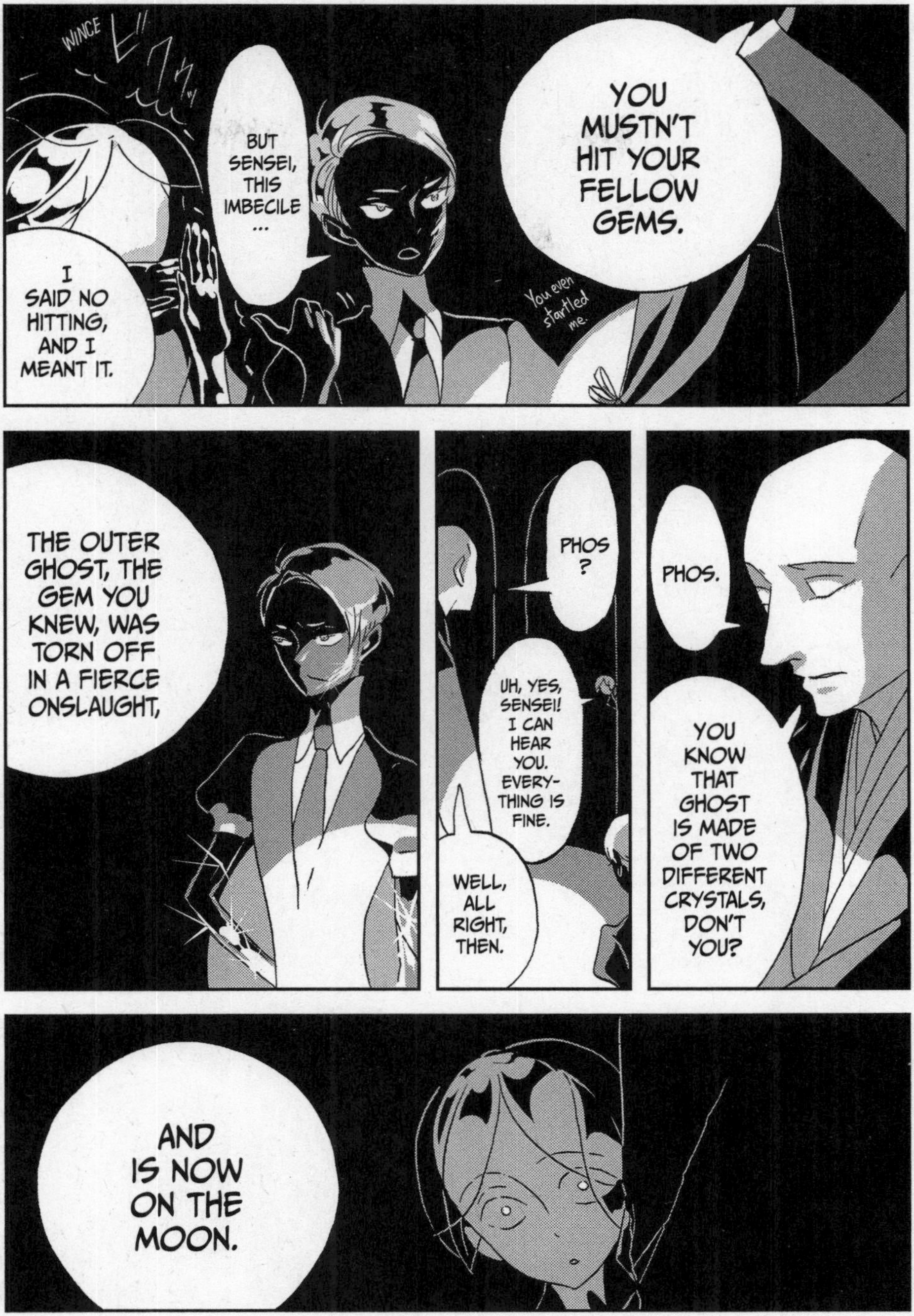
YOU MUSTN'T HIT YOUR FELLOW GEMS.
BUT SENSEI, THIS IMBECILE ...
WINCE
You even startled me.
I SAID NO HITTING, AND I MEANT IT.
PHOS.
YOU KNOW THAT GHOST IS MADE OF TWO DIFFERENT CRYSTALS, DON'T YOU?
PHOS ?
UH, YES, SENSEI! I CAN HEAR YOU. EVERYTHING IS FINE.
WELL, ALL RIGHT, THEN.
THE OUTER GHOST, THE GEM YOU KNEW, WAS TORN OFF IN A FIERCE ONSLAUGHT,
AND IS NOW ON THE MOON.

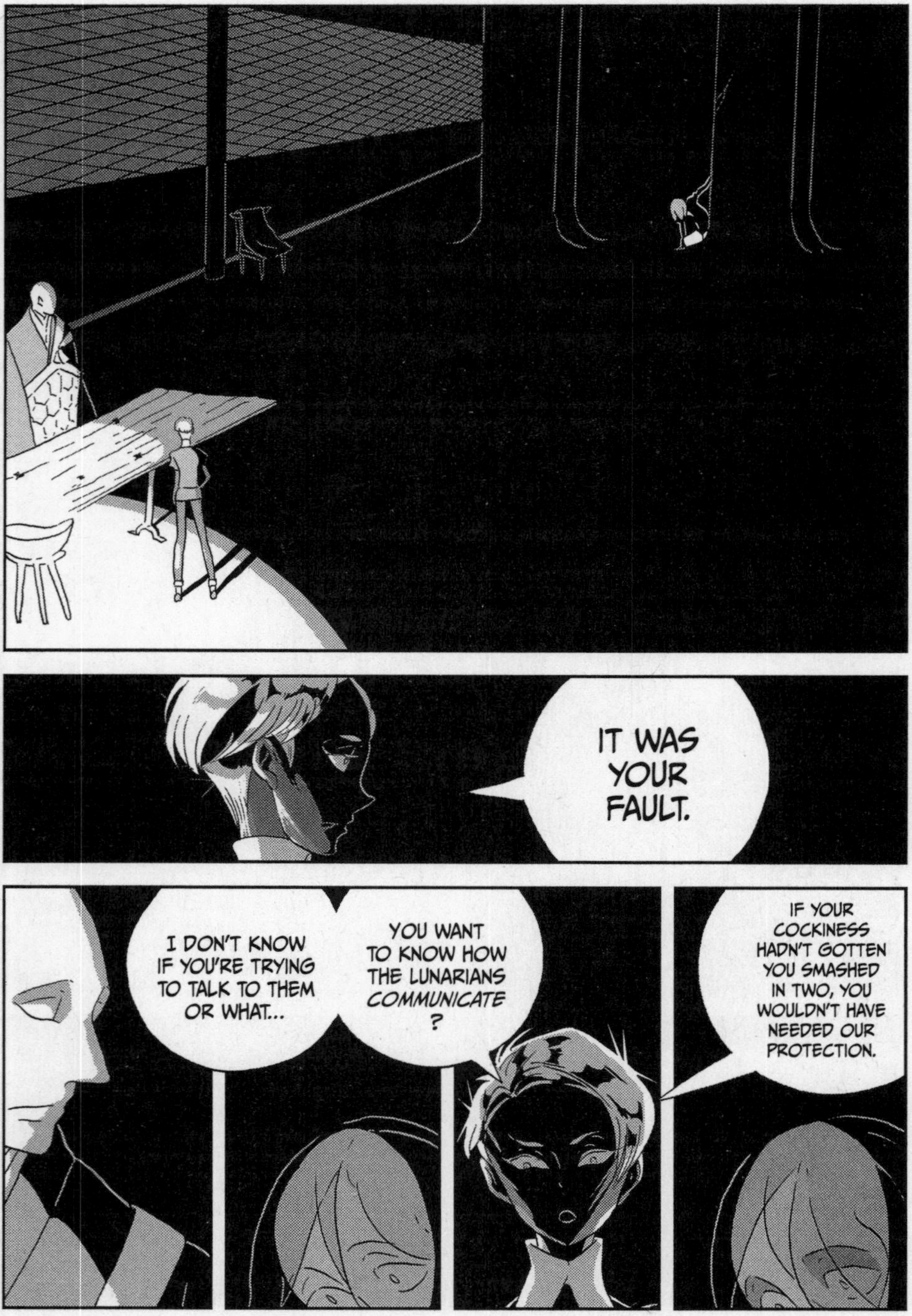
IT WAS YOUR FAULT.
IF YOUR COCKINESS HADN'T GOTTEN YOU SMASHED IN TWO, YOU WOULDN'T HAVE NEEDED OUR PROTECTION.
YOU WANT TO KNOW HOW THE LUNARIANS *COMMUNICATE*?
I DON'T KNOW IF YOU'RE TRYING TO TALK TO THEM OR WHAT...

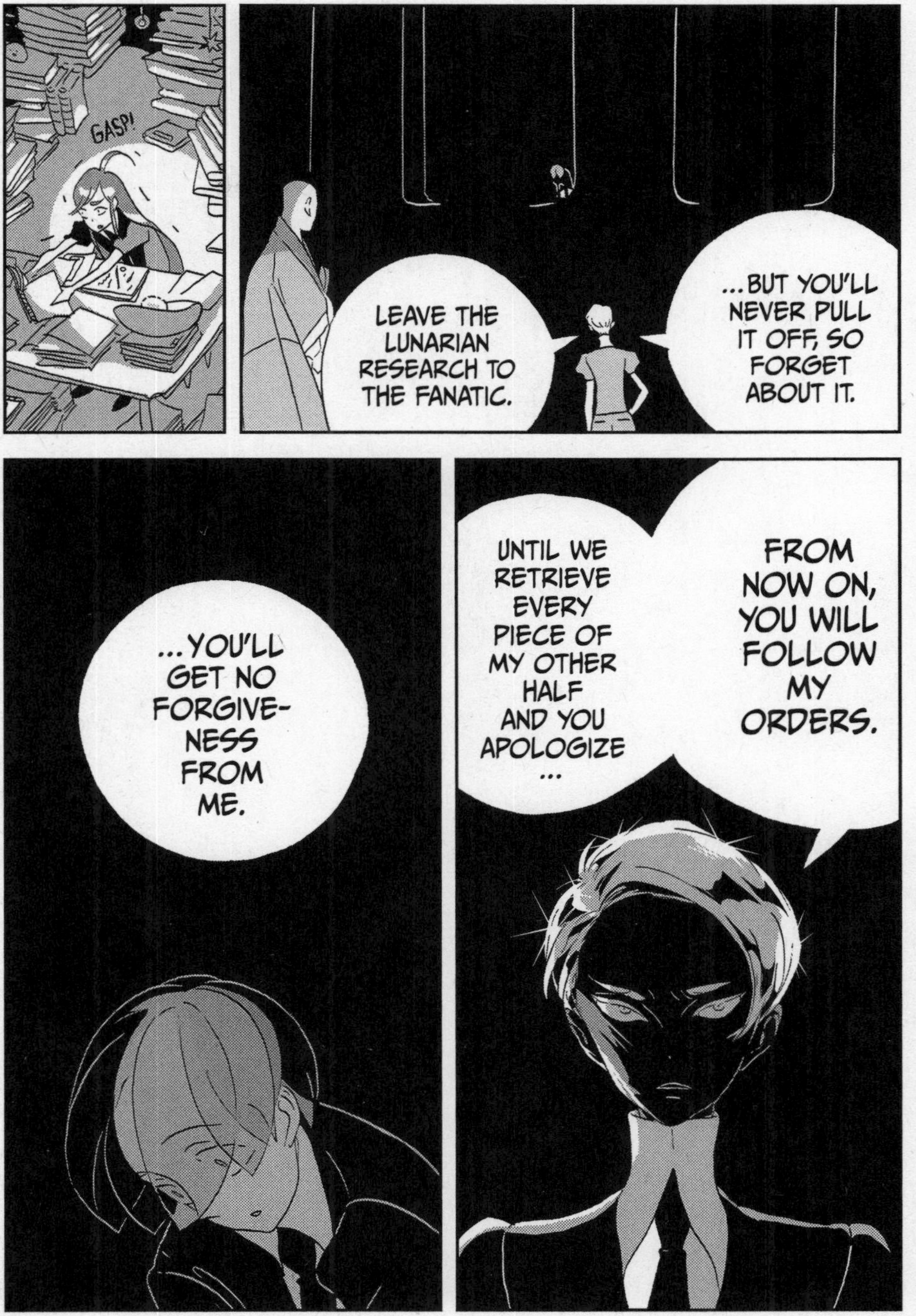
...BUT YOU'LL NEVER PULL IT OFF, SO FORGET ABOUT IT.
LEAVE THE LUNARIAN RESEARCH TO THE FANATIC.
GASP!
FROM NOW ON, YOU WILL FOLLOW MY ORDERS.
UNTIL WE RETRIEVE EVERY PIECE OF MY OTHER HALF AND YOU APOLOGIZE ...
...YOU'LL GET NO FORGIVE-NESS FROM ME.

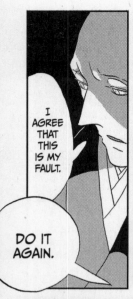

GHOST, YOU SHOULDN'T LAY ALL THE BLAME ON PHOS.
YOU'RE TOO FORGIVING, SENSEI!
THE IDIOT KEEPS TRYING TO GET AWAY WITH EVERYTHING BECAUSE YOU KEEP CODDLING THE LITTLE BABY! IF YOU DON'T LAY DOWN ANY BOUNDARIES, THIS IS ONLY GOING TO HAPPEN AGAIN!
I AGREE THAT THIS IS MY FAULT.
DO IT AGAIN.
HIT ME AGAIN.
MAYBE THIS IS ANOTHER DREAM.
DON'T THINK *I'M* GOING TO SPOIL YOU, TOO.
NO TRAMPLING, EITHER.

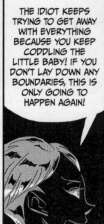

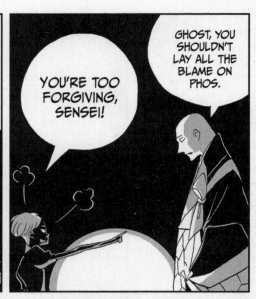

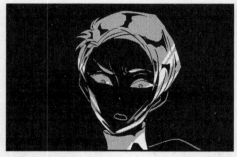

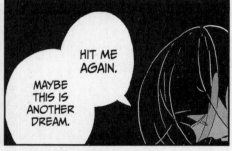

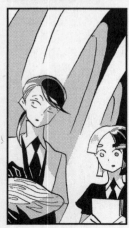

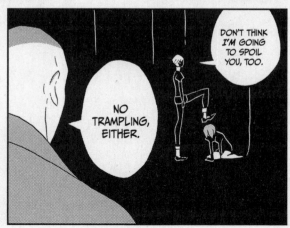

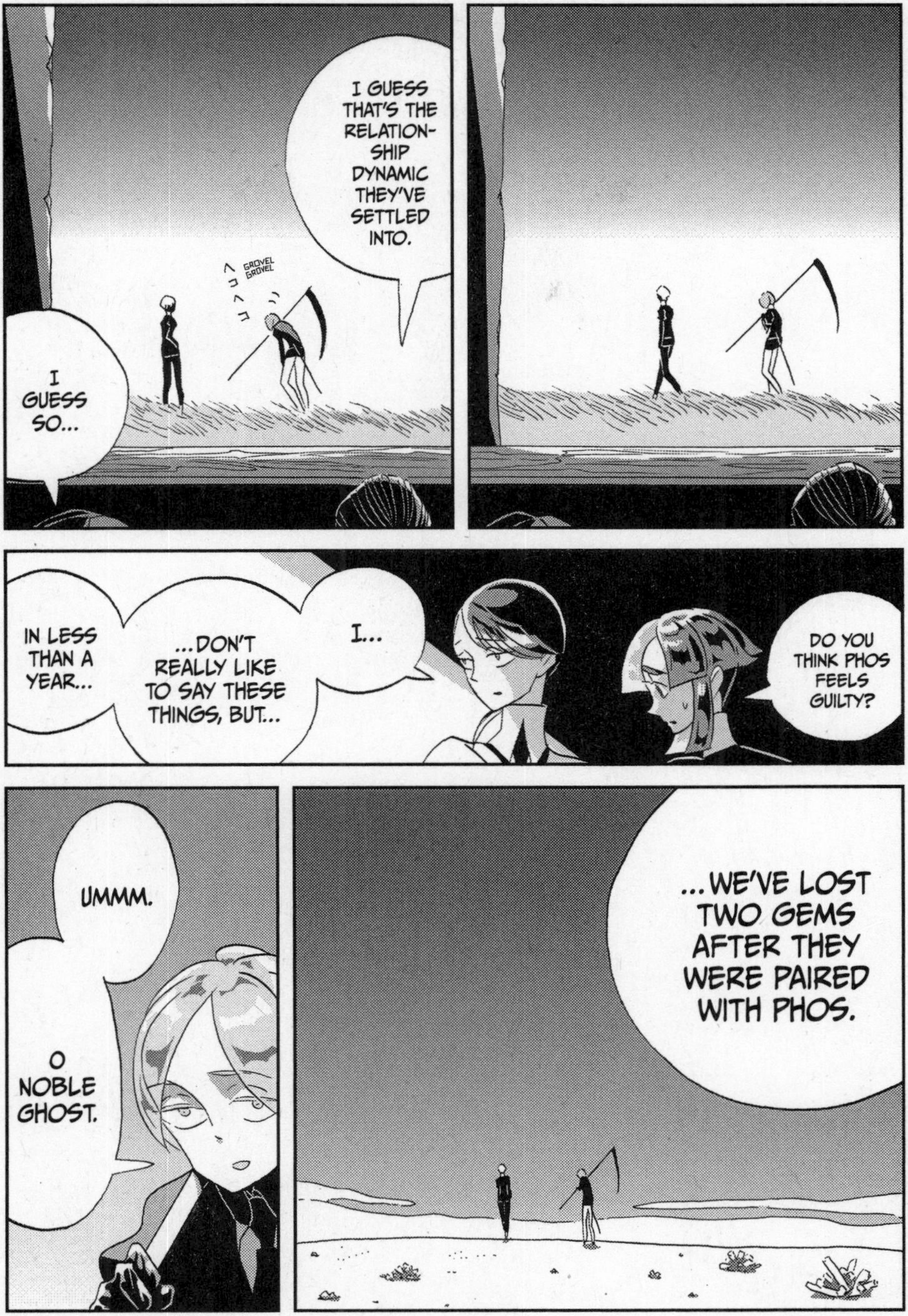
I GUESS THAT'S THE RELATION-SHIP DYNAMIC THEY'VE SETTLED INTO.
GROVEL GROVEL
I GUESS SO...
DO YOU THINK PHOS FEELS GUILTY?
I...
...DON'T REALLY LIKE TO SAY THESE THINGS, BUT...
IN LESS THAN A YEAR...
...WE'VE LOST TWO GEMS AFTER THEY WERE PAIRED WITH PHOS.
UMMM.
O NOBLE GHOST.

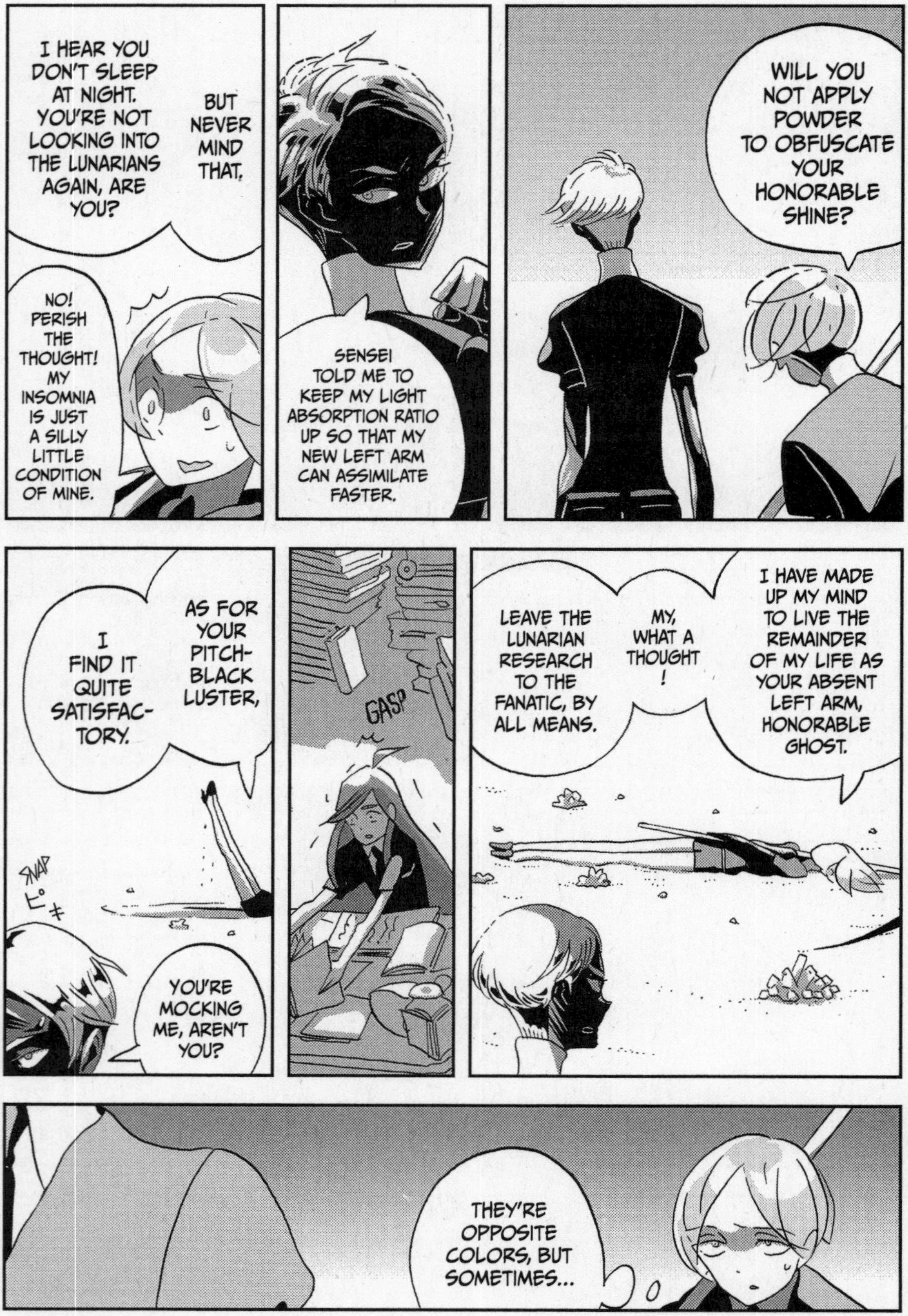
WILL YOU NOT APPLY POWDER TO OBFUSCATE YOUR HONORABLE SHINE?
SENSEI TOLD ME TO KEEP MY LIGHT ABSORPTION RATIO UP SO THAT MY NEW LEFT ARM CAN ASSIMILATE FASTER.
BUT NEVER MIND THAT.
I HEAR YOU DON'T SLEEP AT NIGHT. YOU'RE NOT LOOKING INTO THE LUNARIANS AGAIN, ARE YOU?
NO! PERISH THE THOUGHT! MY INSOMNIA IS JUST A SILLY LITTLE CONDITION OF MINE.
I HAVE MADE UP MY MIND TO LIVE THE REMAINDER OF MY LIFE AS YOUR ABSENT LEFT ARM, HONORABLE GHOST.
MY, WHAT A THOUGHT!
LEAVE THE LUNARIAN RESEARCH TO THE FANATIC, BY ALL MEANS.
GASP
AS FOR YOUR PITCH-BLACK LUSTER,
I FIND IT QUITE SATISFACTORY.
SNAP
ピキ
YOU'RE MOCKING ME, AREN'T YOU?
THEY'RE OPPOSITE COLORS, BUT SOMETIMES...

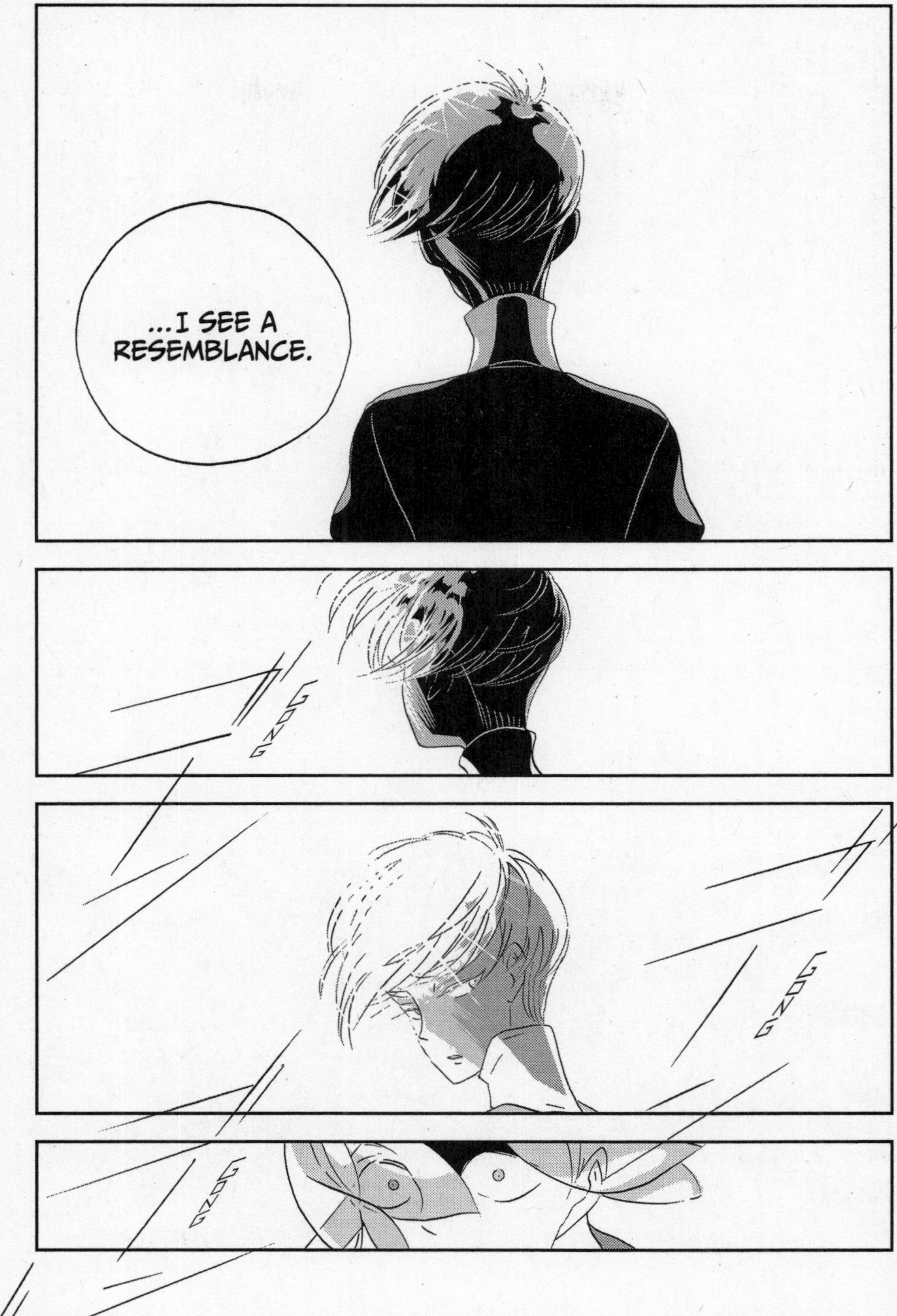
...I SEE A RESEMBLANCE.
GONG
GONG
GONG

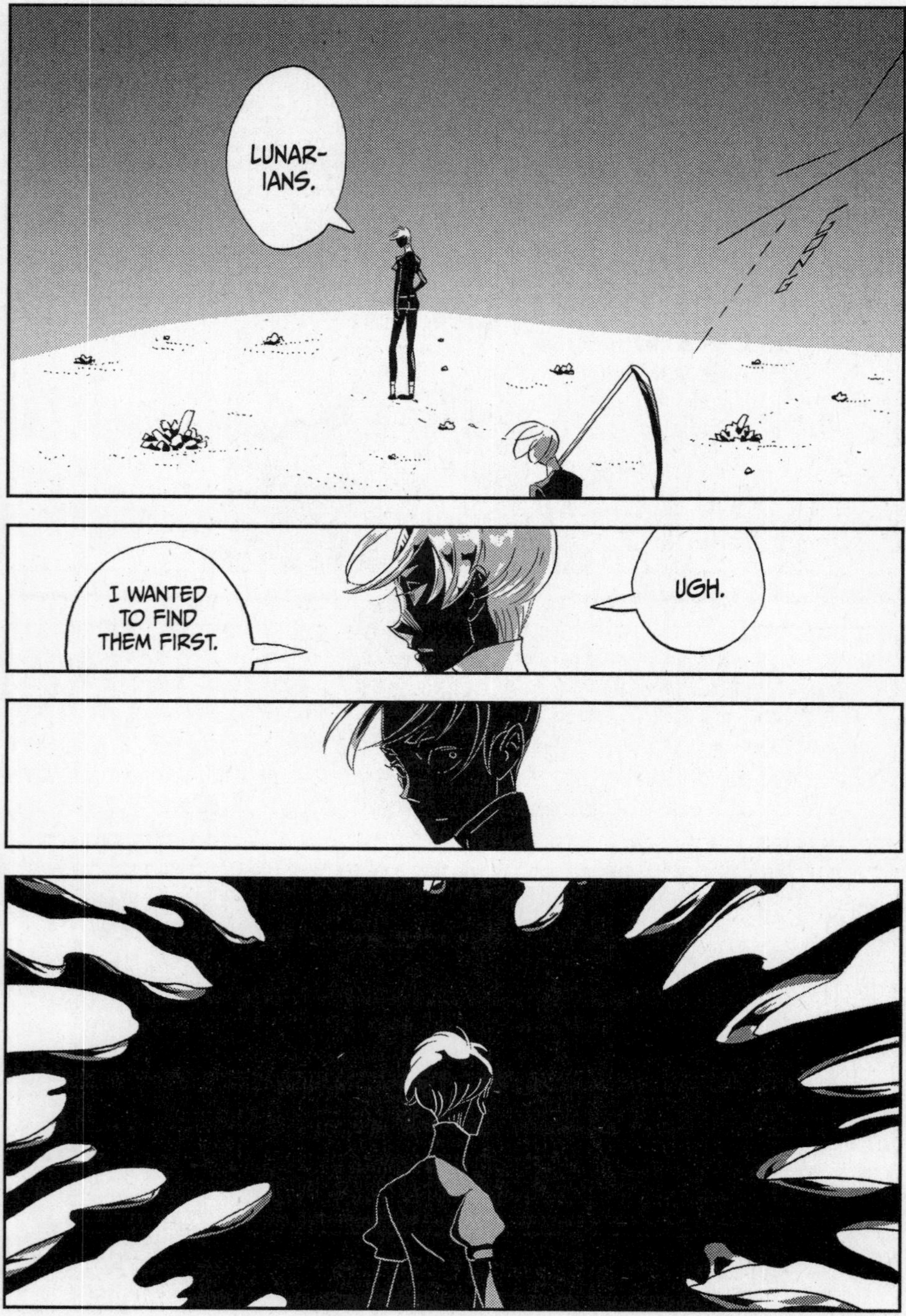
GONG
LUNAR-IANS.
UGH.
I WANTED TO FIND THEM FIRST.

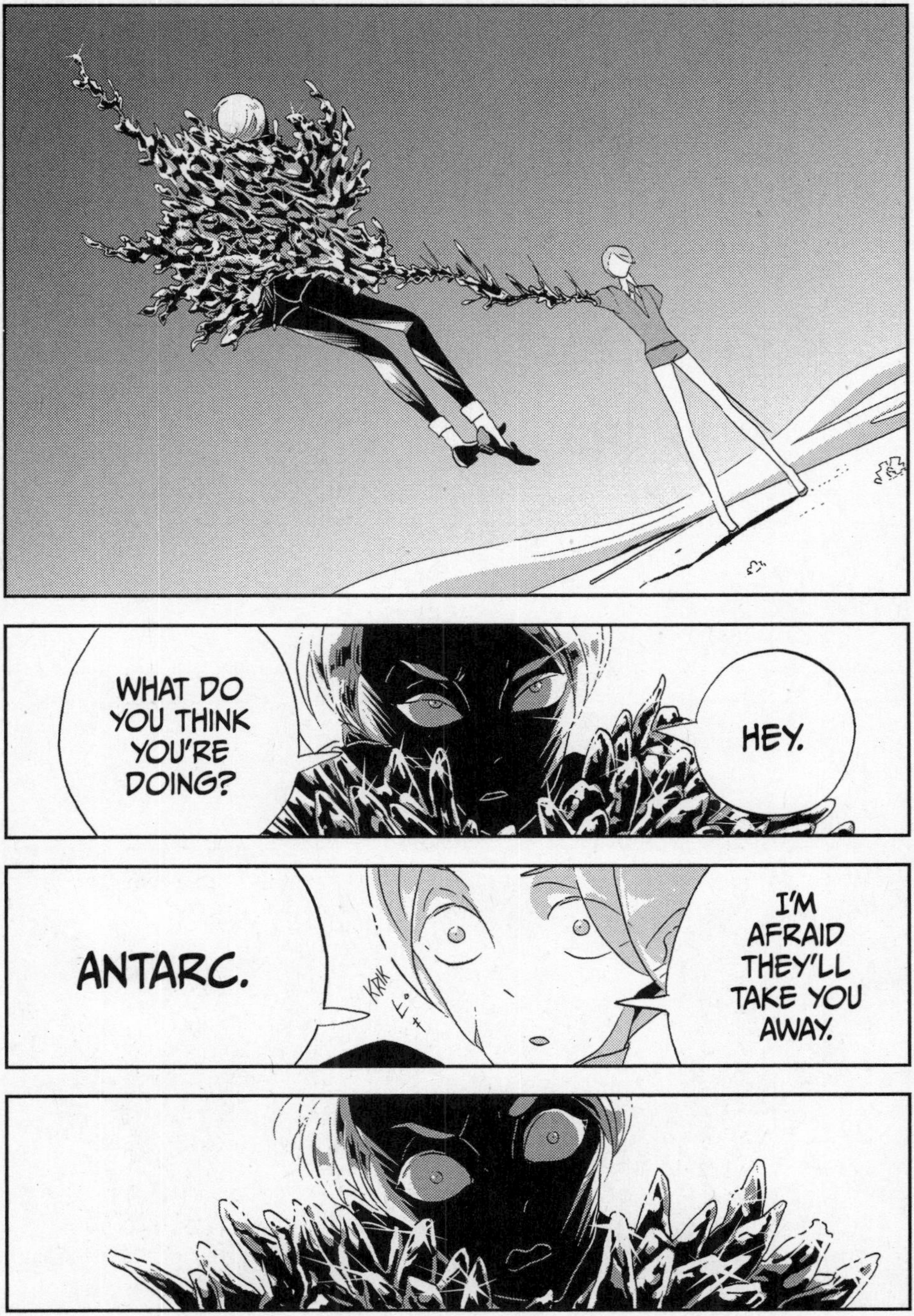
HEY.
WHAT DO YOU THINK YOU'RE DOING?
I'M AFRAID THEY'LL TAKE YOU AWAY.
KRIK
ANTARC.

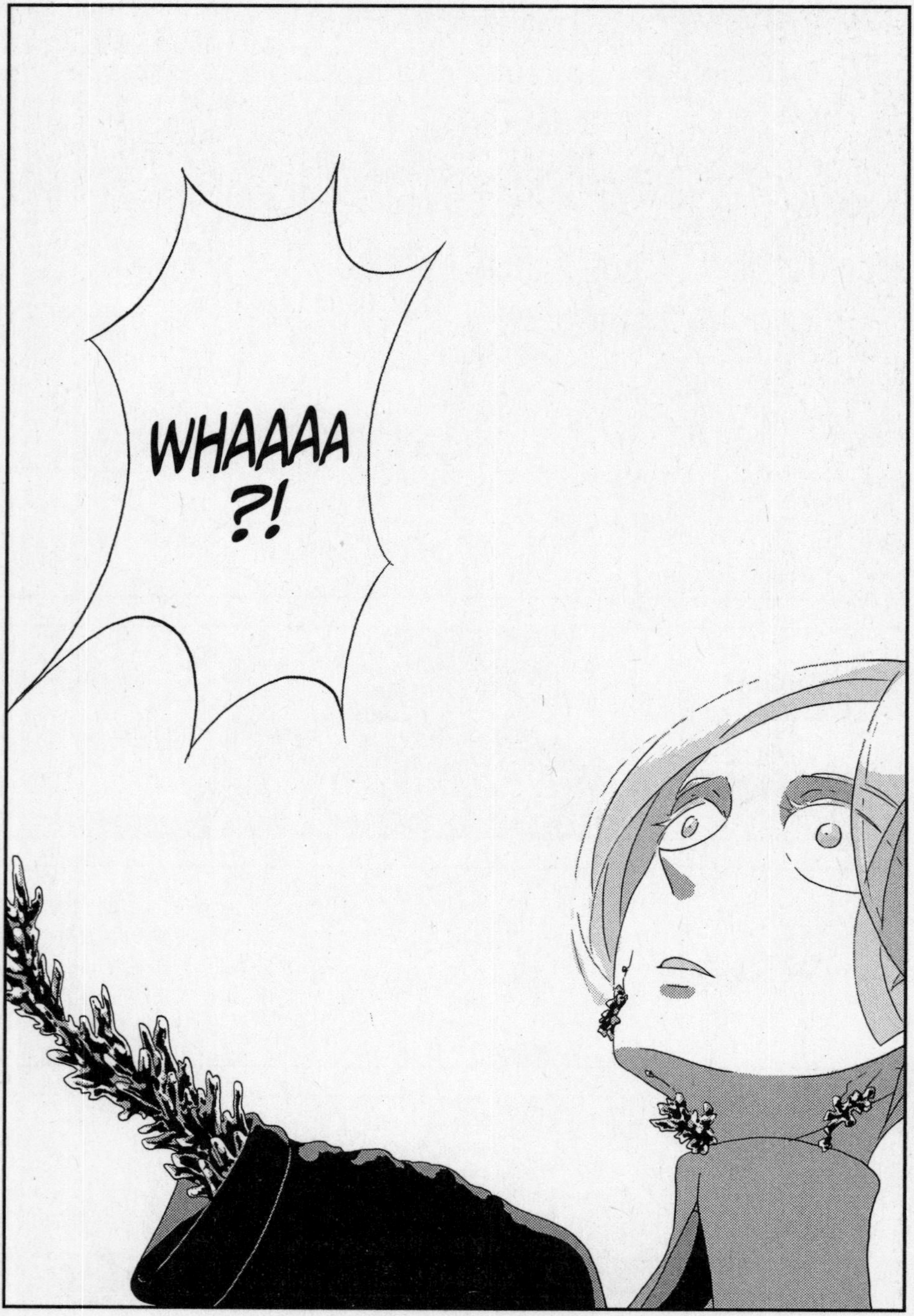
WHAAAA
?!

CHAPTER 38: Ghost Quartz END

CHAPTER 39:

Self-Admonition

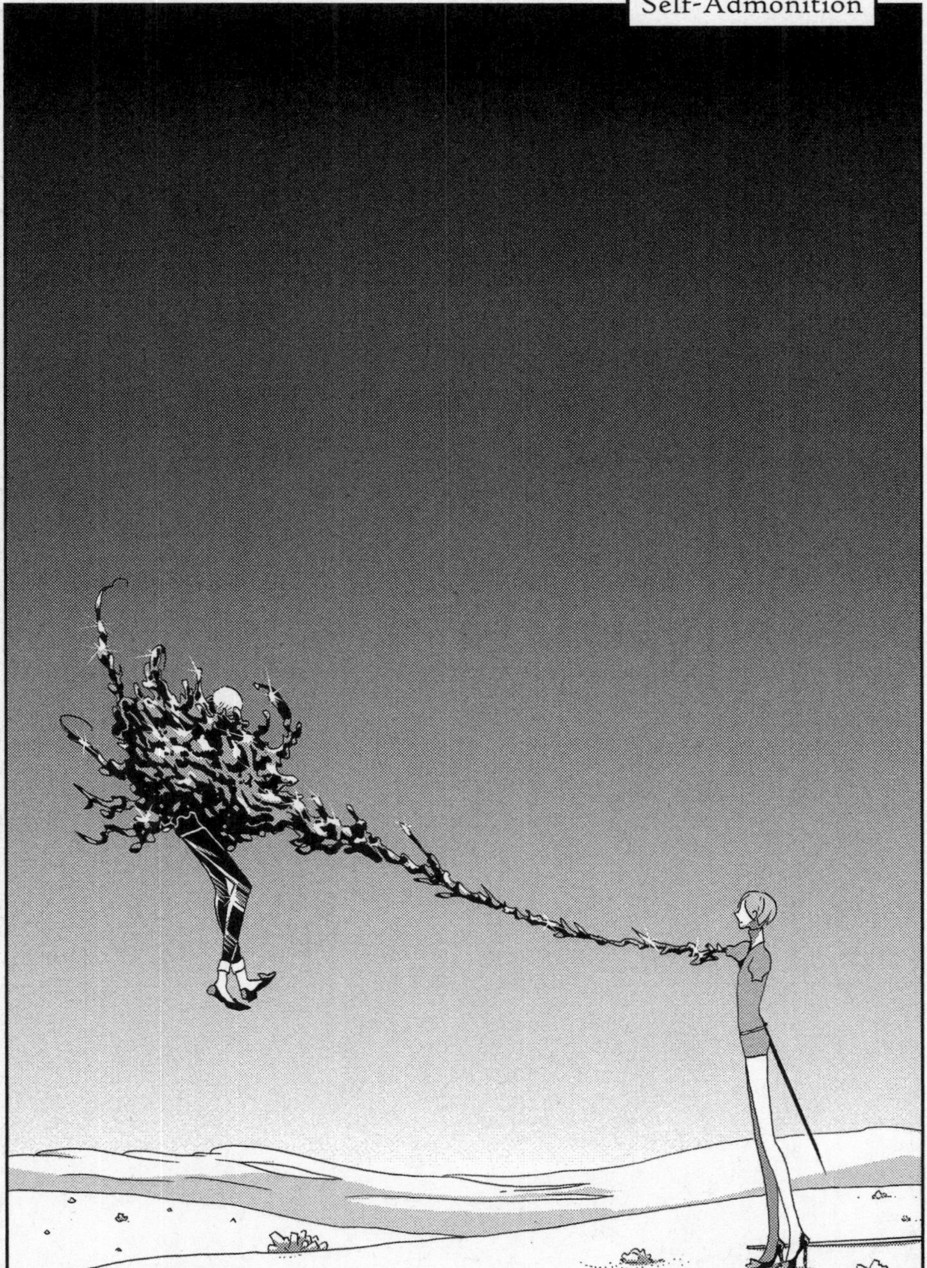

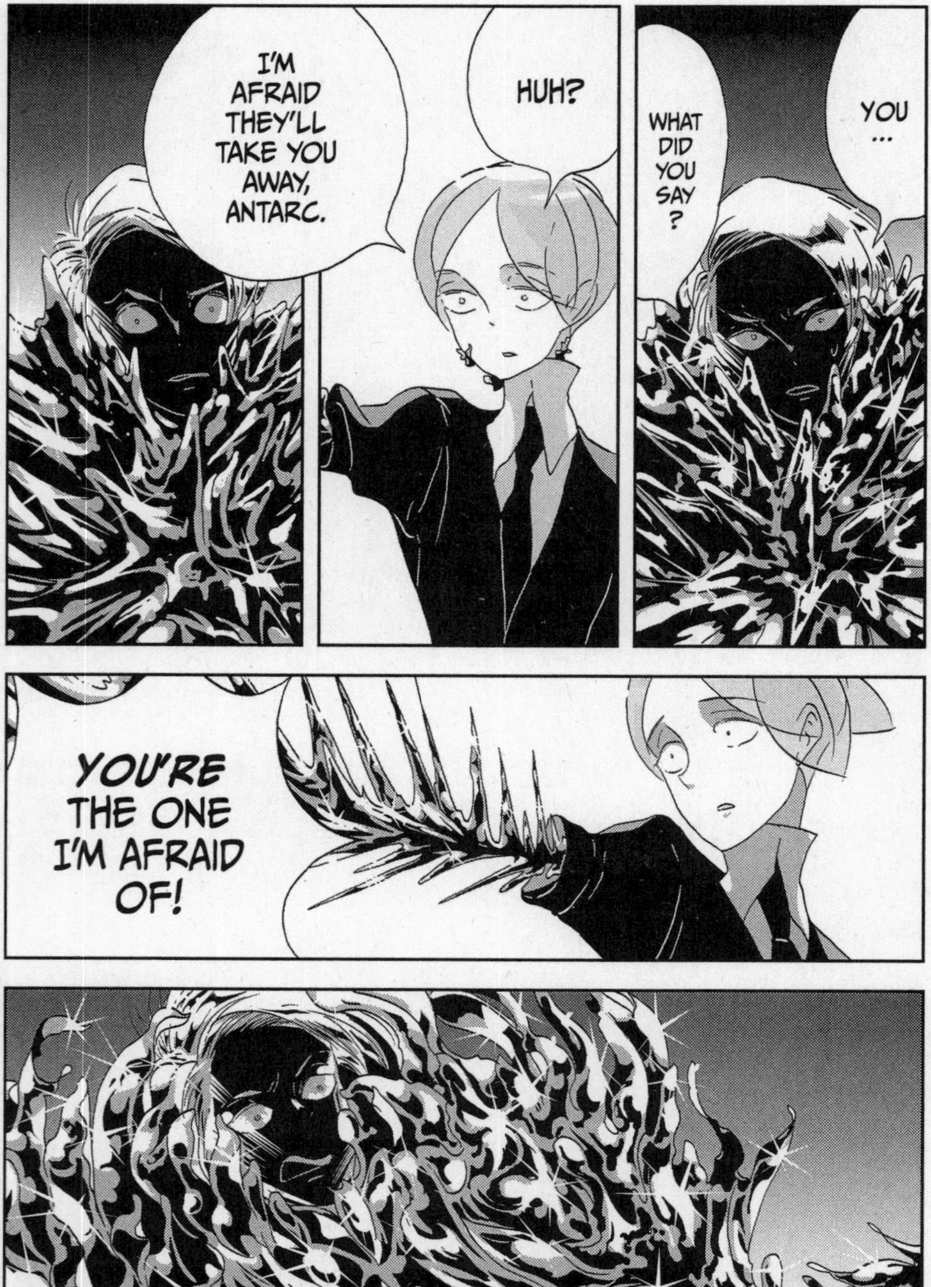
I'M AFRAID THEY'LL TAKE YOU AWAY, ANTARC.
HUH?
WHAT DID YOU SAY ?
YOU ...
YOU'RE THE ONE I'M AFRAID OF!

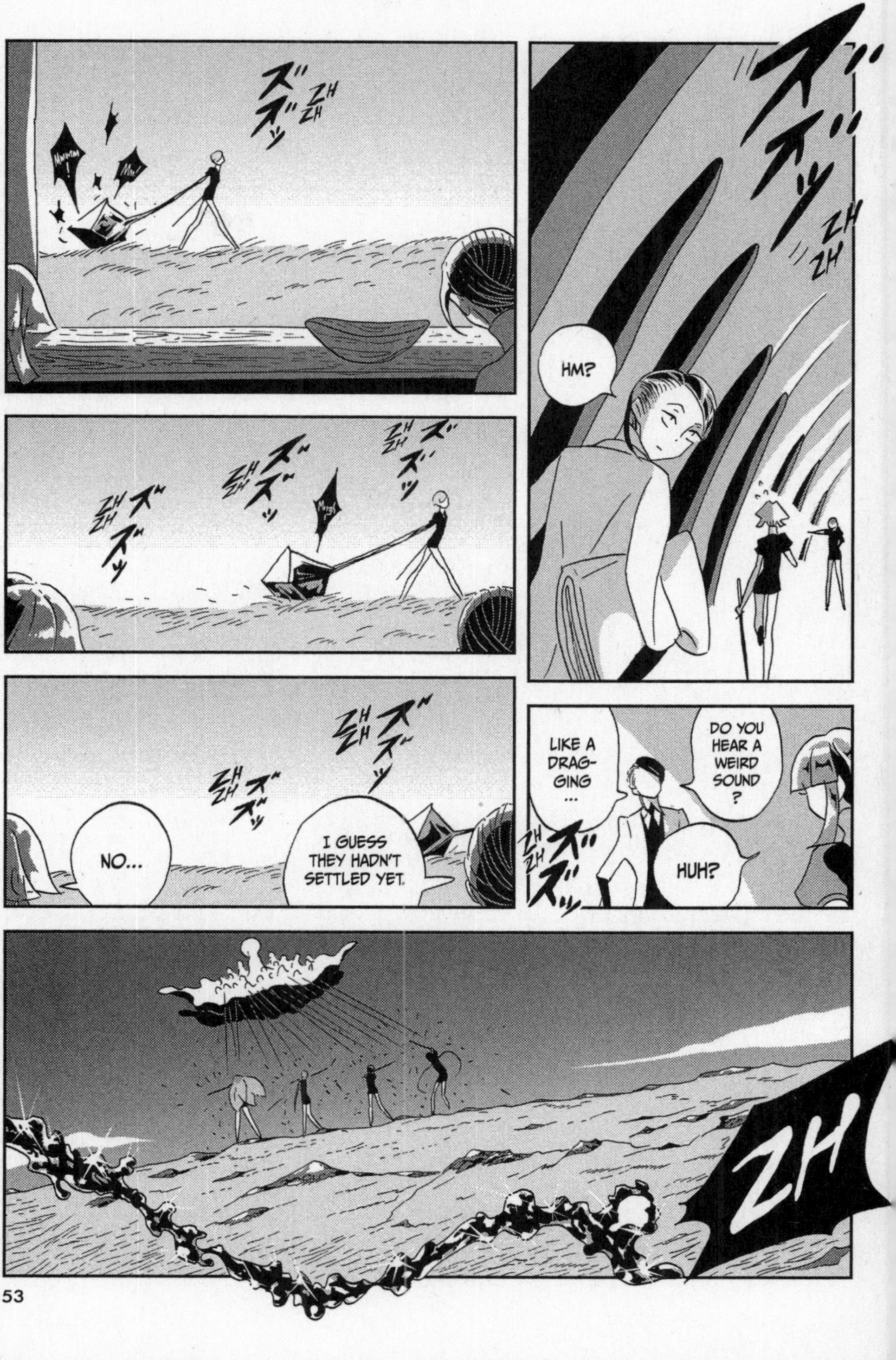
ZH ZH
HM?
ZH ZH
ZH ZH
ZH ZH
ZH ZH
DO YOU HEAR A WEIRD SOUND?
LIKE A DRAG-GING...
HUH?
ZH ZH
ZH ZH
ZH ZH
I GUESS THEY HADN'T SETTLED YET.
NO...
ZH

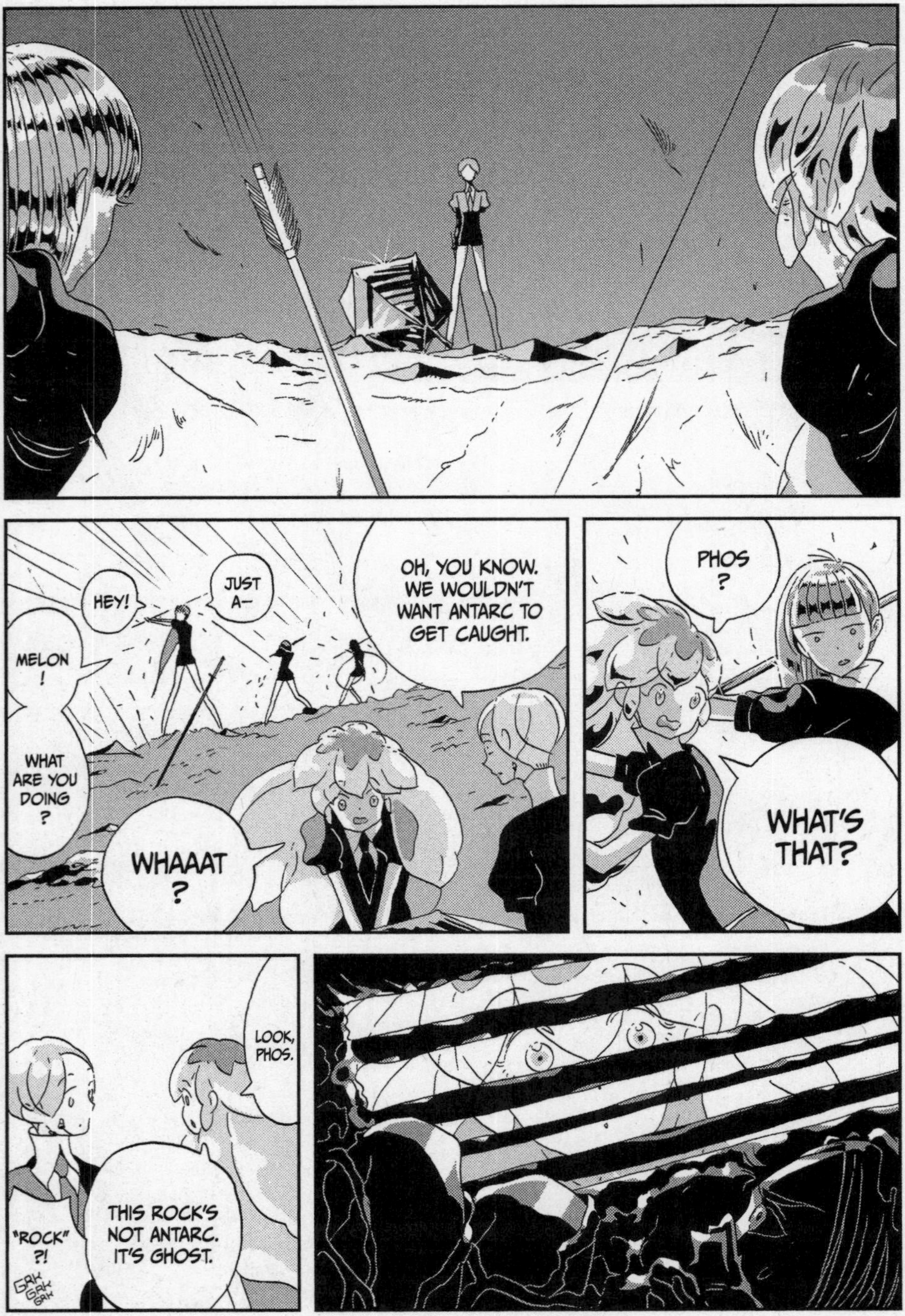
PHOS ?
WHAT'S THAT?
OH, YOU KNOW. WE WOULDN'T WANT ANTARC TO GET CAUGHT.
JUST A–
HEY!
MELON !
WHAT ARE YOU DOING ?
WHAAAT ?
LOOK, PHOS.
THIS ROCK'S NOT ANTARC. IT'S GHOST.
"ROCK" ?!
GRK GRK GRK

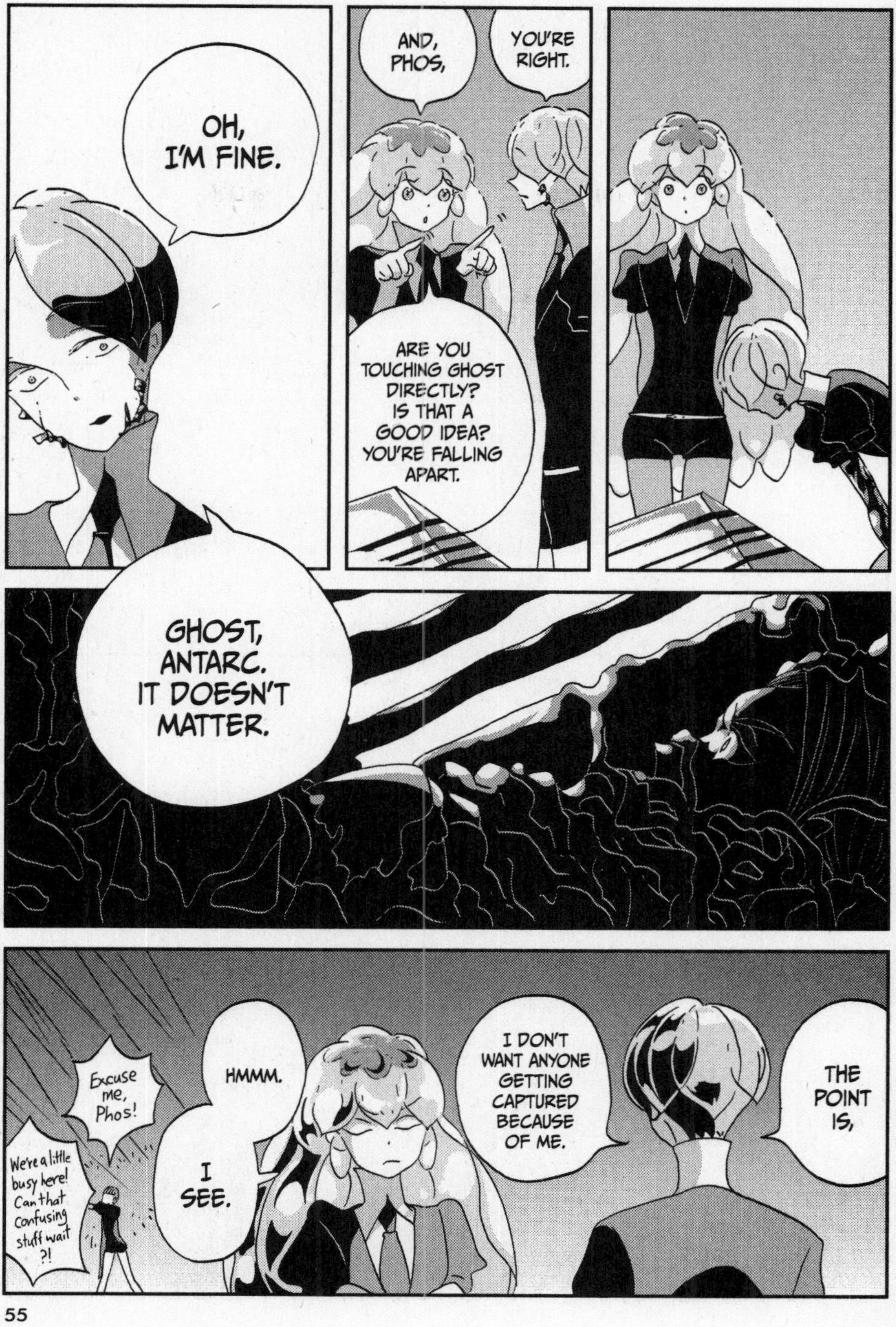
YOU'RE RIGHT.
AND, PHOS,
ARE YOU TOUCHING GHOST DIRECTLY? IS THAT A GOOD IDEA? YOU'RE FALLING APART.
OH, I'M FINE.
GHOST, ANTARC. IT DOESN'T MATTER.
THE POINT IS,
I DON'T WANT ANYONE GETTING CAPTURED BECAUSE OF ME.
HMMM.
I SEE.
Excuse me, Phos!
We're a little busy here! Can that confusing stuff wait ?!

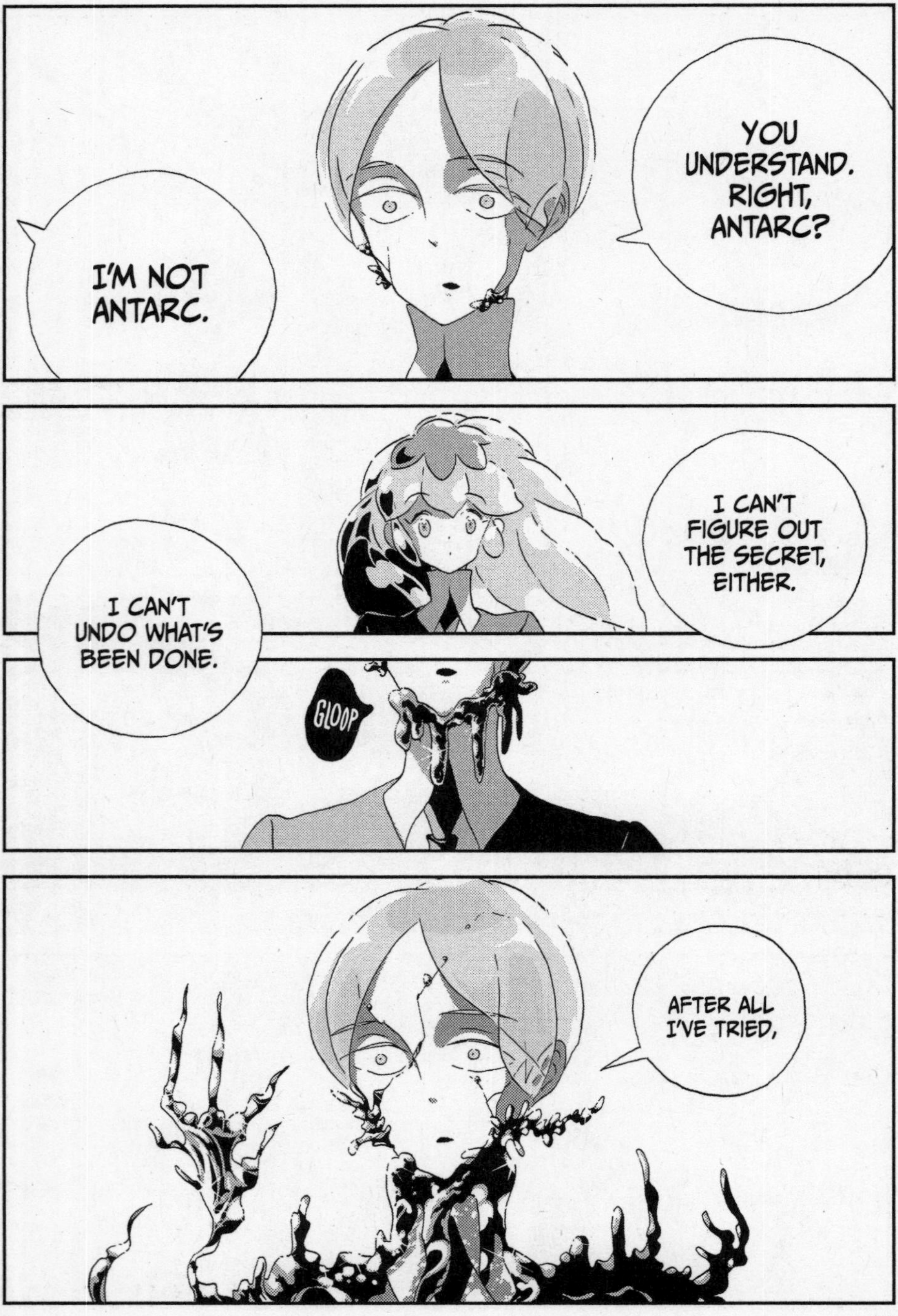
YOU UNDERSTAND. RIGHT, ANTARC?
I'M NOT ANTARC.
I CAN'T FIGURE OUT THE SECRET, EITHER.
I CAN'T UNDO WHAT'S BEEN DONE.
GLOOP
AFTER ALL I'VE TRIED,

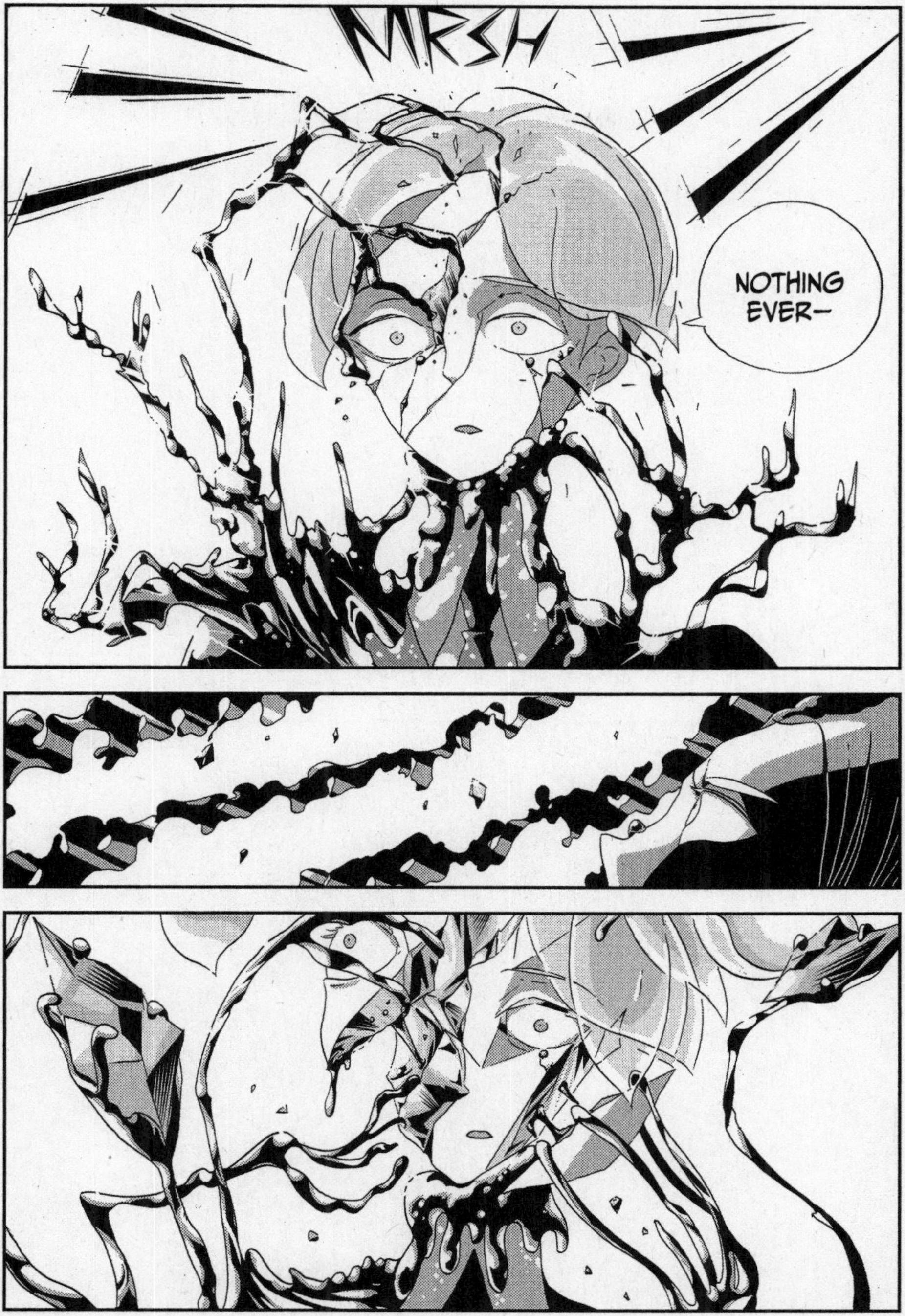
KRSH
NOTHING EVER—

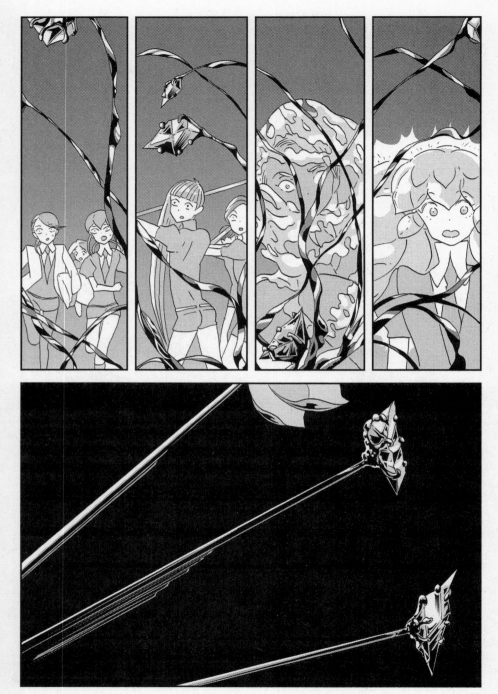

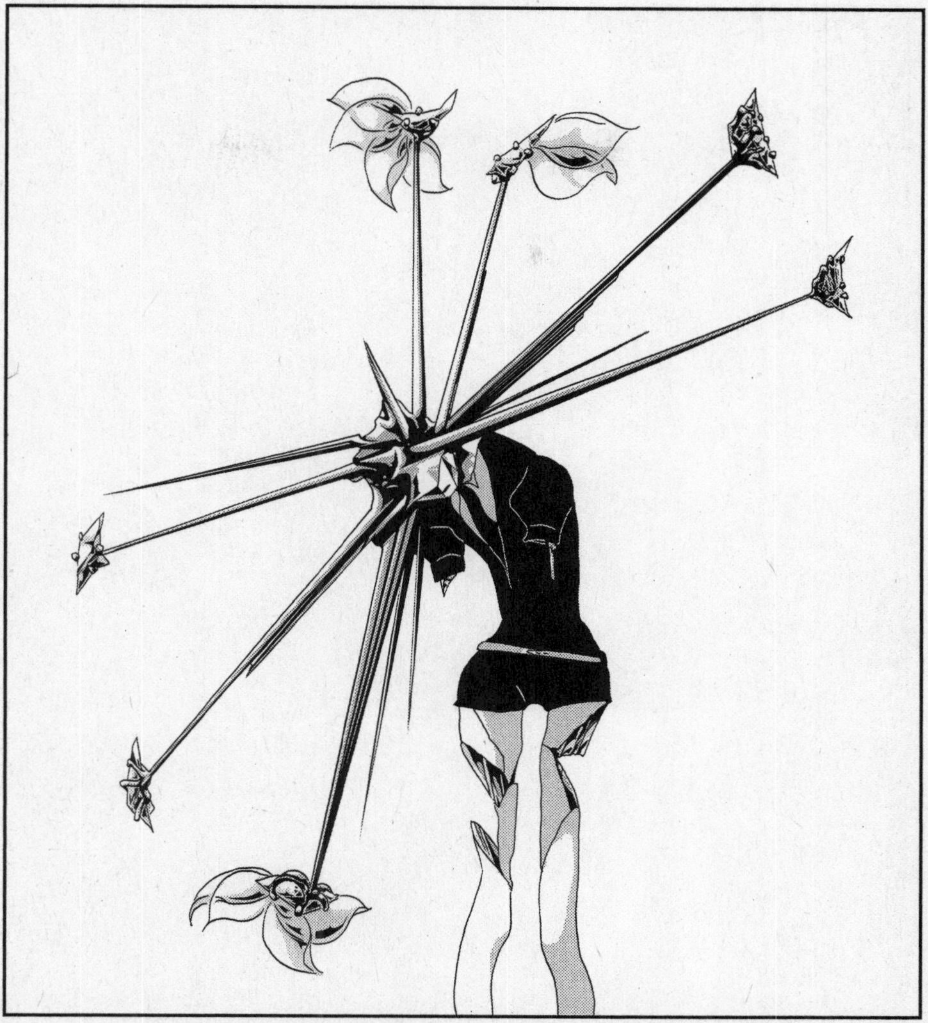

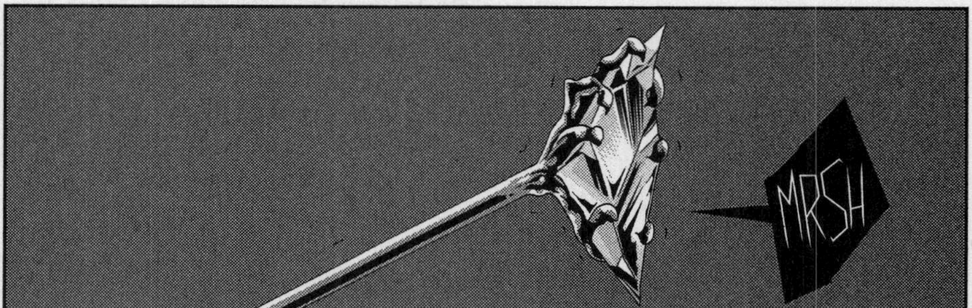
MRSH

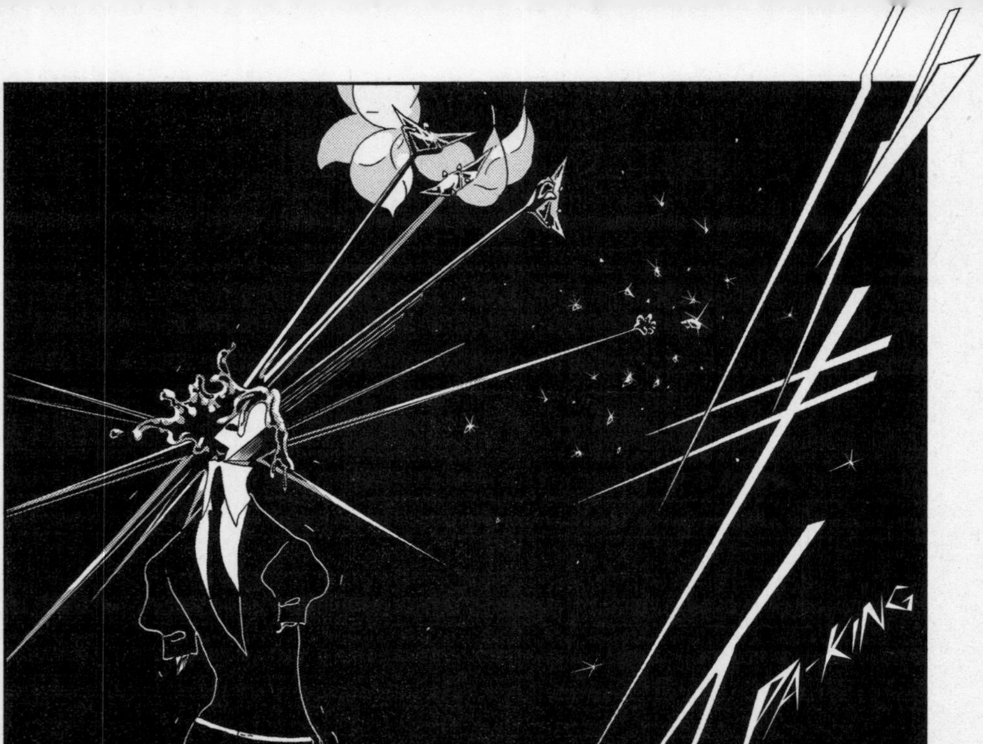
PA-KING
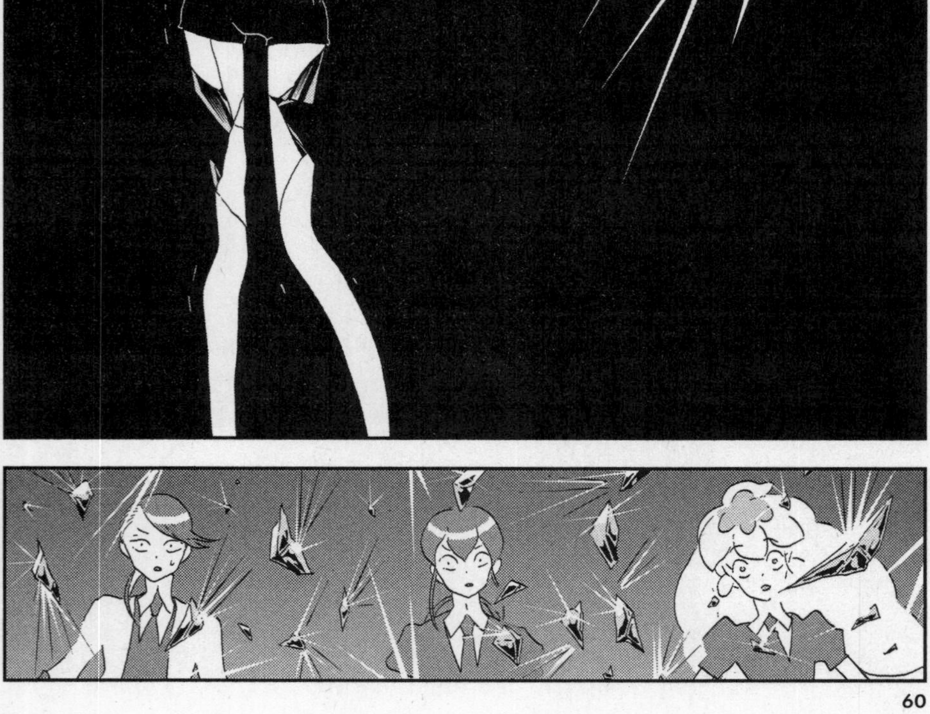

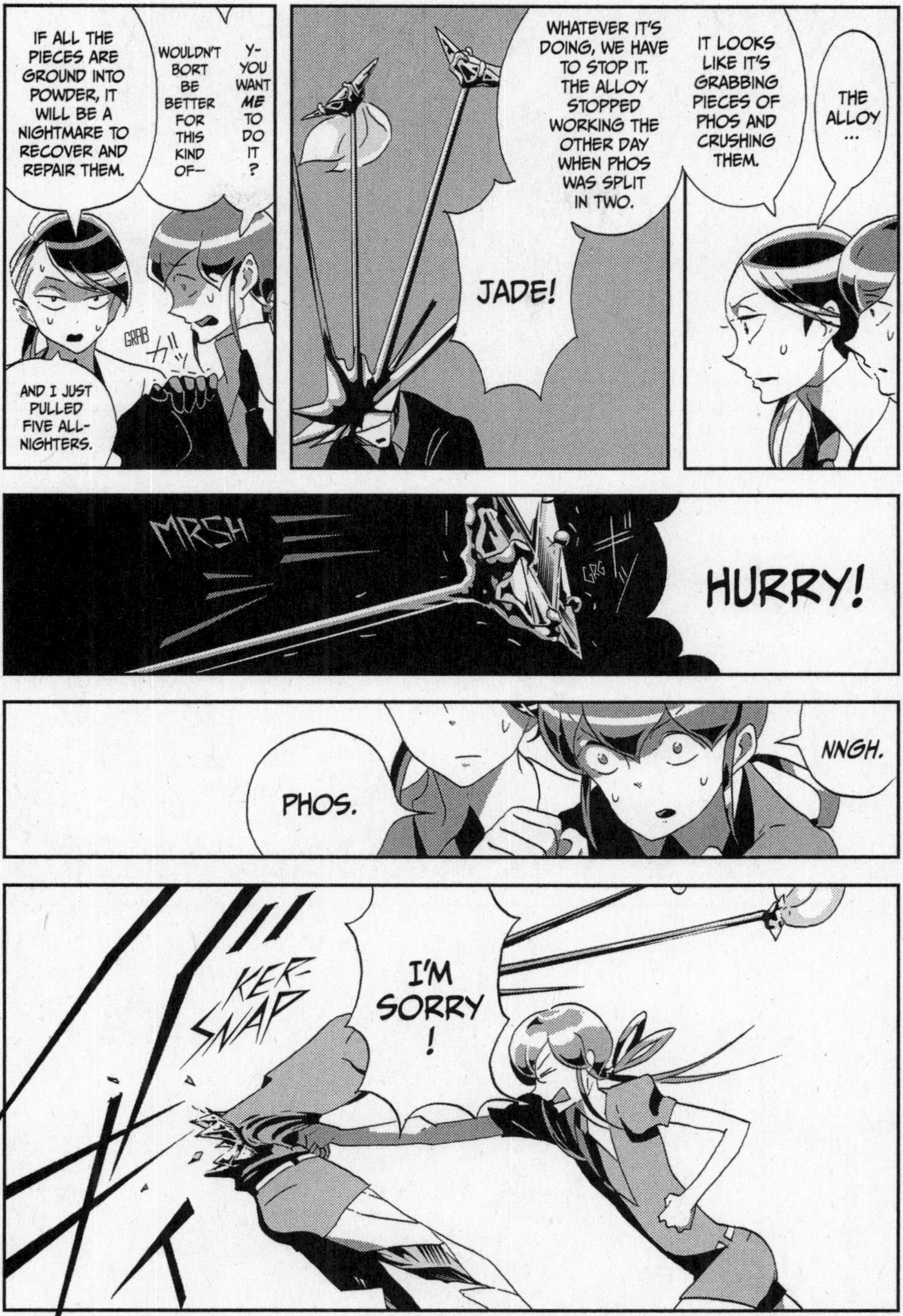
THE ALLOY ...
IT LOOKS LIKE IT'S GRABBING PIECES OF PHOS AND CRUSHING THEM.
WHATEVER IT'S DOING, WE HAVE TO STOP IT. THE ALLOY STOPPED WORKING THE OTHER DAY WHEN PHOS WAS SPLIT IN TWO.
JADE!
Y-YOU WANT ME TO DO IT?
WOULDN'T BORT BE BETTER FOR THIS KIND OF—
IF ALL THE PIECES ARE GROUND INTO POWDER, IT WILL BE A NIGHTMARE TO RECOVER AND REPAIR THEM.
GRAB
AND I JUST PULLED FIVE ALL-NIGHTERS.
HURRY!
GRG
MRSH
NNGH.
PHOS.
I'M SORRY!
KER-SNAP

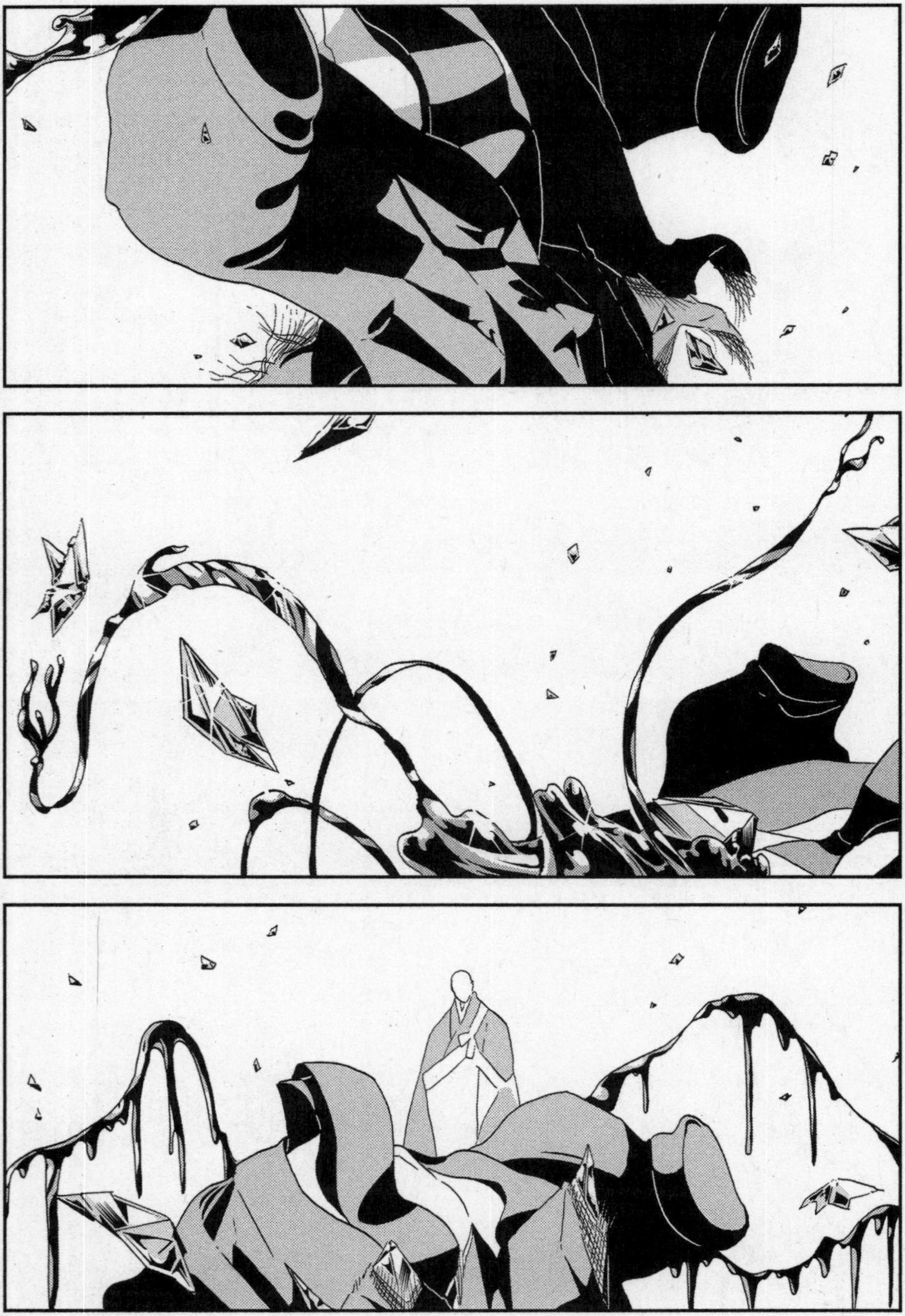

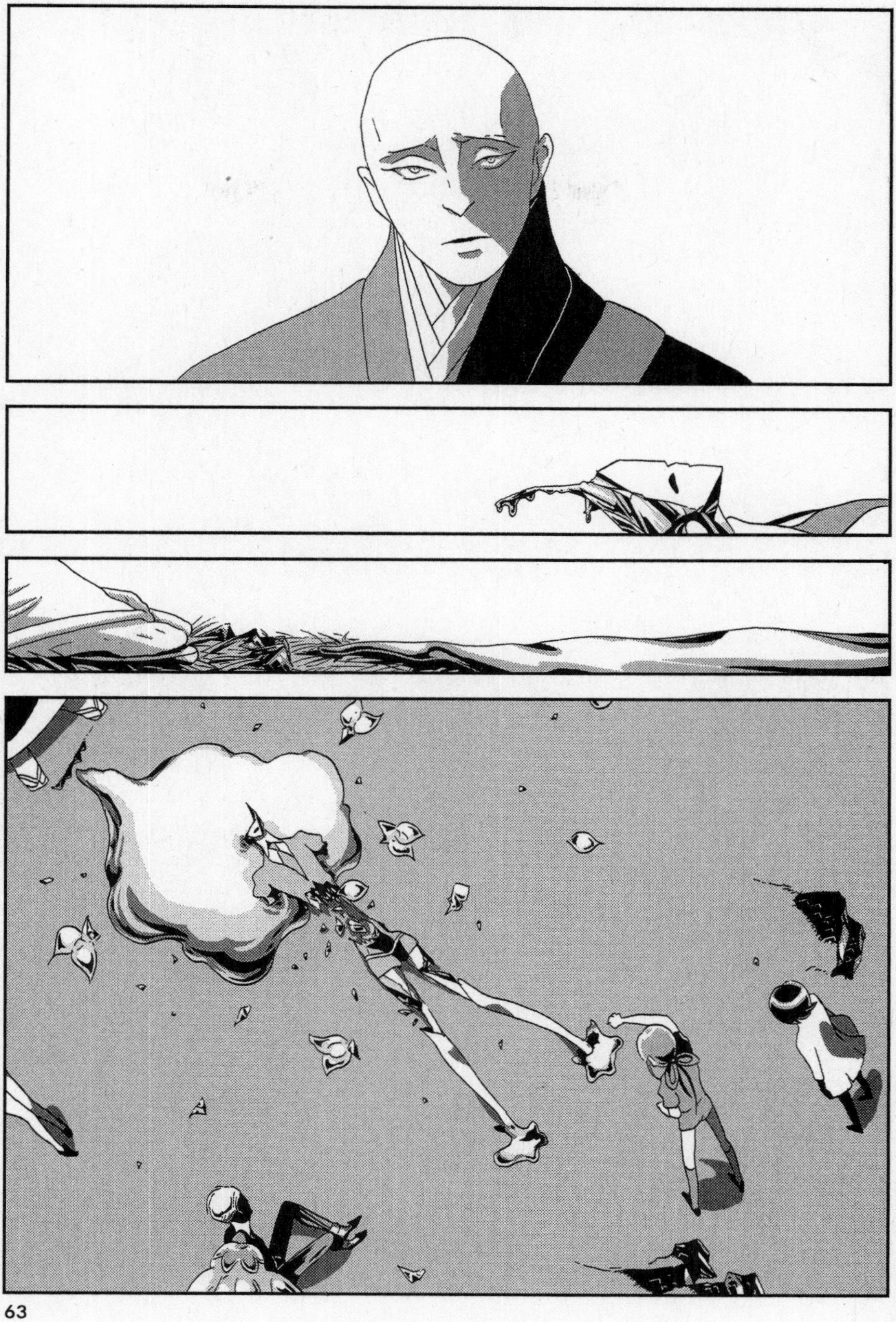

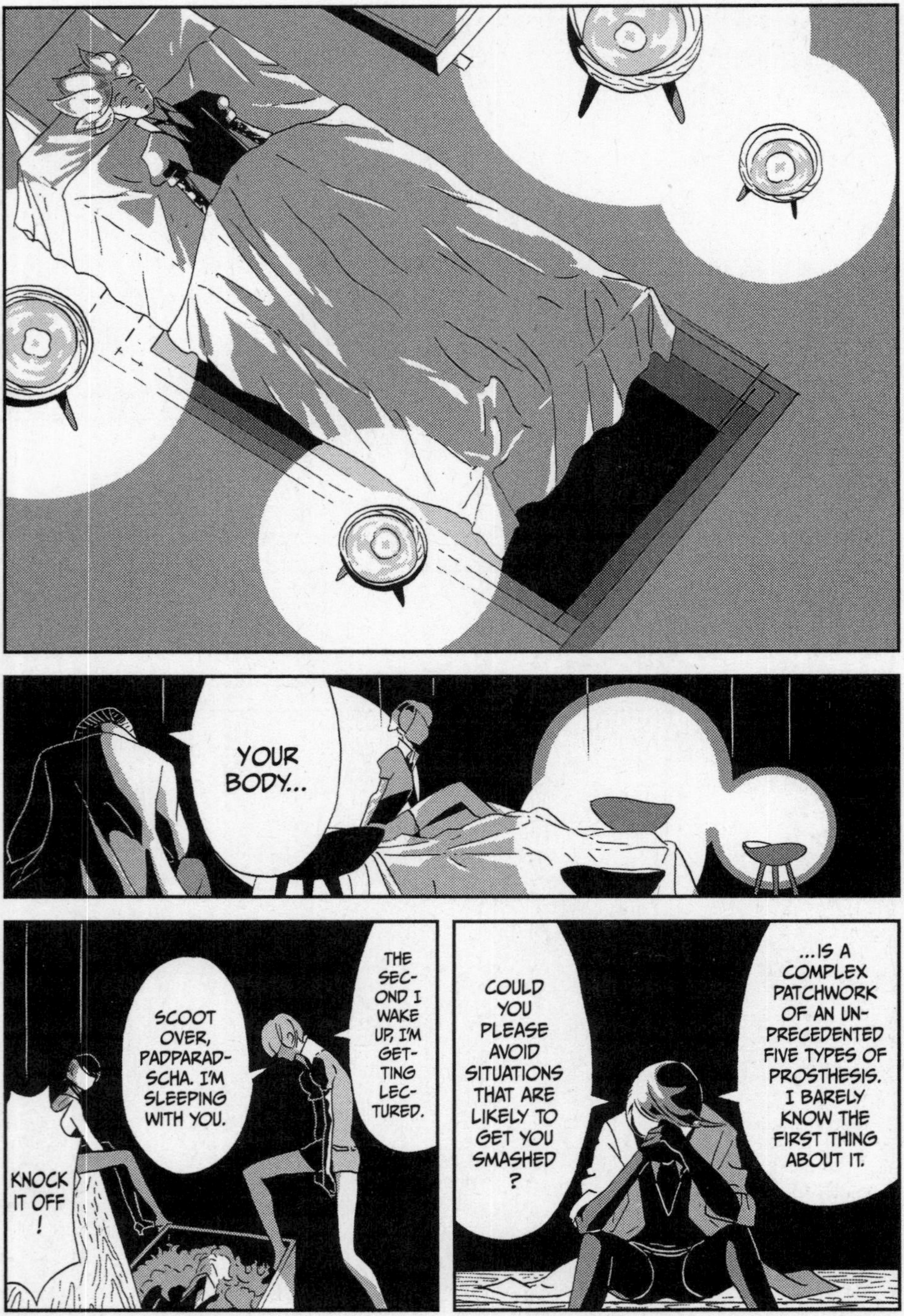
YOUR BODY...
...IS A COMPLEX PATCHWORK OF AN UNPRECEDENTED FIVE TYPES OF PROSTHESIS. I BARELY KNOW THE FIRST THING ABOUT IT.
COULD YOU PLEASE AVOID SITUATIONS THAT ARE LIKELY TO GET YOU SMASHED?
THE SECOND I WAKE UP, I'M GETTING LECTURED.
SCOOT OVER, PADPARADSCHA. I'M SLEEPING WITH YOU.
KNOCK IT OFF!

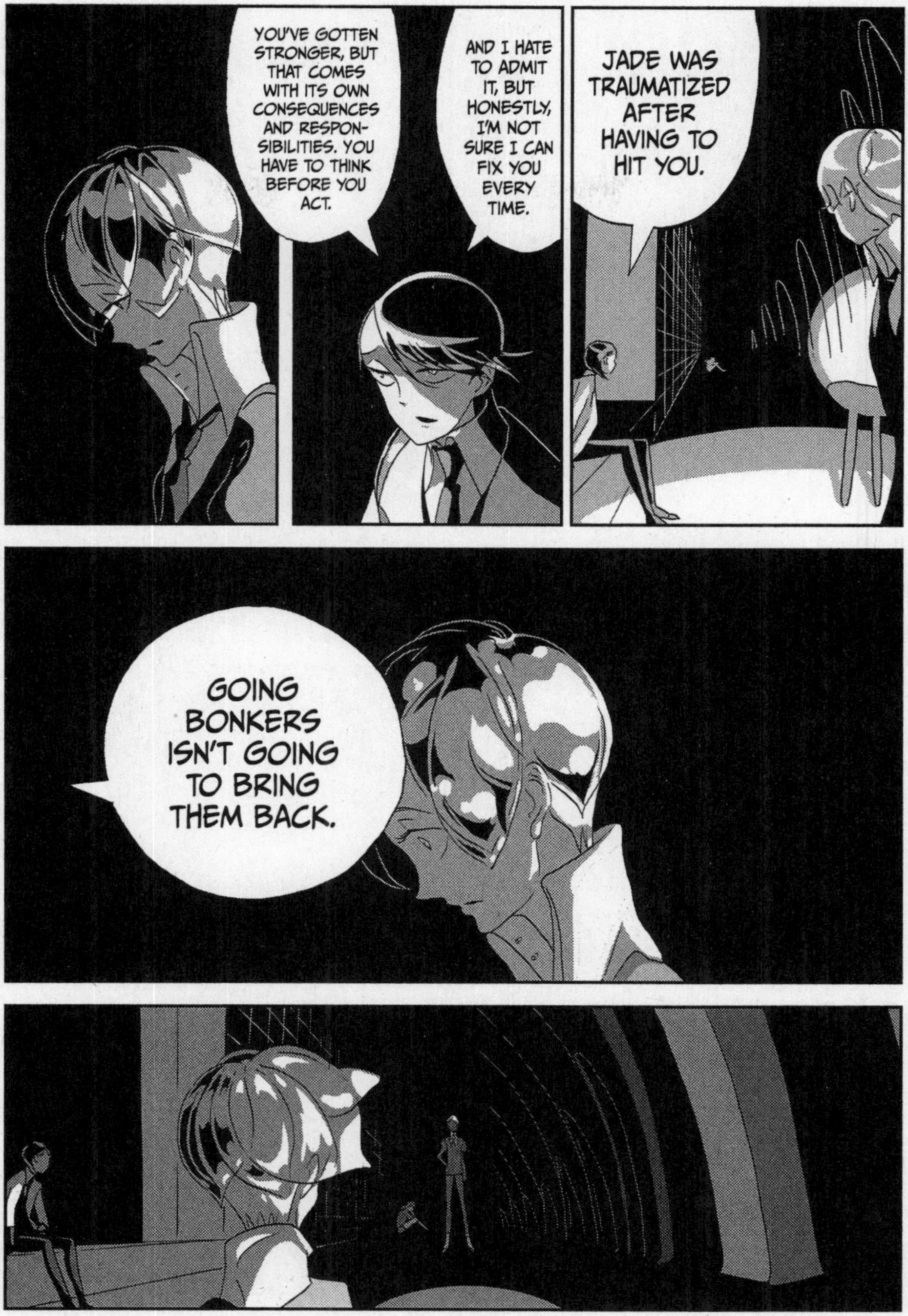
JADE WAS TRAUMATIZED AFTER HAVING TO HIT YOU.
AND I HATE TO ADMIT IT, BUT HONESTLY, I'M NOT SURE I CAN FIX YOU EVERY TIME.
YOU'VE GOTTEN STRONGER, BUT THAT COMES WITH ITS OWN CONSEQUENCES AND RESPON-SIBILITIES. YOU HAVE TO THINK BEFORE YOU ACT.
GOING BONKERS ISN'T GOING TO BRING THEM BACK.

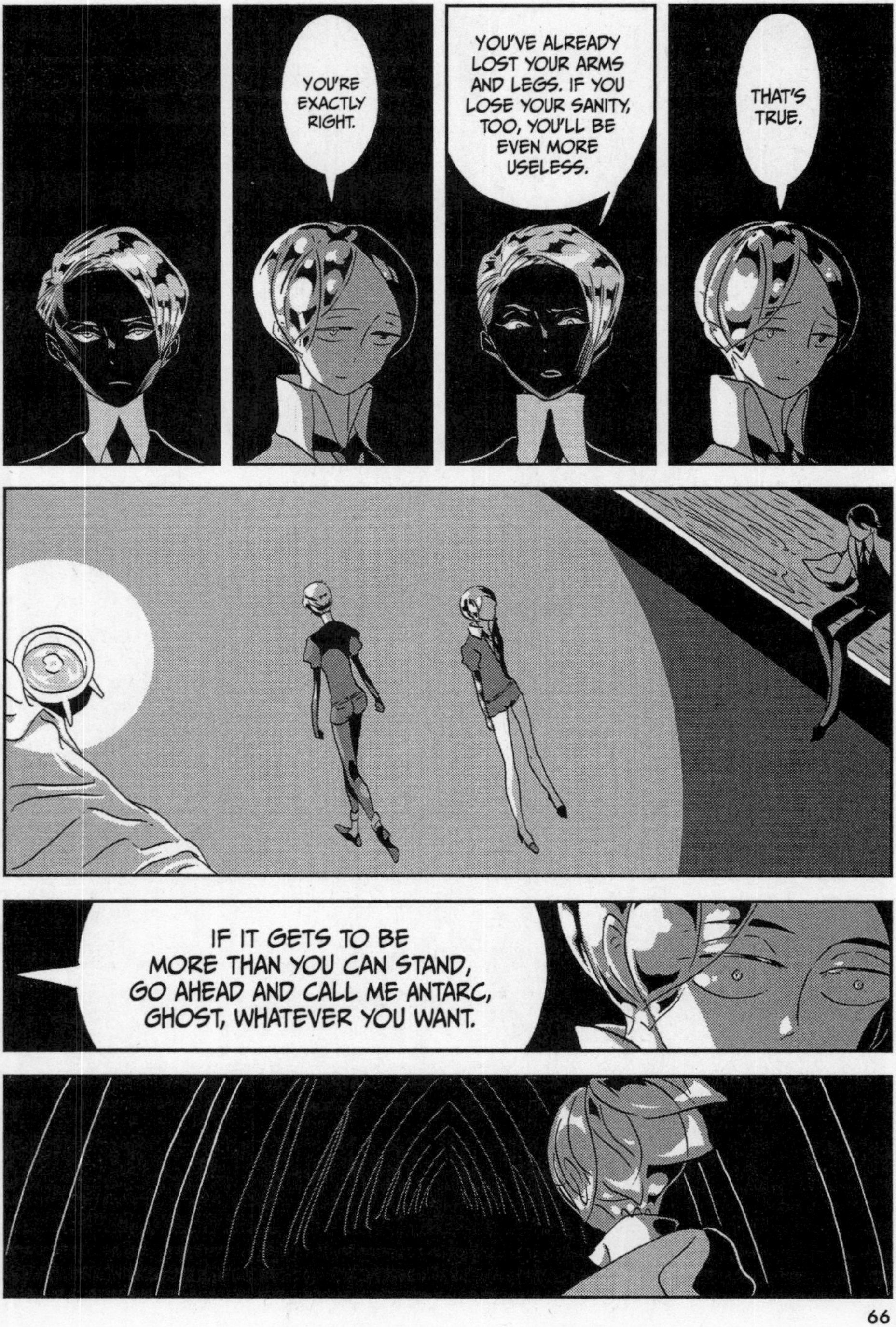
THAT'S TRUE.
YOU'VE ALREADY LOST YOUR ARMS AND LEGS. IF YOU LOSE YOUR SANITY, TOO, YOU'LL BE EVEN MORE USELESS.
YOU'RE EXACTLY RIGHT.
IF IT GETS TO BE MORE THAN YOU CAN STAND, GO AHEAD AND CALL ME ANTARC, GHOST, WHATEVER YOU WANT.

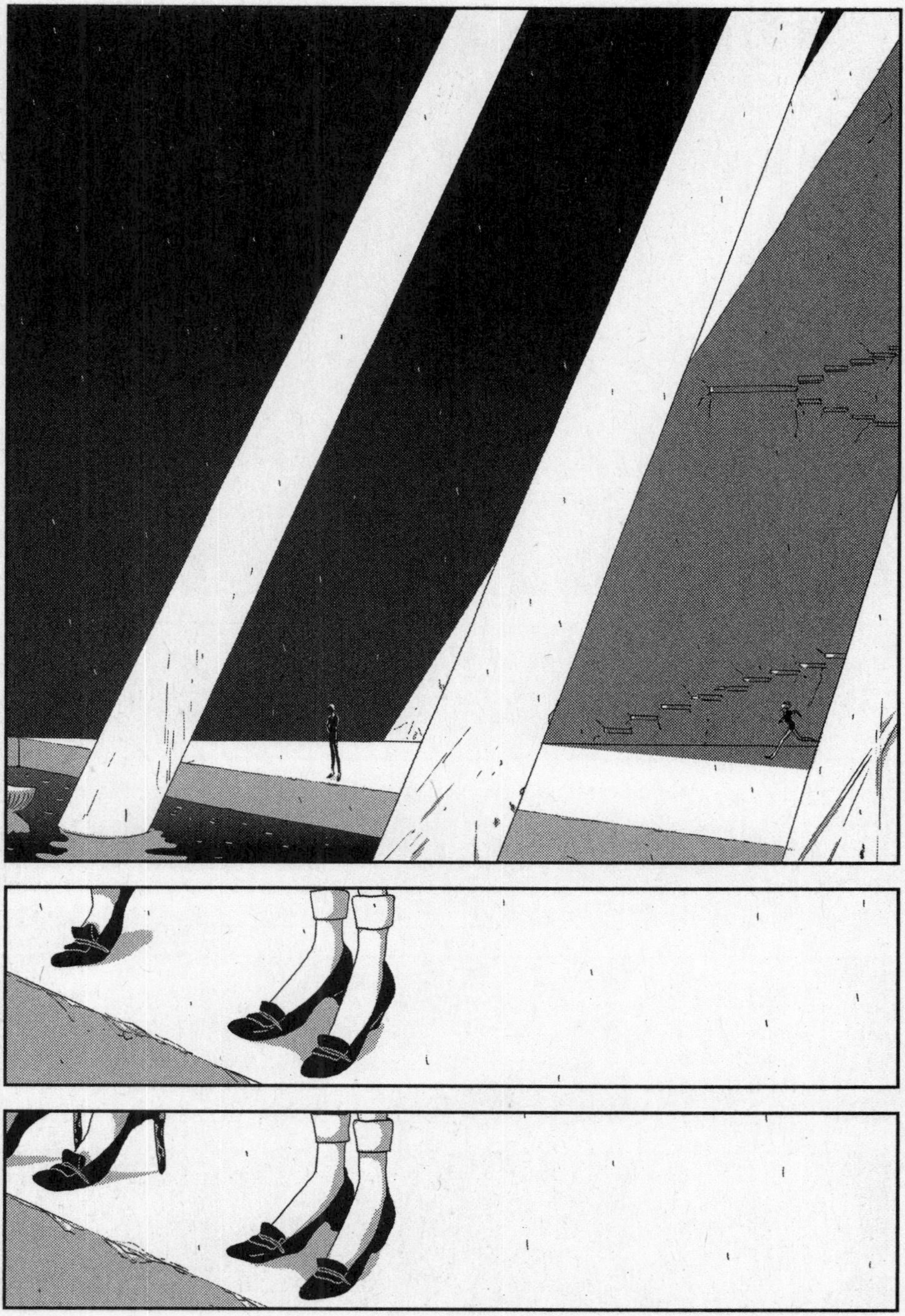

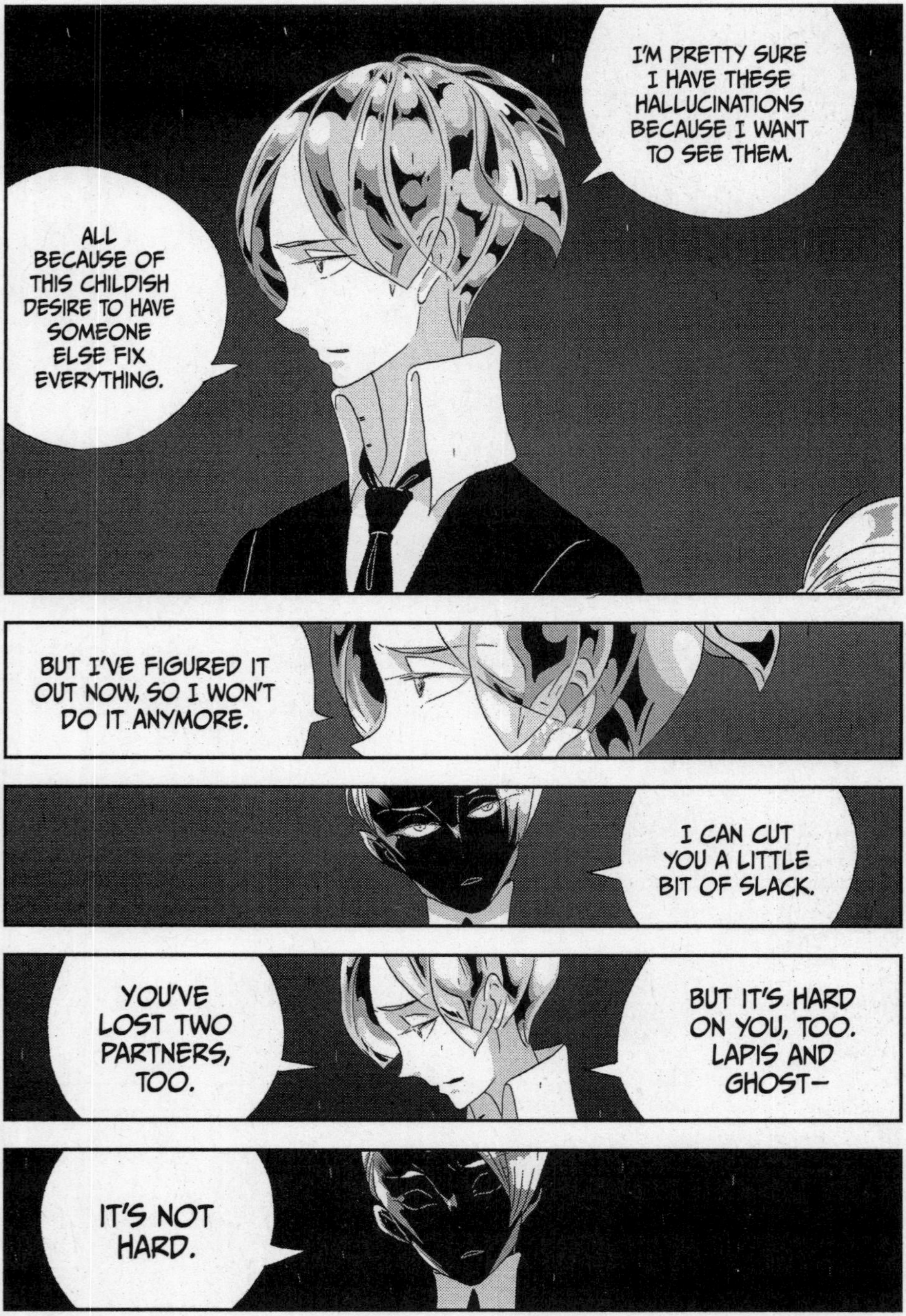
I'M PRETTY SURE I HAVE THESE HALLUCINATIONS BECAUSE I WANT TO SEE THEM.
ALL BECAUSE OF THIS CHILDISH DESIRE TO HAVE SOMEONE ELSE FIX EVERYTHING.
BUT I'VE FIGURED IT OUT NOW, SO I WON'T DO IT ANYMORE.
I CAN CUT YOU A LITTLE BIT OF SLACK.
BUT IT'S HARD ON YOU, TOO. LAPIS AND GHOST–
YOU'VE LOST TWO PARTNERS, TOO.
IT'S NOT HARD.

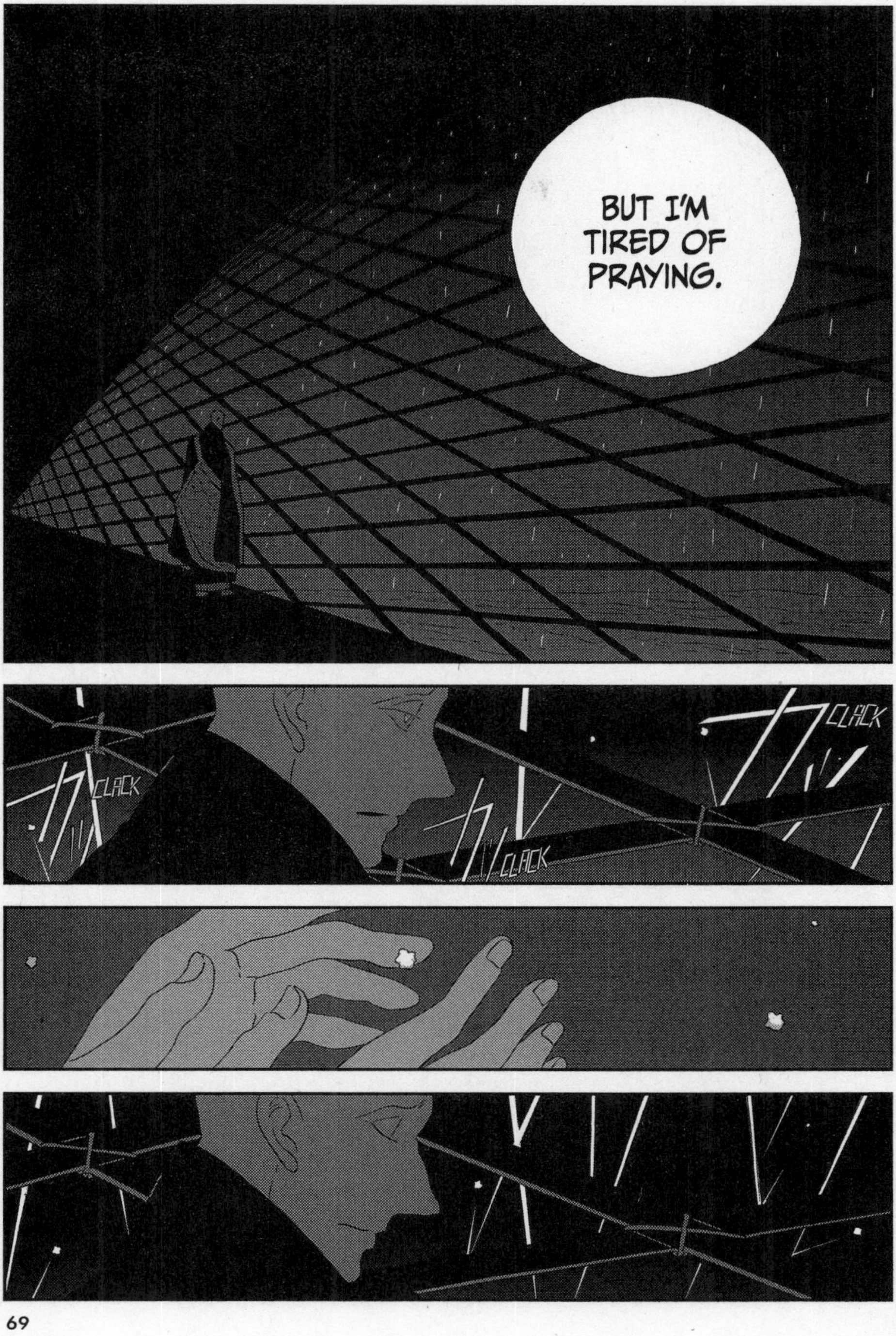
BUT I'M TIRED OF PRAYING.
CLACK
CLACK
CLACK

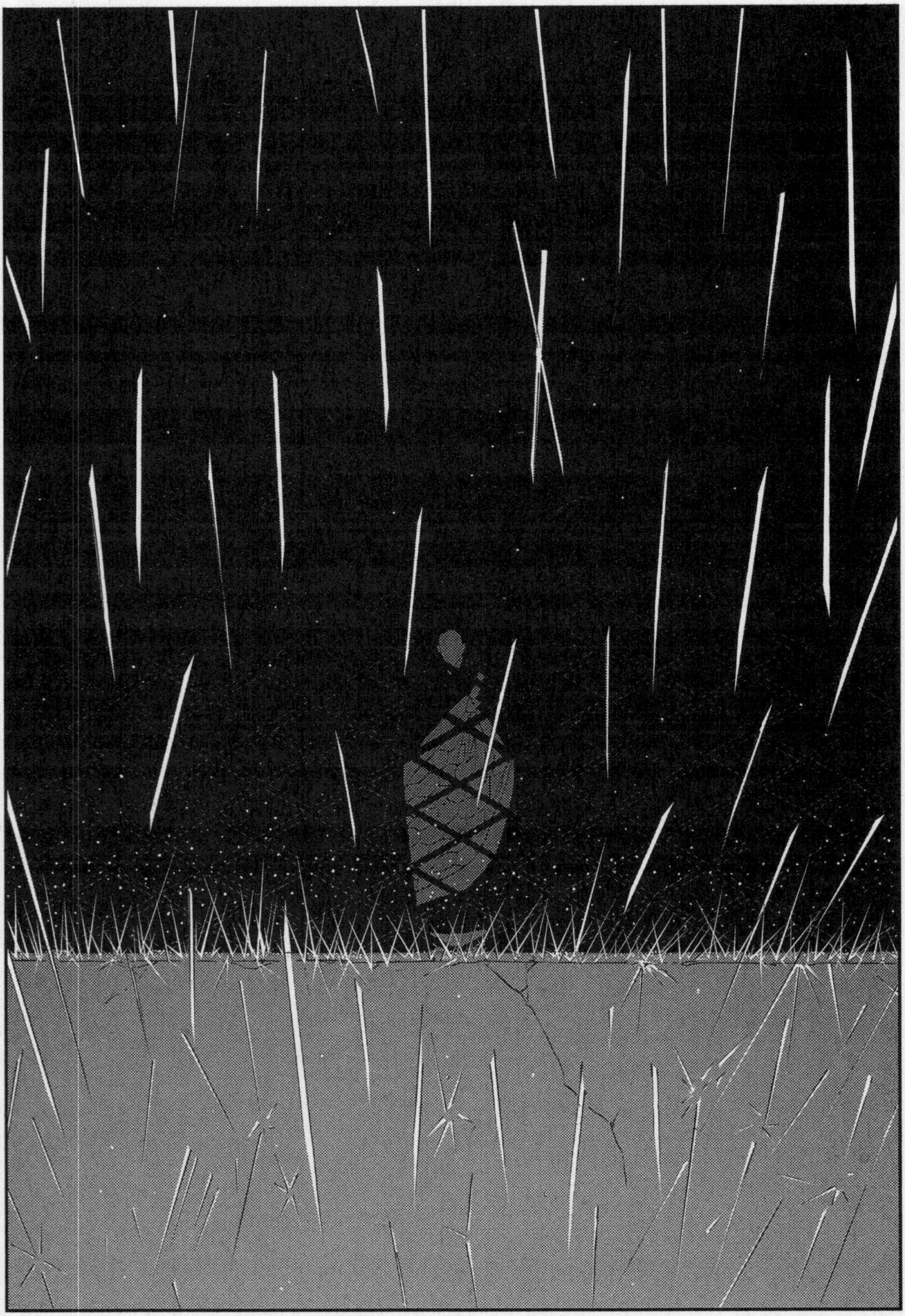

CHAPTER 39: Self-Admonition END

CHAPTER 40:

A Name

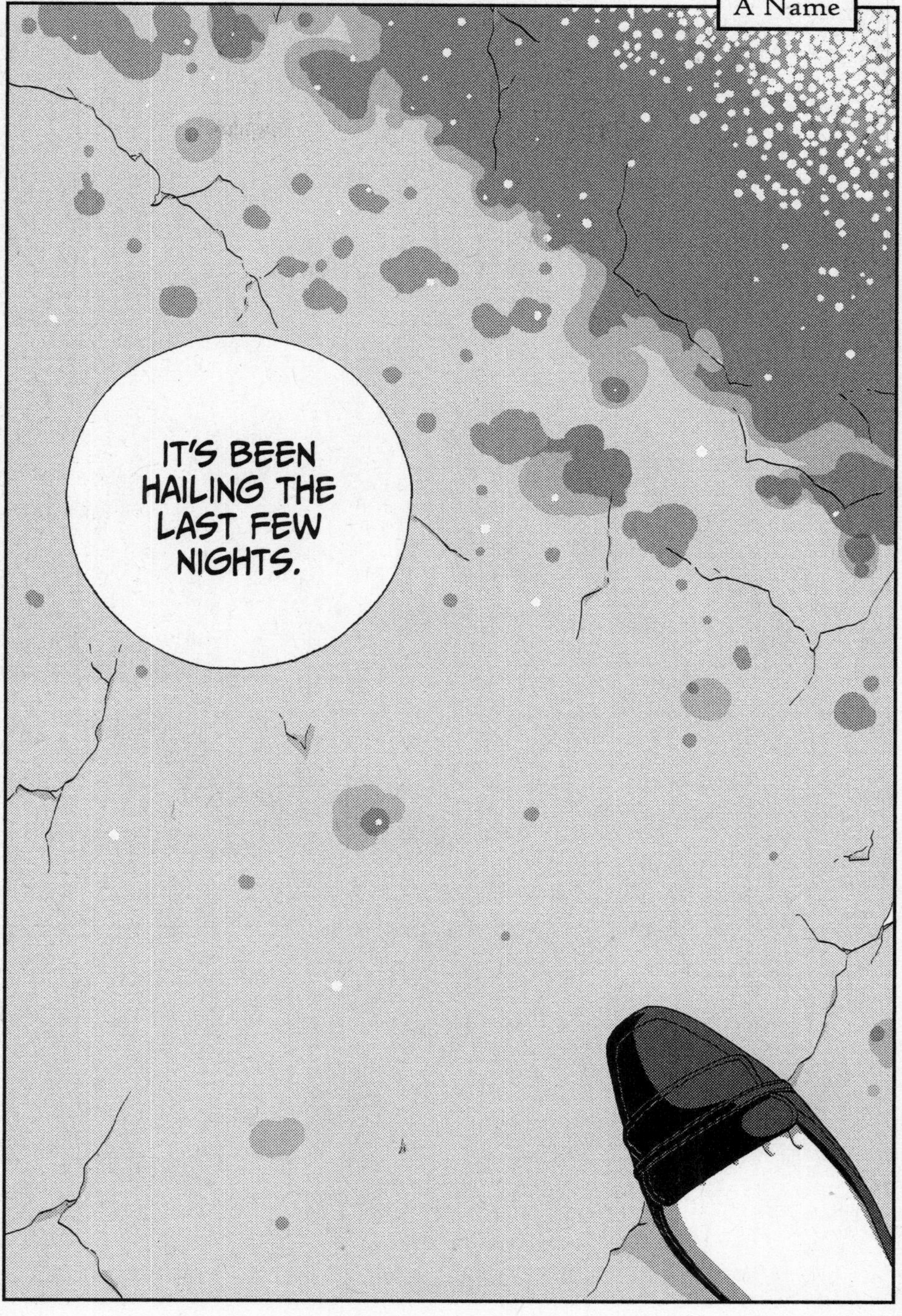
IT'S BEEN HAILING THE LAST FEW NIGHTS.

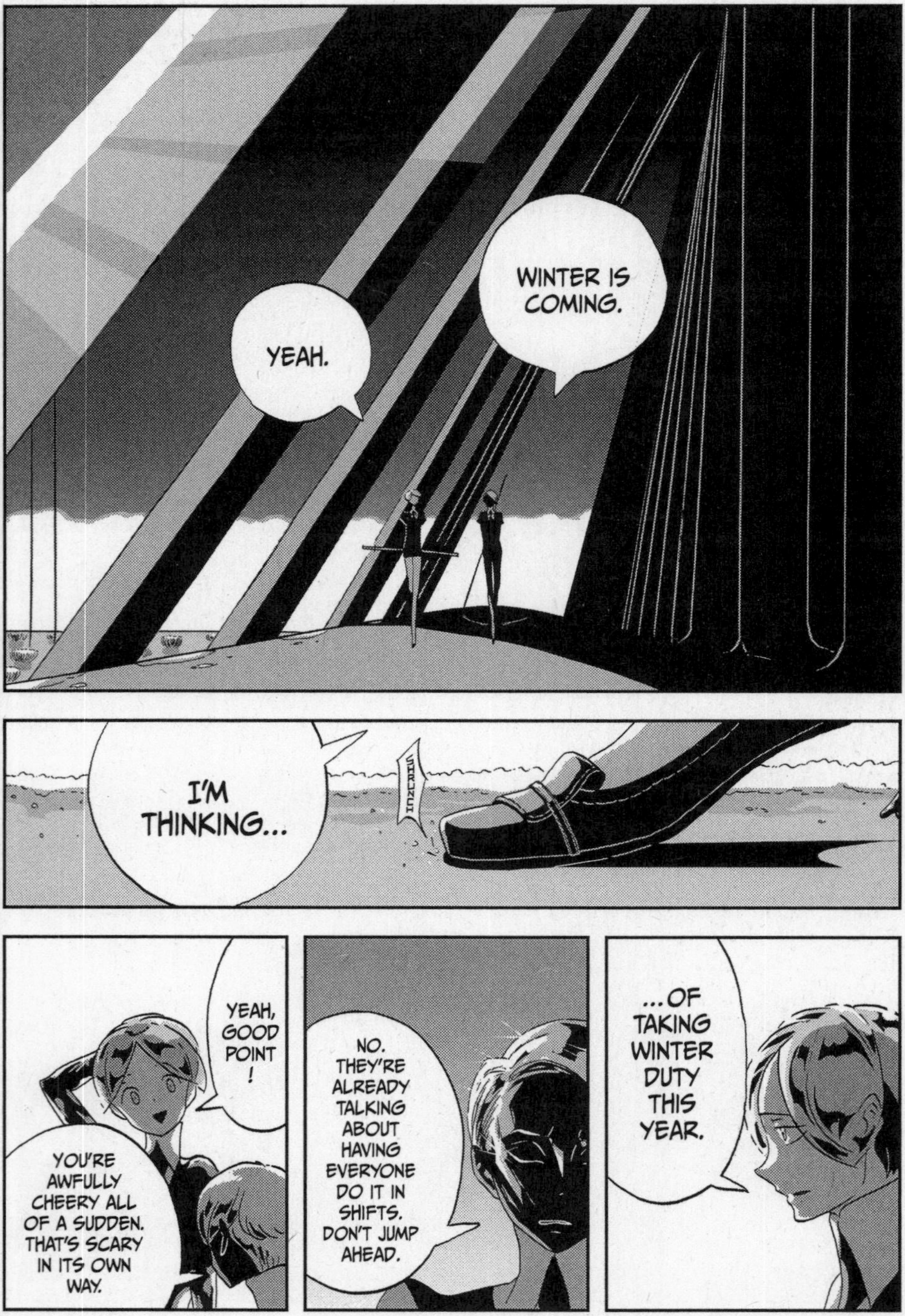
WINTER IS COMING.
YEAH.
SHRUNCH
I'M THINKING...
...OF TAKING WINTER DUTY THIS YEAR.
NO. THEY'RE ALREADY TALKING ABOUT HAVING EVERYONE DO IT IN SHIFTS. DON'T JUMP AHEAD.
YEAH, GOOD POINT!
YOU'RE AWFULLY CHEERY ALL OF A SUDDEN. THAT'S SCARY IN ITS OWN WAY.

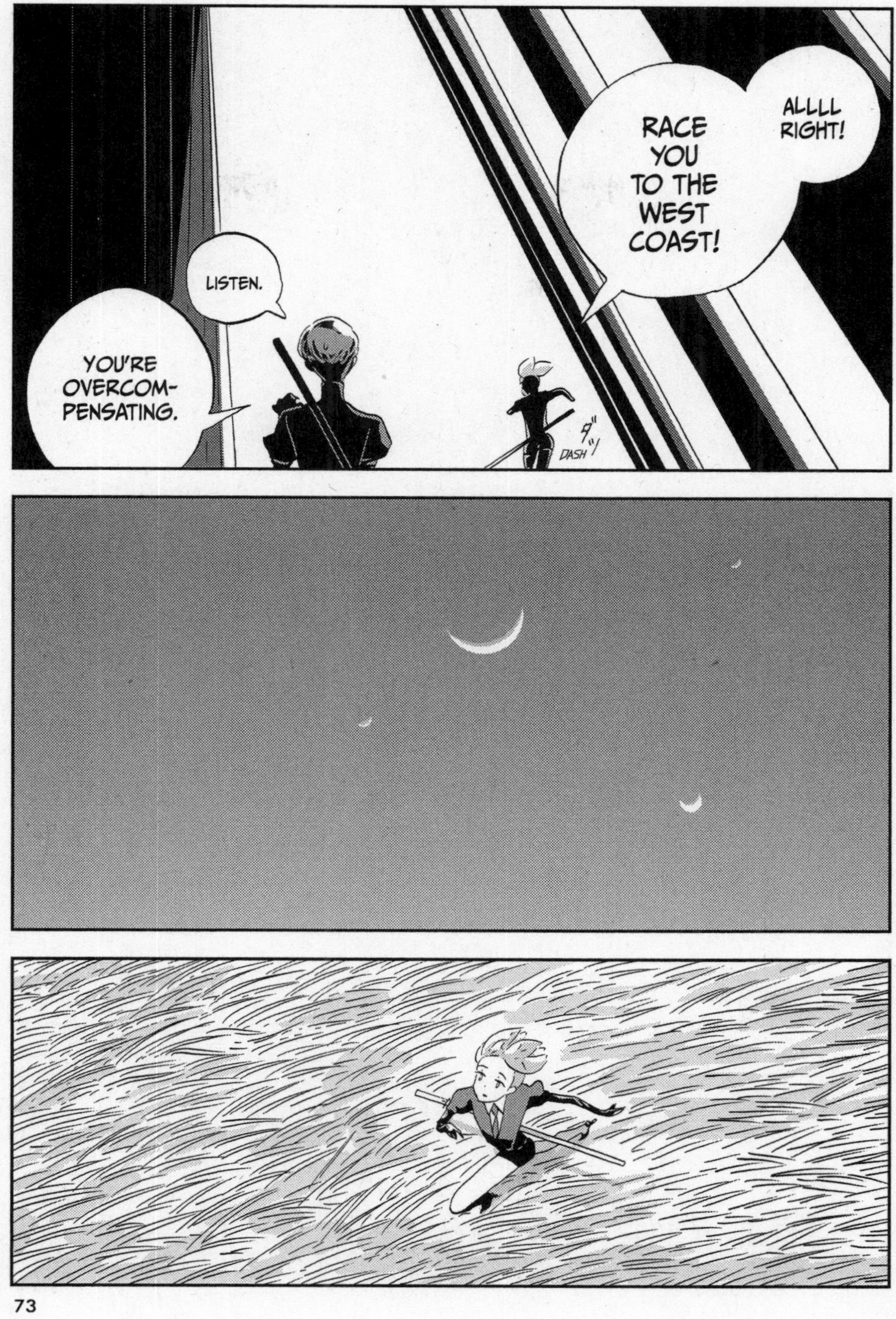
ALLLL RIGHT!
RACE YOU TO THE WEST COAST!
ダッ
DASH
LISTEN.
YOU'RE OVERCOM-PENSATING.

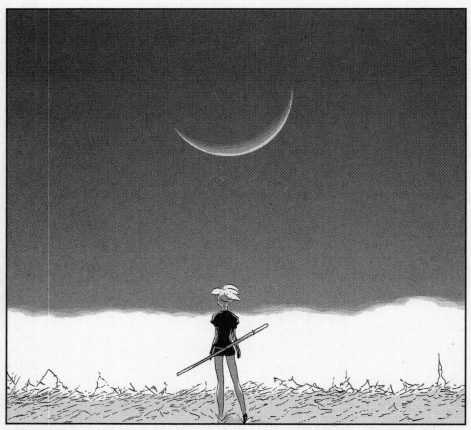

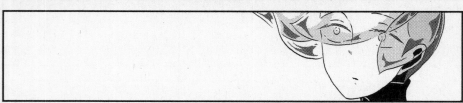

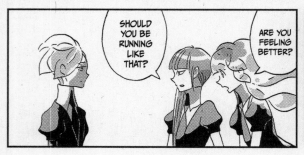

PHOS!
ARE YOU FEELING BETTER?
SHOULD YOU BE RUNNING LIKE THAT?

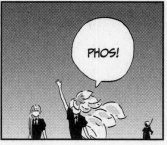

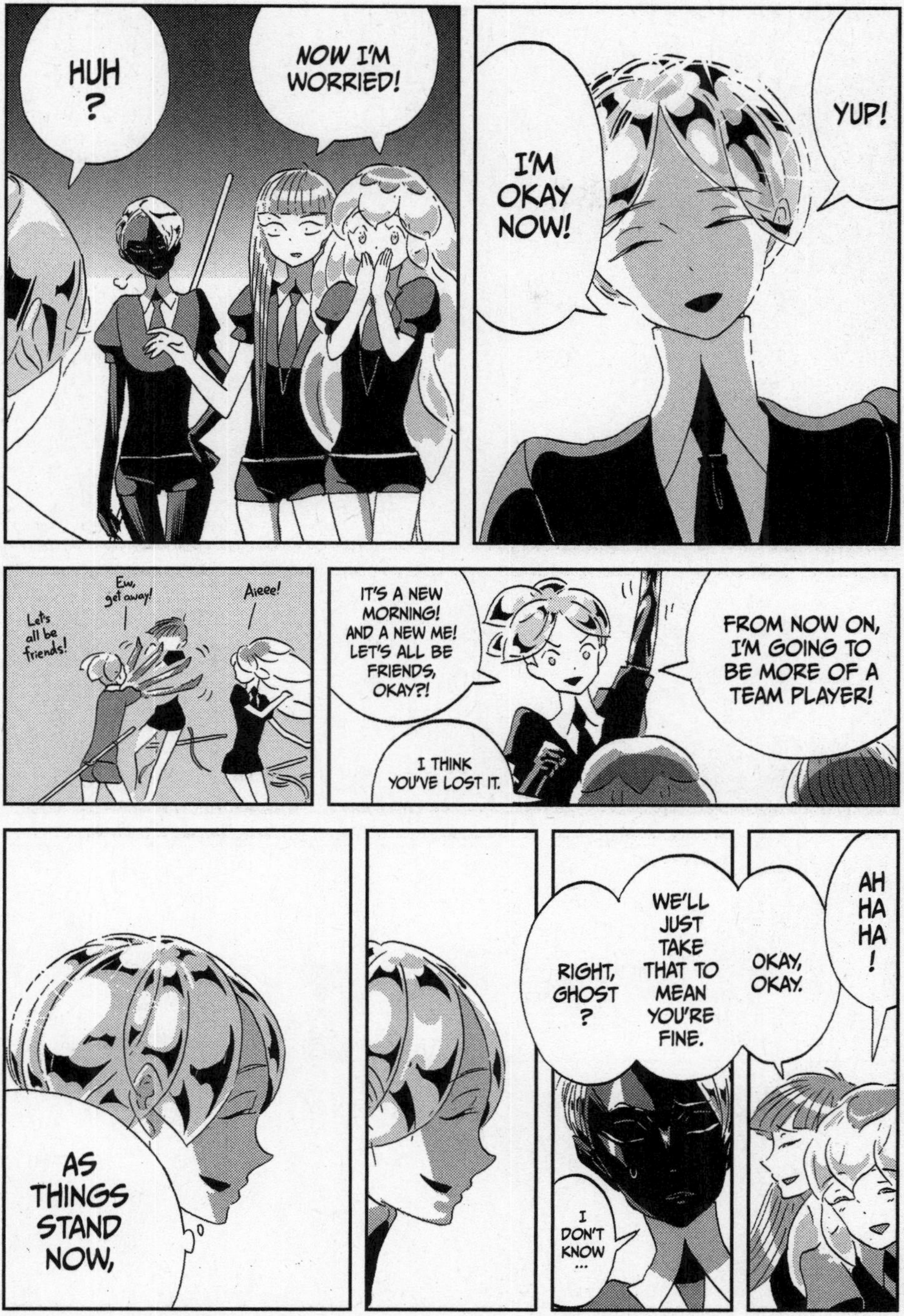
YUP!
I'M OKAY NOW!
NOW I'M WORRIED!
HUH?
FROM NOW ON, I'M GOING TO BE MORE OF A TEAM PLAYER!
IT'S A NEW MORNING! AND A NEW ME! LET'S ALL BE FRIENDS, OKAY?!
I THINK YOU'VE LOST IT.
Aieee!
Ew, get away!
Let's all be friends!
AH HA HA!
OKAY, OKAY.
WE'LL JUST TAKE THAT TO MEAN YOU'RE FINE.
RIGHT, GHOST?
I DON'T KNOW...
AS THINGS STAND NOW,

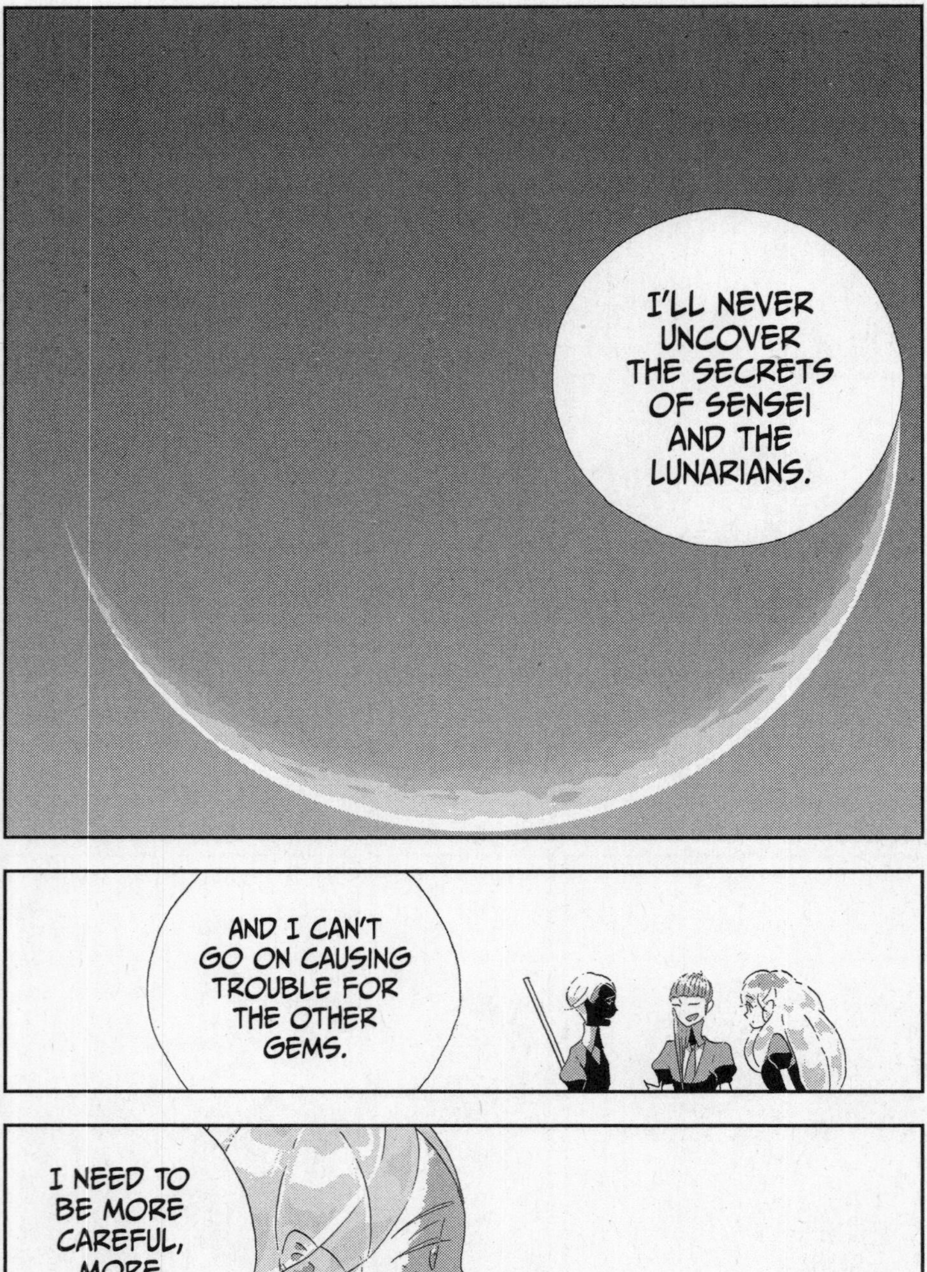
I'LL NEVER UNCOVER THE SECRETS OF SENSEI AND THE LUNARIANS.
AND I CAN'T GO ON CAUSING TROUBLE FOR THE OTHER GEMS.
I NEED TO BE MORE CAREFUL, MORE CALM.

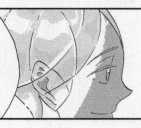

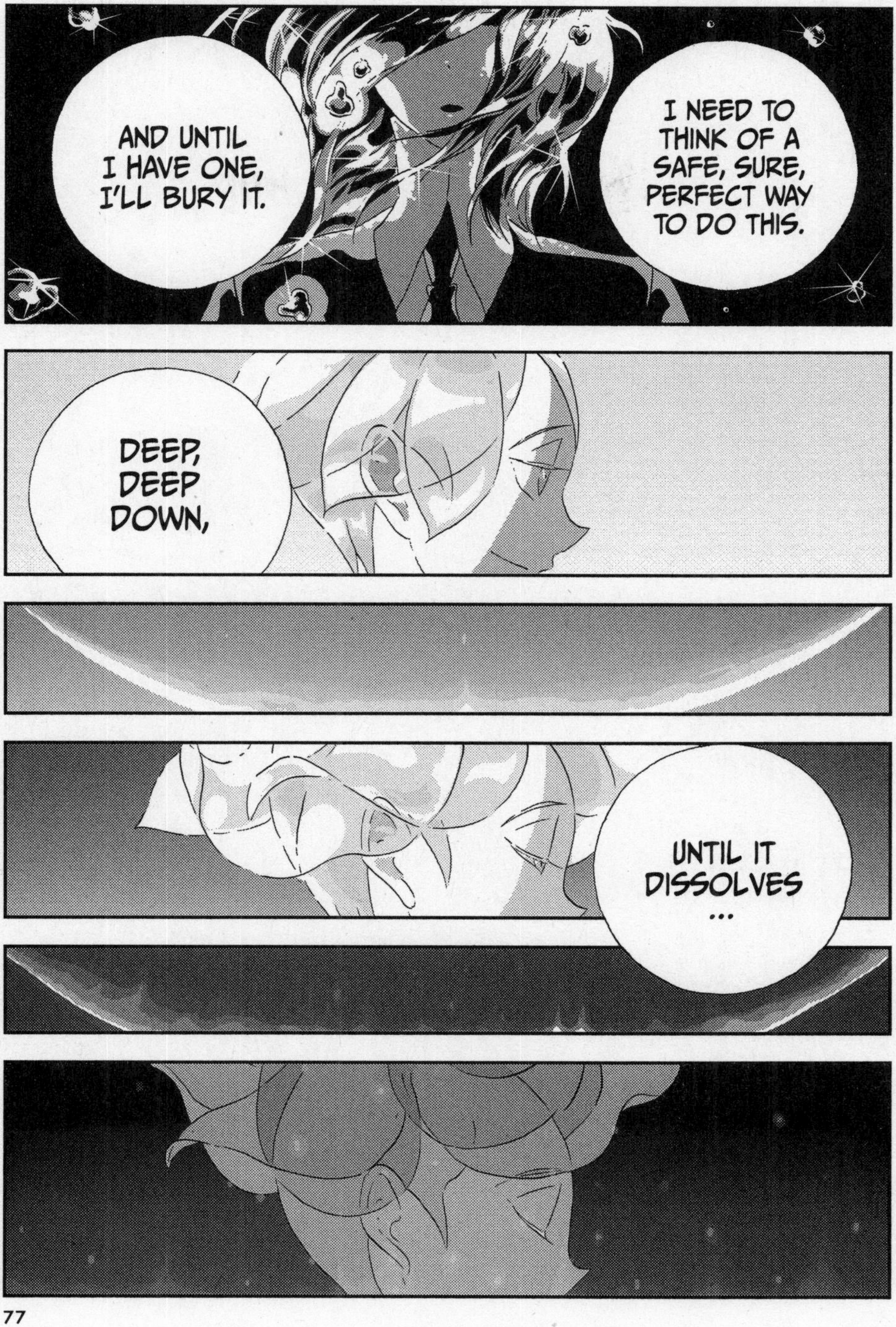
I NEED TO THINK OF A SAFE, SURE, PERFECT WAY TO DO THIS.
AND UNTIL I HAVE ONE, I'LL BURY IT.
DEEP, DEEP DOWN,
UNTIL IT DISSOLVES ...

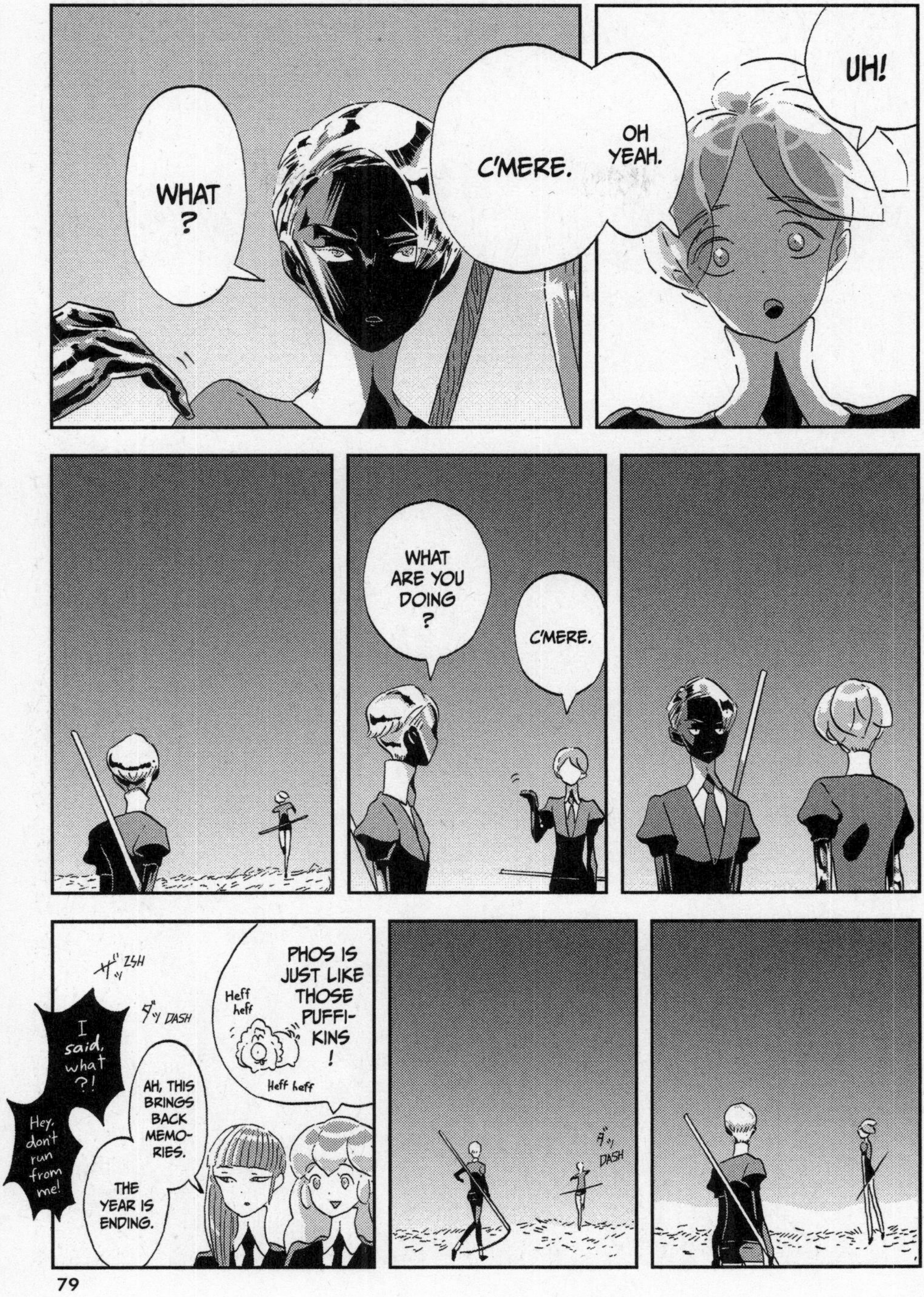
UH!
OH YEAH.
C'MERE.
WHAT ?
WHAT ARE YOU DOING ?
C'MERE.
DASH
PHOS IS JUST LIKE THOSE PUFFI- KINS !
Heff heff
Heff heff
ZSH
DASH
AH, THIS BRINGS BACK MEMO- RIES.
THE YEAR IS ENDING.
I said, what ?!
Hey, don't run from me!

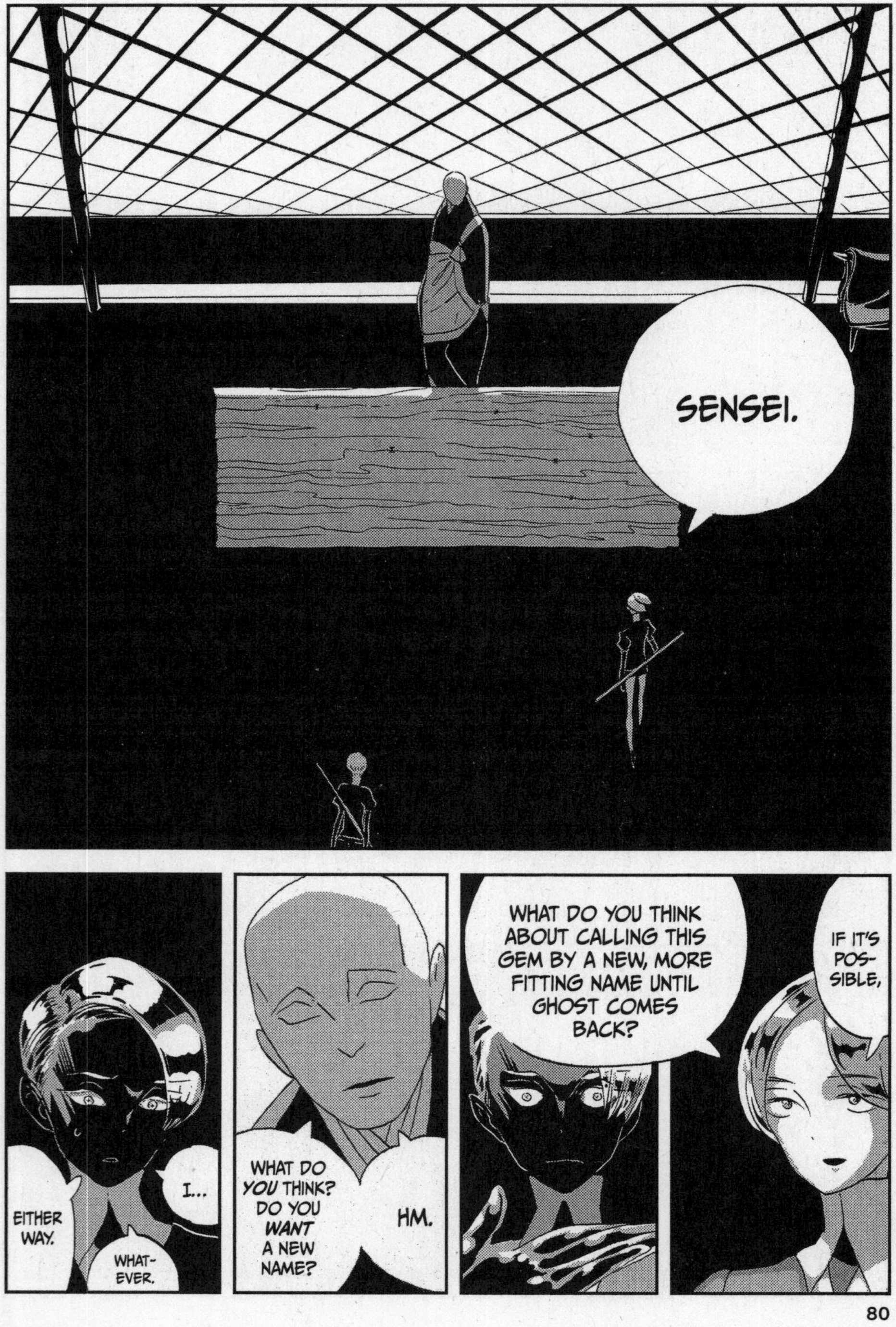
SENSEI.
IF IT'S POS-SIBLE,
WHAT DO YOU THINK ABOUT CALLING THIS GEM BY A NEW, MORE FITTING NAME UNTIL GHOST COMES BACK?
HM.
WHAT DO *YOU* THINK? DO YOU *WANT* A NEW NAME?
I...
EITHER WAY.
WHAT-EVER.

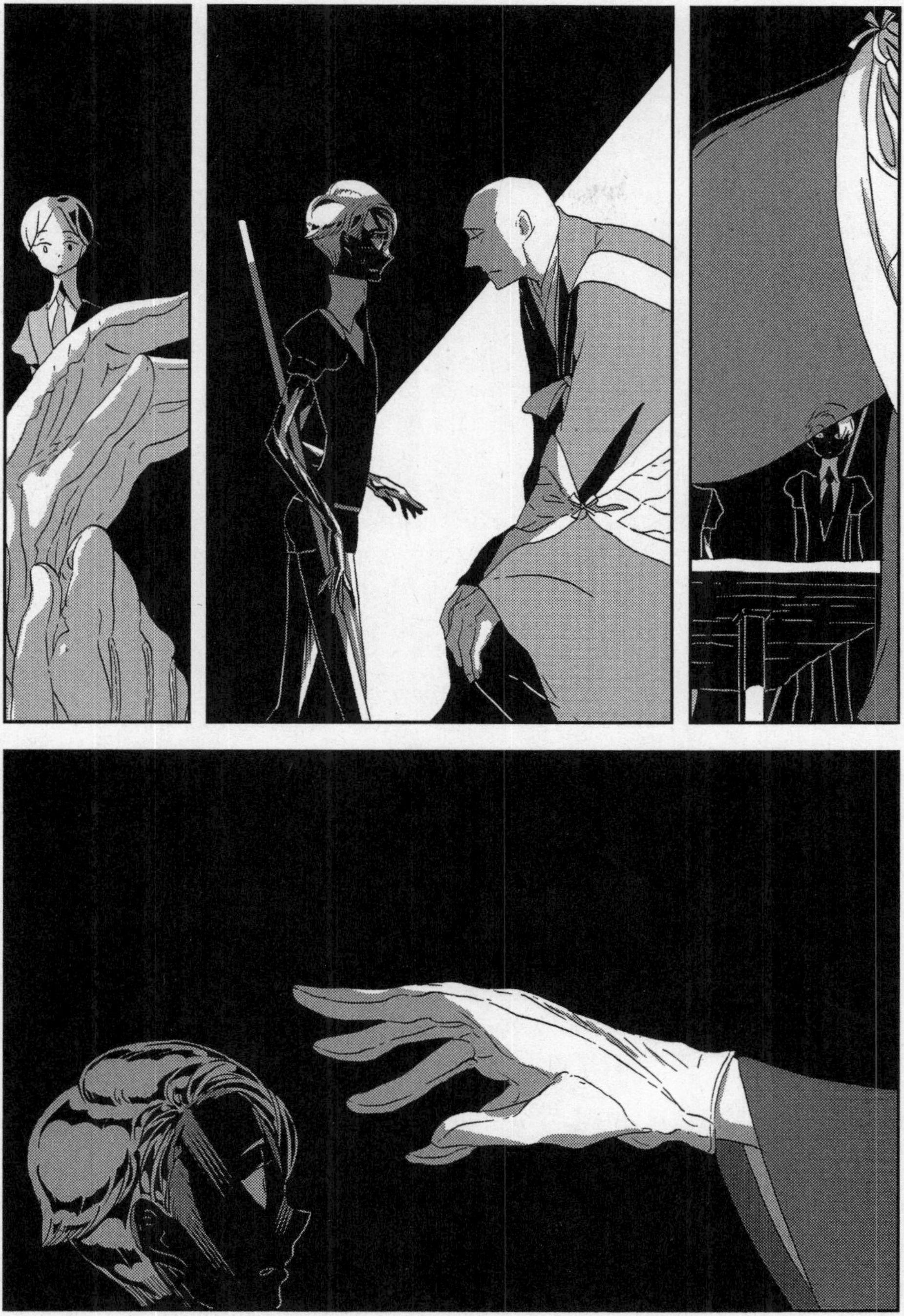

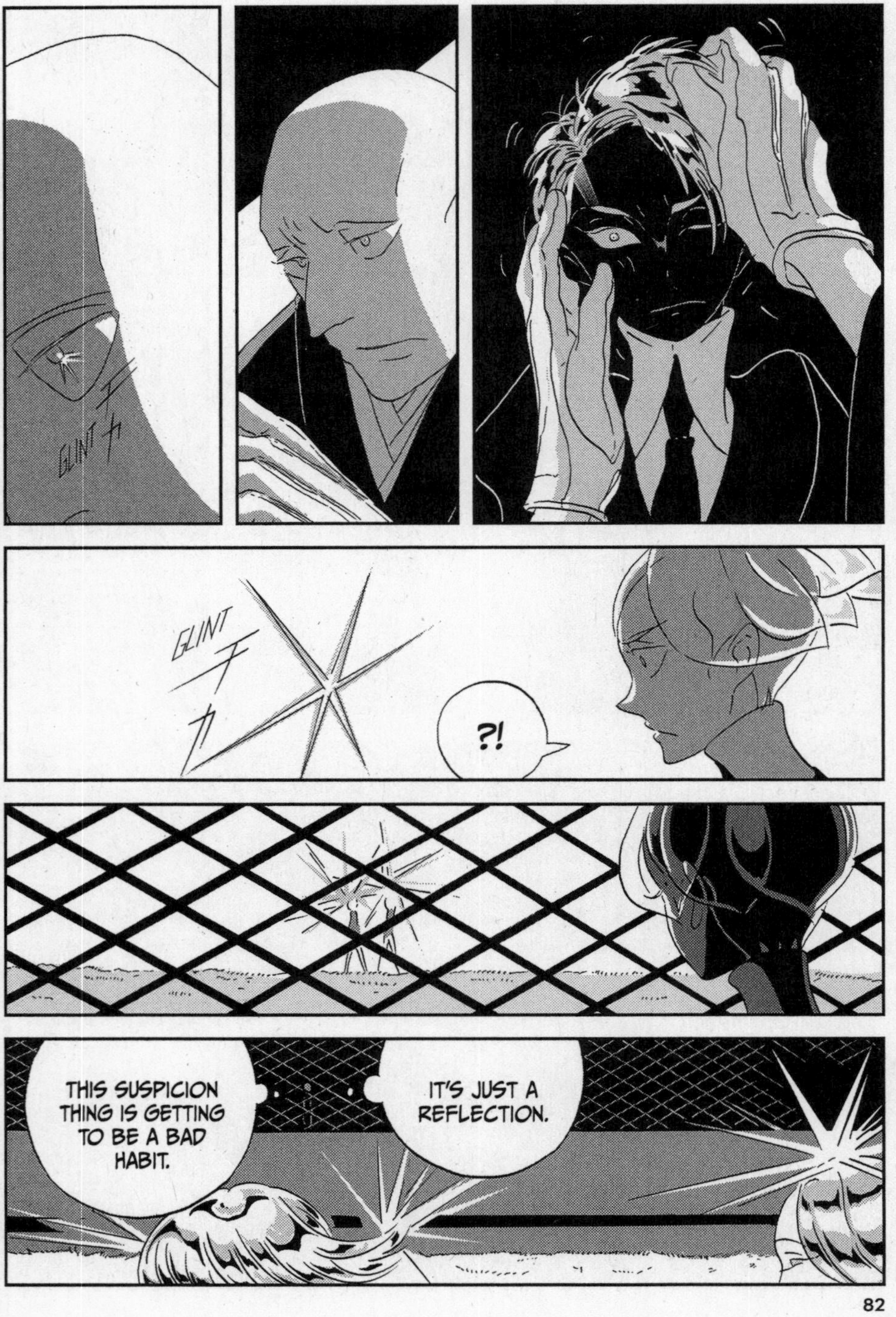
GLINT
チカ
GLINT
チカ
?!
IT'S JUST A REFLECTION.
THIS SUSPICION THING IS GETTING TO BE A BAD HABIT.

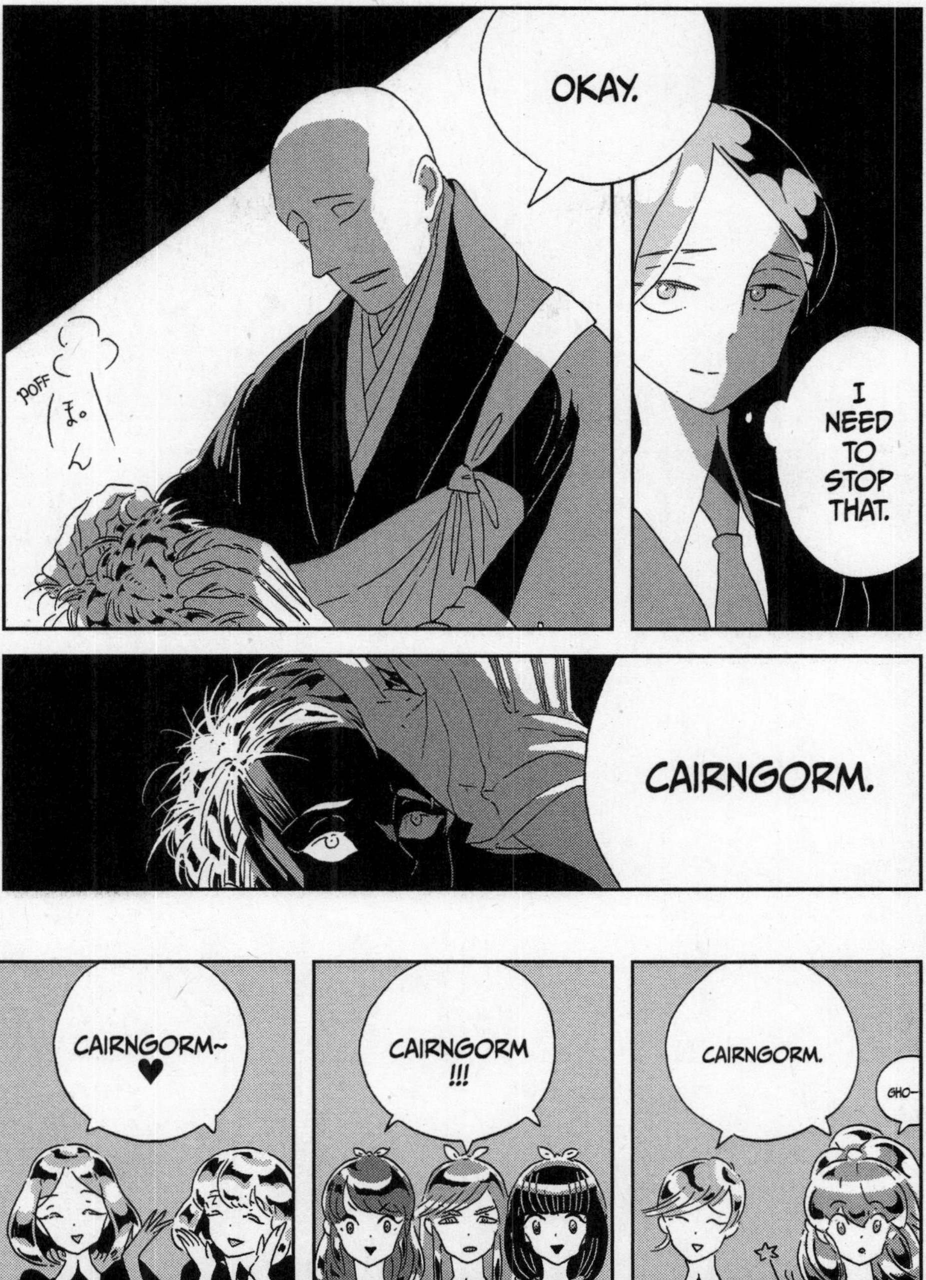
I NEED TO STOP THAT.
OKAY.
POFF
ぽん
CAIRNGORM.
CAIRNGORM.
GHO-
CAIRNGORM !!!
CAIRNGORM~ ♥

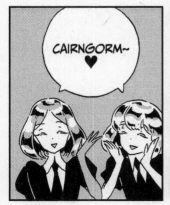

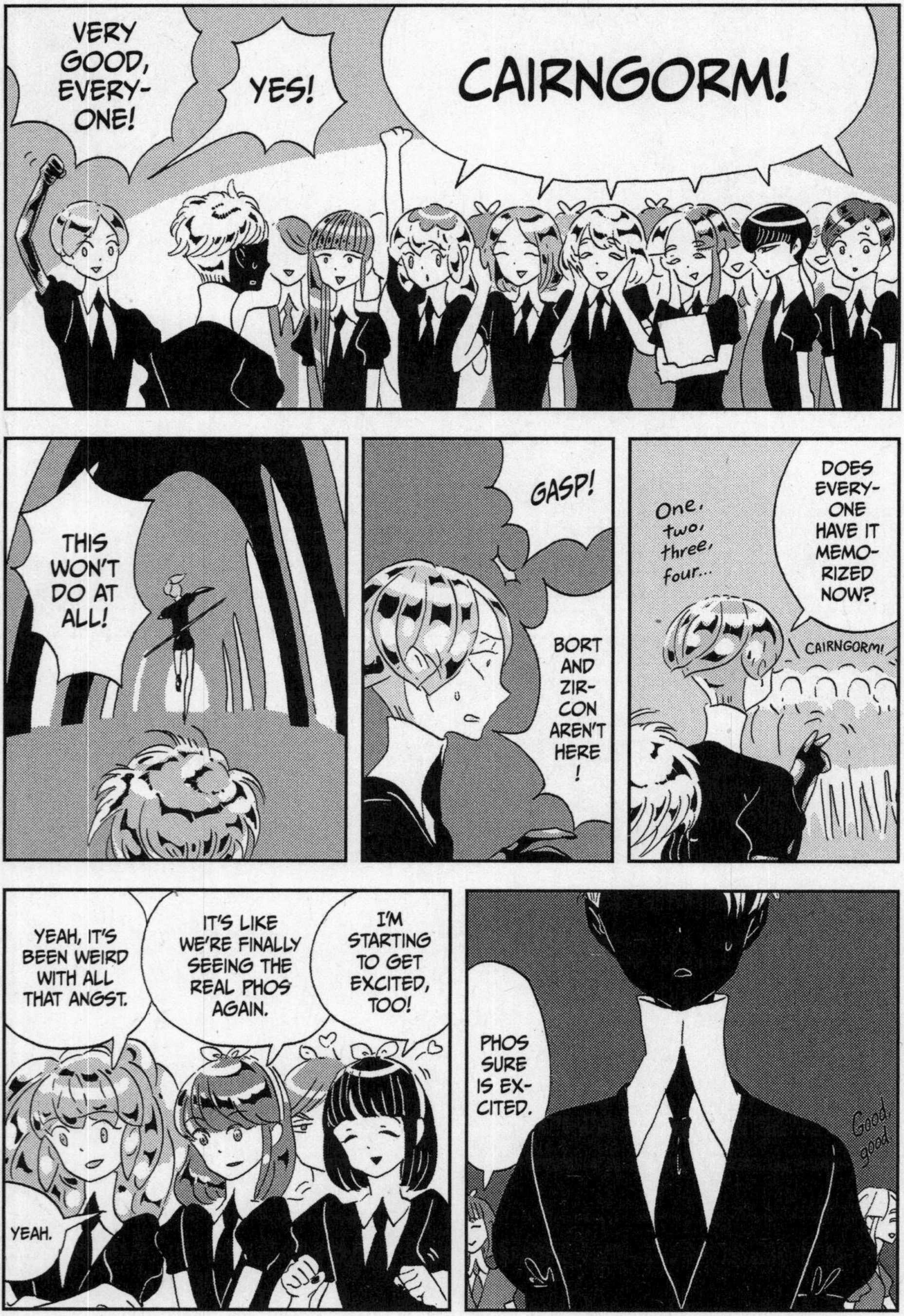

CAIRNGORM!
YES!
VERY GOOD, EVERY-ONE!
DOES EVERY-ONE HAVE IT MEMO-RIZED NOW?
One, two, three, four...
CAIRNGORM!
GASP!
BORT AND ZIR-CON AREN'T HERE!
THIS WON'T DO AT ALL!
Good, good.
PHOS SURE IS EX-CITED.
I'M STARTING TO GET EXCITED, TOO!
IT'S LIKE WE'RE FINALLY SEEING THE REAL PHOS AGAIN.
YEAH, IT'S BEEN WEIRD WITH ALL THAT ANGST.
YEAH.

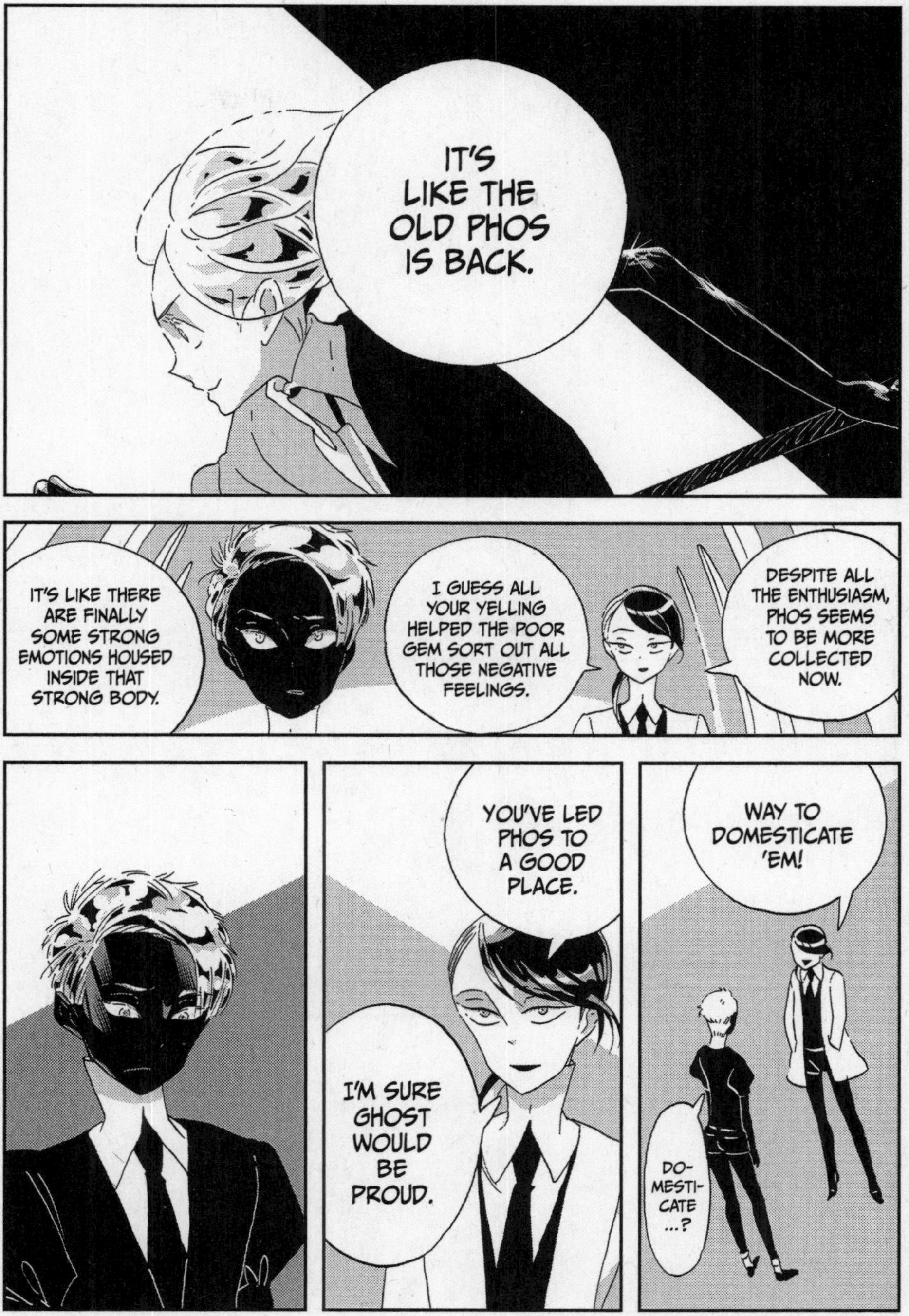
IT'S LIKE THE OLD PHOS IS BACK.
DESPITE ALL THE ENTHUSIASM, PHOS SEEMS TO BE MORE COLLECTED NOW.
I GUESS ALL YOUR YELLING HELPED THE POOR GEM SORT OUT ALL THOSE NEGATIVE FEELINGS.
IT'S LIKE THERE ARE FINALLY SOME STRONG EMOTIONS HOUSED INSIDE THAT STRONG BODY.
WAY TO DOMESTICATE 'EM!
DO-MESTI-CATE ...?
YOU'VE LED PHOS TO A GOOD PLACE.
I'M SURE GHOST WOULD BE PROUD.

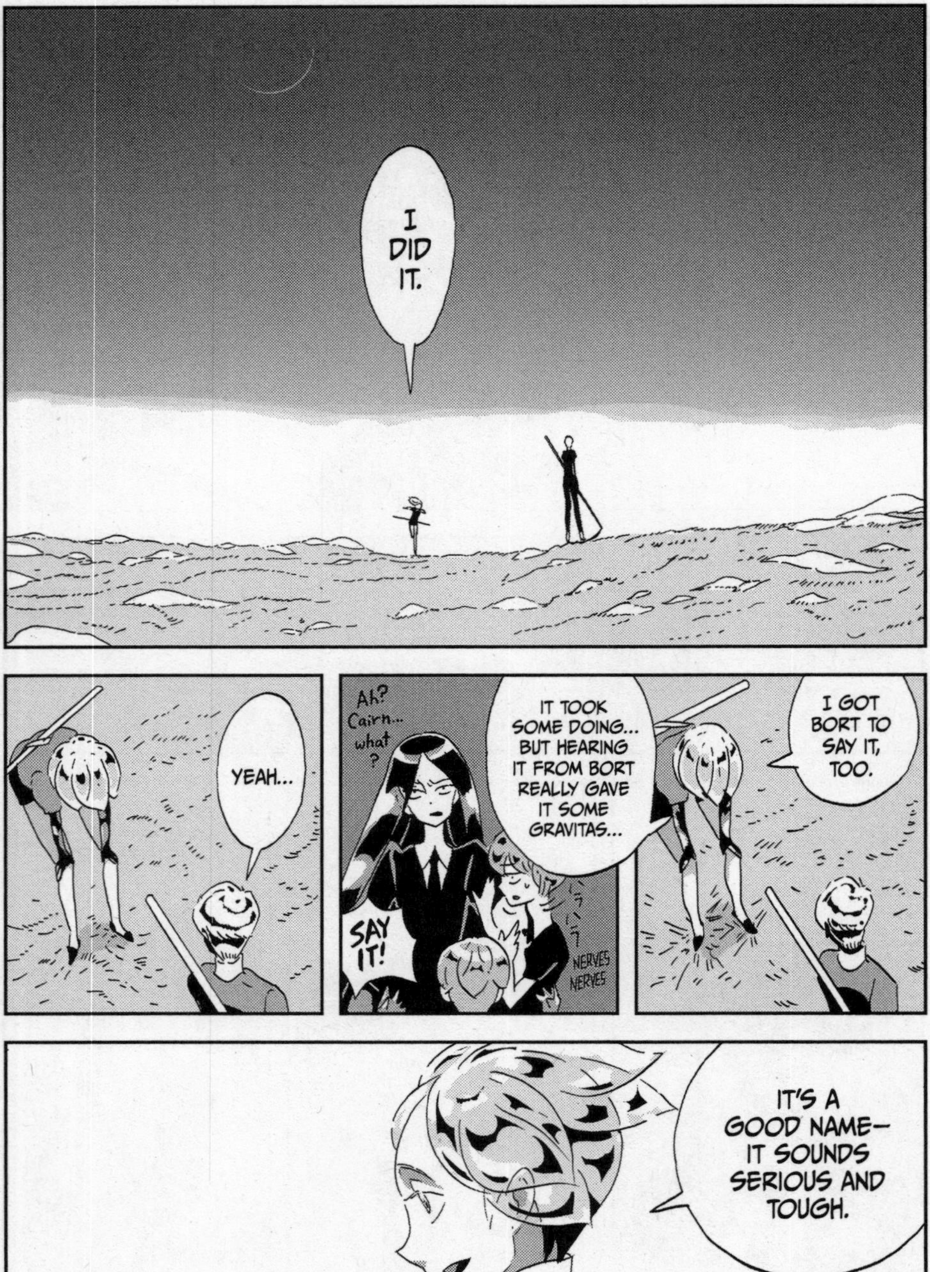
I DID IT.
I GOT BORT TO SAY IT, TOO.
IT TOOK SOME DOING... BUT HEARING IT FROM BORT REALLY GAVE IT SOME GRAVITAS...
Ah? Cairn... what?
NERVES NERVES
SAY IT!
YEAH...
IT'S A GOOD NAME— IT SOUNDS SERIOUS AND TOUGH.

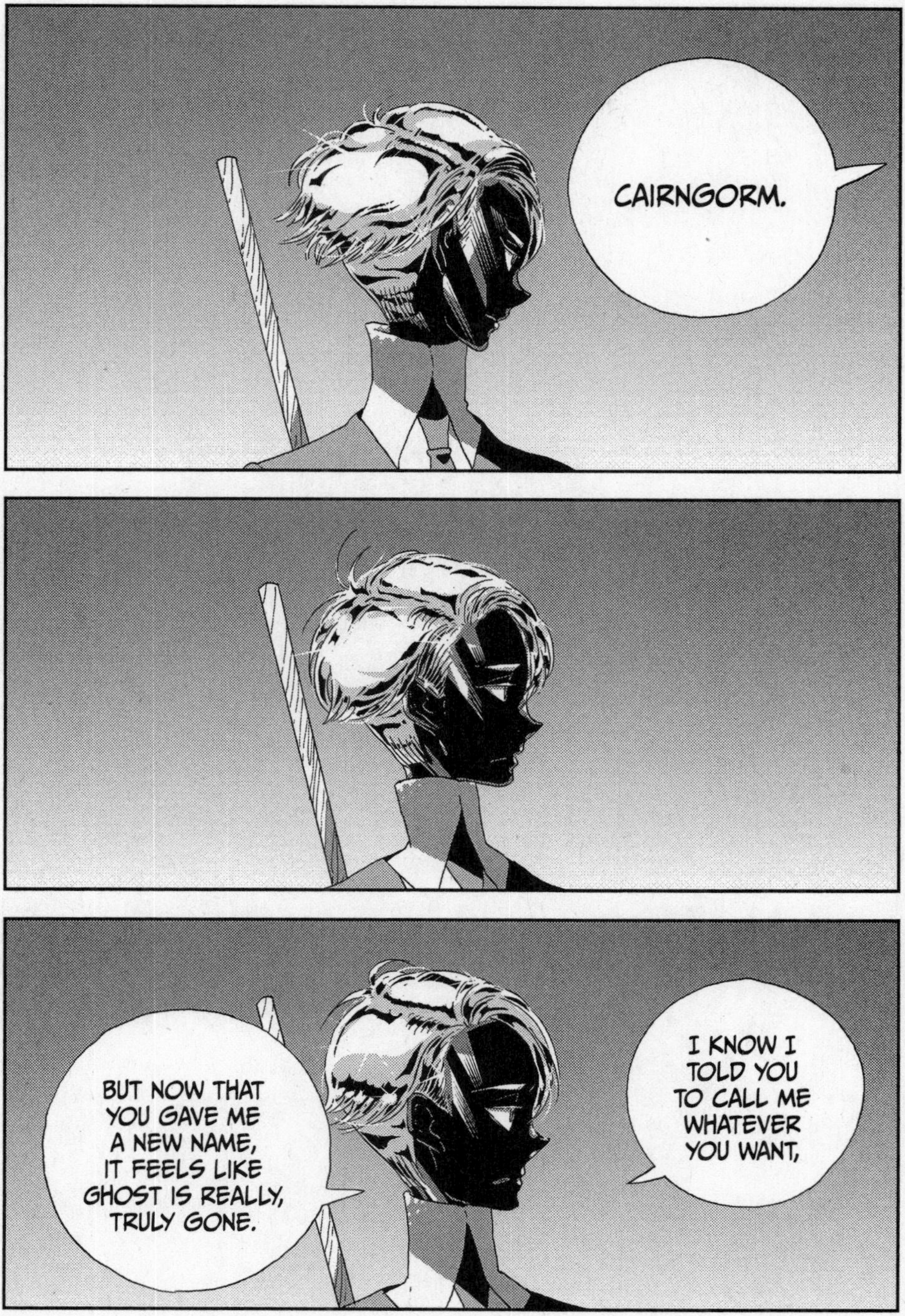
CAIRNGORM.
I KNOW I TOLD YOU TO CALL ME WHATEVER YOU WANT,
BUT NOW THAT YOU GAVE ME A NEW NAME, IT FEELS LIKE GHOST IS REALLY, TRULY GONE.

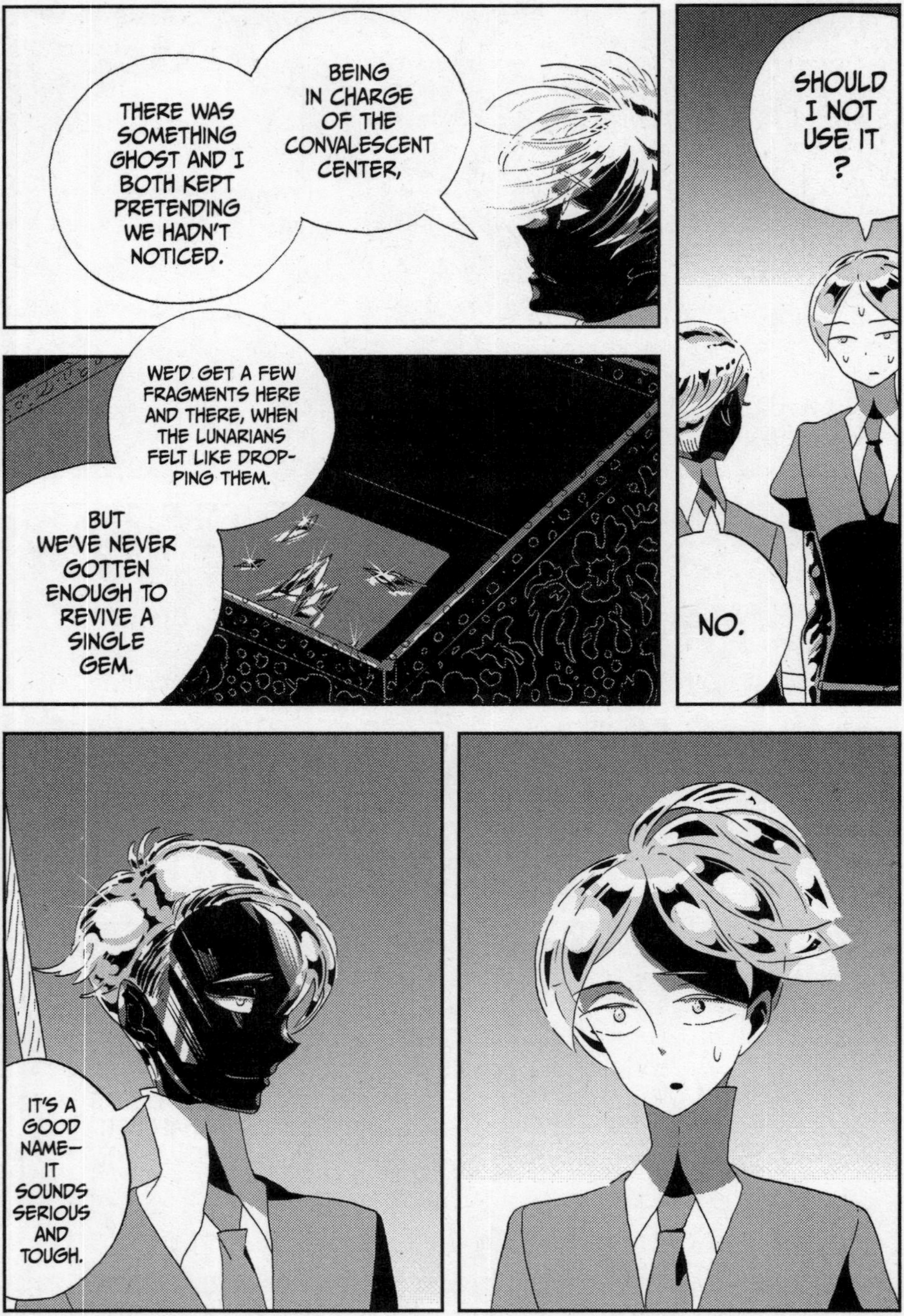
SHOULD I NOT USE IT?
NO.
BEING IN CHARGE OF THE CONVALESCENT CENTER,
THERE WAS SOMETHING GHOST AND I BOTH KEPT PRETENDING WE HADN'T NOTICED.
WE'D GET A FEW FRAGMENTS HERE AND THERE, WHEN THE LUNARIANS FELT LIKE DROP-PING THEM.
BUT WE'VE NEVER GOTTEN ENOUGH TO REVIVE A SINGLE GEM.
IT'S A GOOD NAME—IT SOUNDS SERIOUS AND TOUGH.

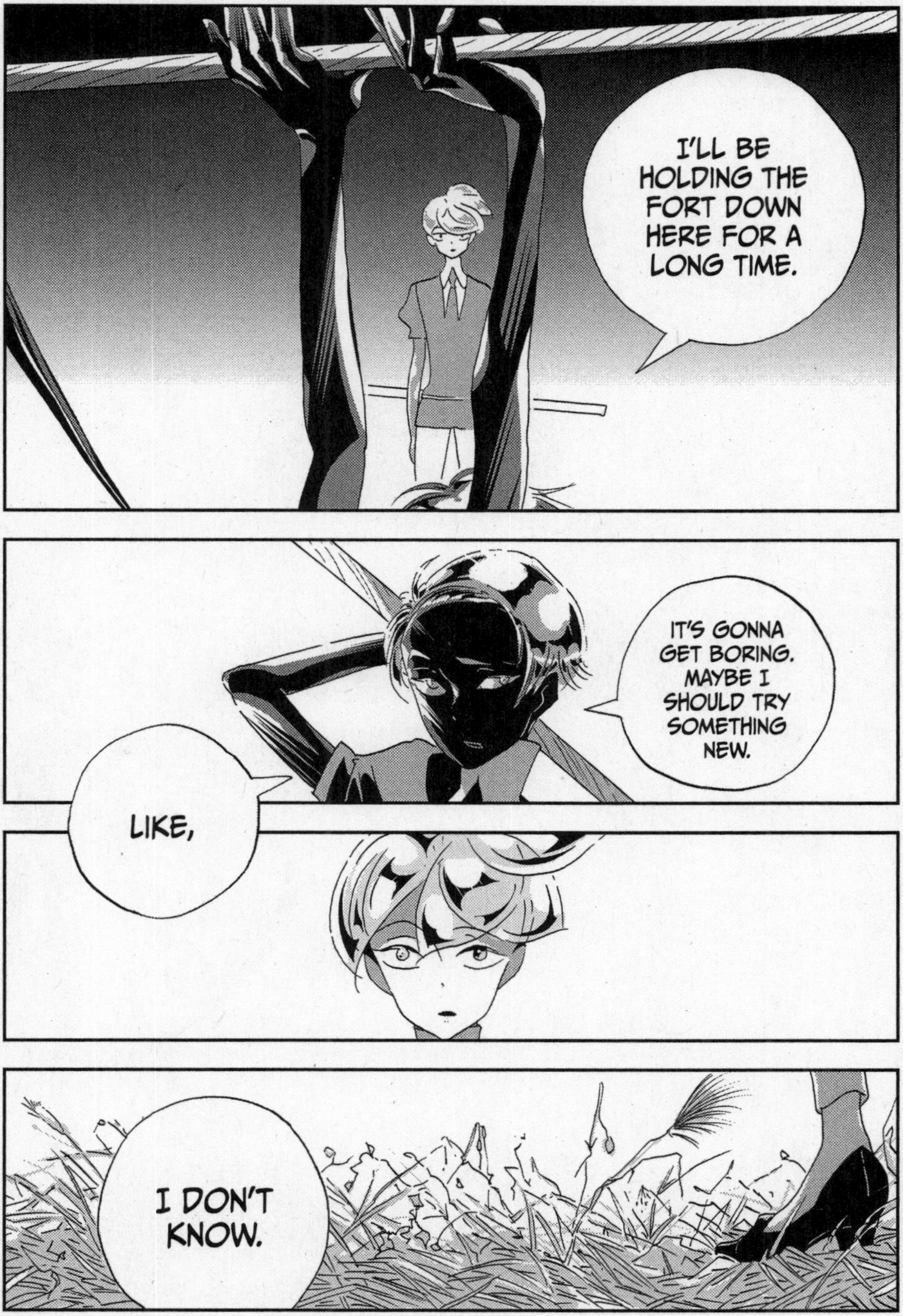
I'LL BE HOLDING THE FORT DOWN HERE FOR A LONG TIME.
IT'S GONNA GET BORING. MAYBE I SHOULD TRY SOMETHING NEW.
LIKE,
I DON'T KNOW.

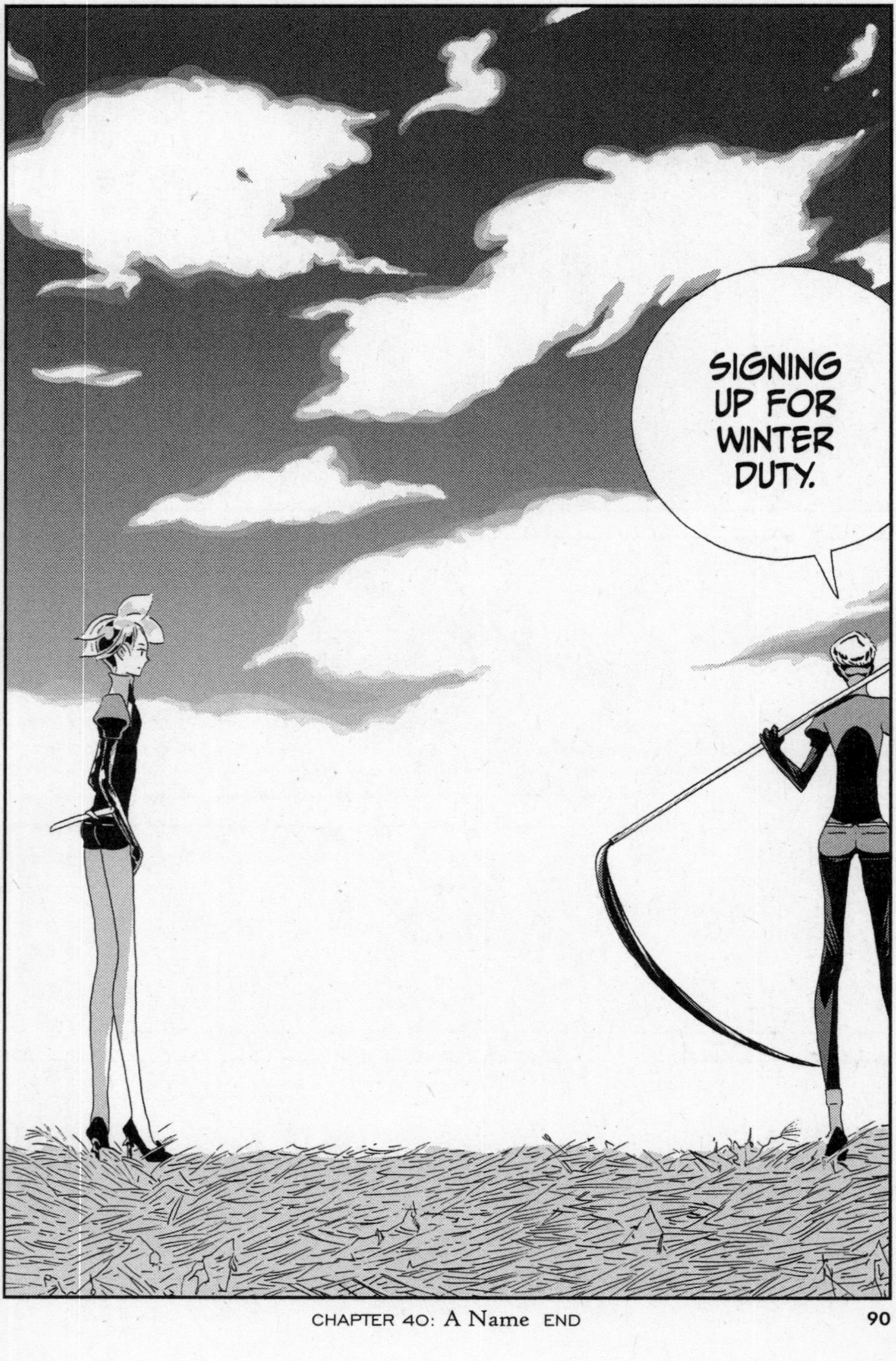
SIGNING UP FOR WINTER DUTY.

CHAPTER 40: A Name END

CHAPTER 41:

Scene

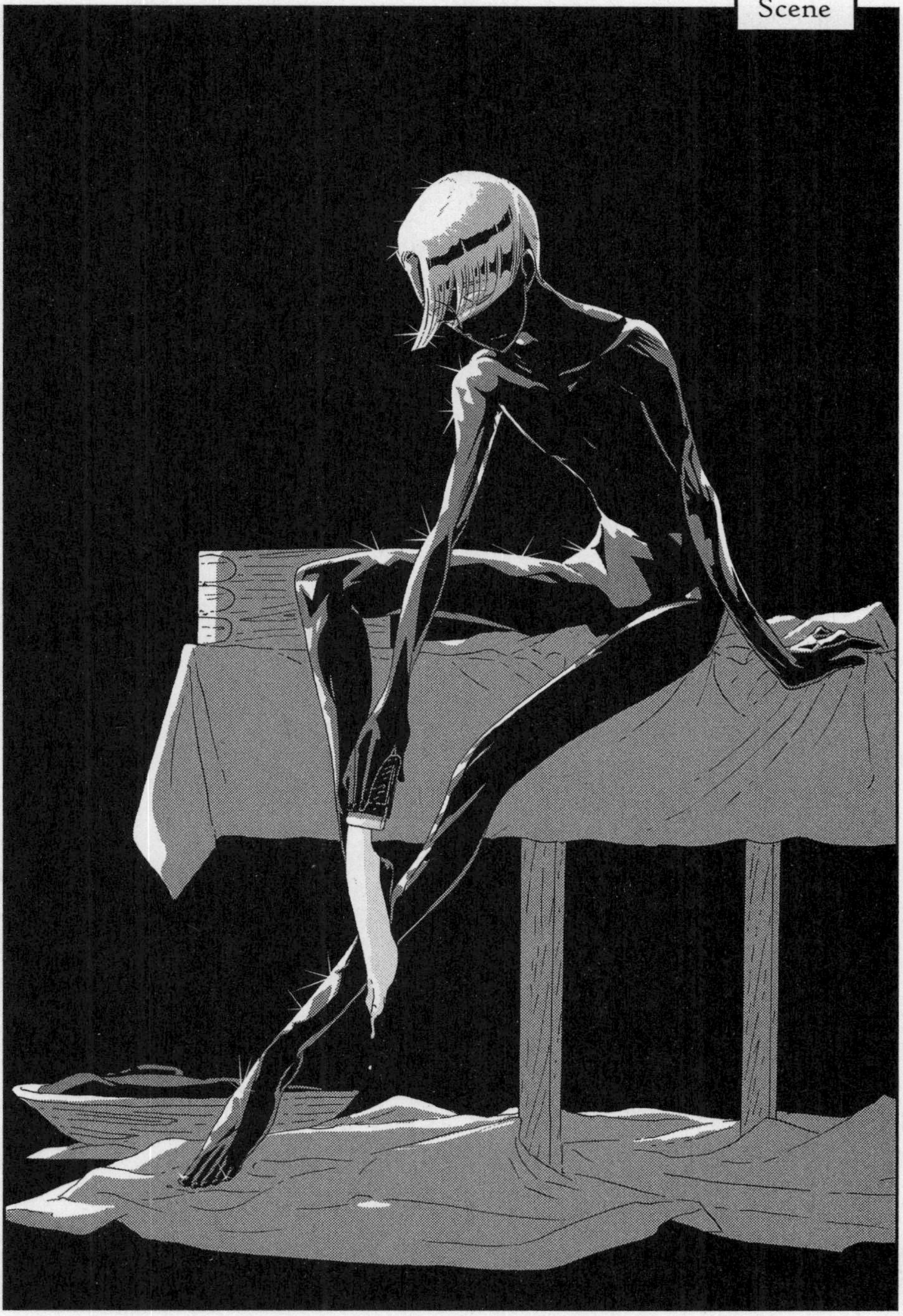

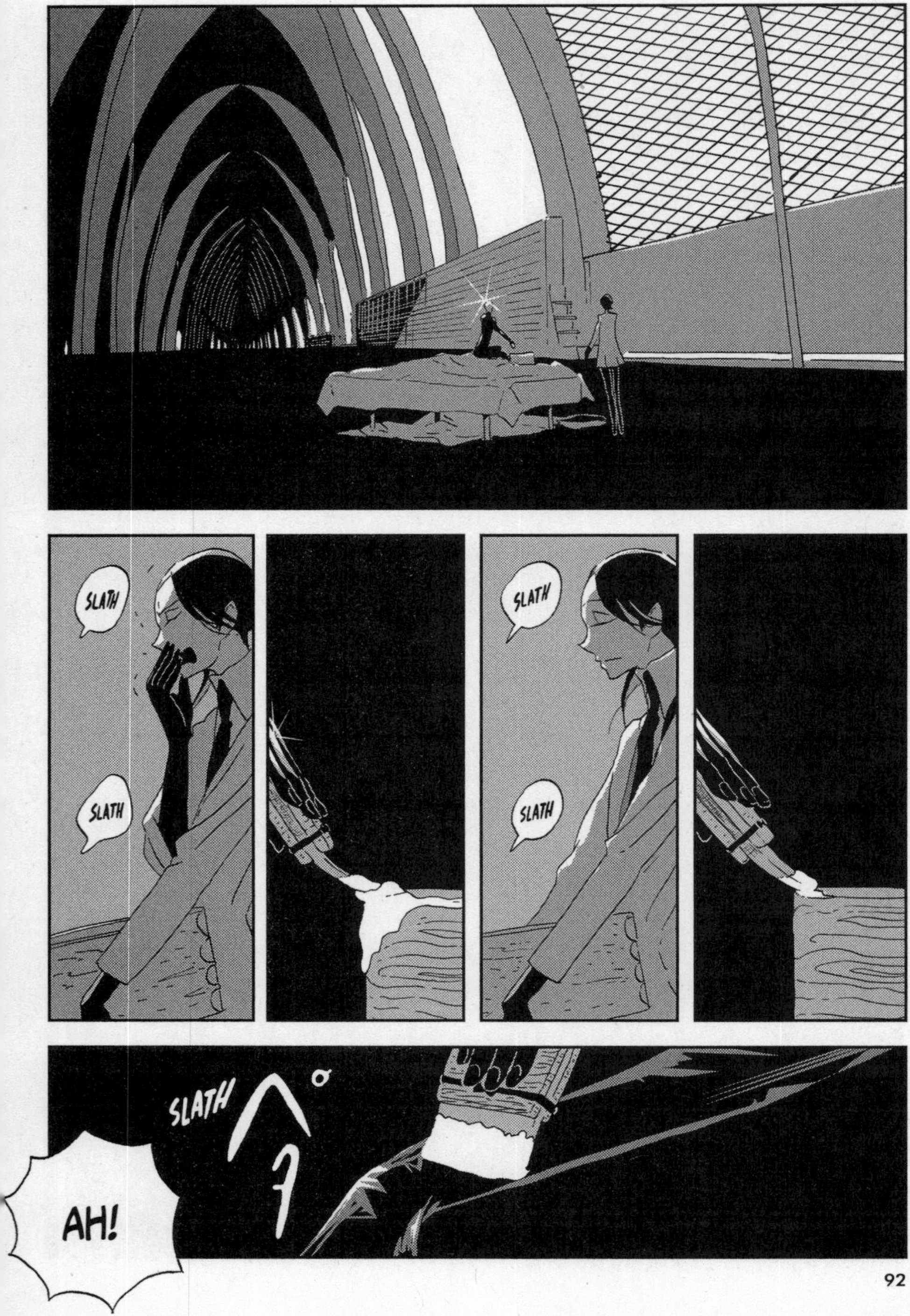
SLATH
SLATH
SLATH
SLATH
SLATH
AH!

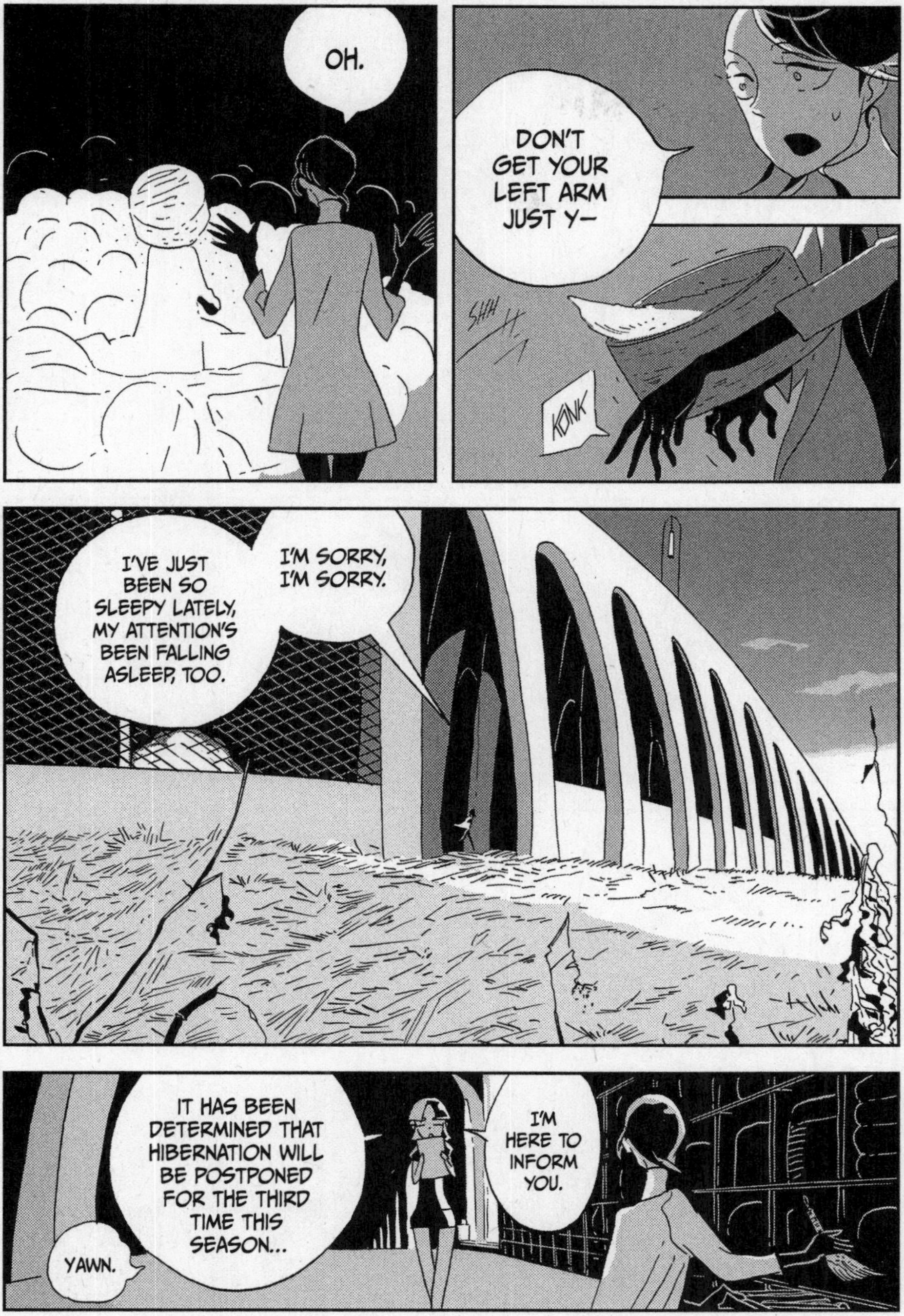
DON'T GET YOUR LEFT ARM JUST Y—
SHH
KONK
OH.
I'M SORRY, I'M SORRY.
I'VE JUST BEEN SO SLEEPY LATELY, MY ATTENTION'S BEEN FALLING ASLEEP, TOO.
I'M HERE TO INFORM YOU.
IT HAS BEEN DETERMINED THAT HIBERNATION WILL BE POSTPONED FOR THE THIRD TIME THIS SEASON...
YAWN.

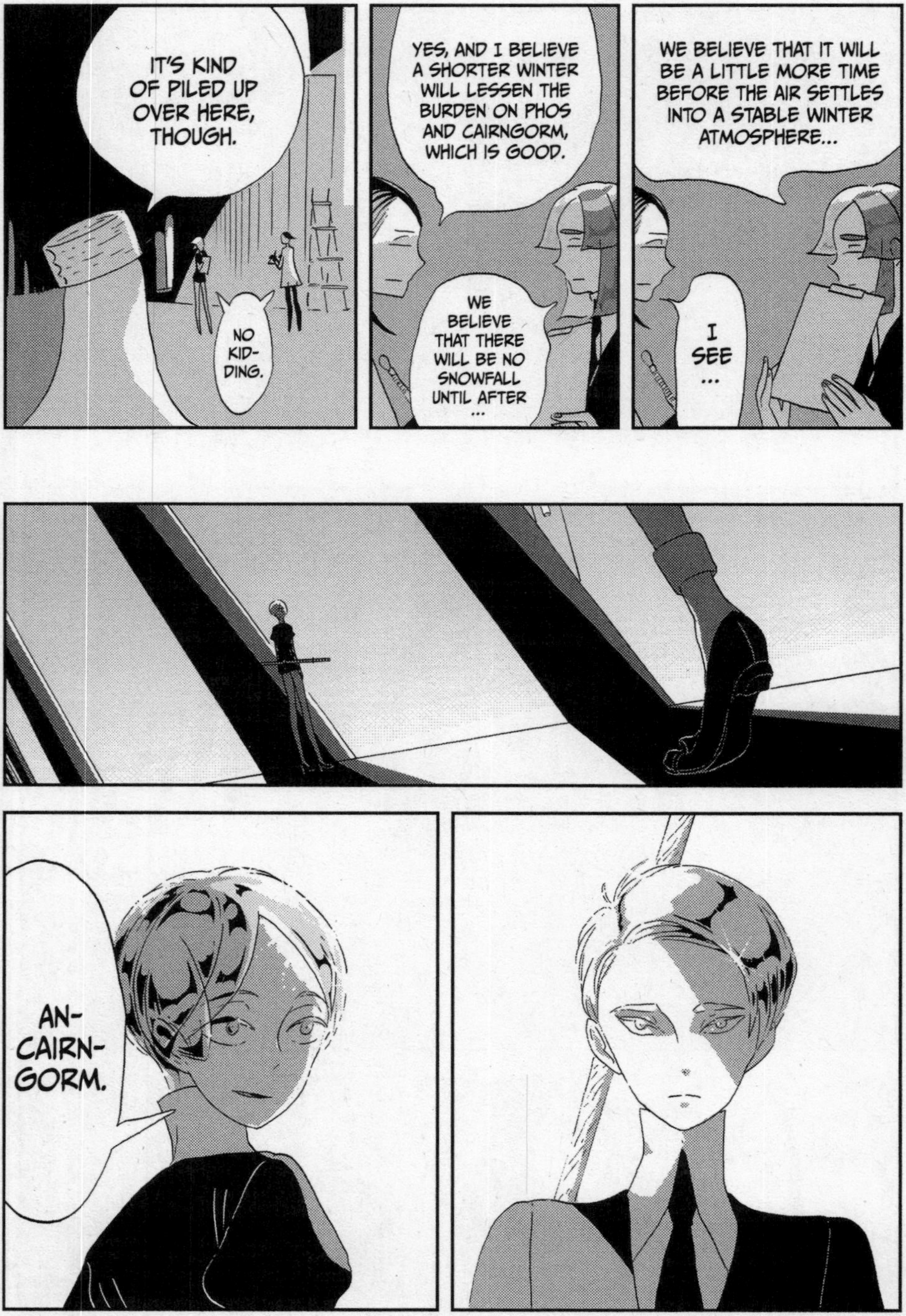
WE BELIEVE THAT IT WILL BE A LITTLE MORE TIME BEFORE THE AIR SETTLES INTO A STABLE WINTER ATMOSPHERE...
I SEE...
YES, AND I BELIEVE A SHORTER WINTER WILL LESSEN THE BURDEN ON PHOS AND CAIRNGORM, WHICH IS GOOD.
WE BELIEVE THAT THERE WILL BE NO SNOWFALL UNTIL AFTER...
IT'S KIND OF PILED UP OVER HERE, THOUGH.
NO KID-DING.
AN-CAIRN-GORM.

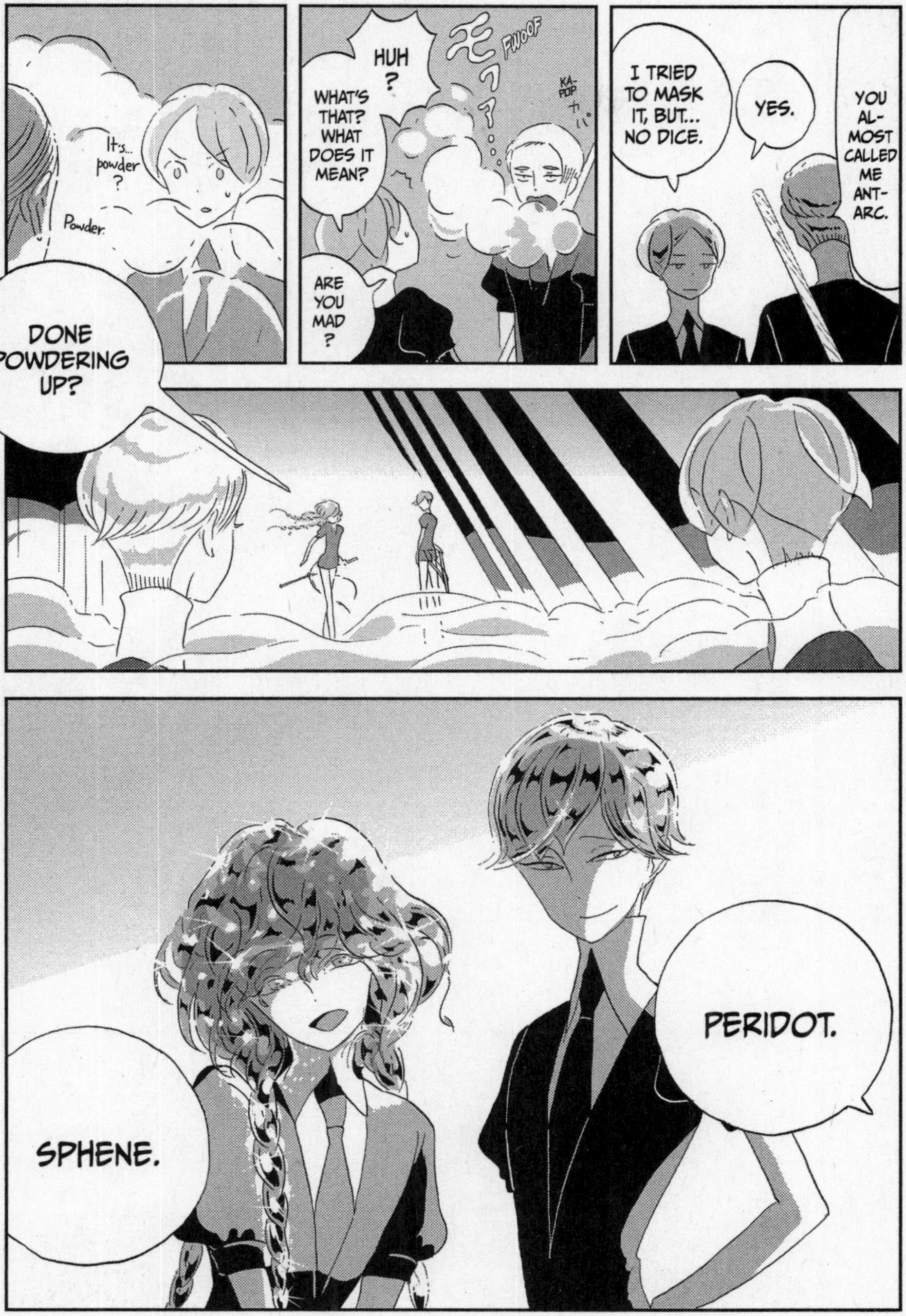
YOU ALMOST CALLED ME ANT-ARC.
YES.
I TRIED TO MASK IT, BUT... NO DICE.
FWOOF
KA-POP
HUH ?
WHAT'S THAT? WHAT DOES IT MEAN?
ARE YOU MAD ?
It's... powder ?
Powder.
DONE POWDERING UP?
PERIDOT.
SPHENE.

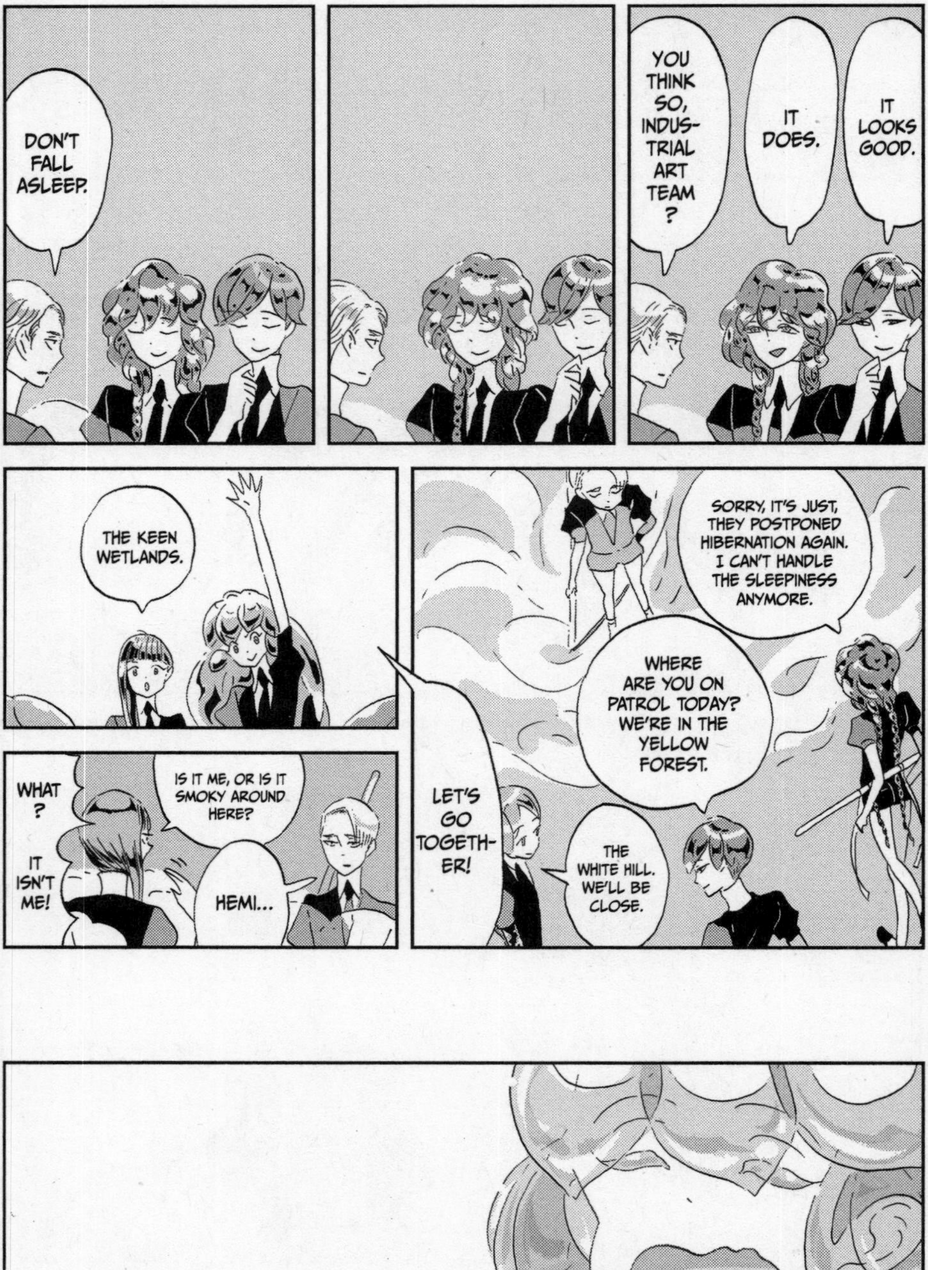
IT LOOKS GOOD.
IT DOES.
YOU THINK SO, INDUS-TRIAL ART TEAM?
DON'T FALL ASLEEP.
SORRY, IT'S JUST, THEY POSTPONED HIBERNATION AGAIN. I CAN'T HANDLE THE SLEEPINESS ANYMORE.
WHERE ARE YOU ON PATROL TODAY? WE'RE IN THE YELLOW FOREST.
THE WHITE HILL. WE'LL BE CLOSE.
LET'S GO TOGETH-ER!
THE KEEN WETLANDS.
IS IT ME, OR IS IT SMOKY AROUND HERE?
HEMI...
WHAT?
IT ISN'T ME!

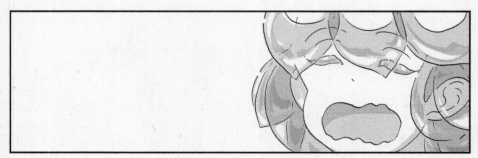

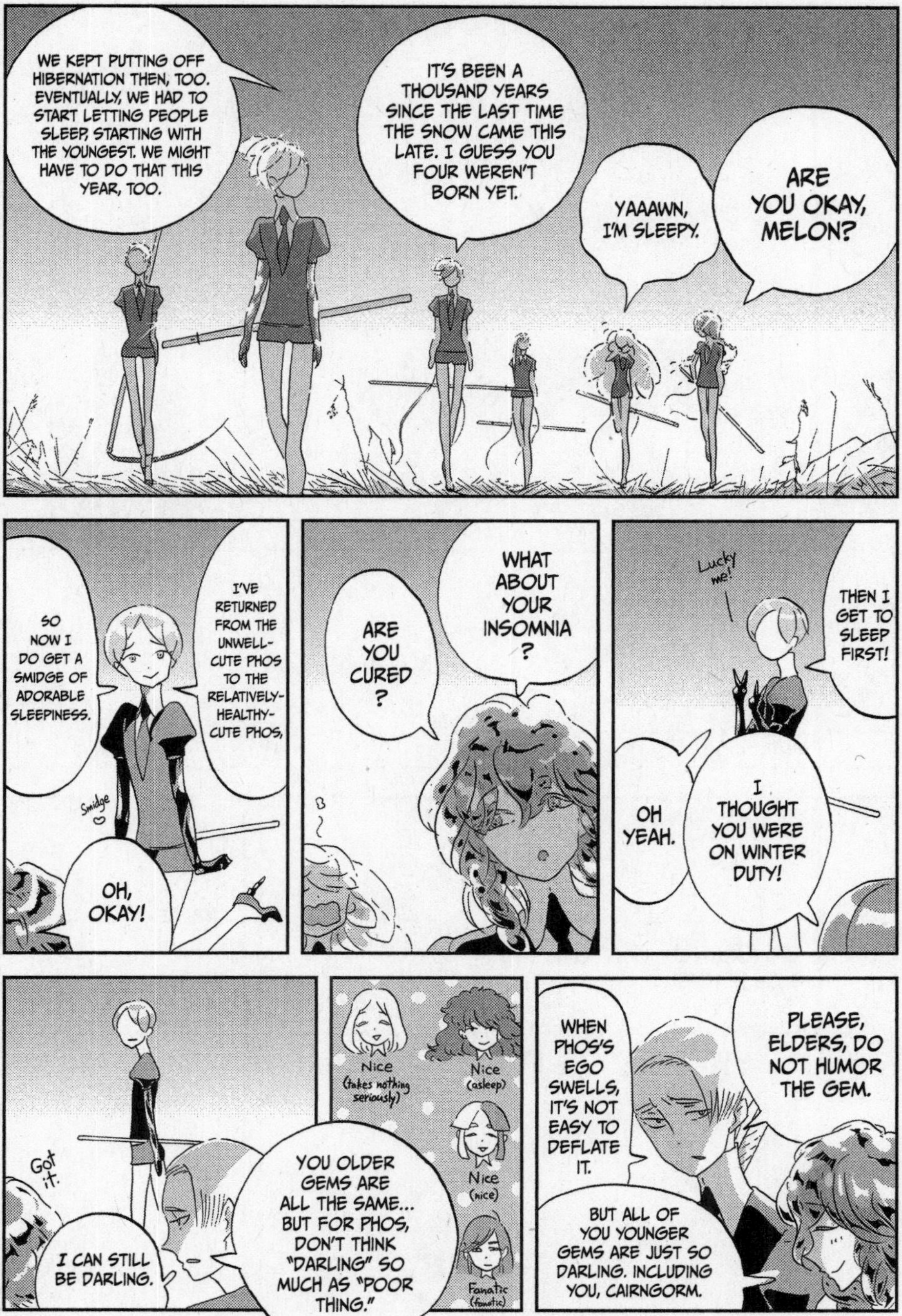
ARE YOU OKAY, MELON?
YAAAWN, I'M SLEEPY.
IT'S BEEN A THOUSAND YEARS SINCE THE LAST TIME THE SNOW CAME THIS LATE. I GUESS YOU FOUR WEREN'T BORN YET.
WE KEPT PUTTING OFF HIBERNATION THEN, TOO. EVENTUALLY, WE HAD TO START LETTING PEOPLE SLEEP, STARTING WITH THE YOUNGEST. WE MIGHT HAVE TO DO THAT THIS YEAR, TOO.
Lucky me!
THEN I GET TO SLEEP FIRST!
I THOUGHT YOU WERE ON WINTER DUTY!
OH YEAH.
WHAT ABOUT YOUR INSOMNIA?
ARE YOU CURED?
I'VE RETURNED FROM THE UNWELL-CUTE PHOS TO THE RELATIVELY-HEALTHY-CUTE PHOS,
SO NOW I DO GET A SMIDGE OF ADORABLE SLEEPINESS.
Smidge
OH, OKAY!
PLEASE, ELDERS, DO NOT HUMOR THE GEM.
WHEN PHOS'S EGO SWELLS, IT'S NOT EASY TO DEFLATE IT.
BUT ALL OF YOU YOUNGER GEMS ARE JUST SO DARLING. INCLUDING YOU, CAIRNGORM.
Nice (asleep)
Nice (takes nothing seriously)
Nice (nice)
Fanatic (fanatic)
YOU OLDER GEMS ARE ALL THE SAME... BUT FOR PHOS, DON'T THINK "DARLING" SO MUCH AS "POOR THING."
Got it.
I CAN STILL BE DARLING.

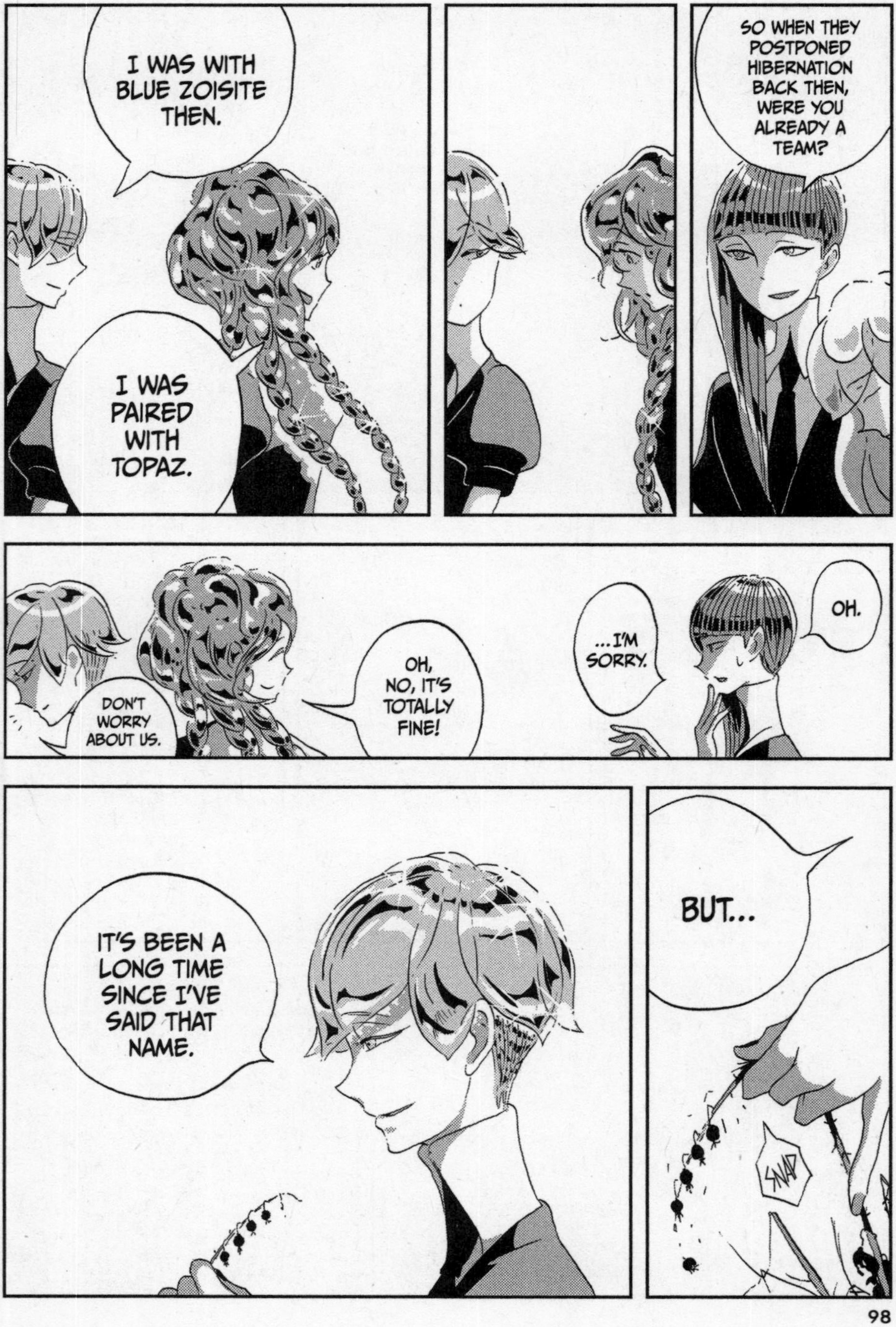
SO WHEN THEY POSTPONED HIBERNATION BACK THEN, WERE YOU ALREADY A TEAM?
I WAS WITH BLUE ZOISITE THEN.
I WAS PAIRED WITH TOPAZ.
OH.
...I'M SORRY.
OH, NO, IT'S TOTALLY FINE!
DON'T WORRY ABOUT US.
BUT...
SNAP
IT'S BEEN A LONG TIME SINCE I'VE SAID THAT NAME.

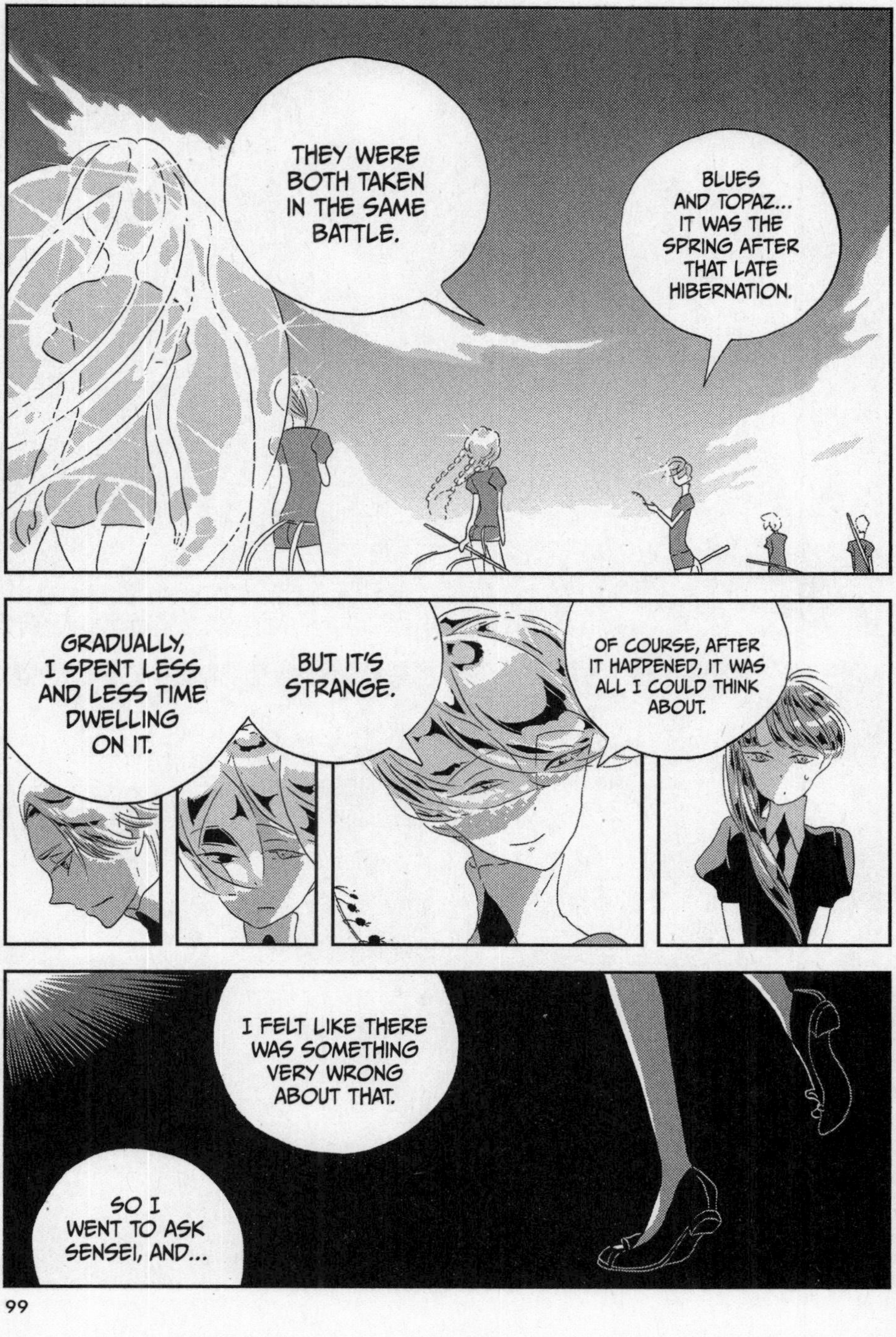
BLUES AND TOPAZ... IT WAS THE SPRING AFTER THAT LATE HIBERNATION.
THEY WERE BOTH TAKEN IN THE SAME BATTLE.
OF COURSE, AFTER IT HAPPENED, IT WAS ALL I COULD THINK ABOUT.
BUT IT'S STRANGE.
GRADUALLY, I SPENT LESS AND LESS TIME DWELLING ON IT.
I FELT LIKE THERE WAS SOMETHING VERY WRONG ABOUT THAT.
SO I WENT TO ASK SENSEI, AND...

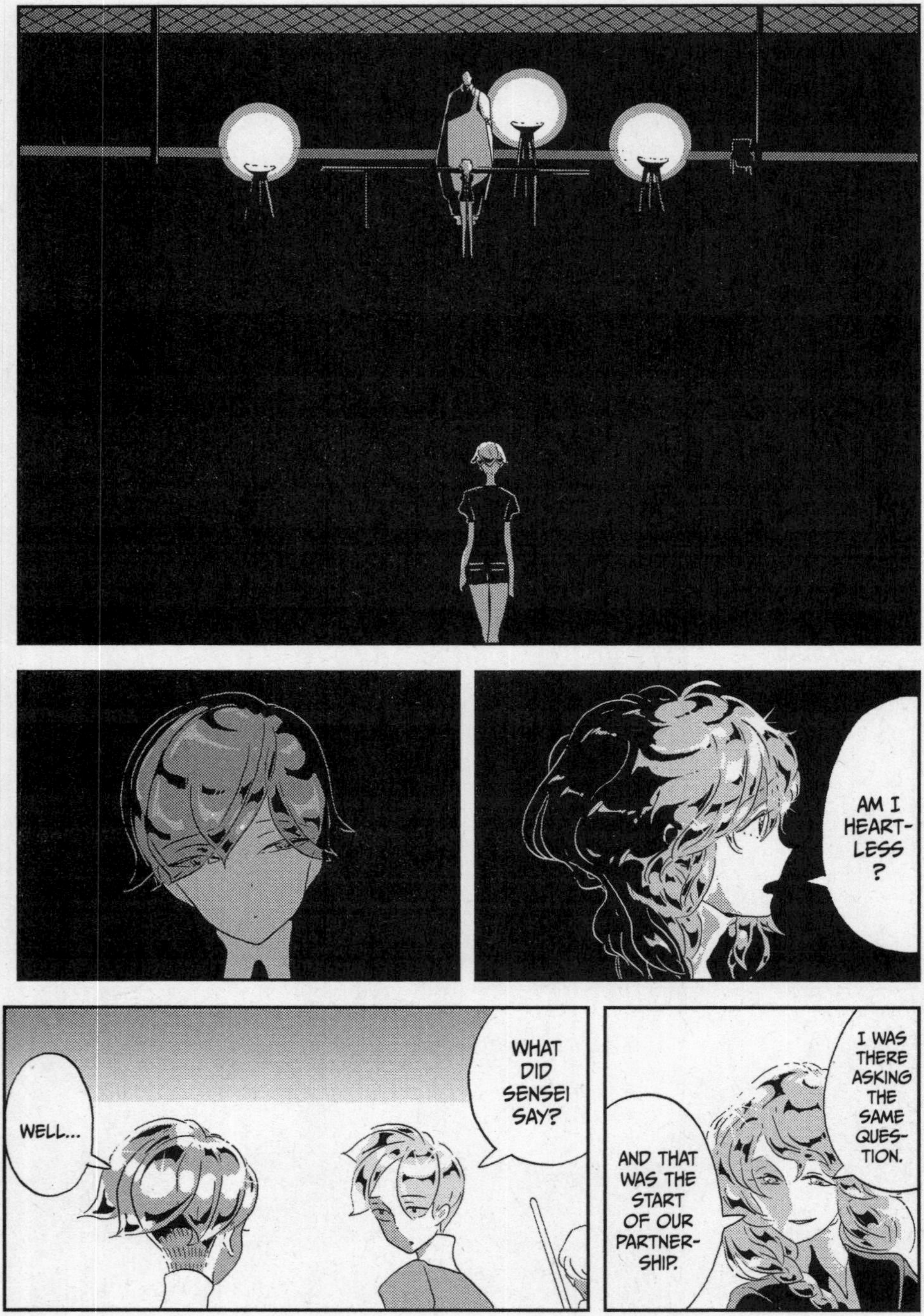
AM I HEARTLESS?
I WAS THERE ASKING THE SAME QUESTION.
AND THAT WAS THE START OF OUR PARTNERSHIP.
WHAT DID SENSEI SAY?
WELL...

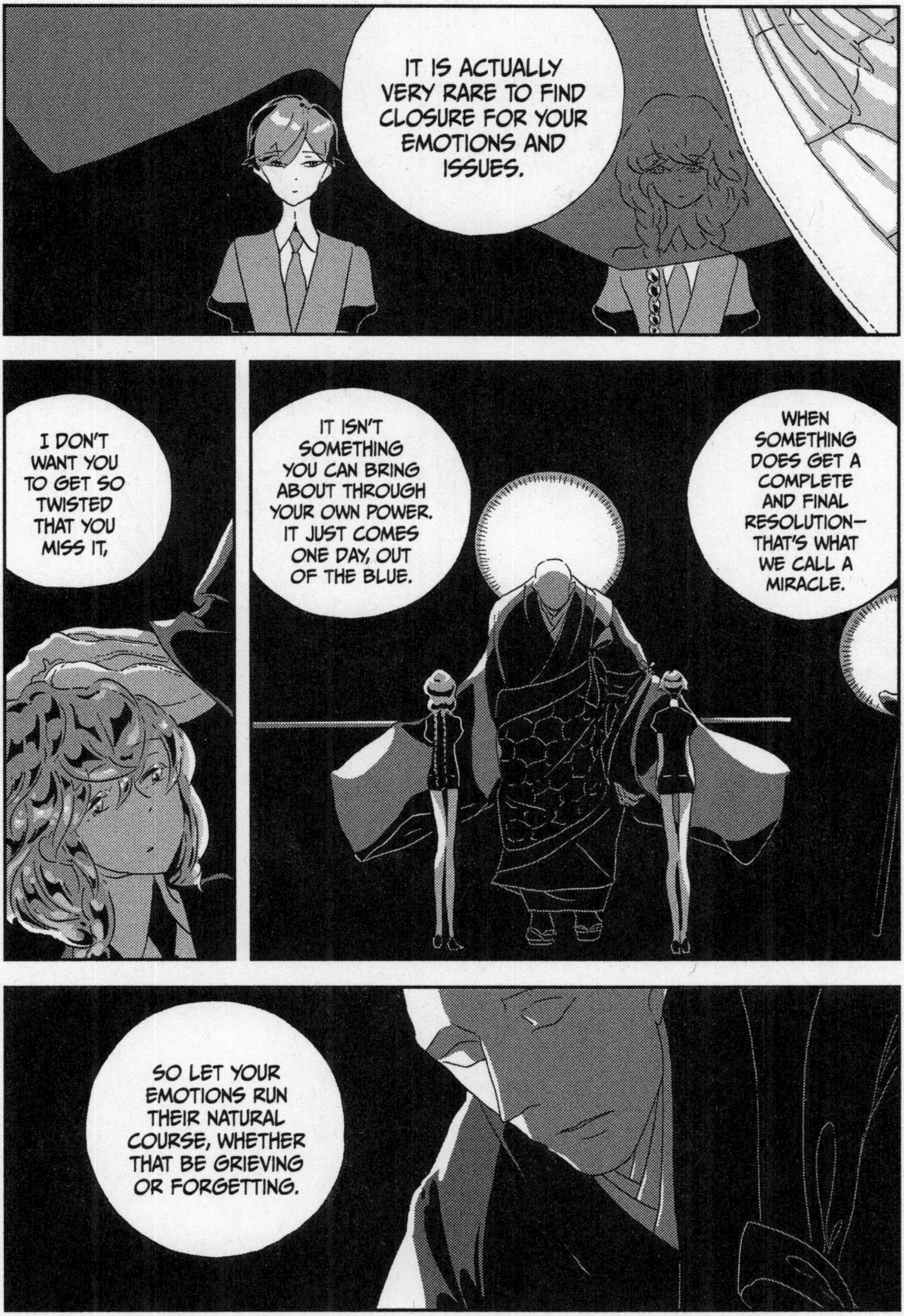
IT IS ACTUALLY VERY RARE TO FIND CLOSURE FOR YOUR EMOTIONS AND ISSUES.
WHEN SOMETHING DOES GET A COMPLETE AND FINAL RESOLUTION—THAT'S WHAT WE CALL A MIRACLE.
IT ISN'T SOMETHING YOU CAN BRING ABOUT THROUGH YOUR OWN POWER. IT JUST COMES ONE DAY, OUT OF THE BLUE.
I DON'T WANT YOU TO GET SO TWISTED THAT YOU MISS IT,
SO LET YOUR EMOTIONS RUN THEIR NATURAL COURSE, WHETHER THAT BE GRIEVING OR FORGETTING.

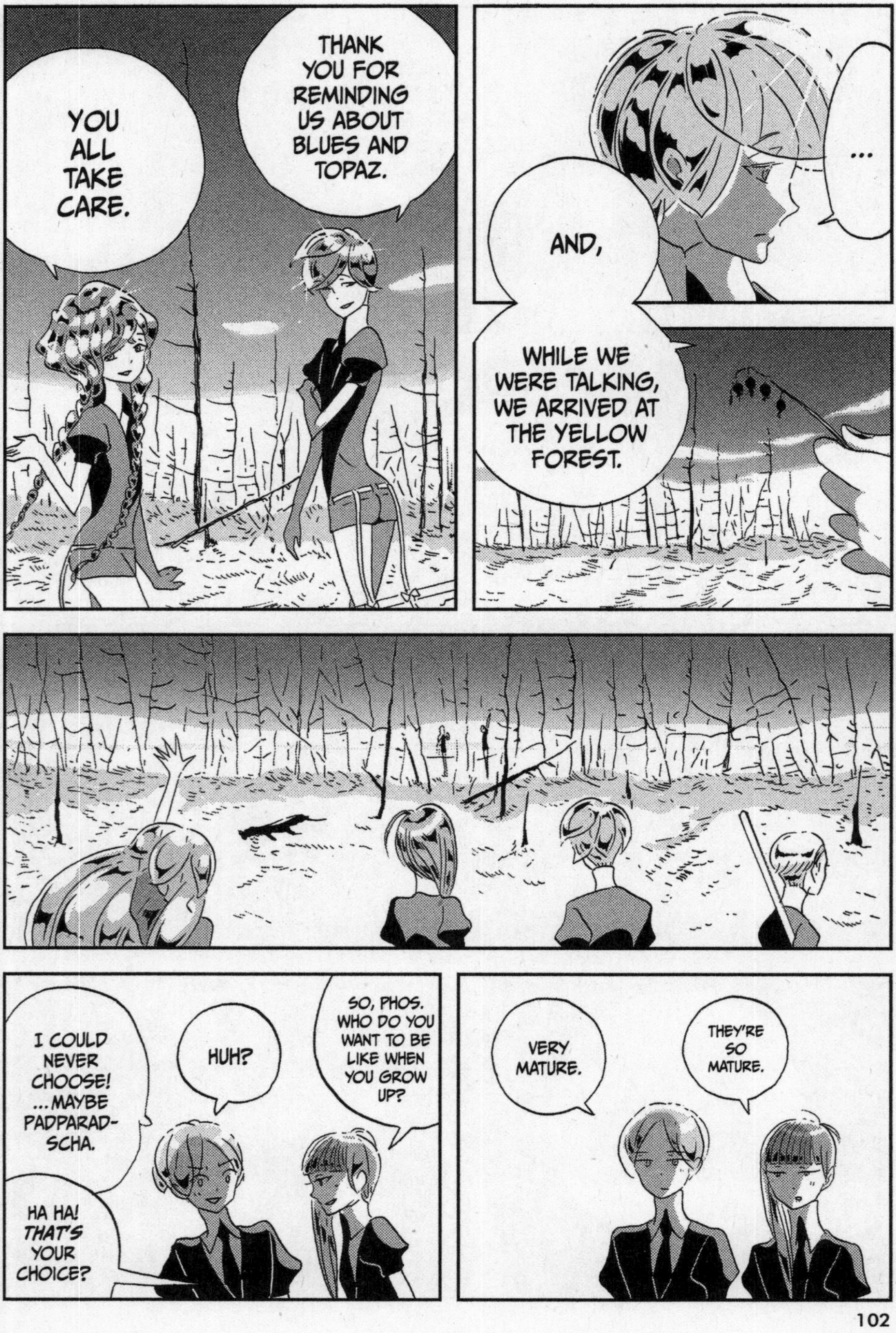
...
AND,
WHILE WE WERE TALKING, WE ARRIVED AT THE YELLOW FOREST.
THANK YOU FOR REMINDING US ABOUT BLUES AND TOPAZ.
YOU ALL TAKE CARE.
THEY'RE SO MATURE.
VERY MATURE.
SO, PHOS. WHO DO YOU WANT TO BE LIKE WHEN YOU GROW UP?
HUH?
I COULD NEVER CHOOSE! ...MAYBE PADPARAD-SCHA.
HA HA! *THAT'S* YOUR CHOICE?

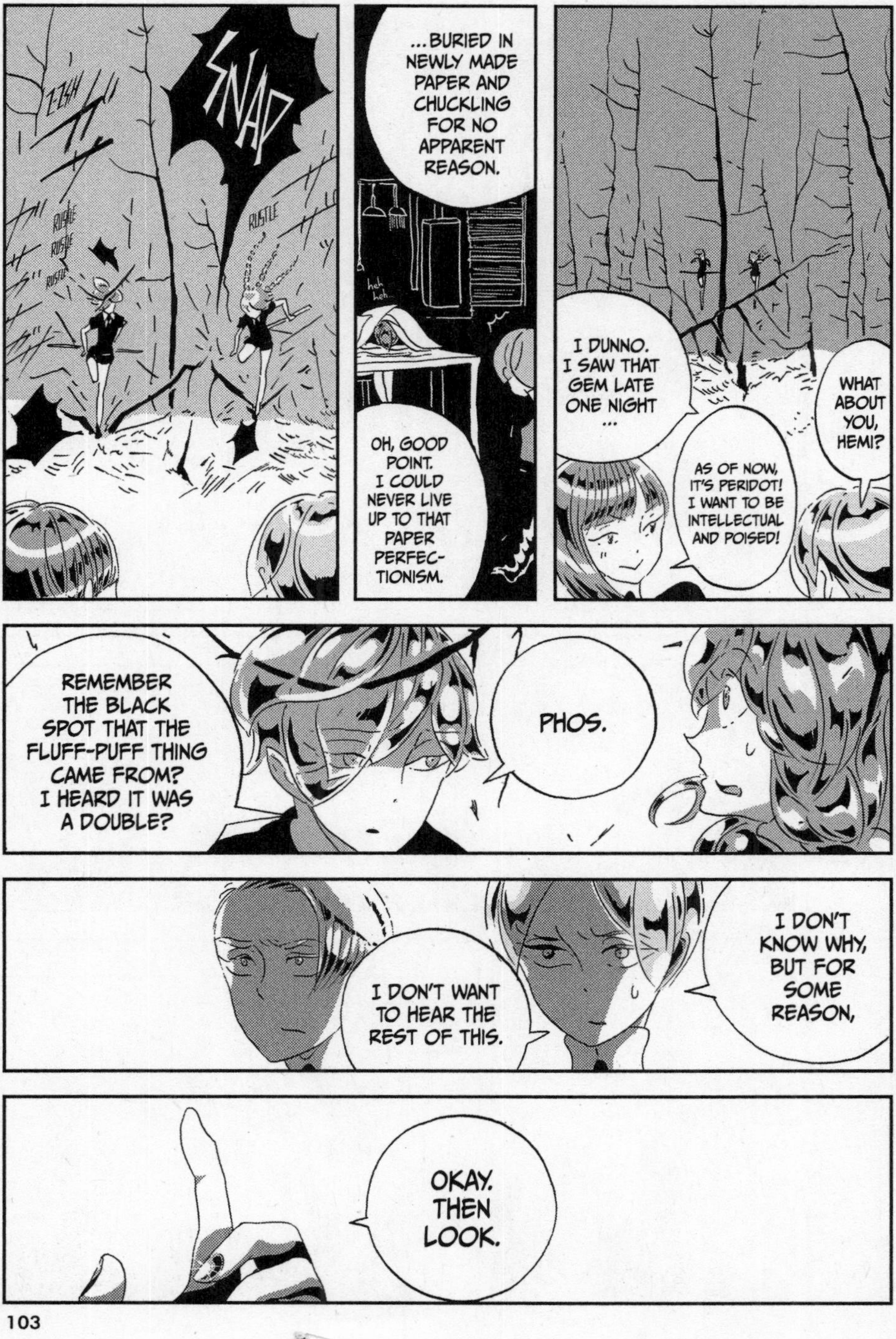
WHAT ABOUT YOU, HEMI?
AS OF NOW, IT'S PERIDOT! I WANT TO BE INTELLECTUAL AND POISED!
I DUNNO. I SAW THAT GEM LATE ONE NIGHT ...
...BURIED IN NEWLY MADE PAPER AND CHUCKLING FOR NO APPARENT REASON.
heh heh...
OH, GOOD POINT. I COULD NEVER LIVE UP TO THAT PAPER PERFECTIONISM.
SNAP
RUSTLE
RUSTLE
RUSTLE
PHOS.
REMEMBER THE BLACK SPOT THAT THE FLUFF-PUFF THING CAME FROM? I HEARD IT WAS A DOUBLE?
I DON'T KNOW WHY, BUT FOR SOME REASON,
I DON'T WANT TO HEAR THE REST OF THIS.
OKAY. THEN LOOK.

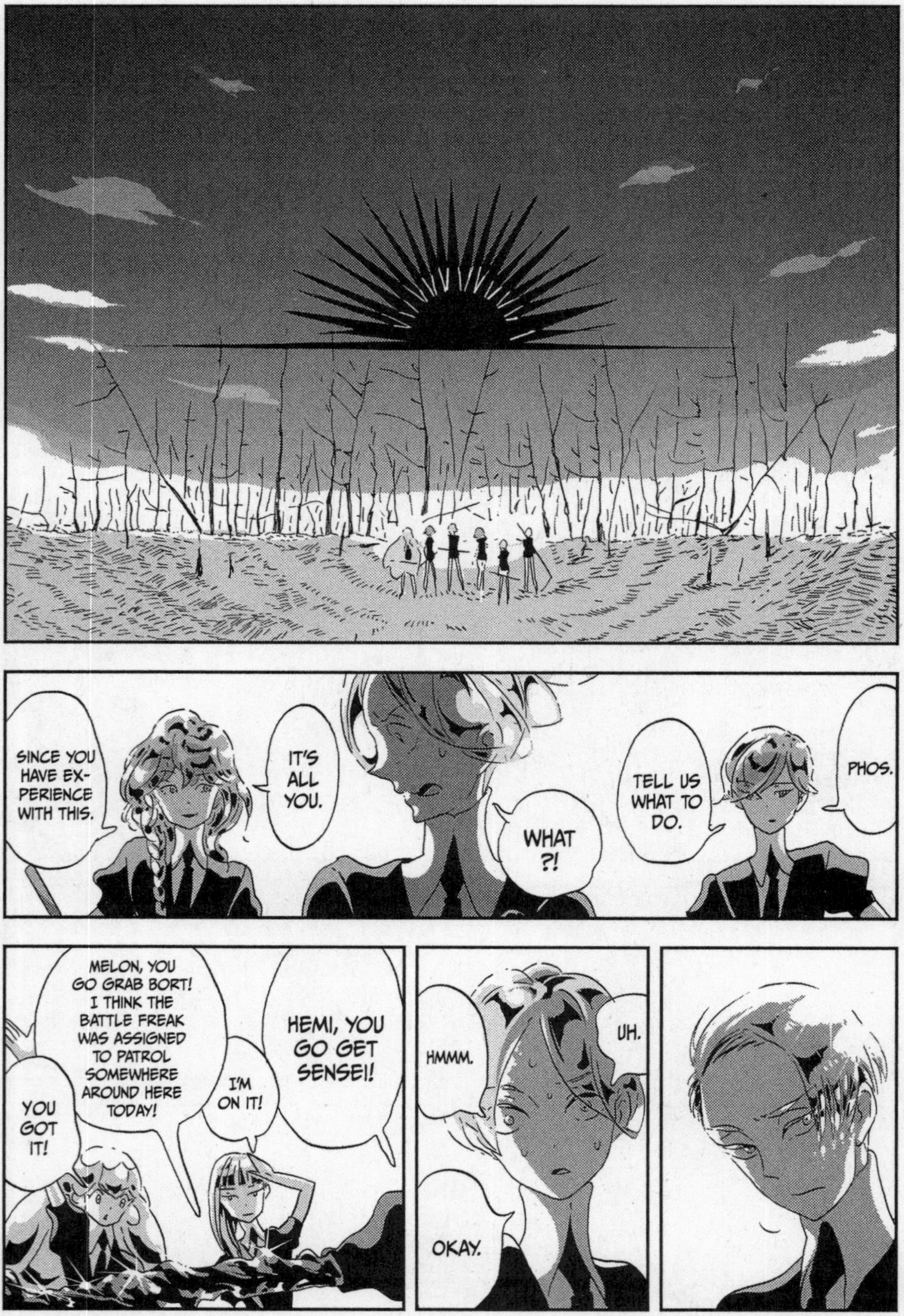
PHOS.
TELL US WHAT TO DO.
WHAT ?!
IT'S ALL YOU.
SINCE YOU HAVE EX-PERIENCE WITH THIS.
UH.
HMMM.
OKAY.
HEMI, YOU GO GET SENSEI!
I'M ON IT!
MELON, YOU GO GRAB BORT! I THINK THE BATTLE FREAK WAS ASSIGNED TO PATROL SOMEWHERE AROUND HERE TODAY!
YOU GOT IT!

IT'S REALLY LOW TO THE GROUND.

HMM.

IS THAT HOW IT WAS LAST TIME?

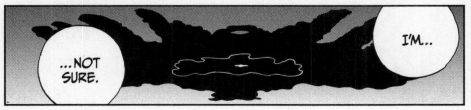

I'M...

...NOT SURE.

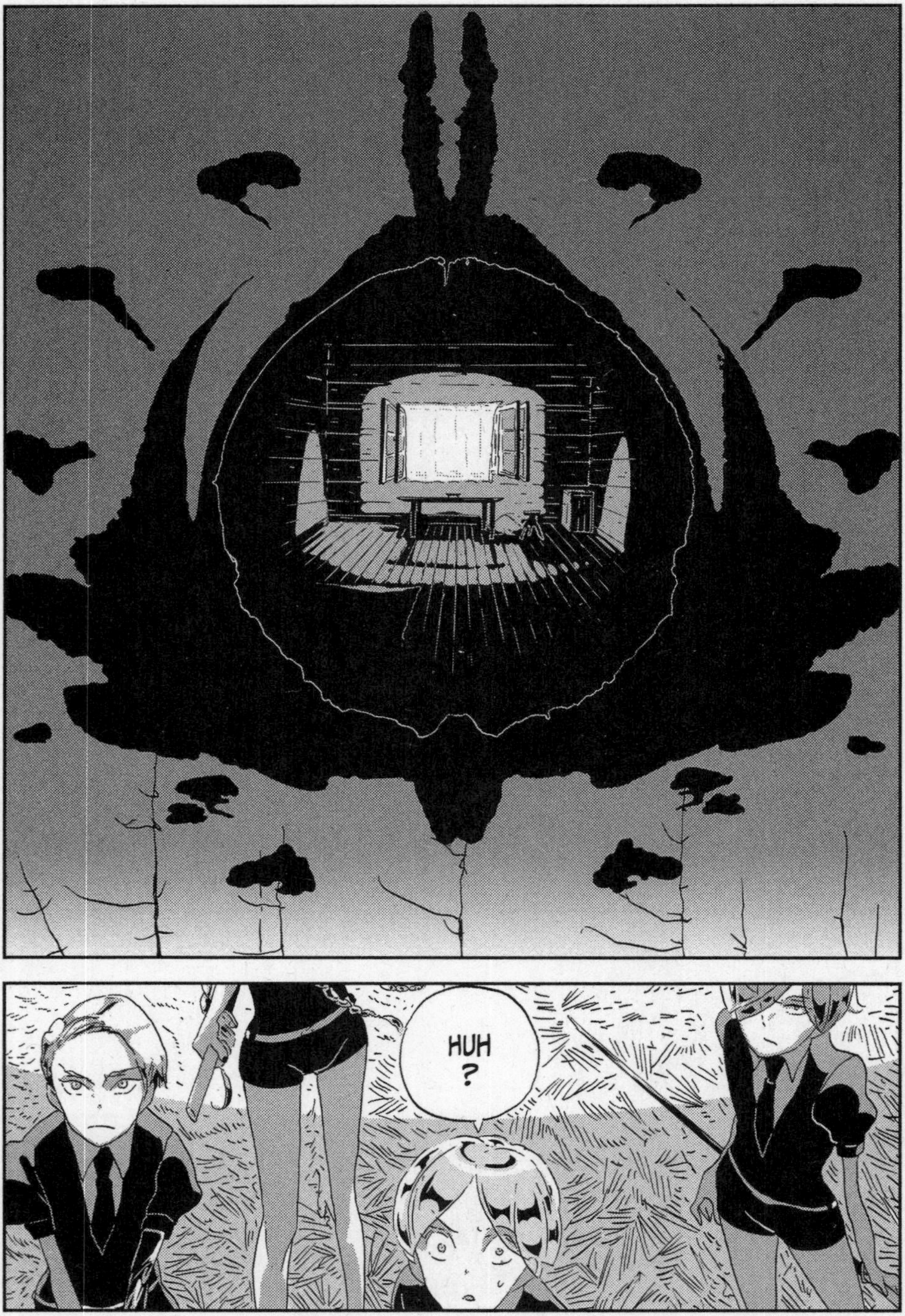
HUH ?

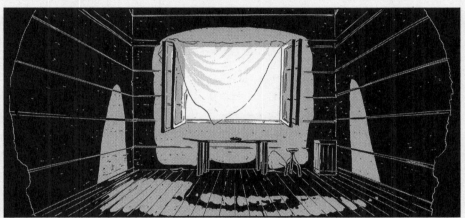

107

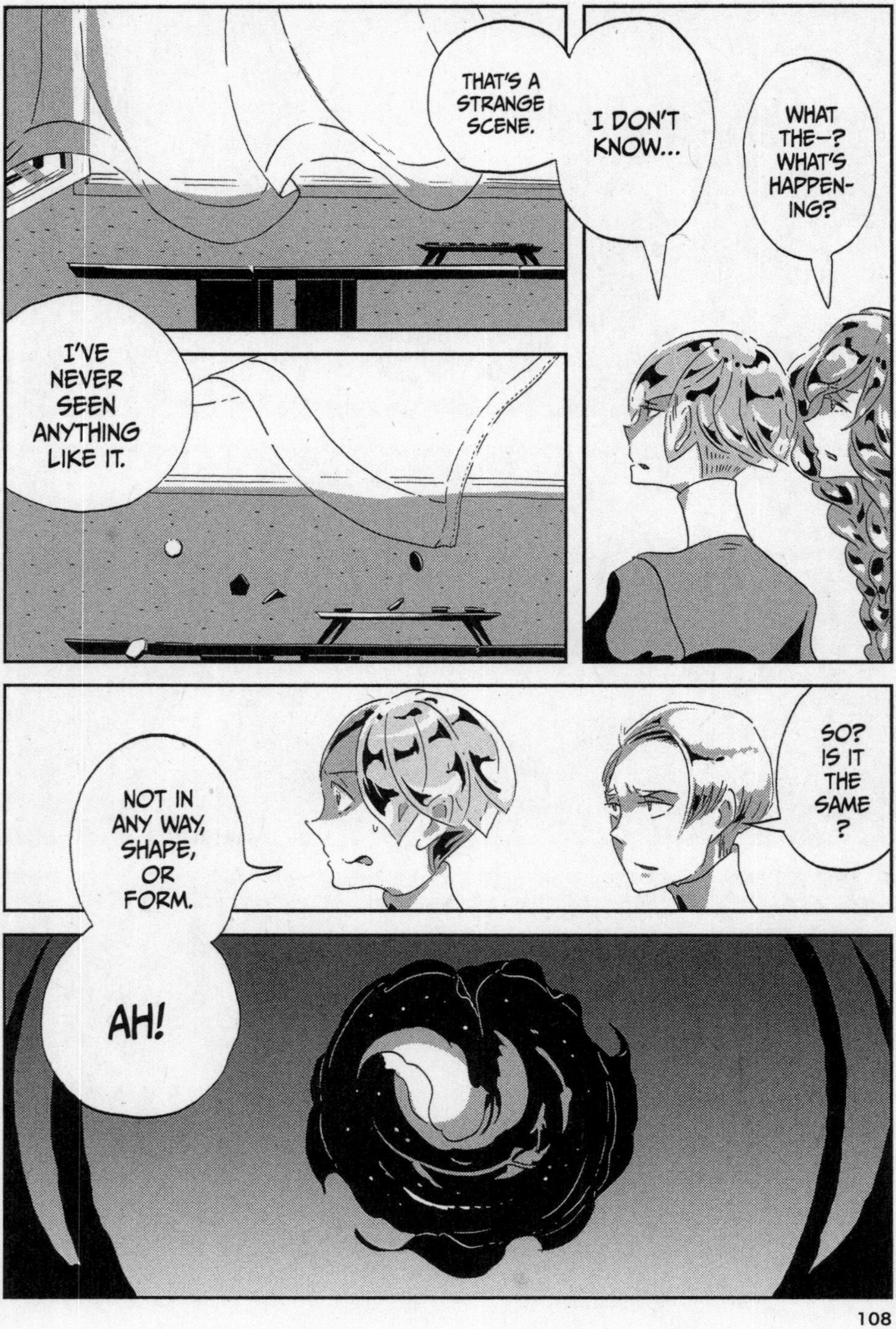
WHAT THE—? WHAT'S HAPPENING?
I DON'T KNOW...
THAT'S A STRANGE SCENE.
I'VE NEVER SEEN ANYTHING LIKE IT.
SO? IS IT THE SAME?
NOT IN ANY WAY, SHAPE, OR FORM.
AH!

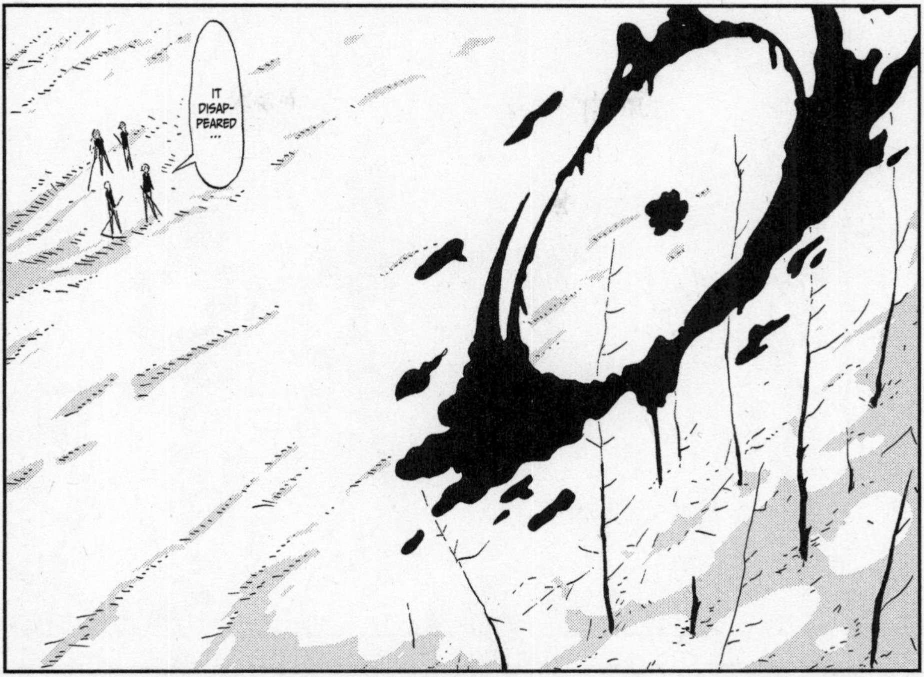
IT DISAP-PEARED...
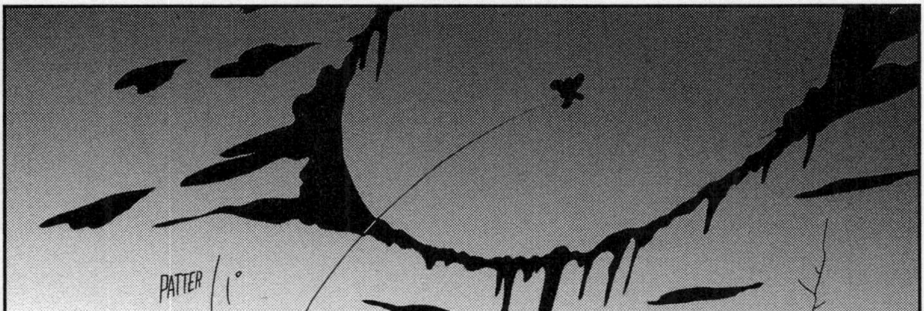
PATTER
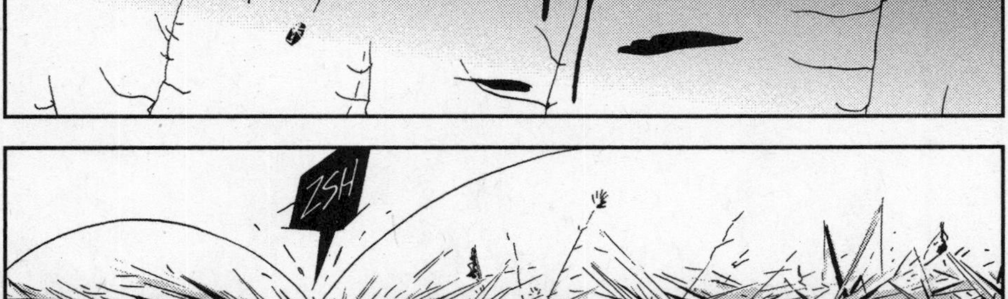
ZSH

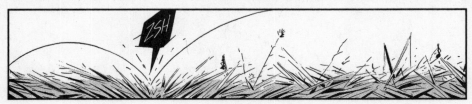

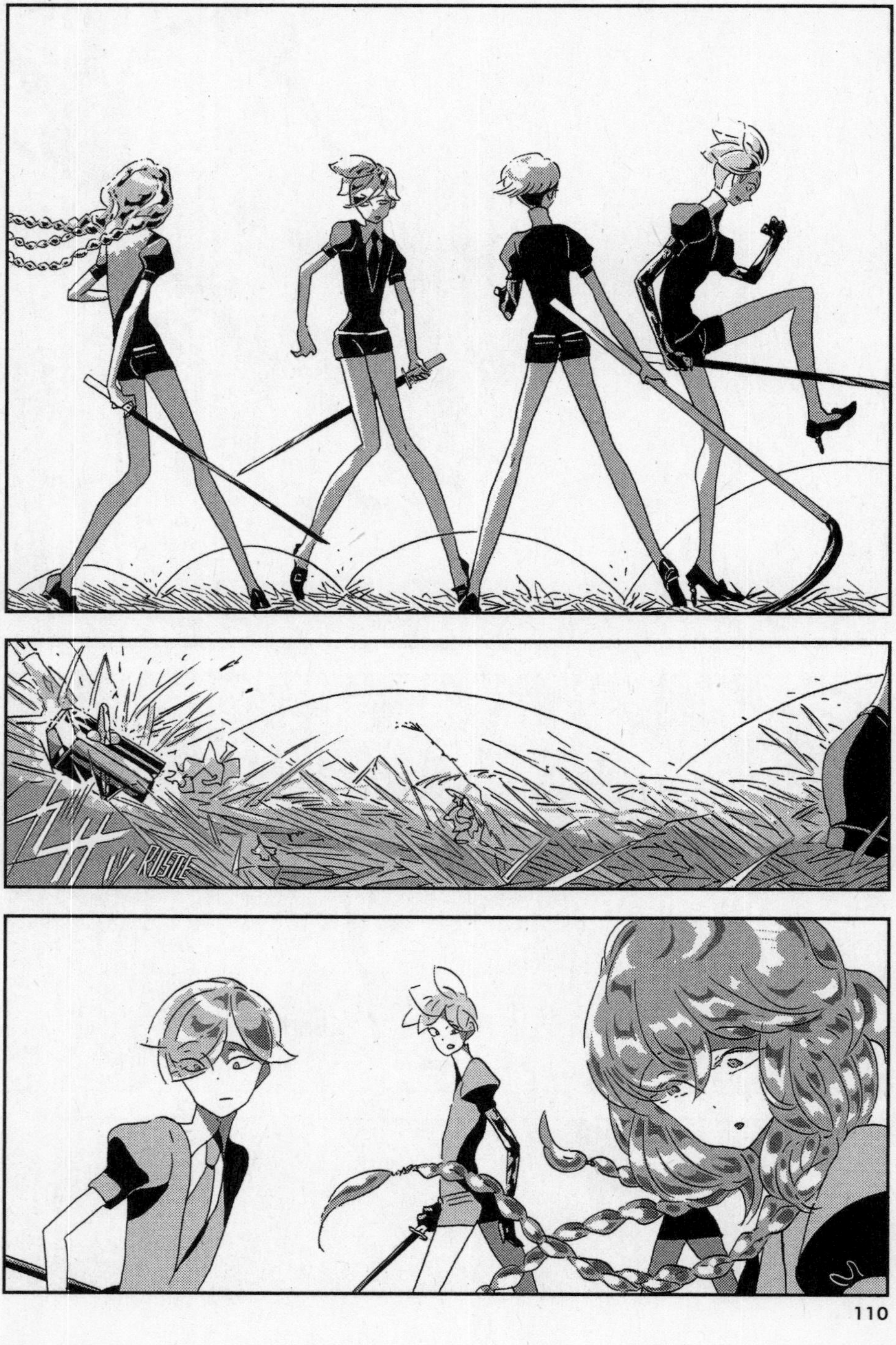
RUSTLE

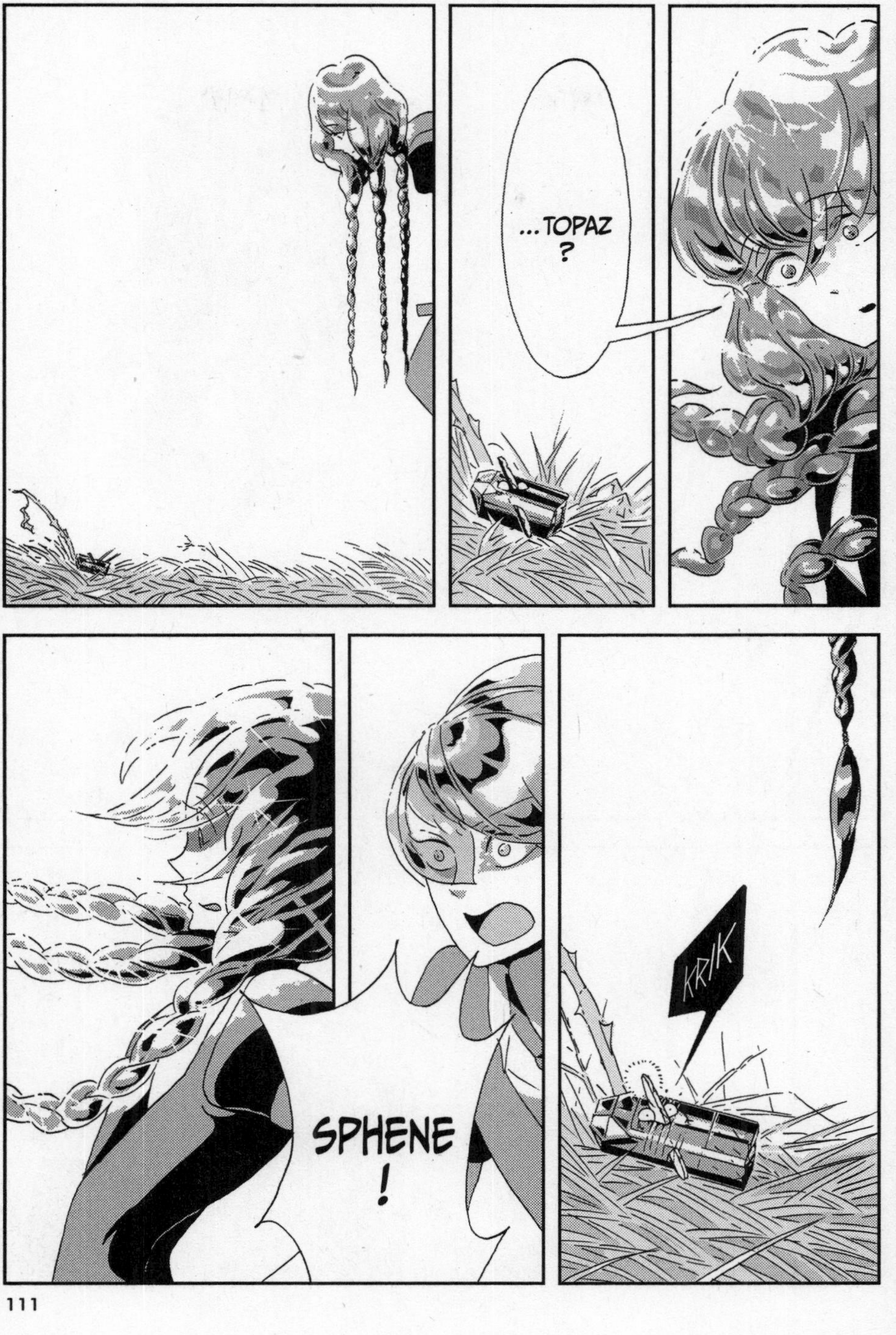
...TOPAZ
?
KRIK
SPHENE
!

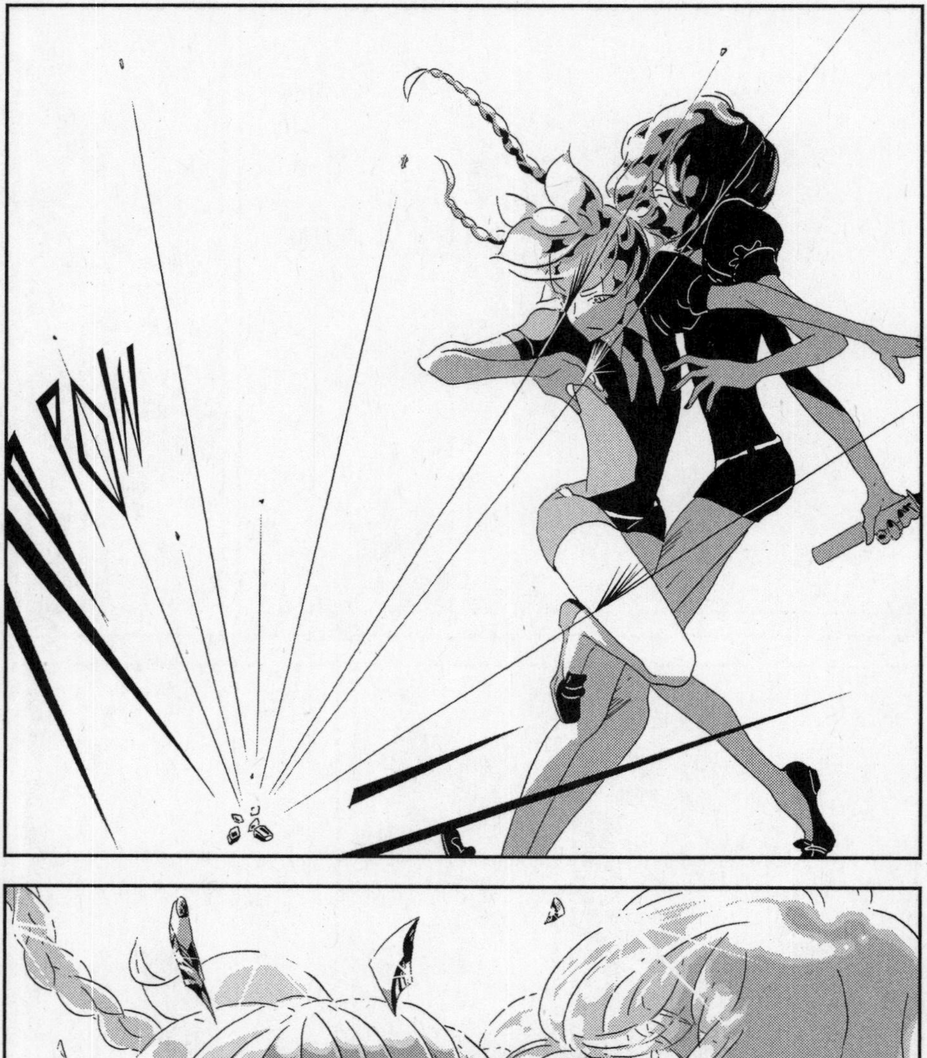
POW
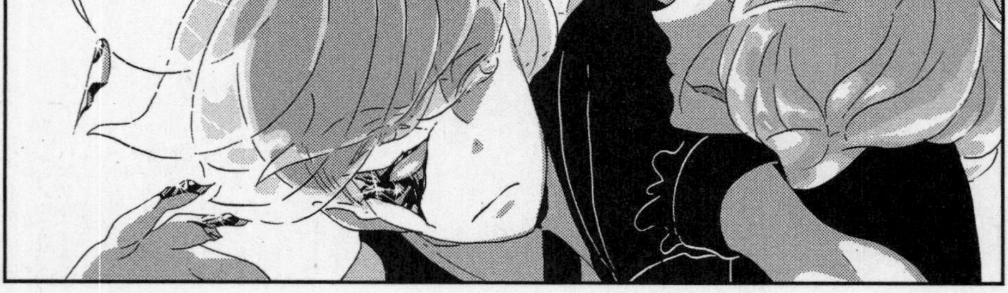

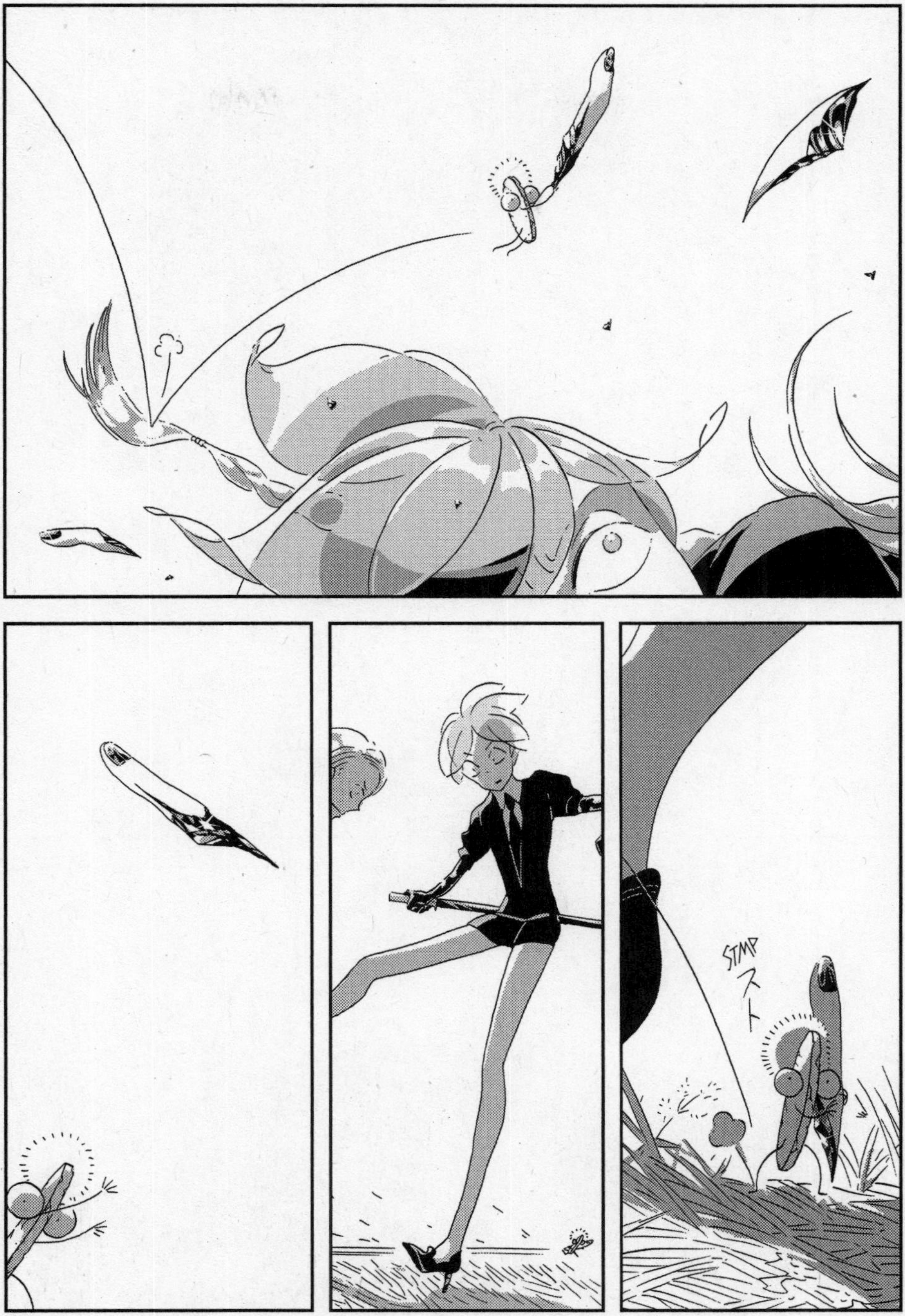
STMP
スト

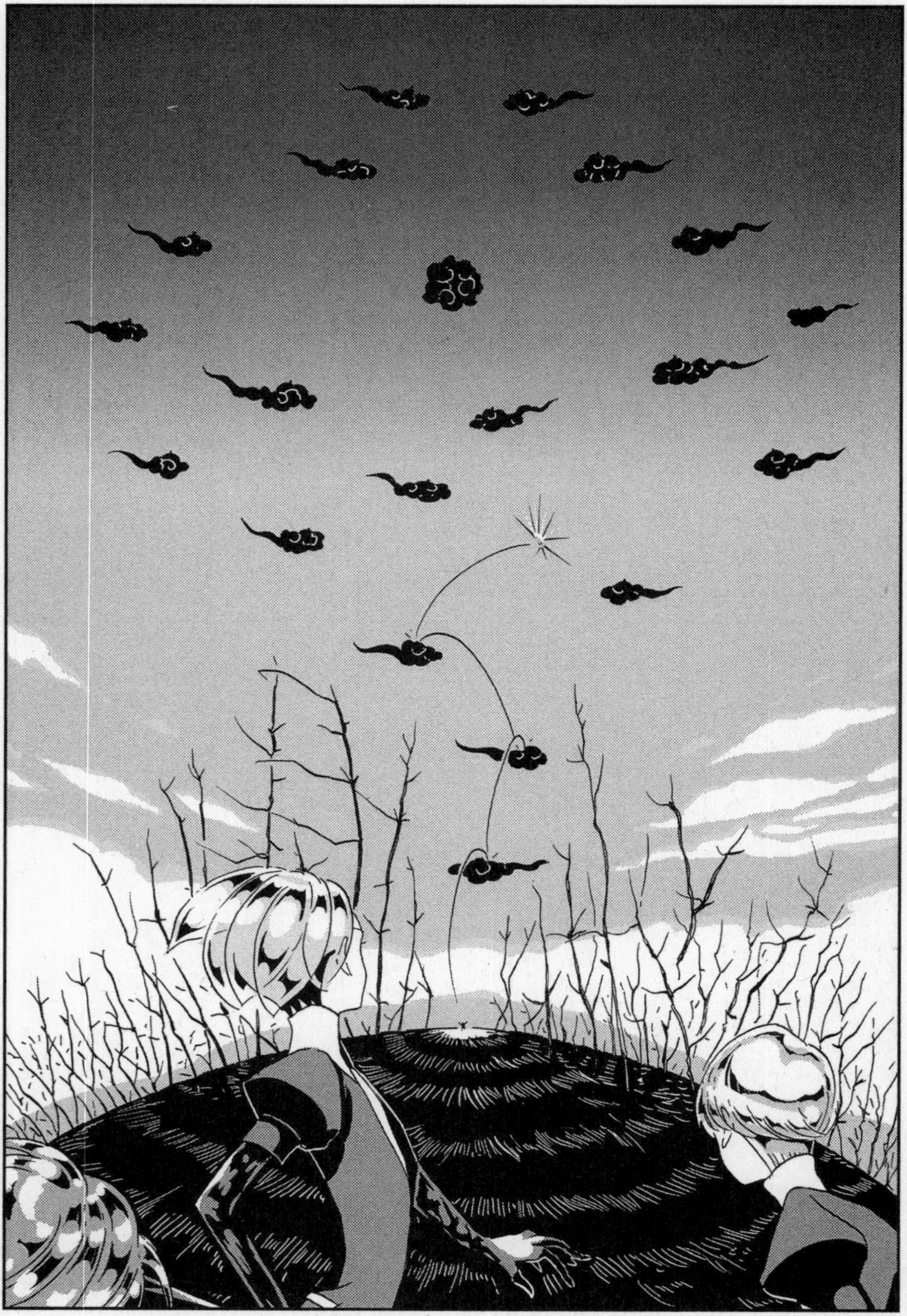

CHAPTER 41: Scene END

CHAPTER 42:

Explosion

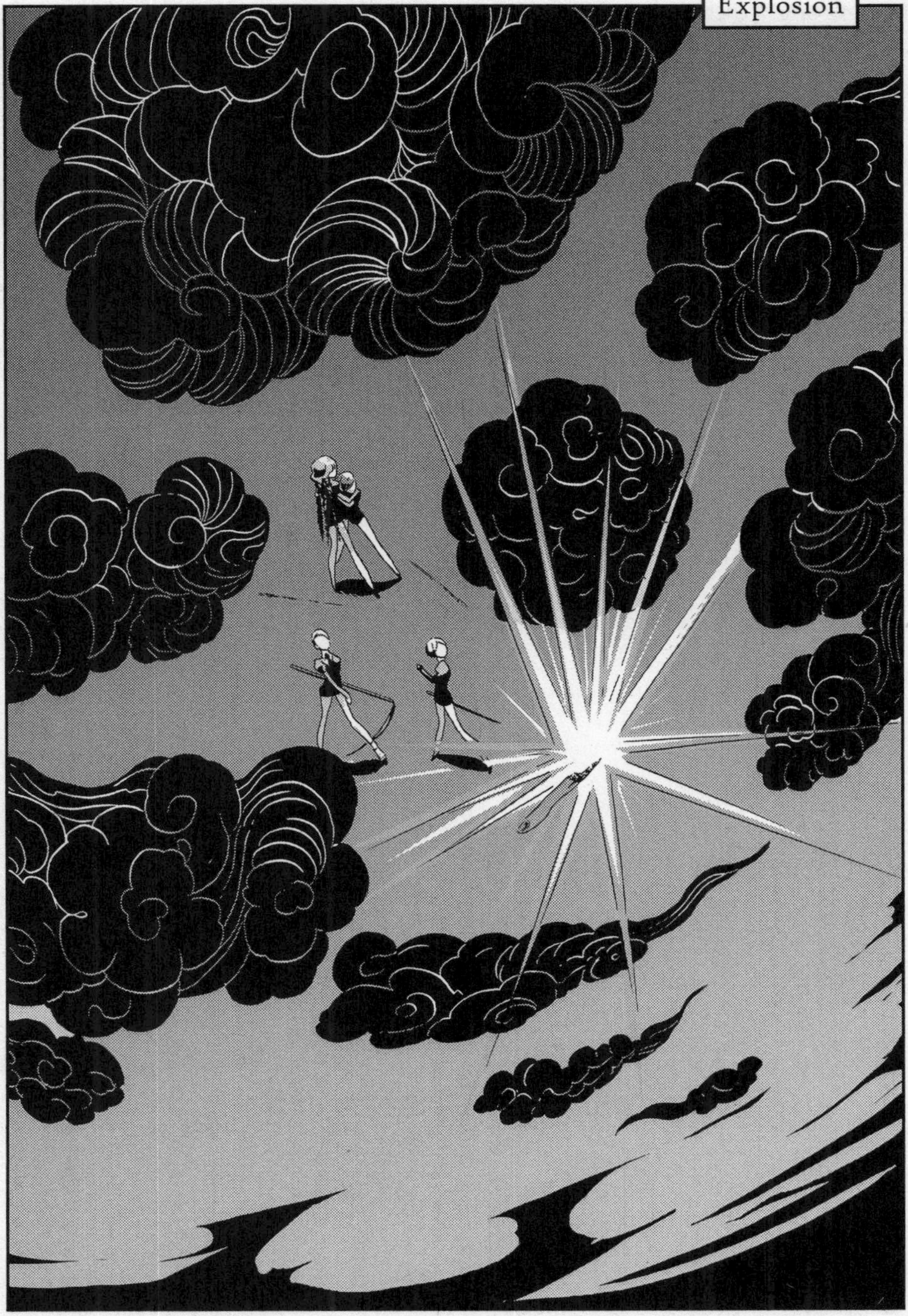

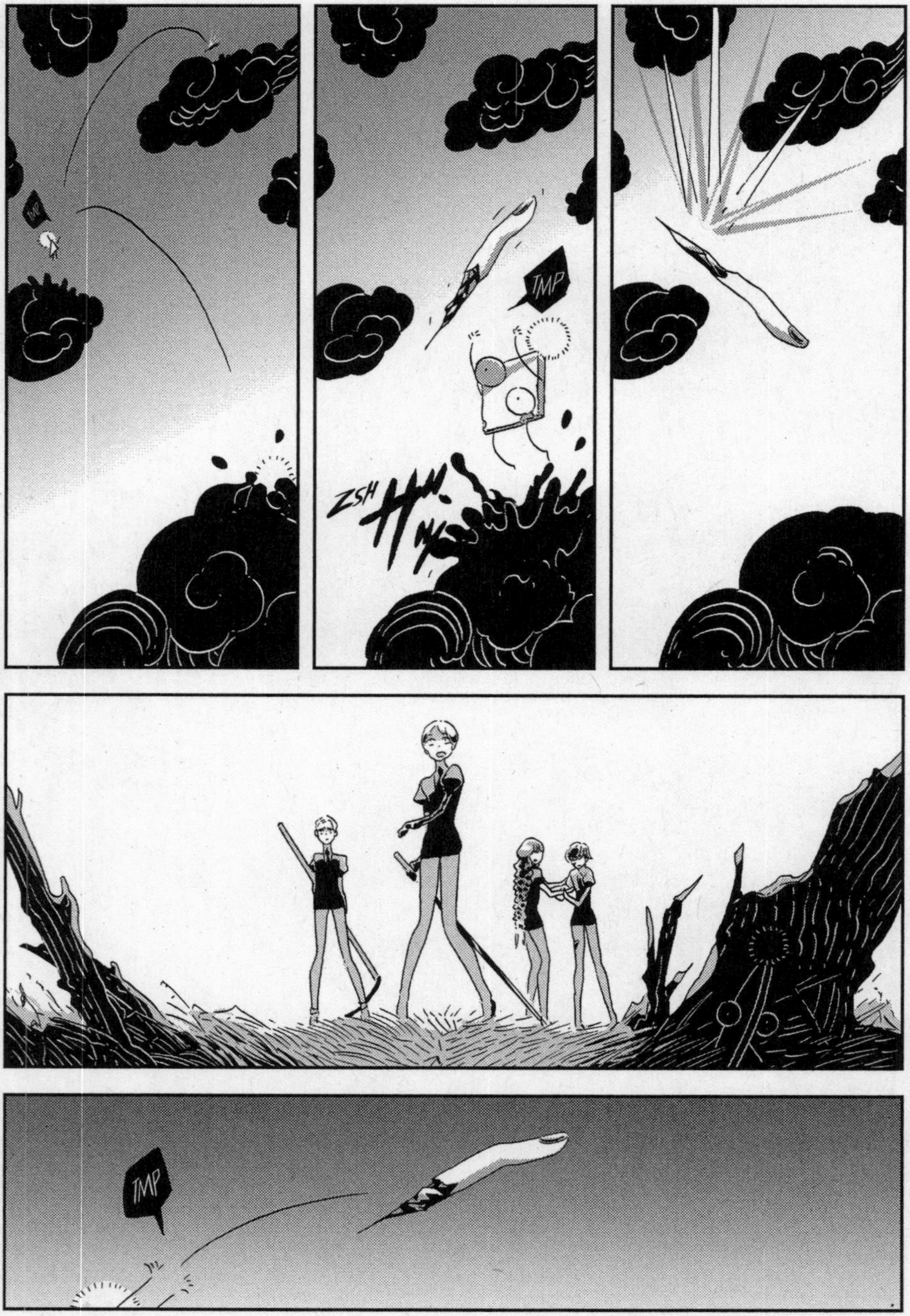
TMP
ZSH
TMP
TMP

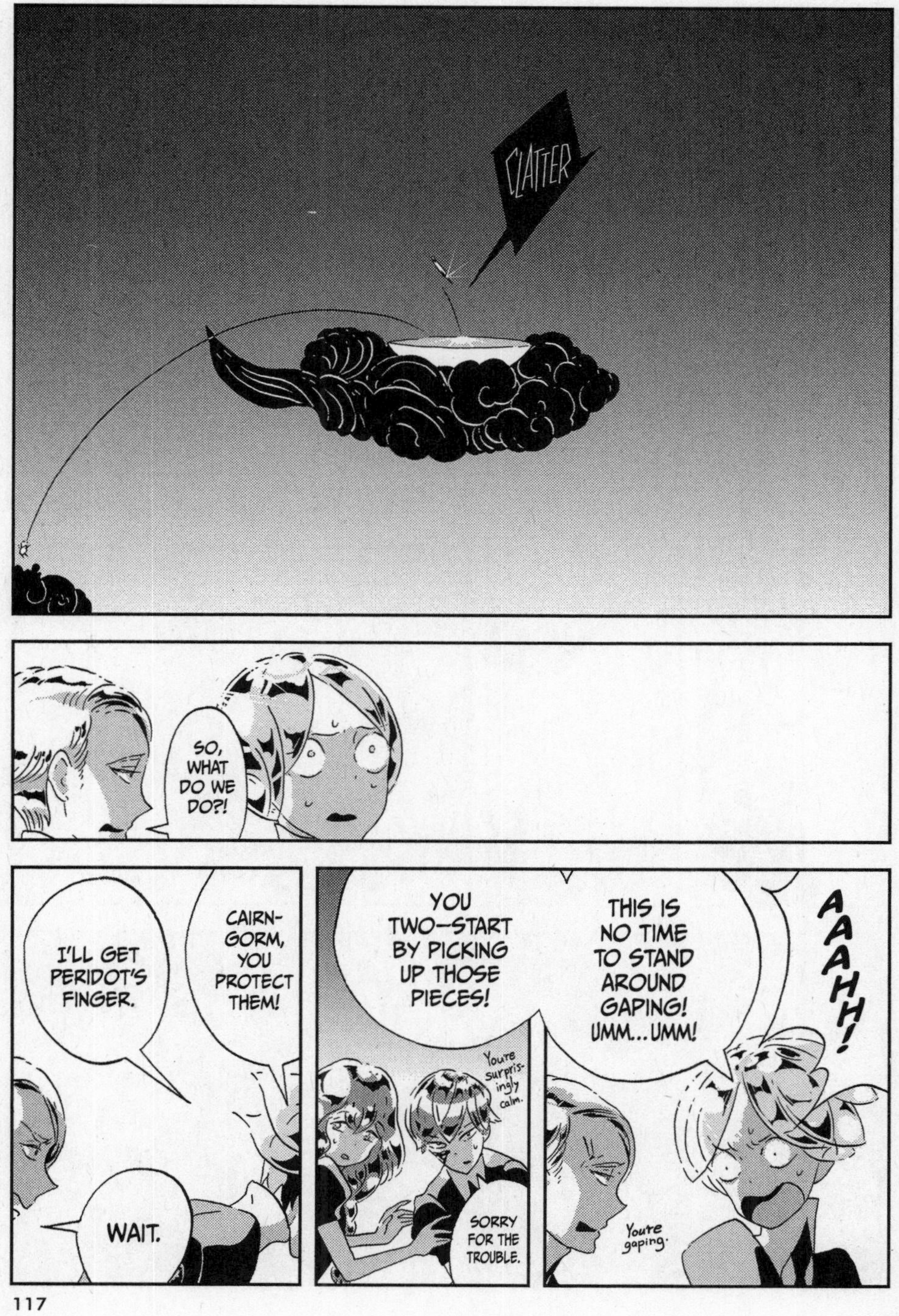
CLATTER
SO, WHAT DO WE DO?!
AAAHH!
THIS IS NO TIME TO STAND AROUND GAPING! UMM...UMM!
You're gaping.
YOU TWO—START BY PICKING UP THOSE PIECES!
You're surprisingly calm.
SORRY FOR THE TROUBLE.
CAIRN-GORM, YOU PROTECT THEM!
I'LL GET PERIDOT'S FINGER.
WAIT.

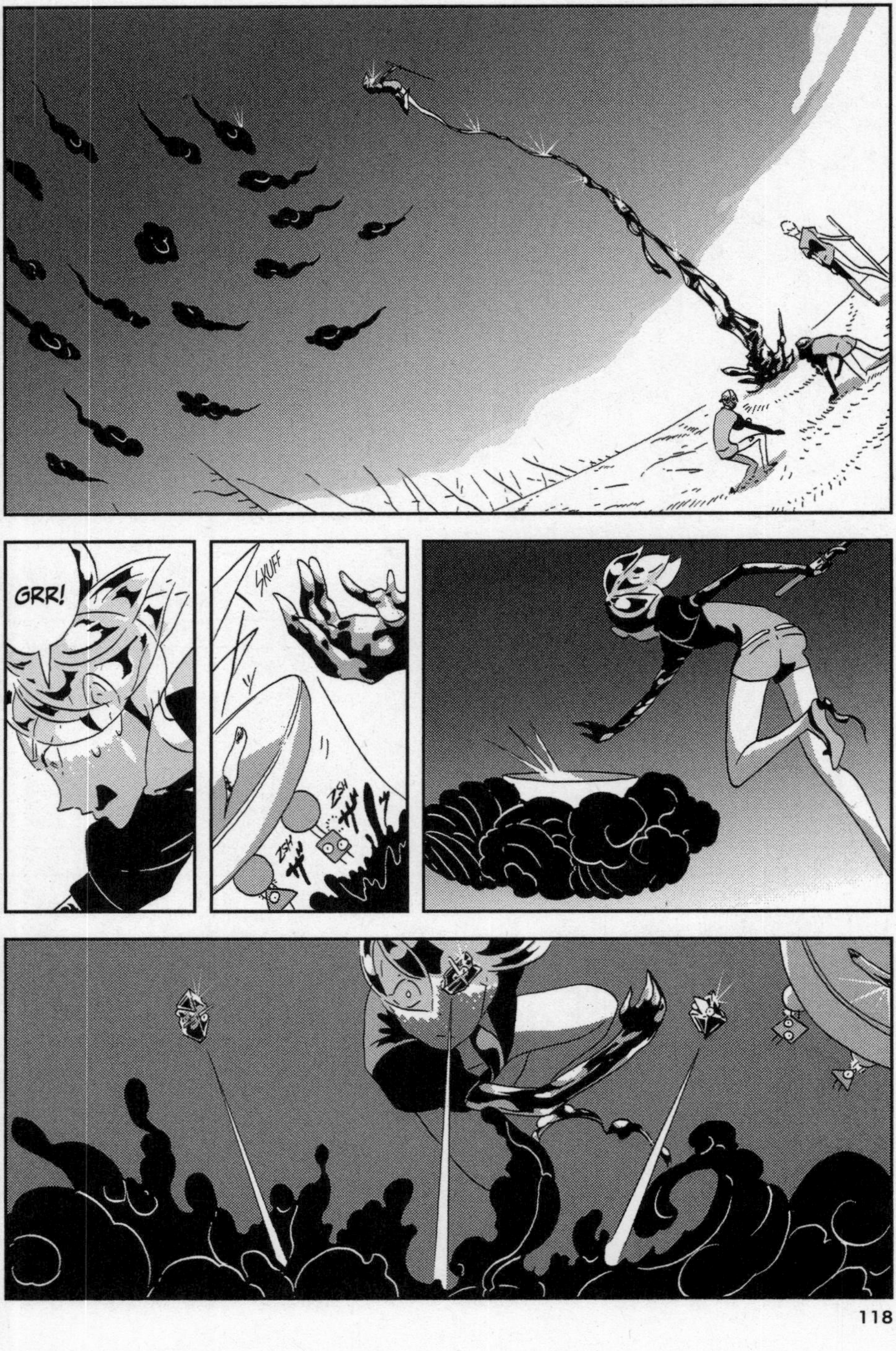
SKUFF
ZSH
ZSH
GRR!

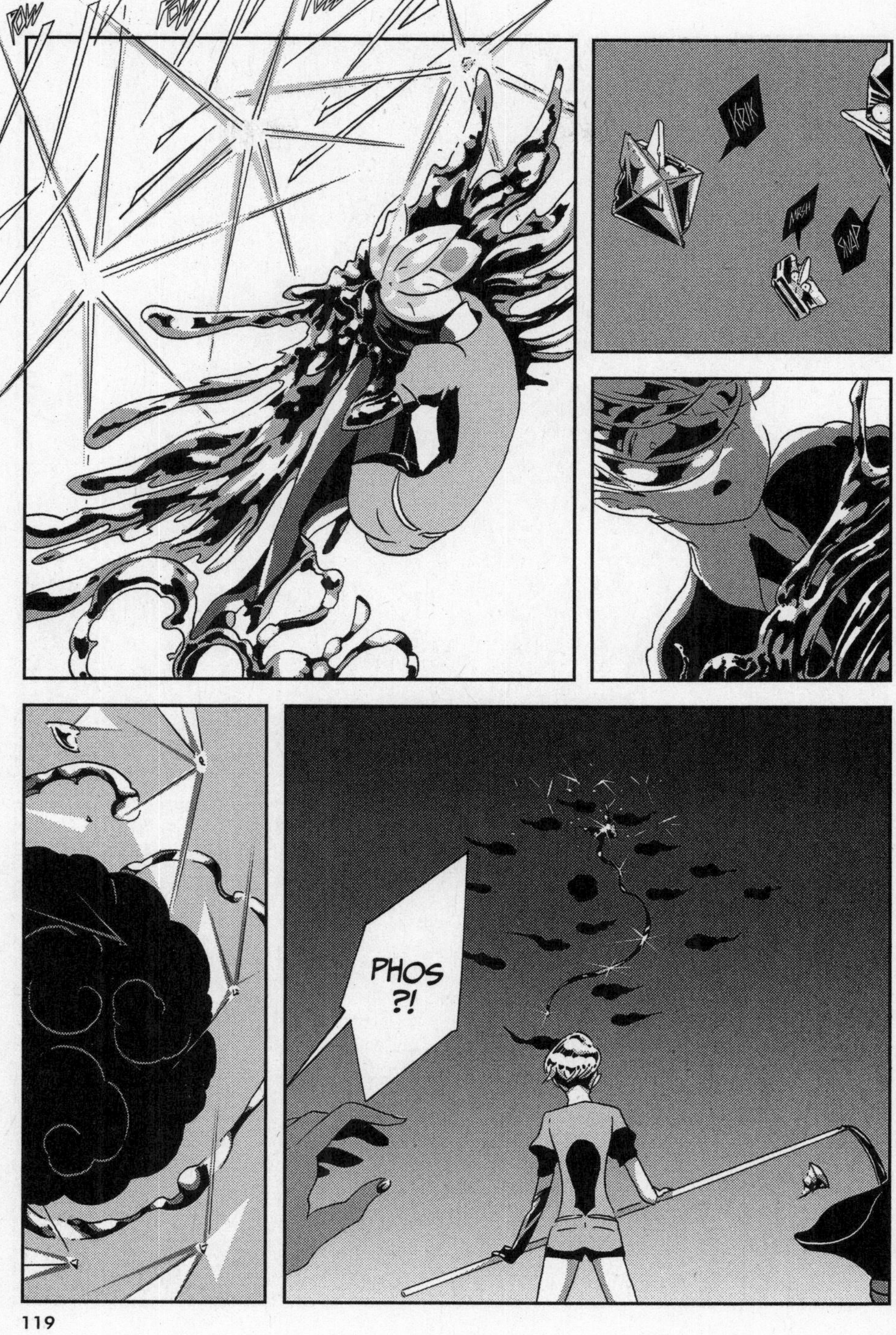
KRIK
MRSH
SNAP
POW
POW
POW
PHOS ?!

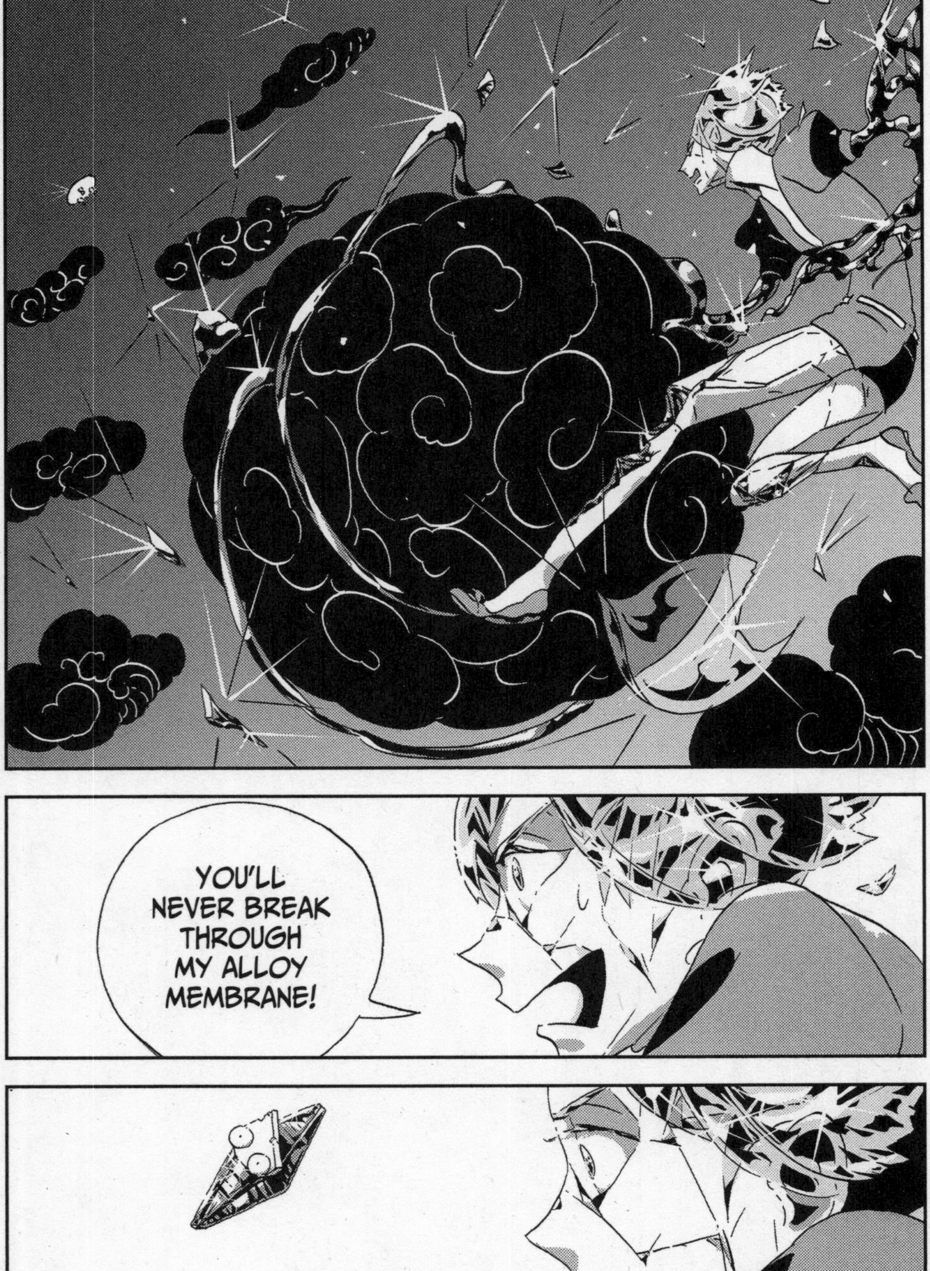
YOU'LL NEVER BREAK THROUGH MY ALLOY MEMBRANE!

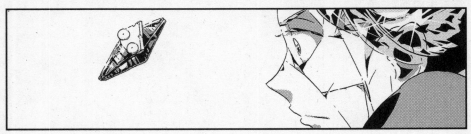

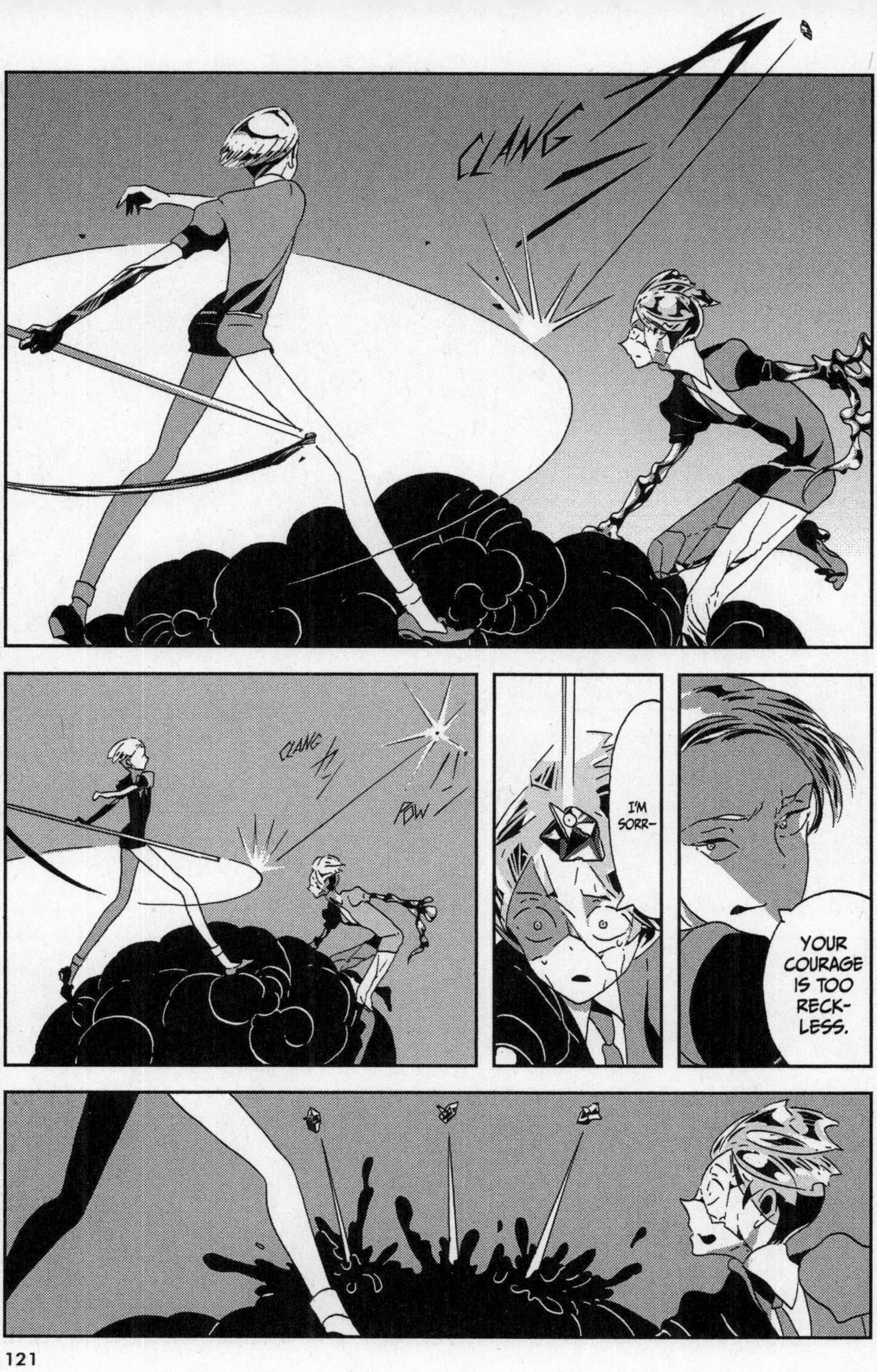
CLANG
YOUR COURAGE IS TOO RECK-LESS.
I'M SORR–
CLANG
POW

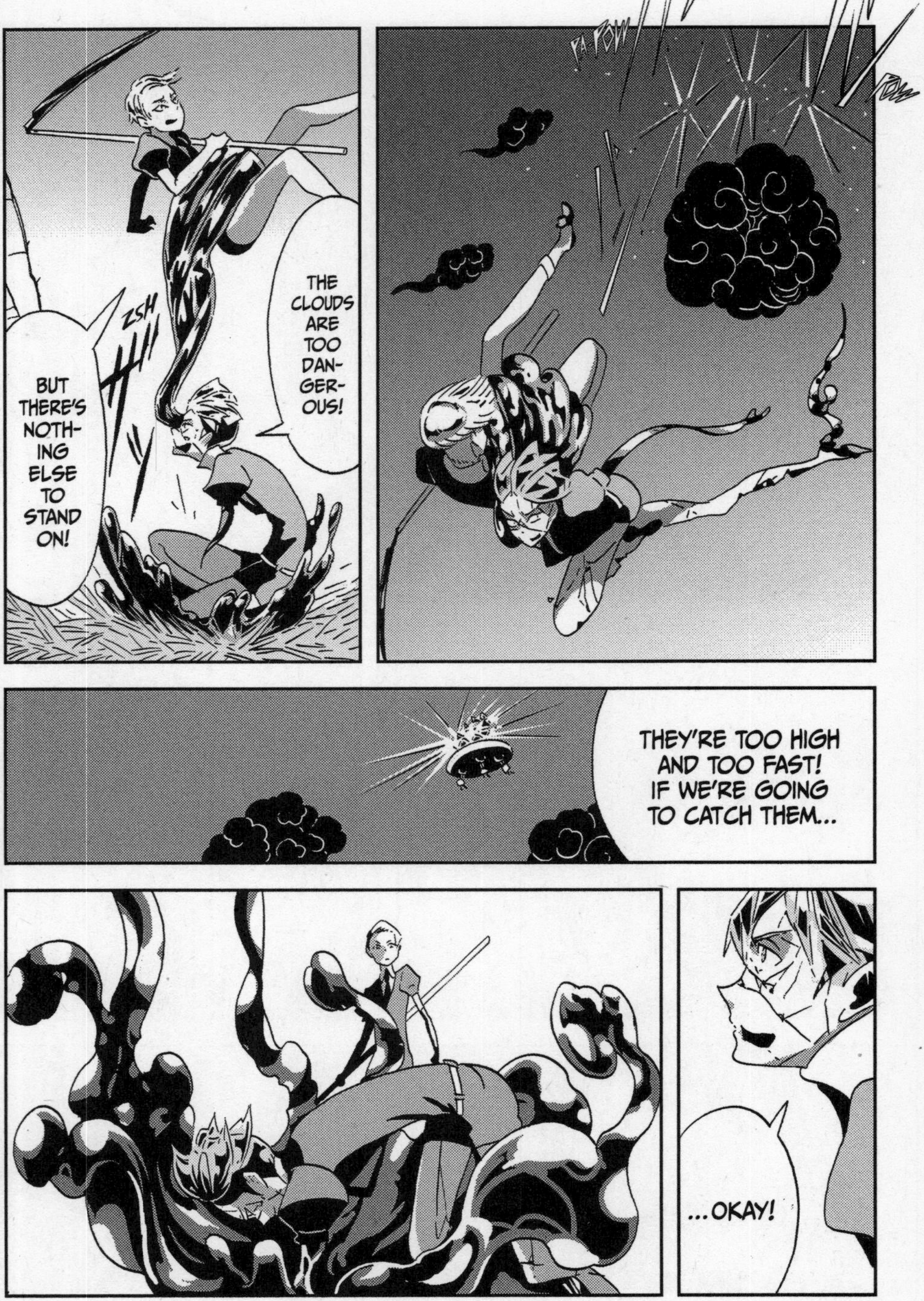
PA-POW
POW
THE CLOUDS ARE TOO DANGEROUS!
ZSH
BUT THERE'S NOTHING ELSE TO STAND ON!
THEY'RE TOO HIGH AND TOO FAST! IF WE'RE GOING TO CATCH THEM...
...OKAY!

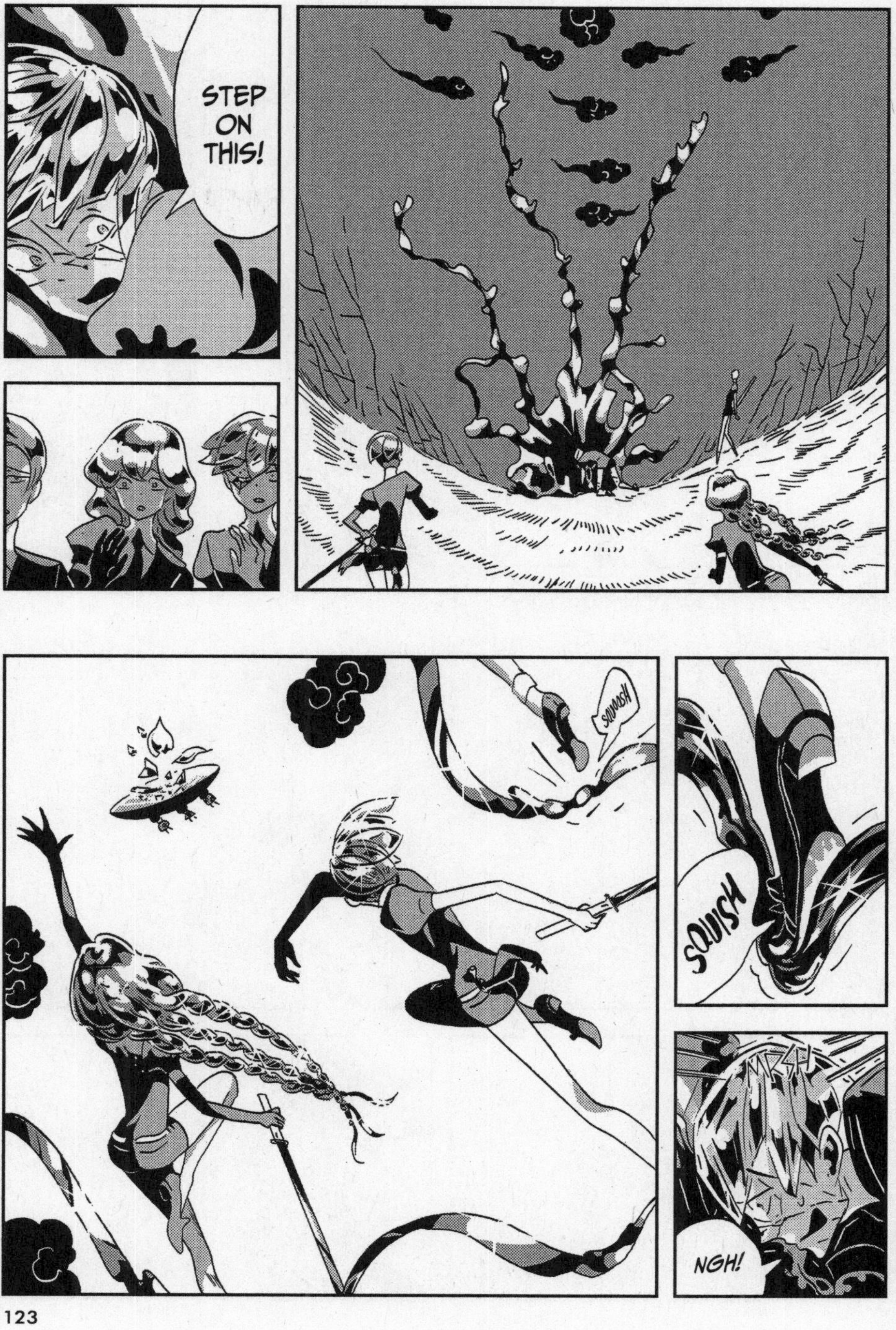
STEP ON THIS!
SQUISH
NGH!
SQUOOSH

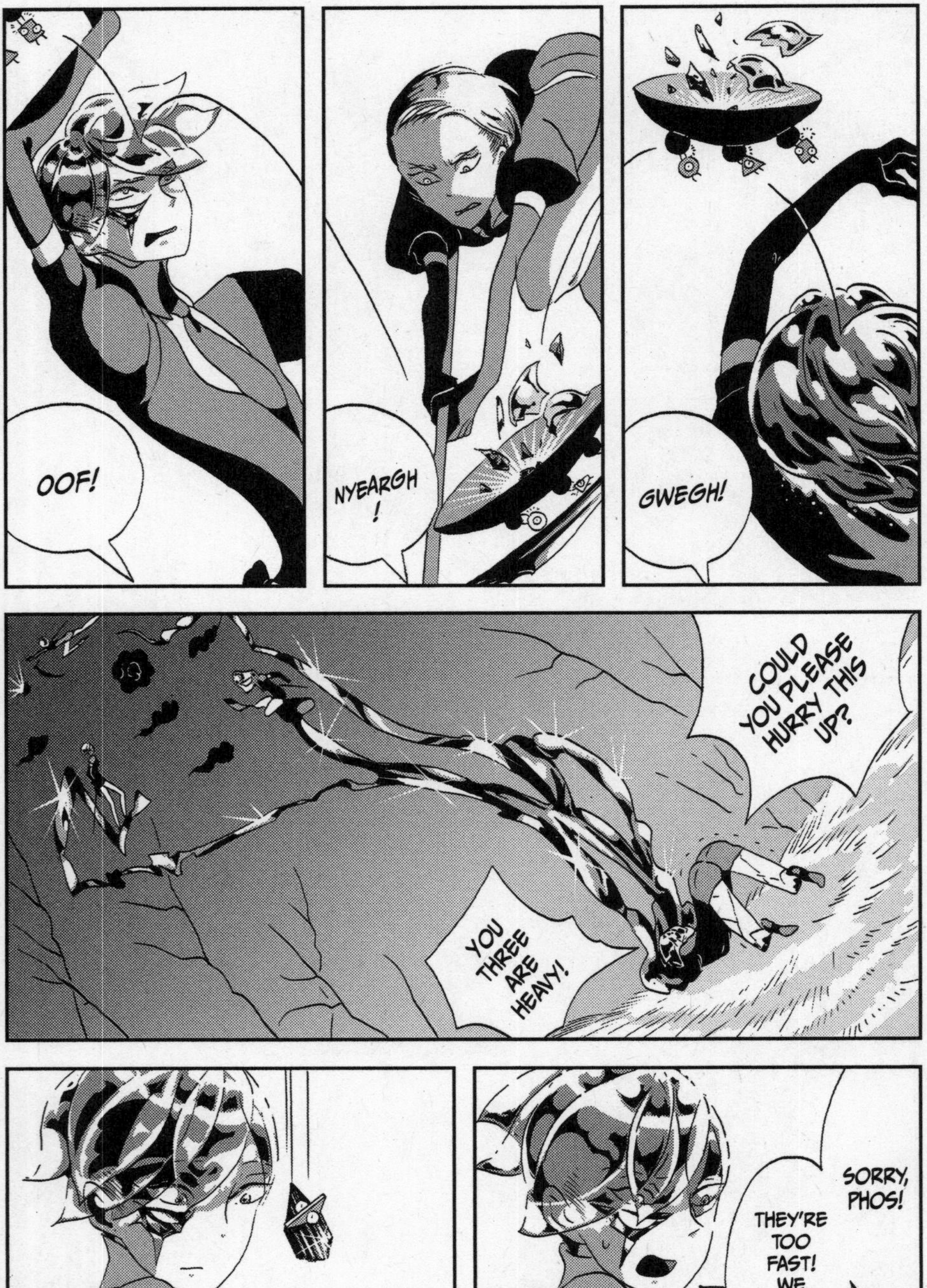
GWEGH!
NYEARGH!
OOF!
COULD YOU PLEASE HURRY THIS UP?
YOU THREE ARE HEAVY!
SORRY, PHOS!
THEY'RE TOO FAST! WE CAN'T—

BLUES.
DAM-MIT!
TAK
ACK!

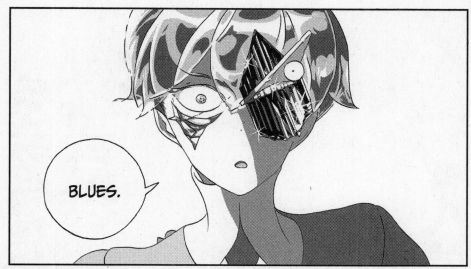

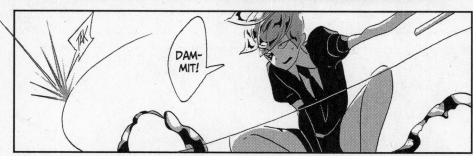

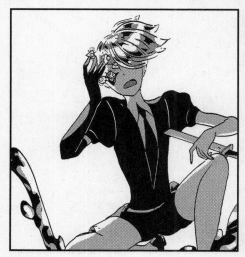

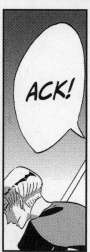

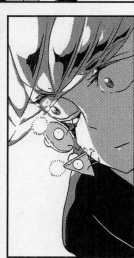

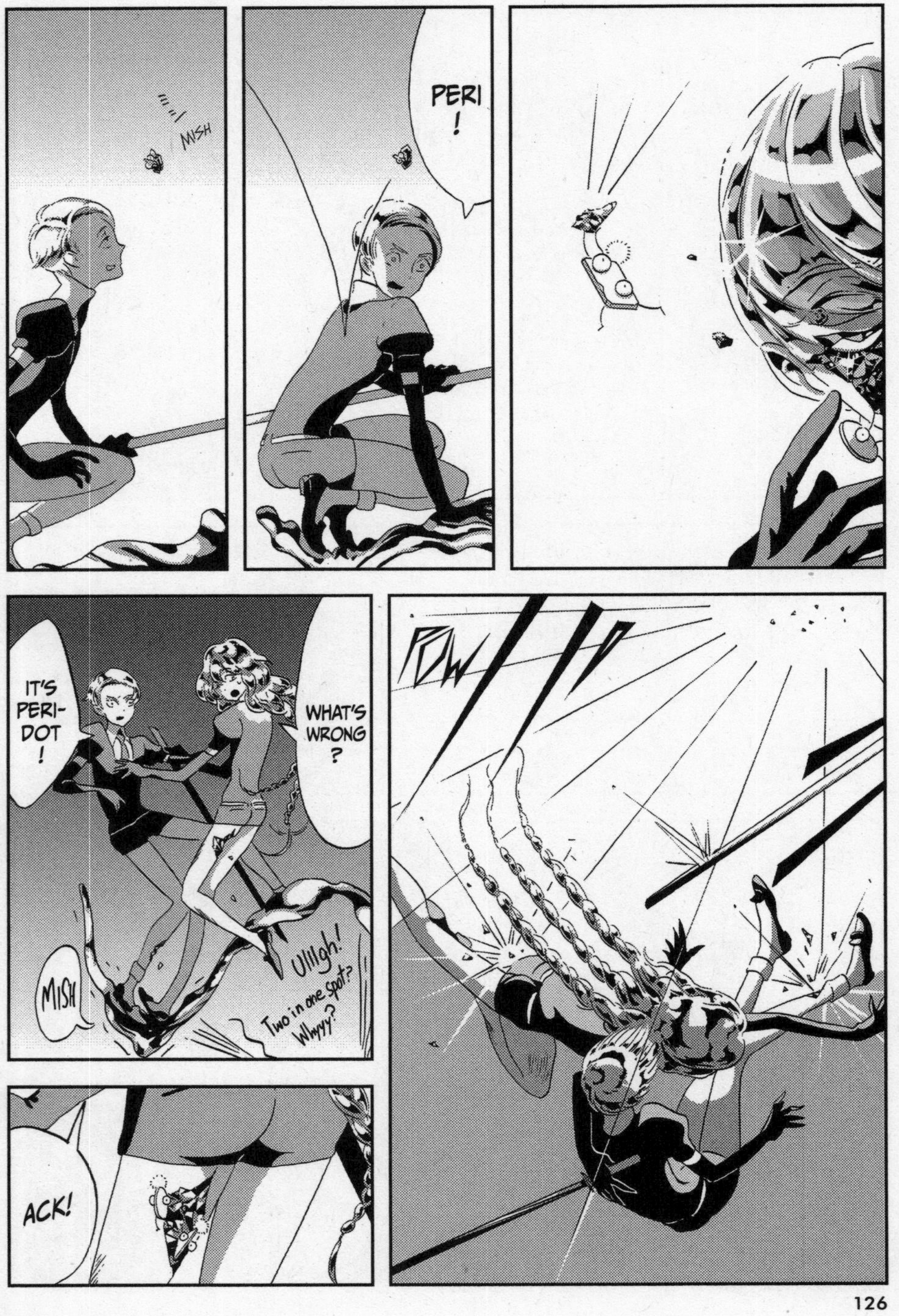
PERI!
MISH
POW
WHAT'S WRONG?
IT'S PERI-DOT!
Ulllgh! Two in one spot? Whyyy?
MISH
ACK!

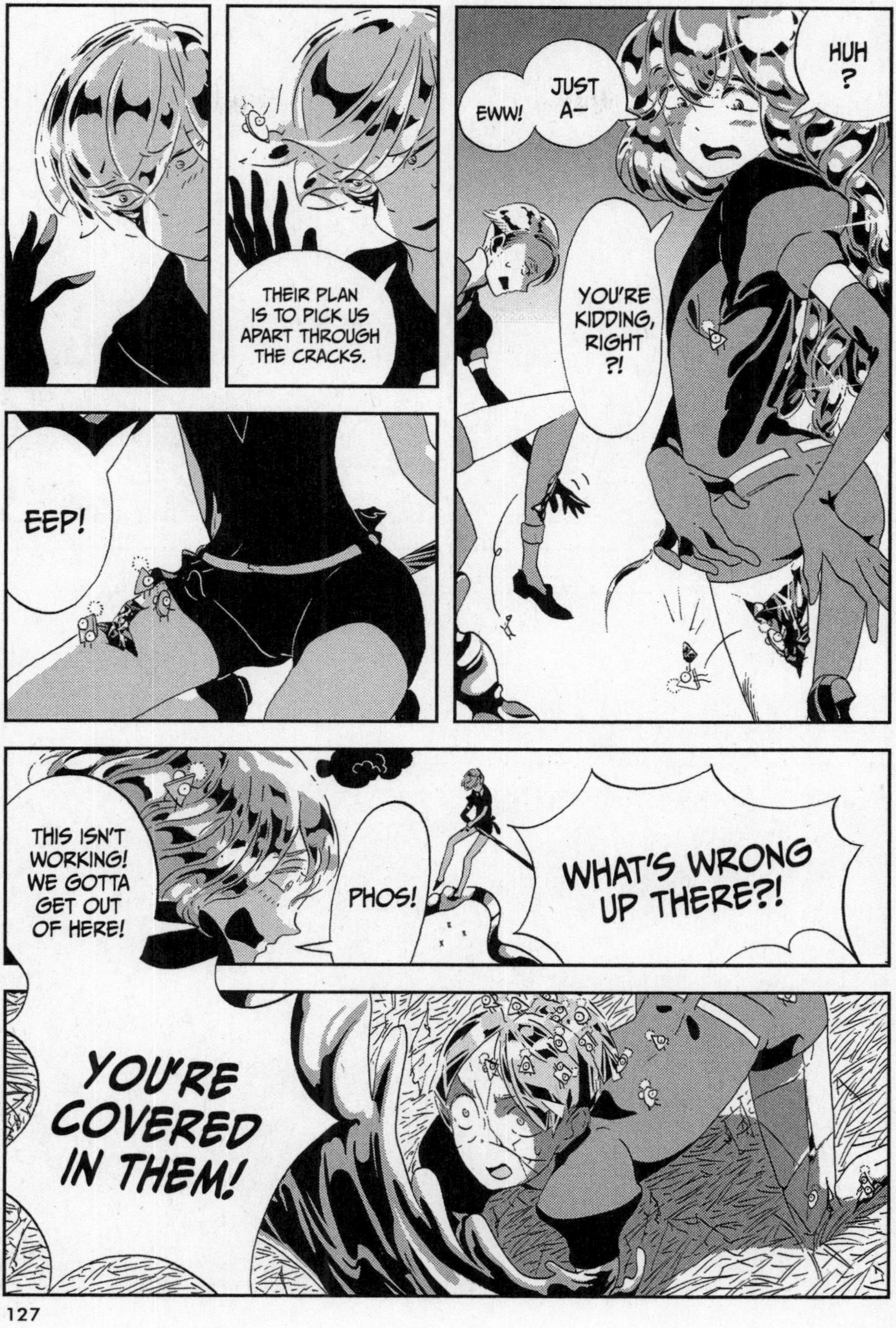
HUH?
JUST A—
EWW!
YOU'RE KIDDING, RIGHT?!
THEIR PLAN IS TO PICK US APART THROUGH THE CRACKS.
EEP!
WHAT'S WRONG UP THERE?!
PHOS!
THIS ISN'T WORKING! WE GOTTA GET OUT OF HERE!
YOU'RE COVERED IN THEM!

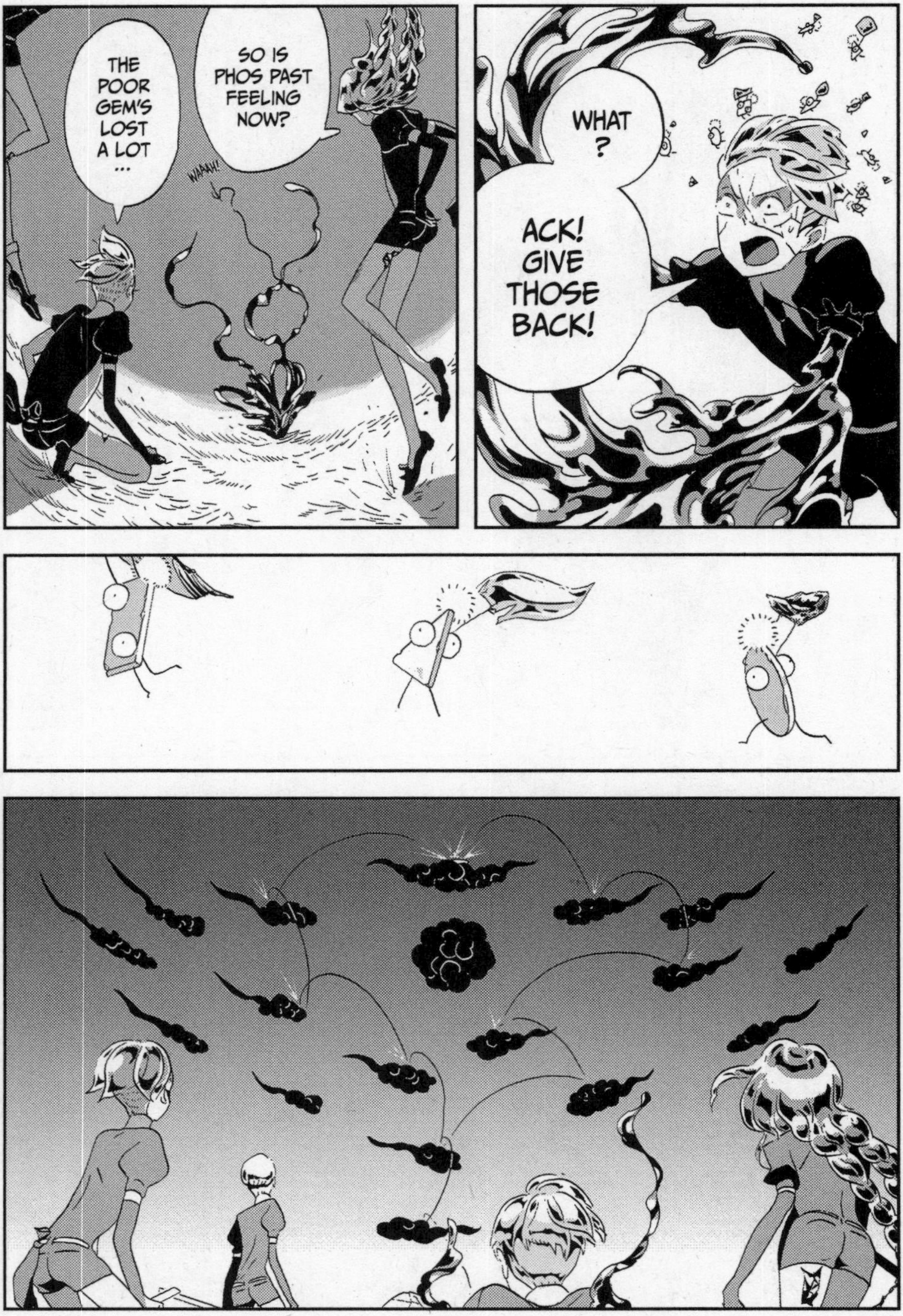
WHAT?
ACK! GIVE THOSE BACK!
SO IS PHOS PAST FEELING NOW?
THE POOR GEM'S LOST A LOT ...
WAAAH!

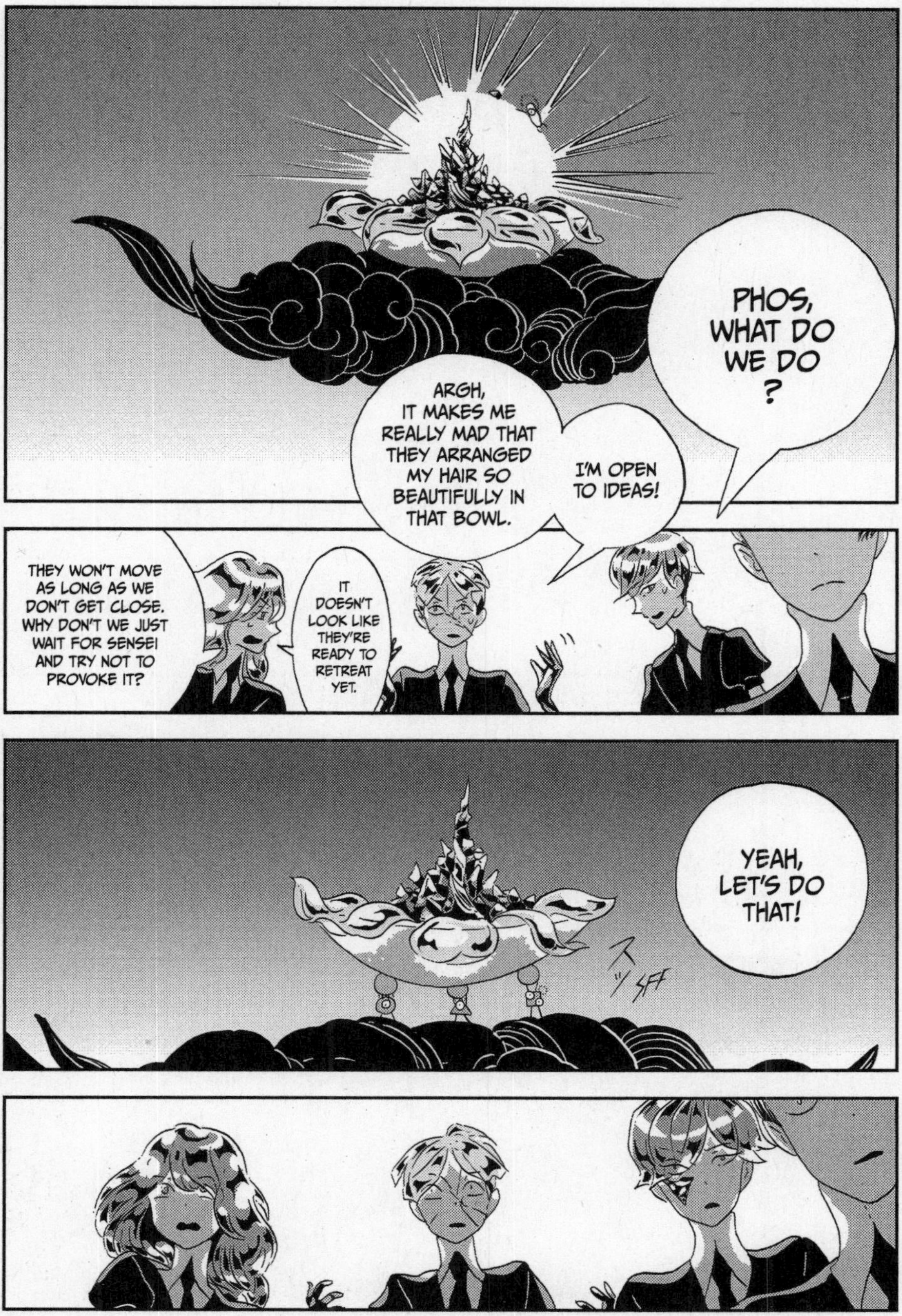
PHOS, WHAT DO WE DO?
I'M OPEN TO IDEAS!
ARGH, IT MAKES ME REALLY MAD THAT THEY ARRANGED MY HAIR SO BEAUTIFULLY IN THAT BOWL.
IT DOESN'T LOOK LIKE THEY'RE READY TO RETREAT YET.
THEY WON'T MOVE AS LONG AS WE DON'T GET CLOSE. WHY DON'T WE JUST WAIT FOR SENSEI AND TRY NOT TO PROVOKE IT?
YEAH, LET'S DO THAT!
スッ
SFF

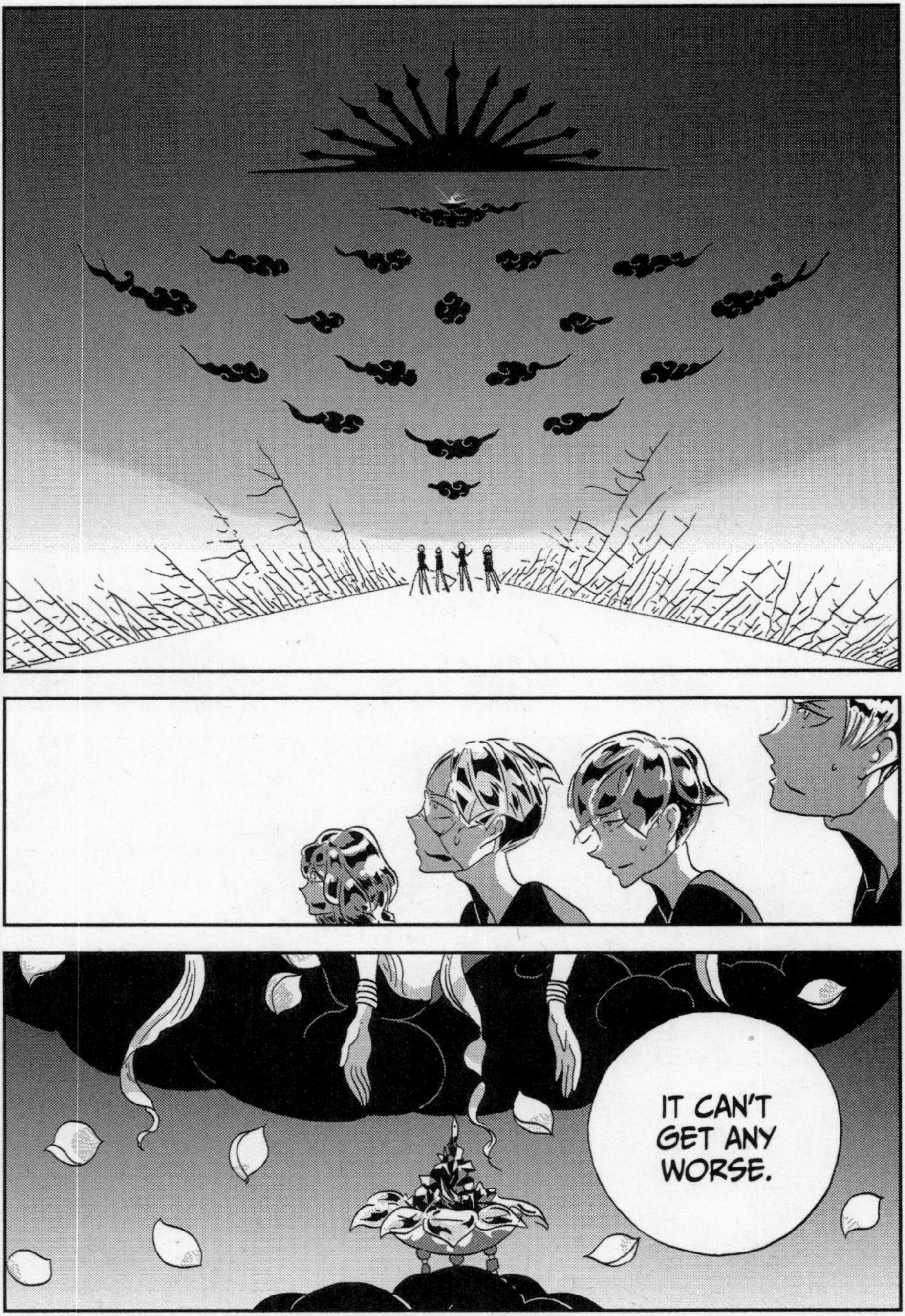
IT CAN'T GET ANY WORSE.

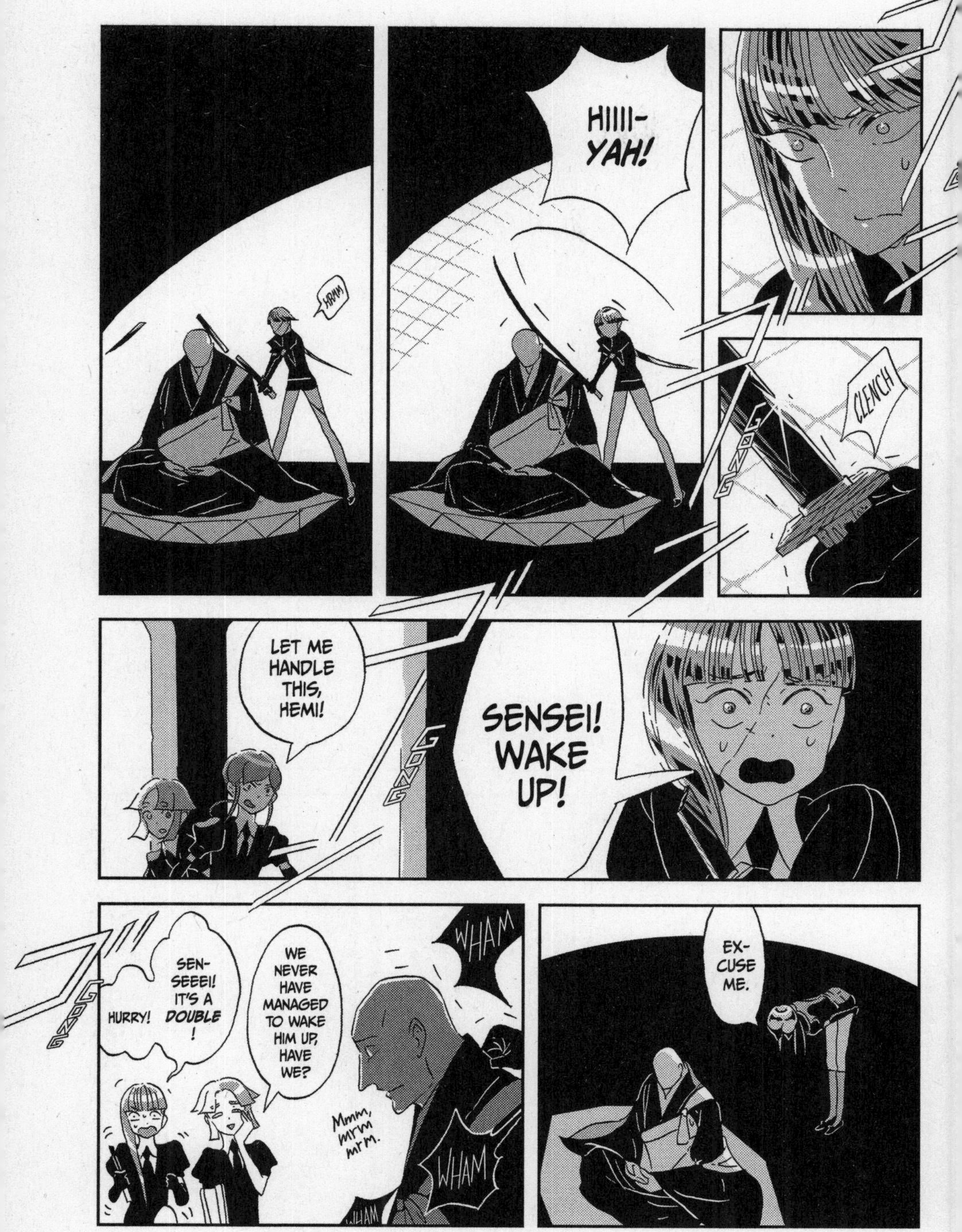

CLENCH
GONG
HIIII-YAH!
HRMM
SENSEI! WAKE UP!
GONG
LET ME HANDLE THIS, HEMI!
EX-CUSE ME.
WHAM
WE NEVER HAVE MANAGED TO WAKE HIM UP, HAVE WE?
SEN-SEEEI! IT'S A *DOUBLE*!
HURRY!
Mmm, mrm mrm.
WHAM
WHAM
GONG

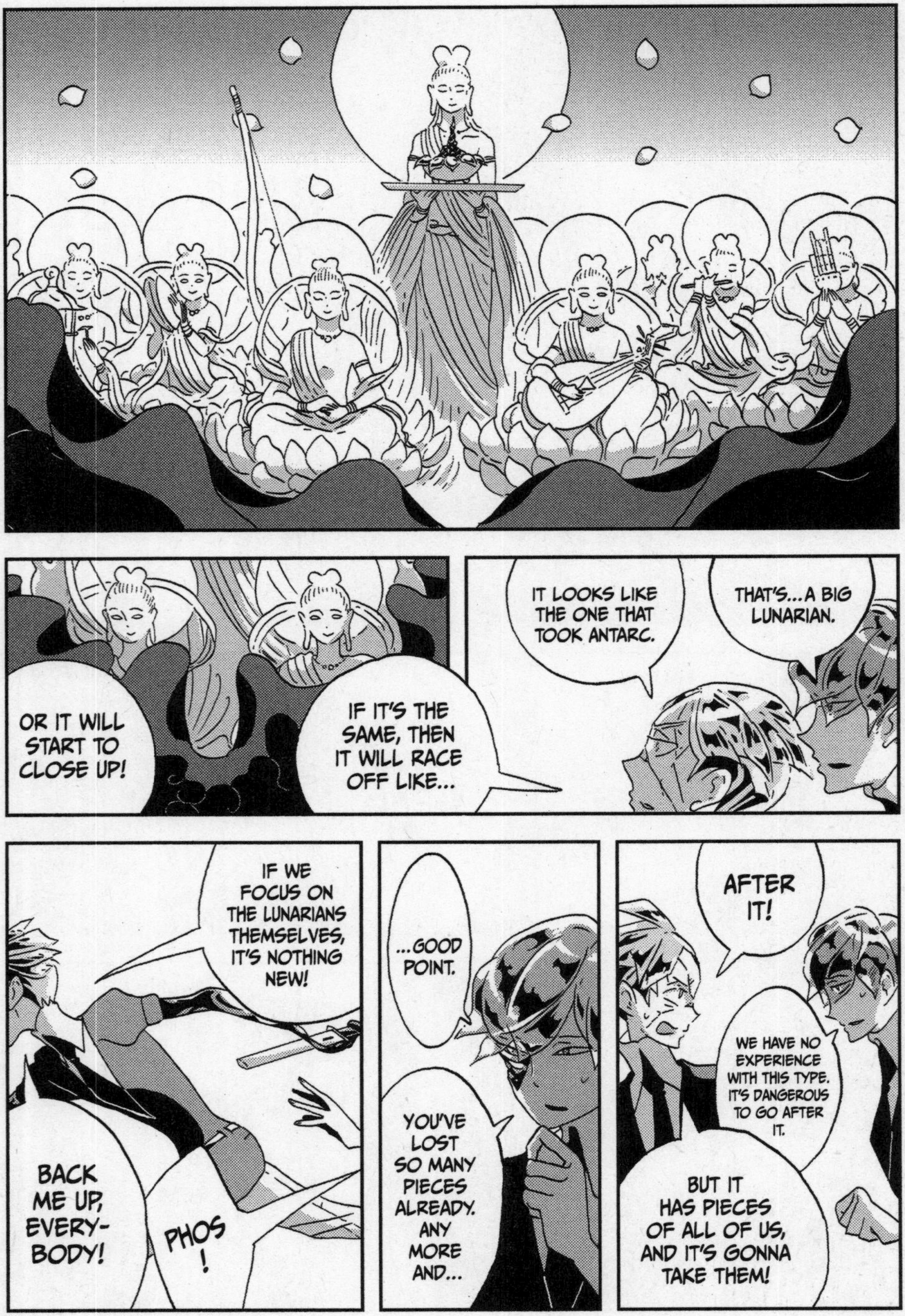

THAT'S...A BIG LUNARIAN.
IT LOOKS LIKE THE ONE THAT TOOK ANTARC.
IF IT'S THE SAME, THEN IT WILL RACE OFF LIKE...
OR IT WILL START TO CLOSE UP!
AFTER IT!
WE HAVE NO EXPERIENCE WITH THIS TYPE. IT'S DANGEROUS TO GO AFTER IT.
BUT IT HAS PIECES OF ALL OF US, AND IT'S GONNA TAKE THEM!
...GOOD POINT.
YOU'VE LOST SO MANY PIECES ALREADY. ANY MORE AND...
IF WE FOCUS ON THE LUNARIANS THEMSELVES, IT'S NOTHING NEW!
BACK ME UP, EVERY-BODY!
PHOS!

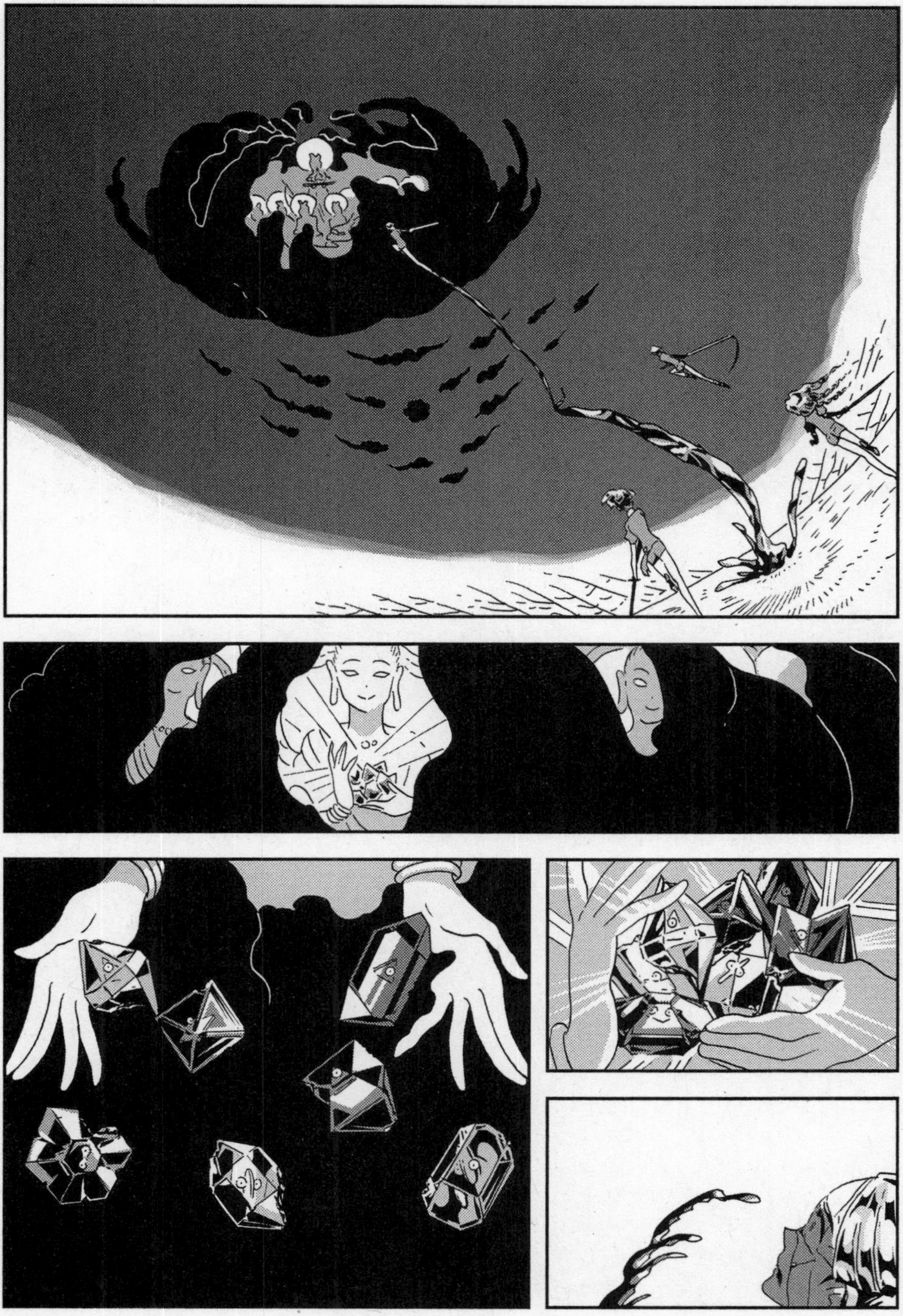

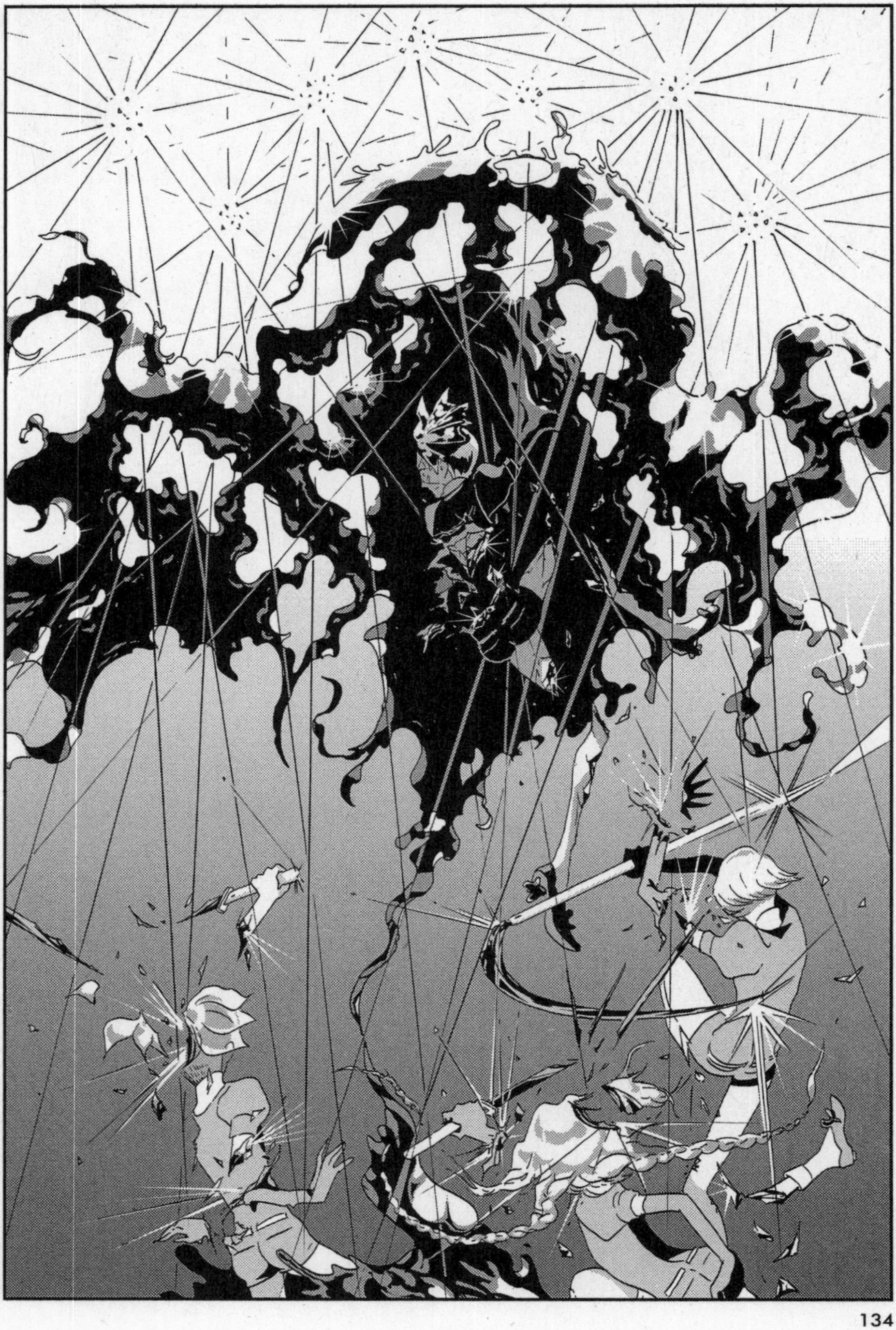

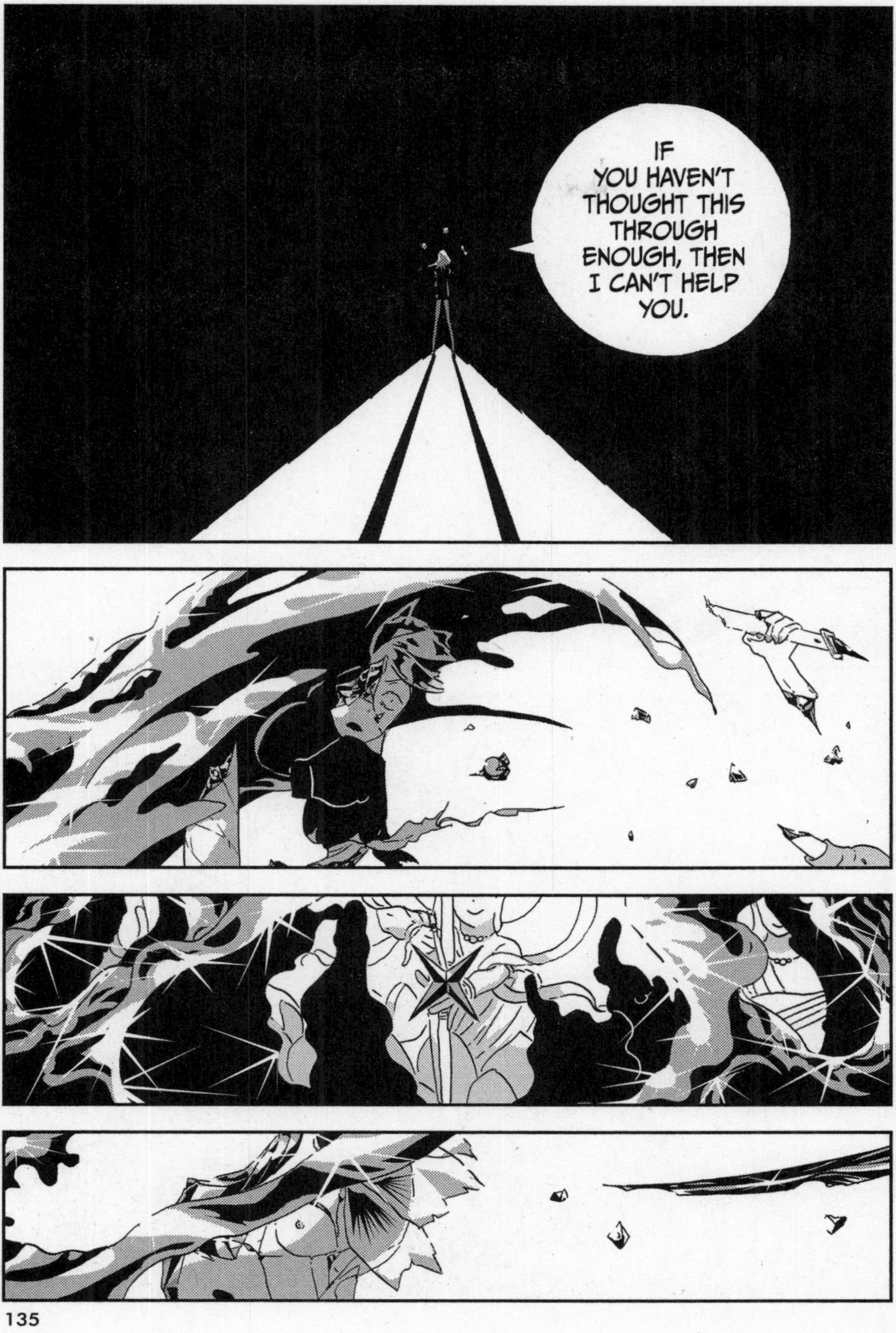
IF YOU HAVEN'T THOUGHT THIS THROUGH ENOUGH, THEN I CAN'T HELP YOU.

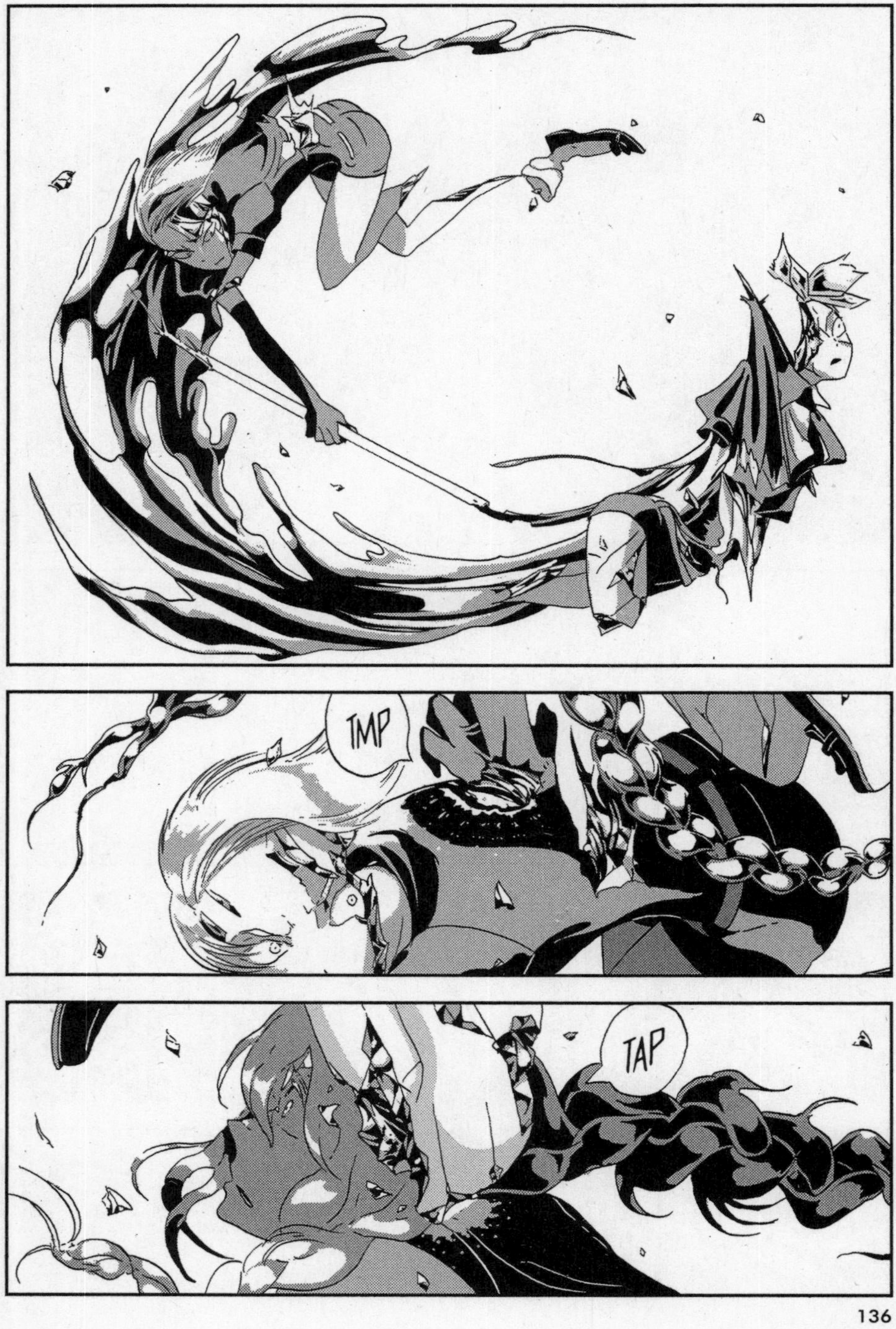
TMP
TAP

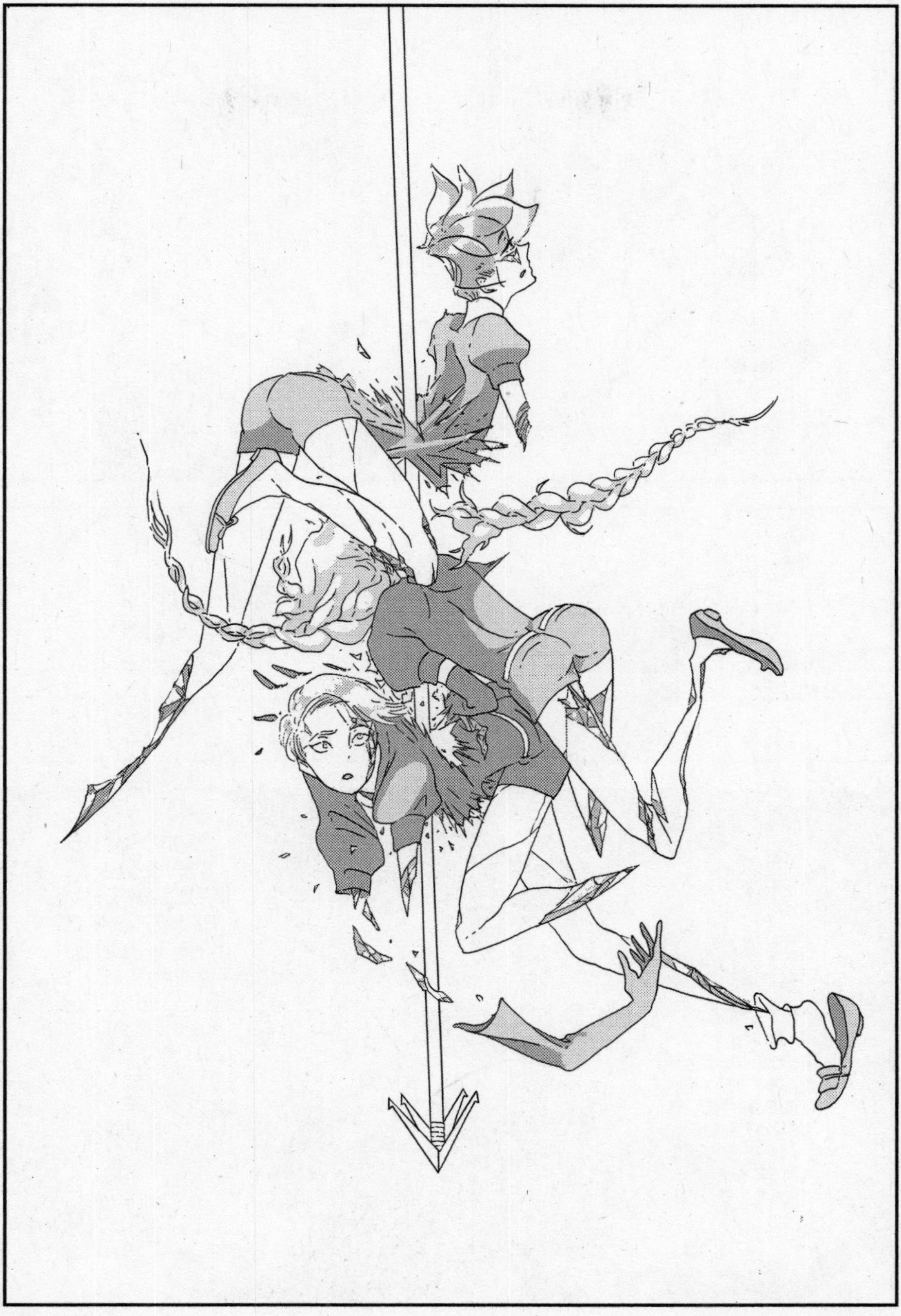

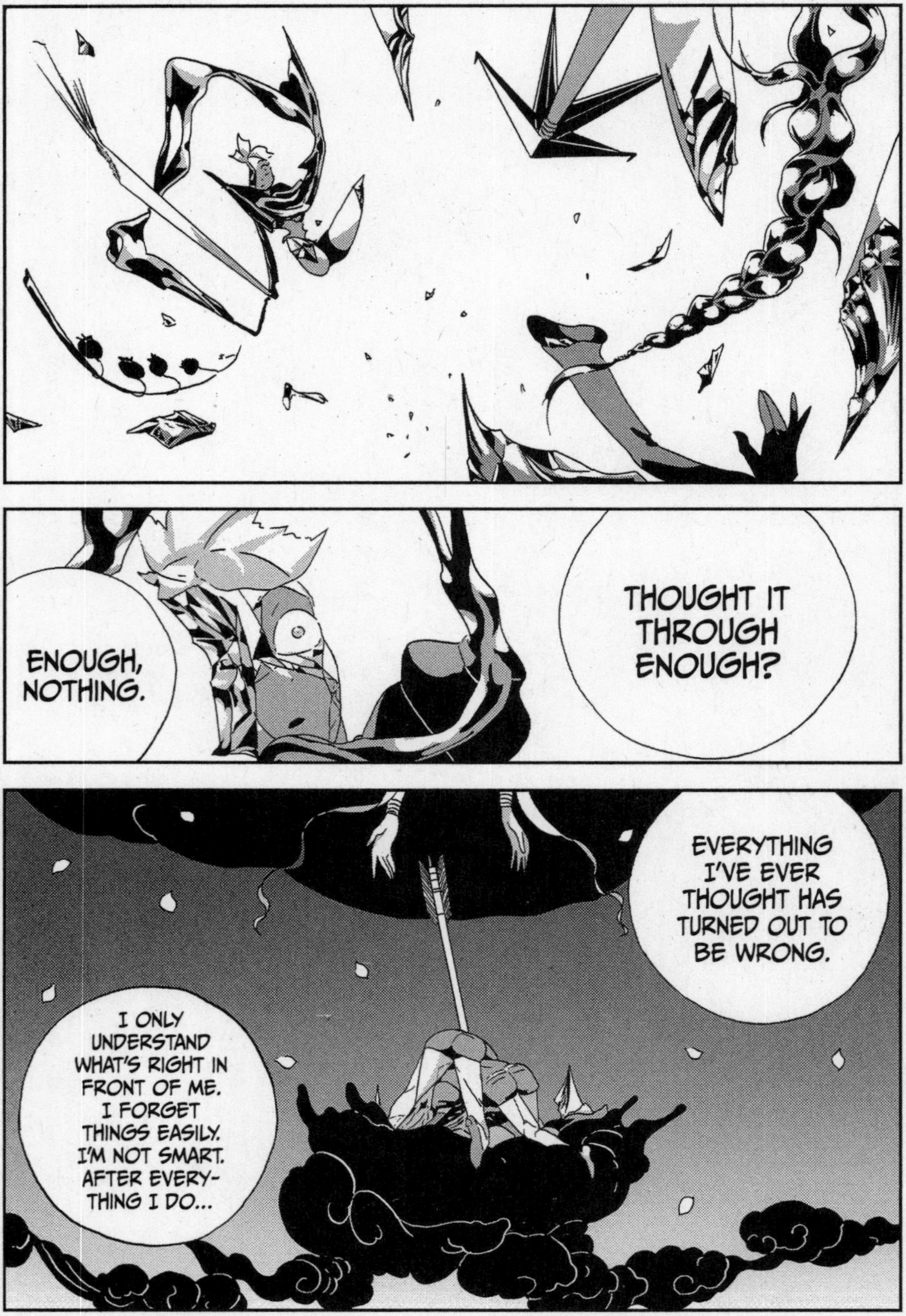
THOUGHT IT THROUGH ENOUGH?
ENOUGH, NOTHING.
EVERYTHING I'VE EVER THOUGHT HAS TURNED OUT TO BE WRONG.
I ONLY UNDERSTAND WHAT'S RIGHT IN FRONT OF ME. I FORGET THINGS EASILY. I'M NOT SMART. AFTER EVERY-THING I DO...

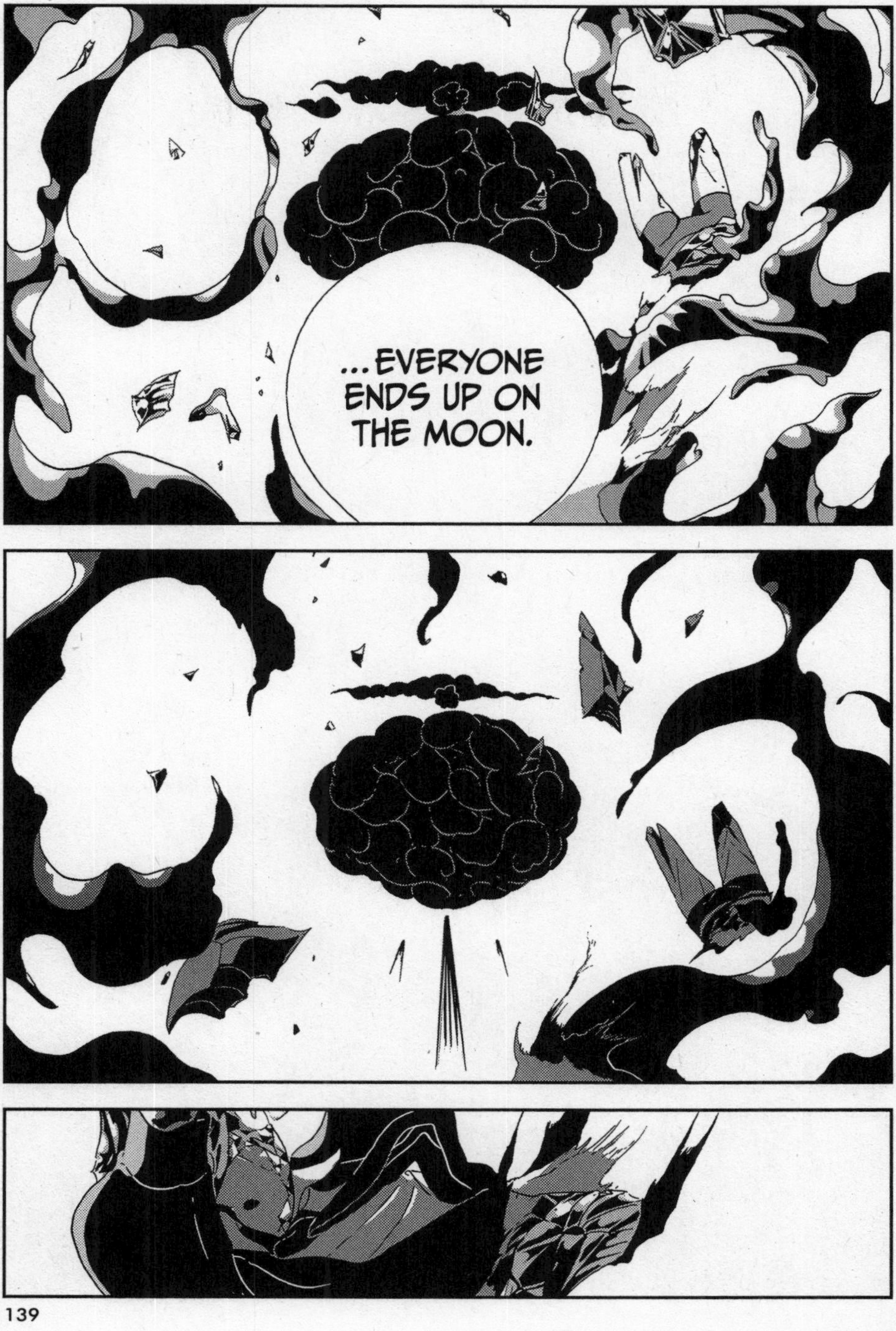
...EVERYONE ENDS UP ON THE MOON.

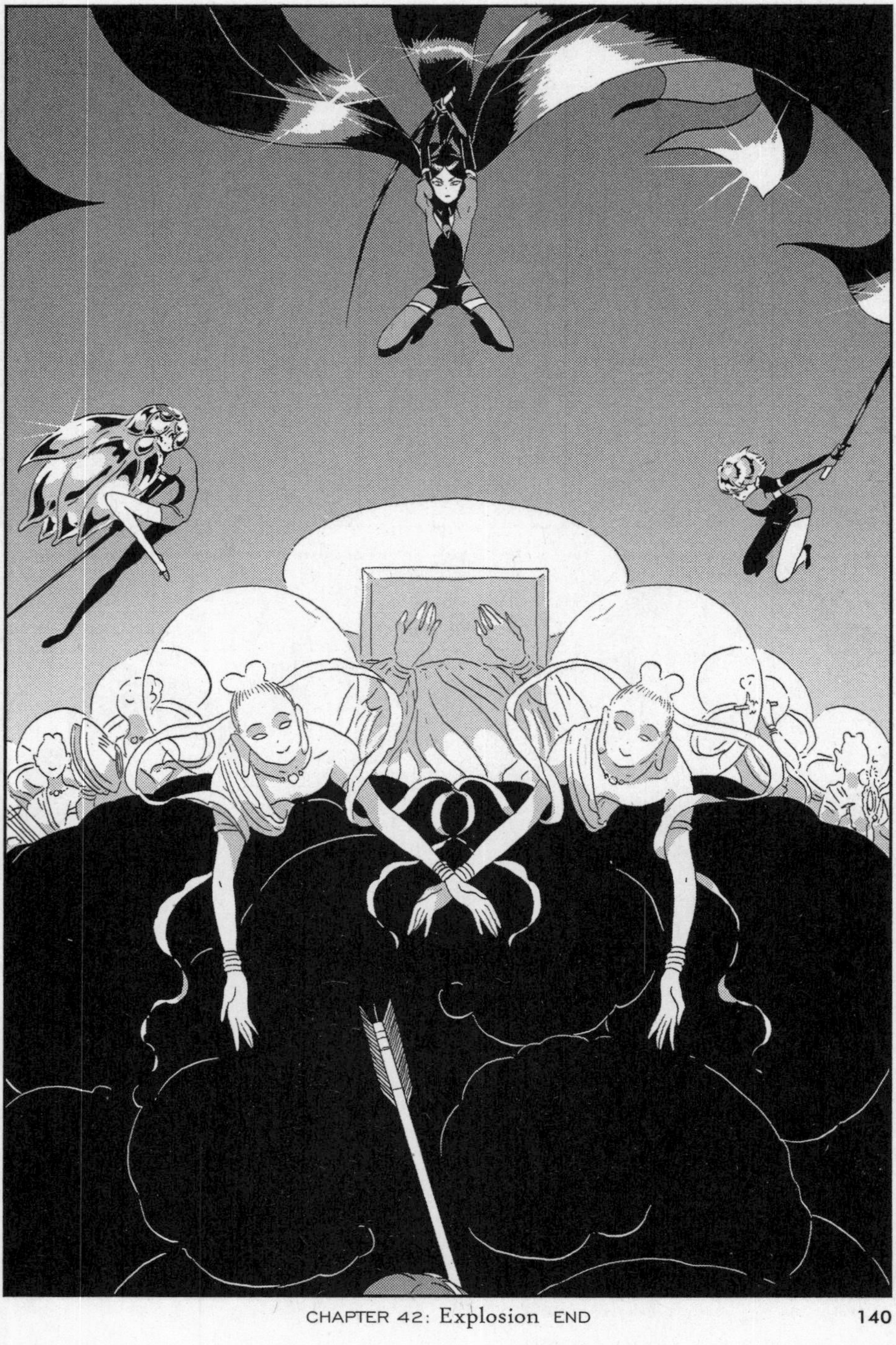

CHAPTER 42: Explosion END

CHAPTER 43:

The Game Board

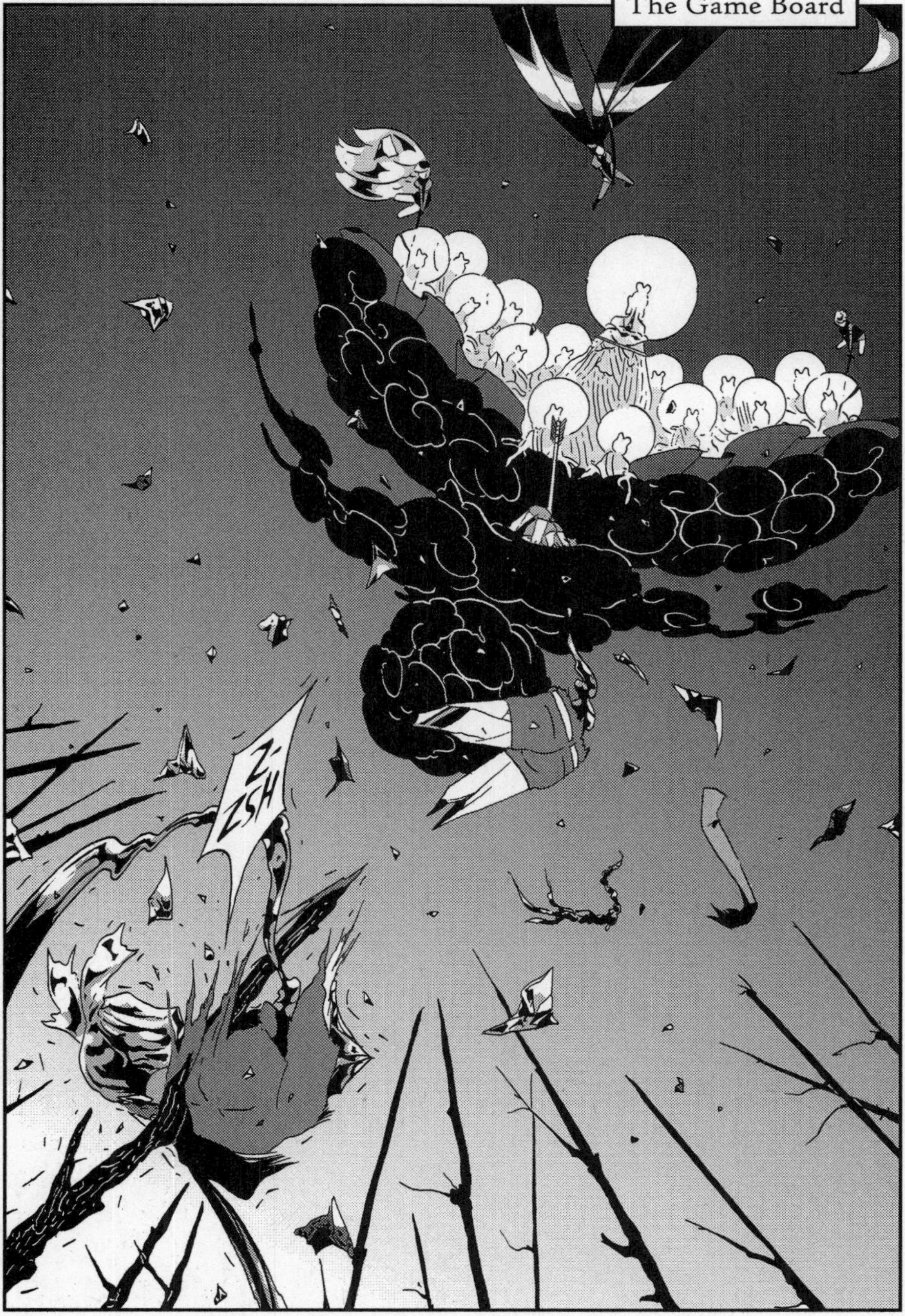
Z-ZSH

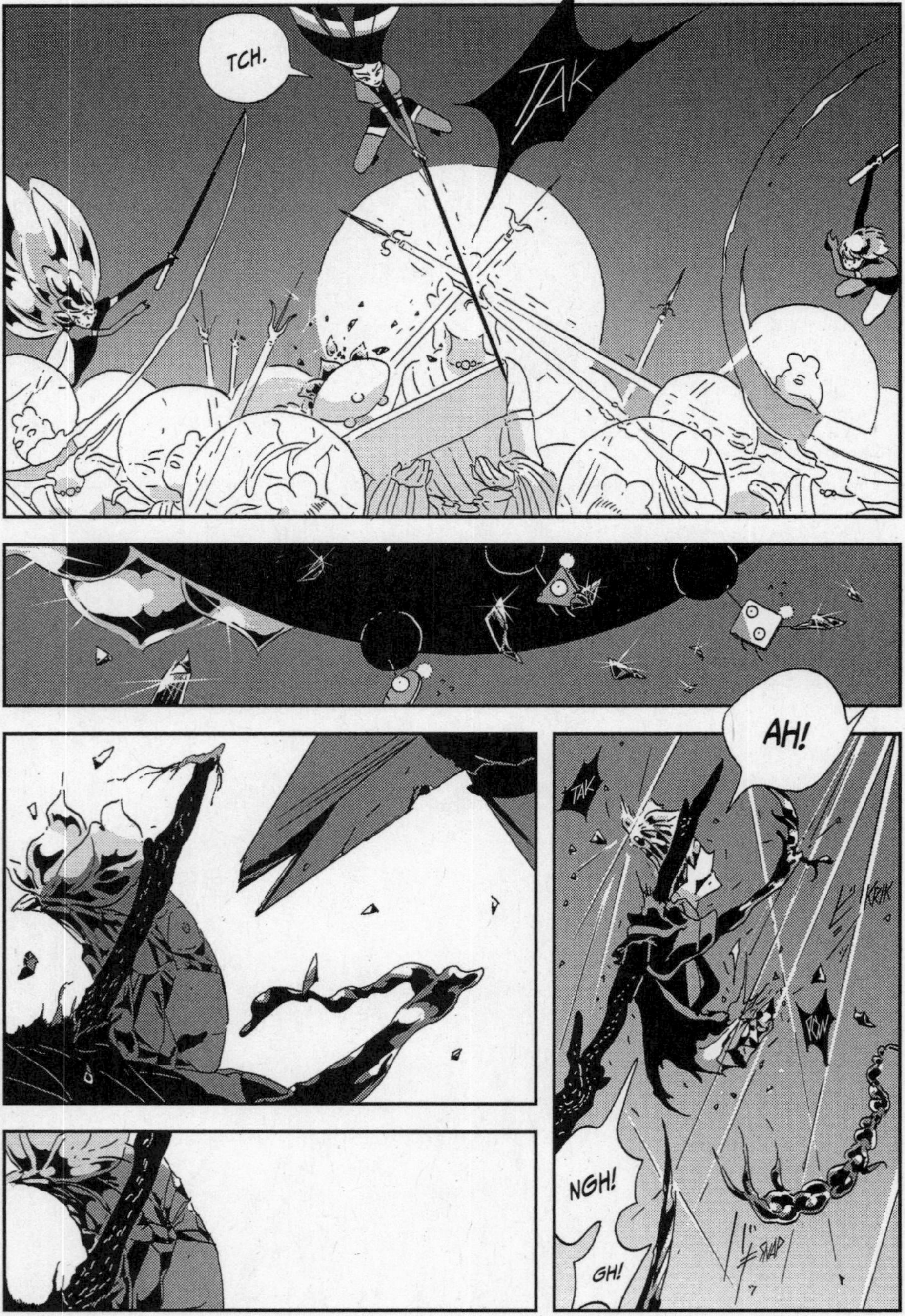
TCH.
TAK
AH!
TAK
KRIK
NGH!
GH!
SNAP

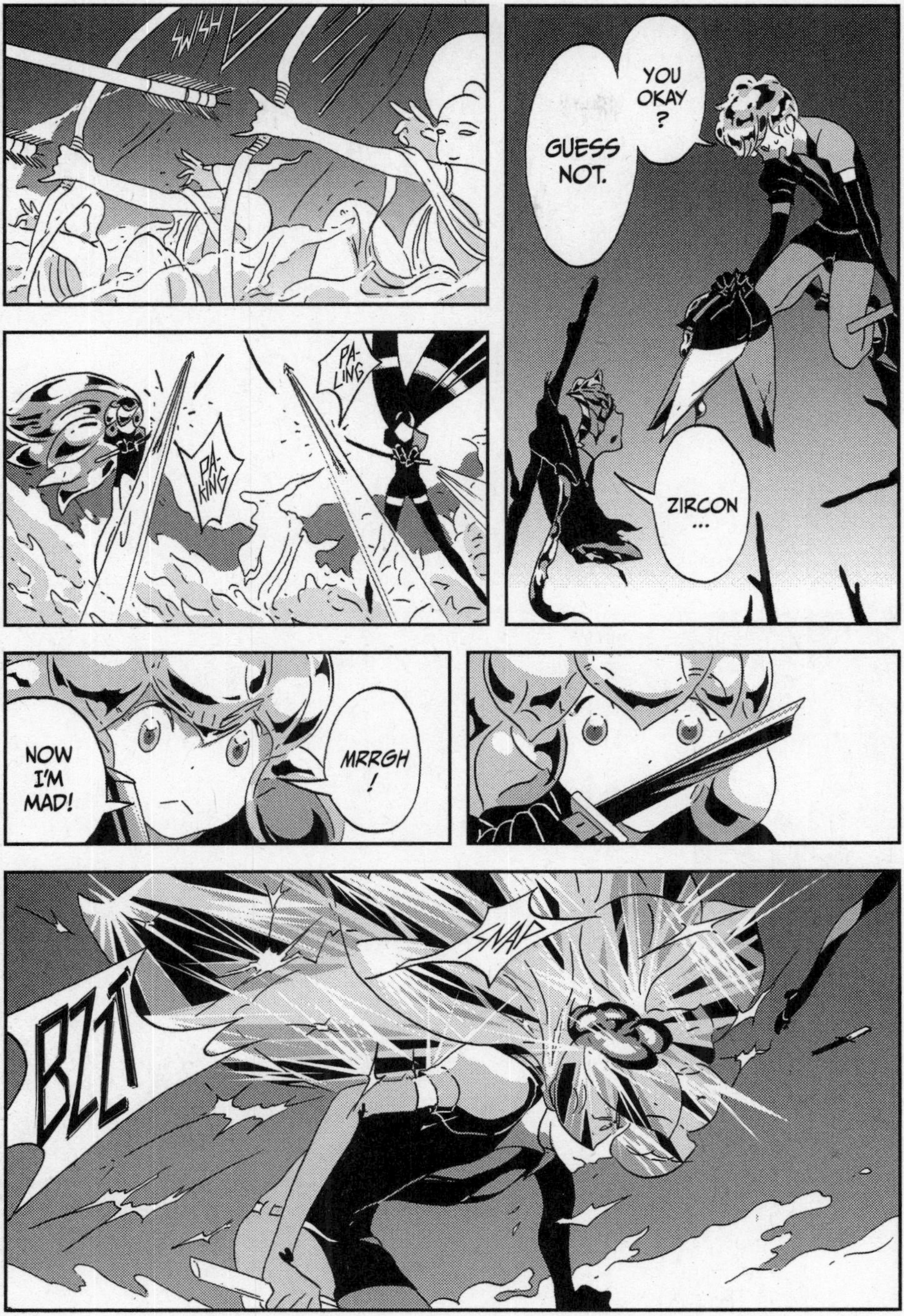
YOU OKAY ?
GUESS NOT.
ZIRCON ...
SWISH
PA-LING
PA-KING
MRRGH !
NOW I'M MAD!
SNAP
BZZT

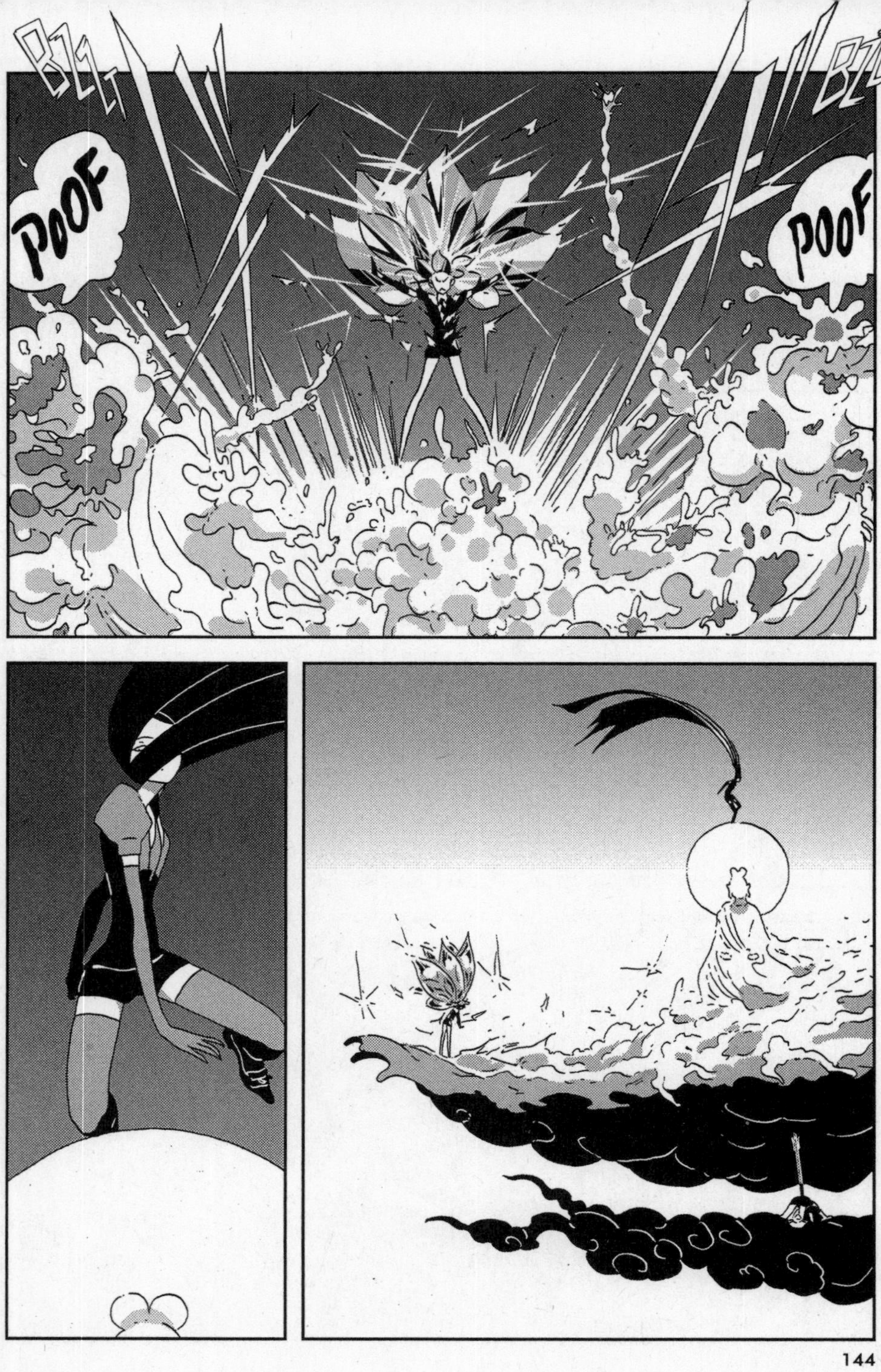
BZZT
POOF
BZZZT
POOF

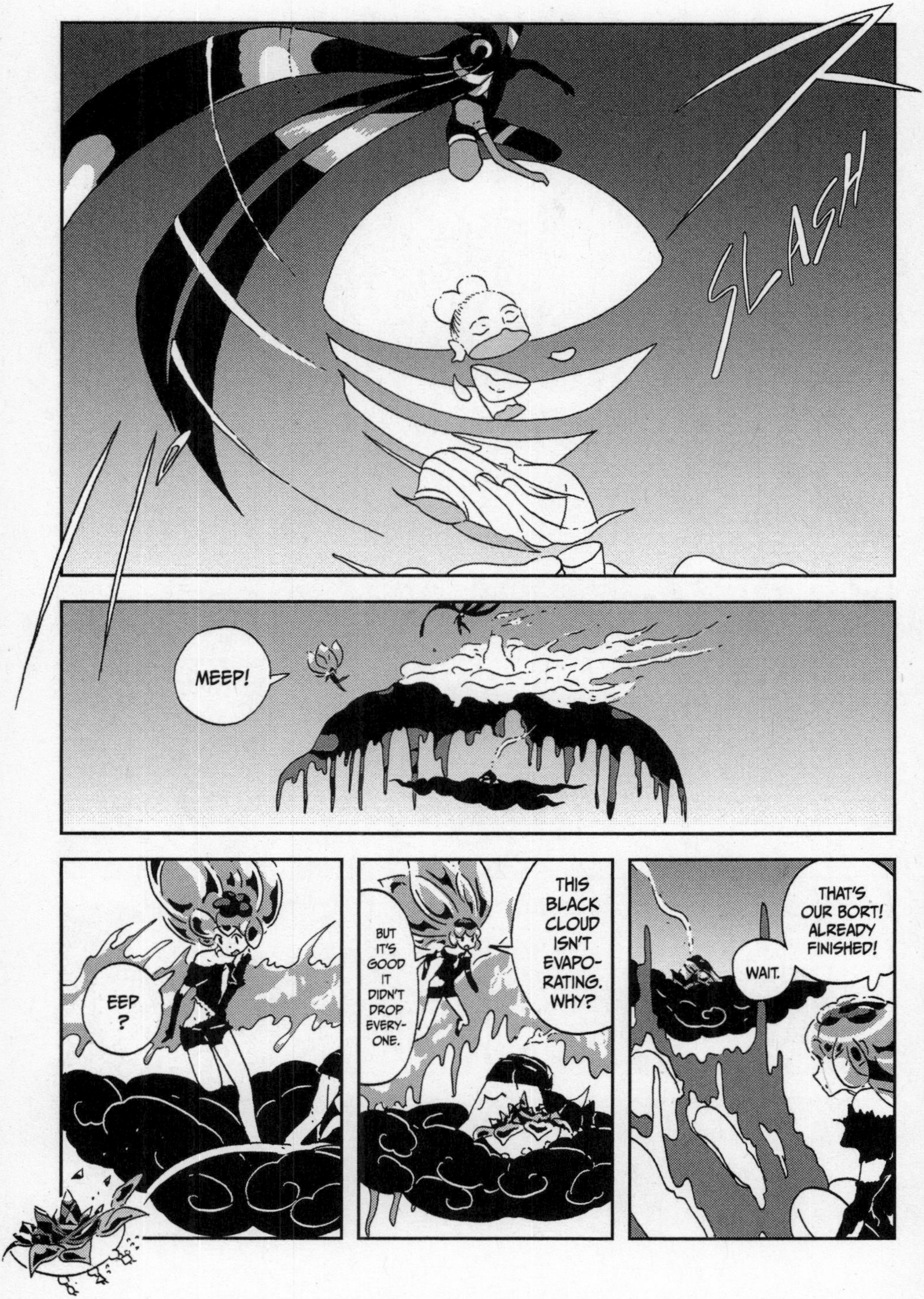
SLASH
MEEP!
THAT'S OUR BORT! ALREADY FINISHED!
WAIT.
THIS BLACK CLOUD ISN'T EVAPO-RATING. WHY?
BUT IT'S GOOD IT DIDN'T DROP EVERY-ONE.
EEP ?

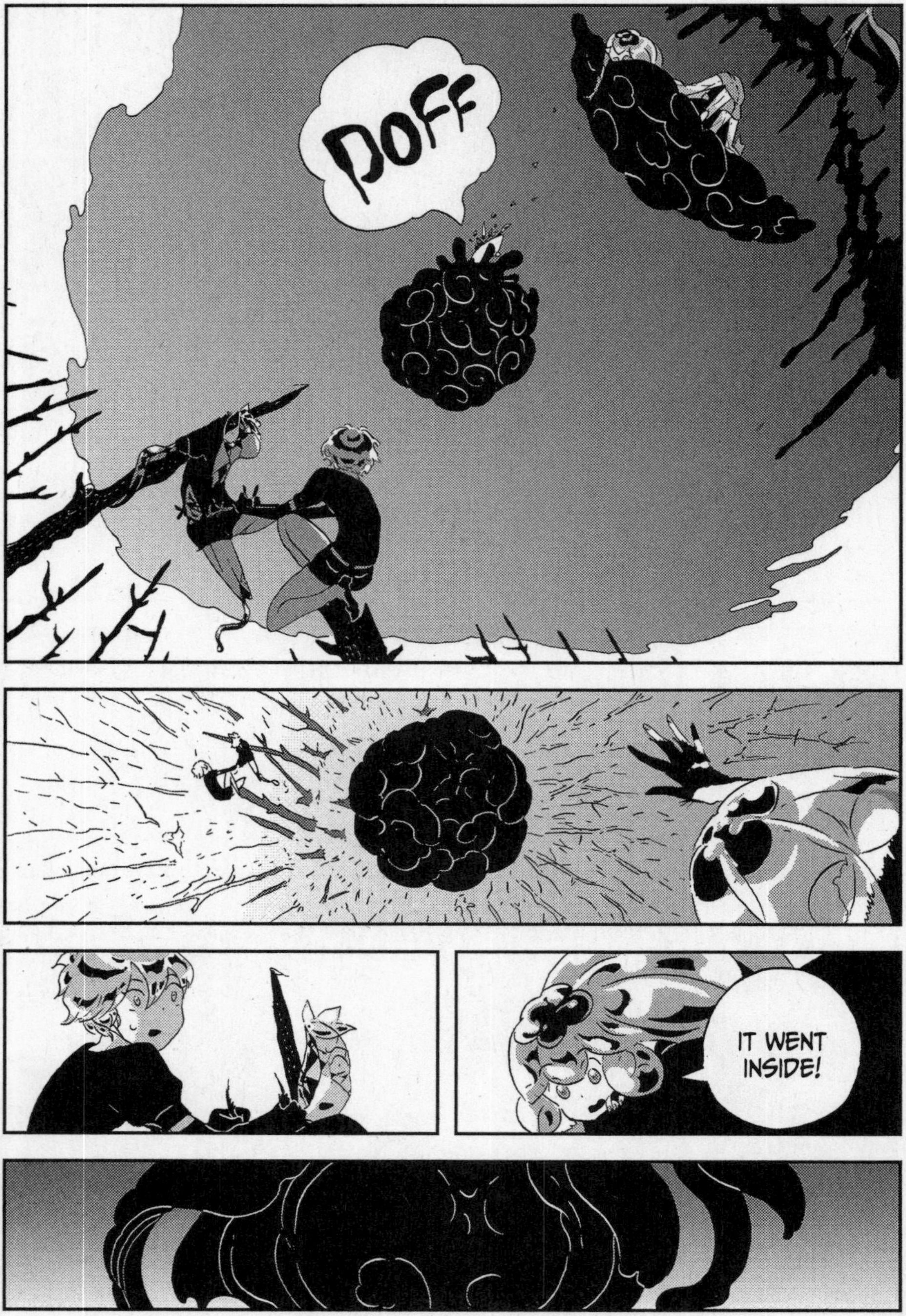
DOFF
IT WENT INSIDE!

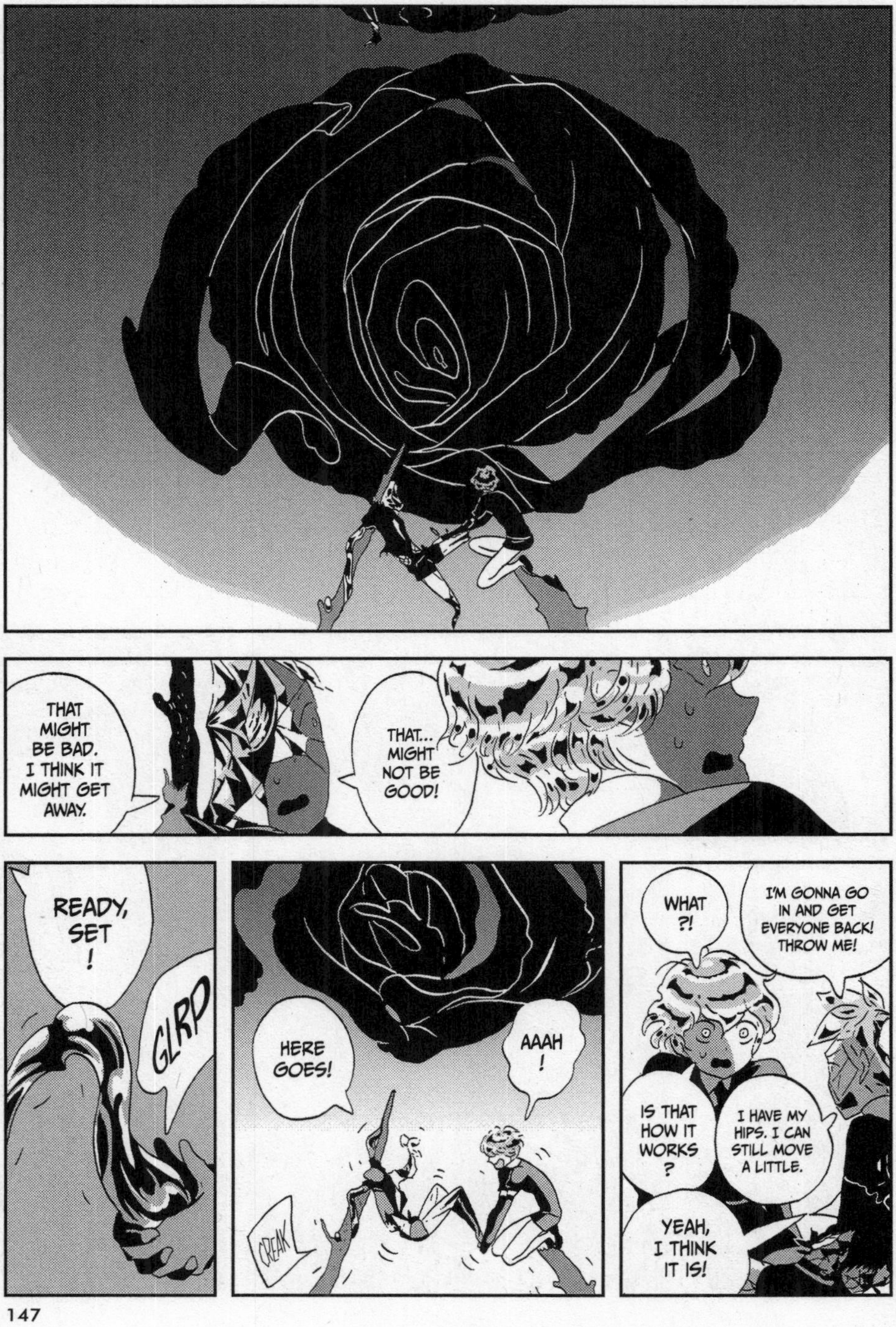

THAT... MIGHT NOT BE GOOD!
THAT MIGHT BE BAD. I THINK IT MIGHT GET AWAY.
I'M GONNA GO IN AND GET EVERYONE BACK! THROW ME!
WHAT?!
I HAVE MY HIPS. I CAN STILL MOVE A LITTLE.
IS THAT HOW IT WORKS?
YEAH, I THINK IT IS!
AAAH!
HERE GOES!
CREAK
READY, SET!
GLRP

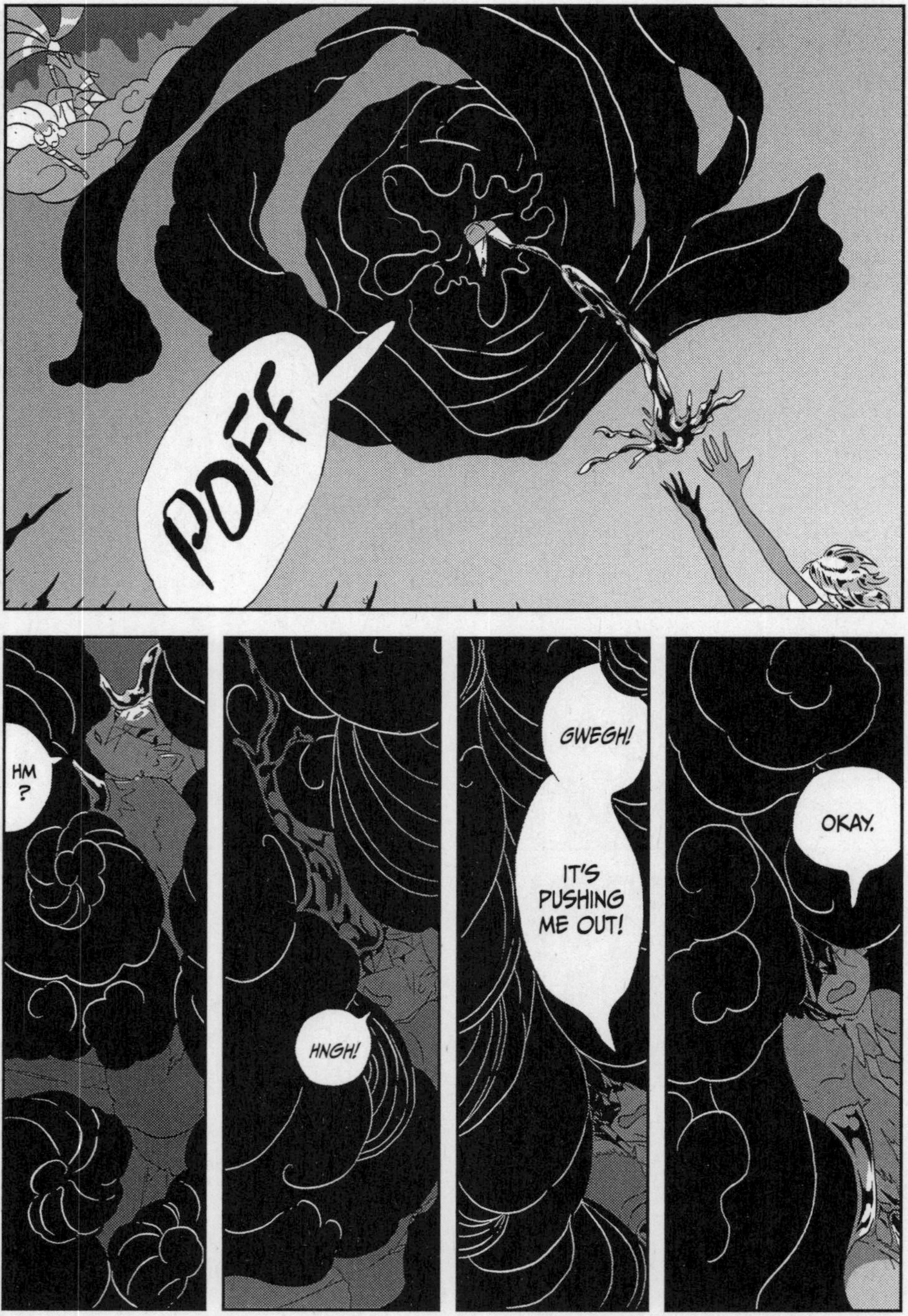
PDFF
OKAY.
GWEGH!
IT'S PUSHING ME OUT!
HNGH!
HM ?

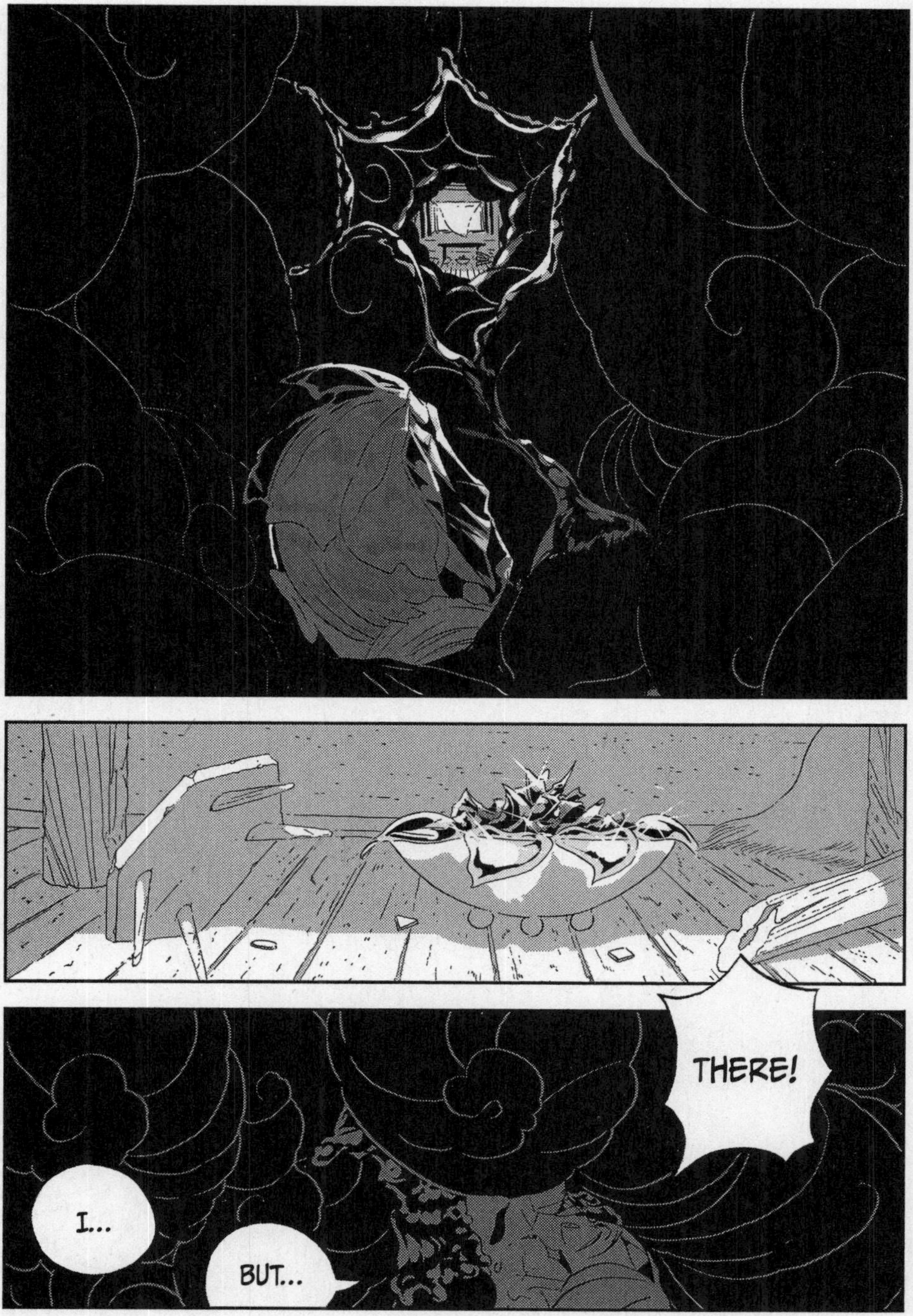
THERE!
I...
BUT...

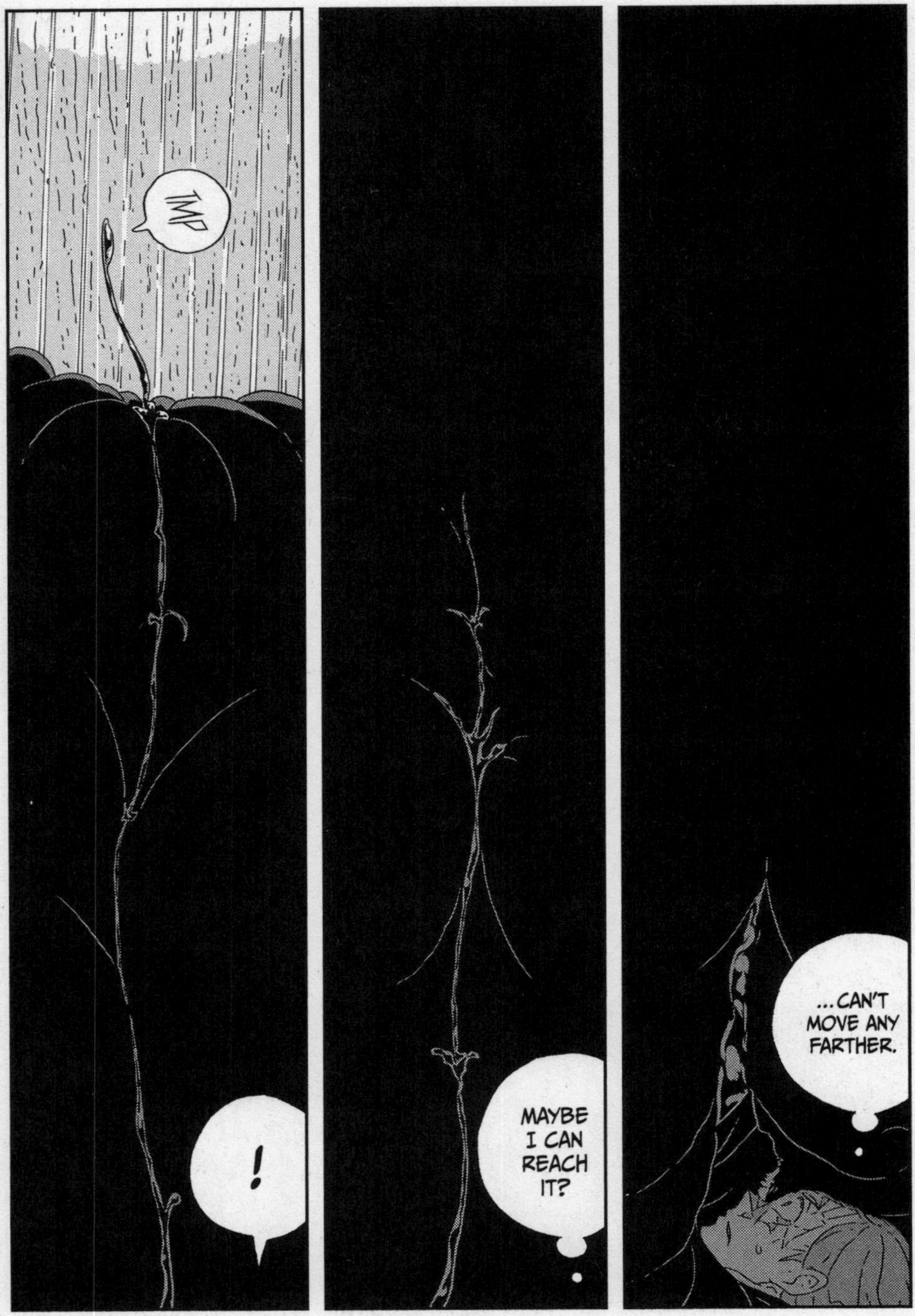
...CAN'T MOVE ANY FARTHER.
MAYBE I CAN REACH IT?
TMP
!

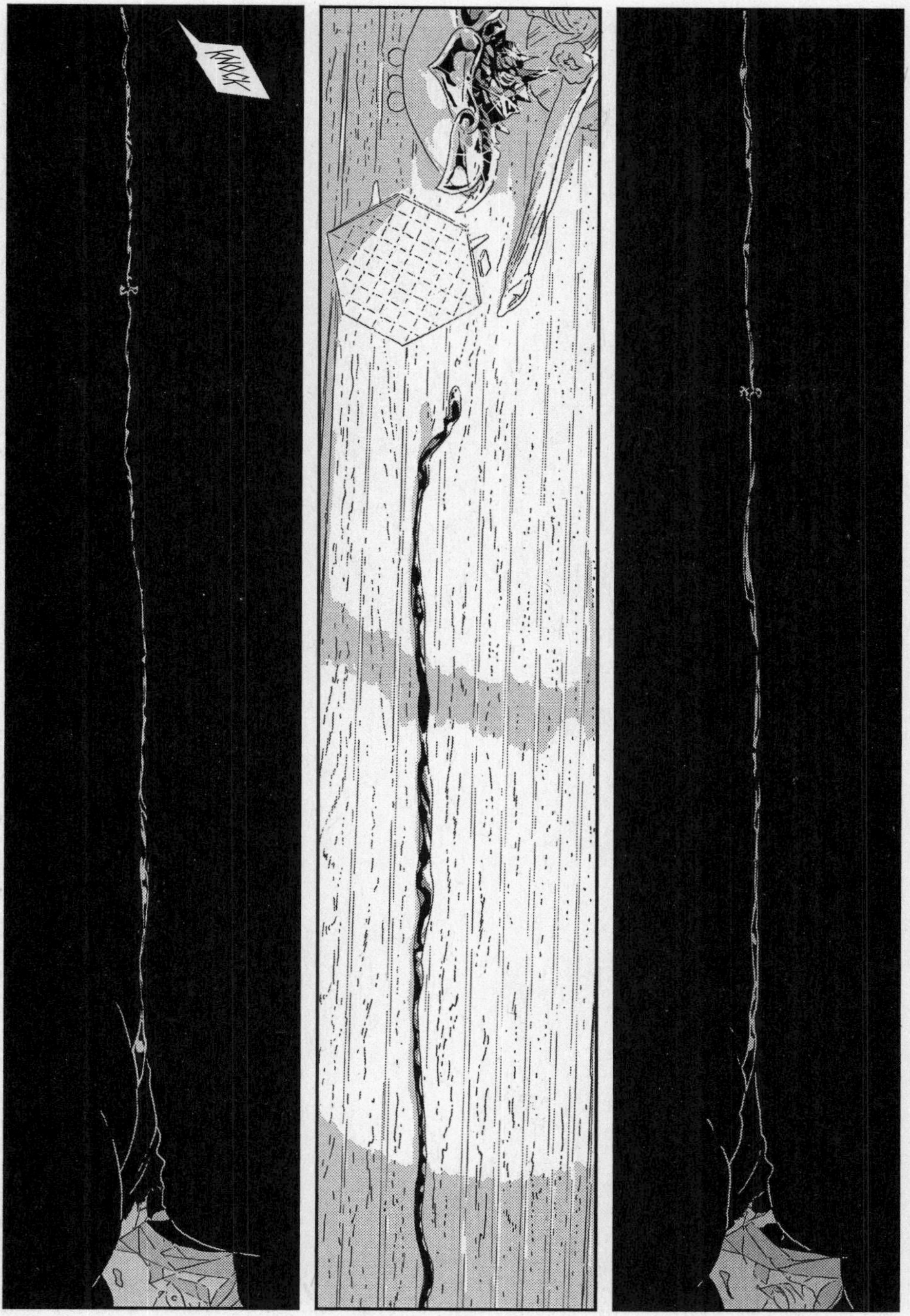
KNOCK

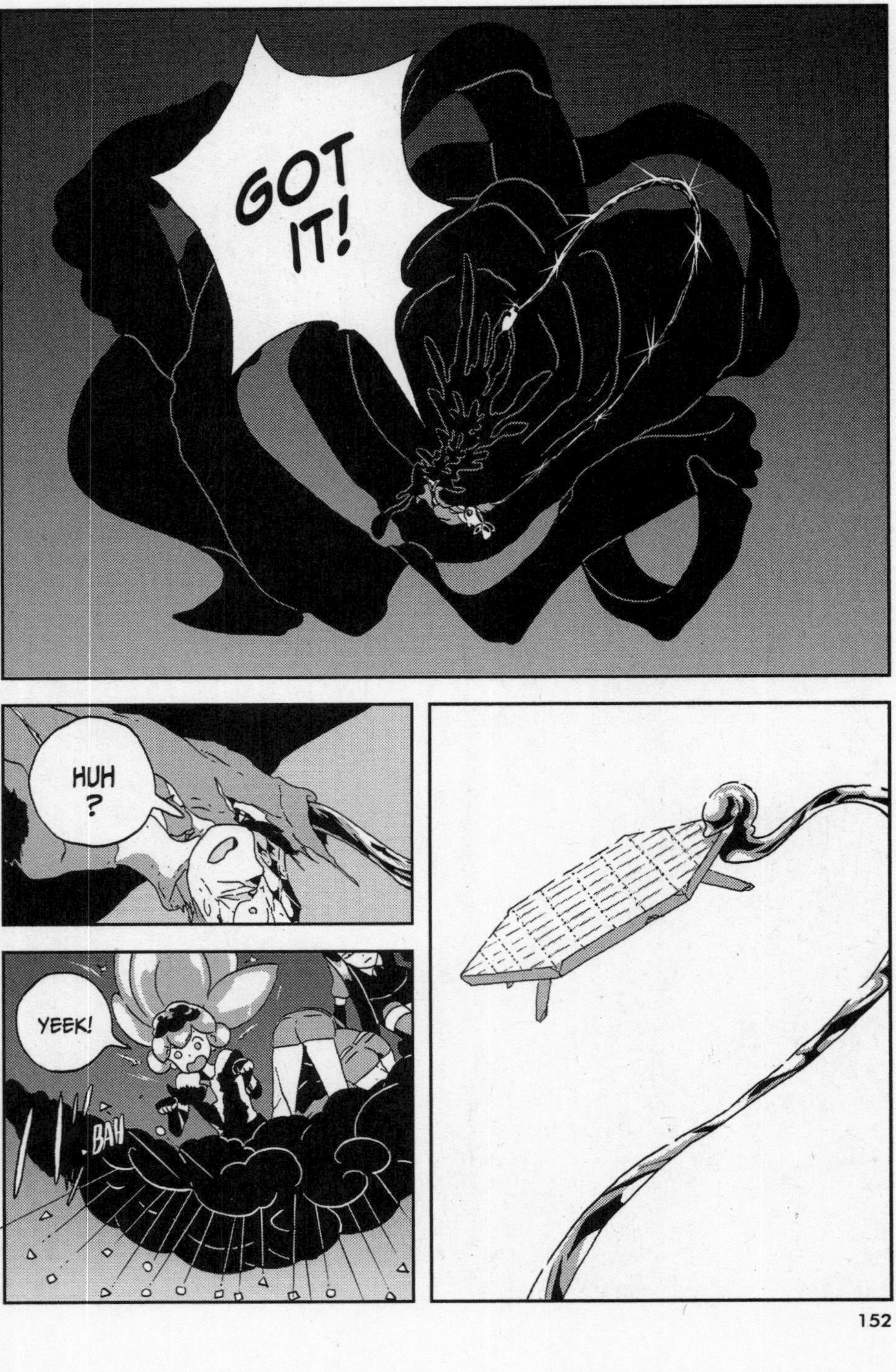
GOT IT!
HUH ?
YEEK!
BAH

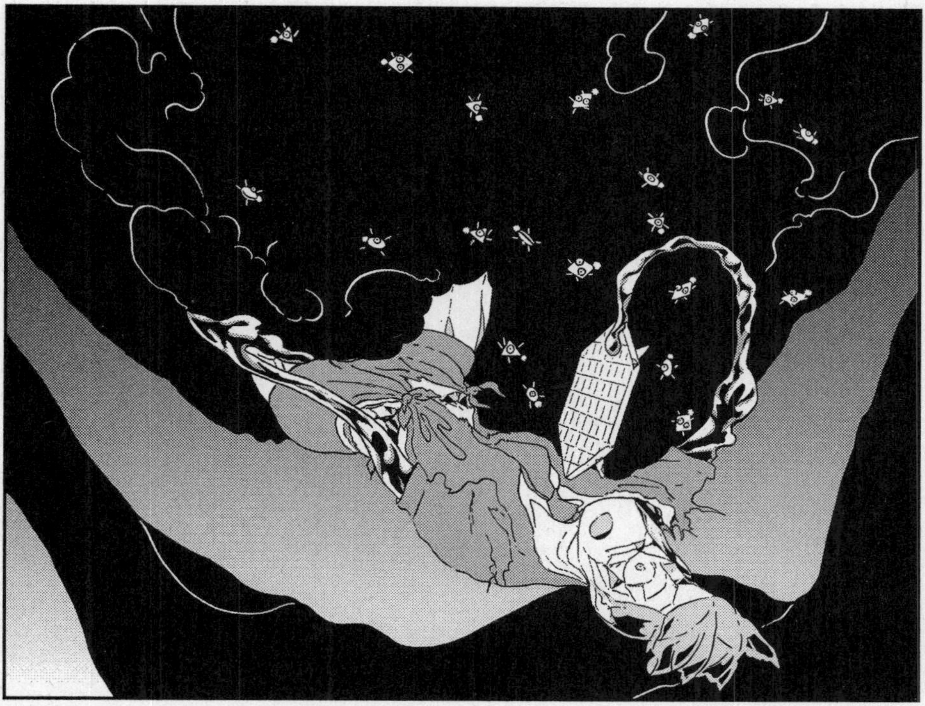

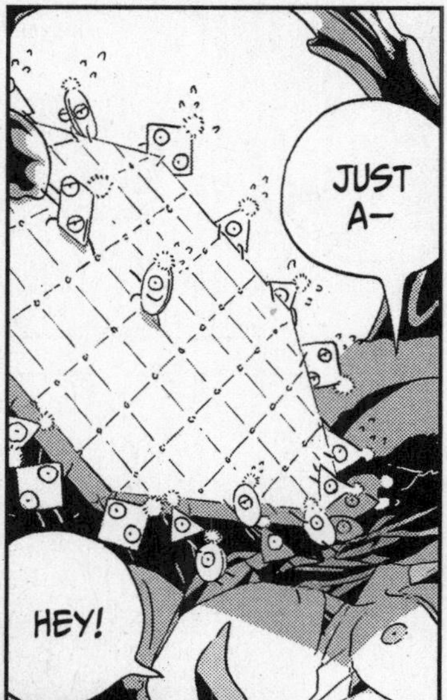
JUST A—
HEY!

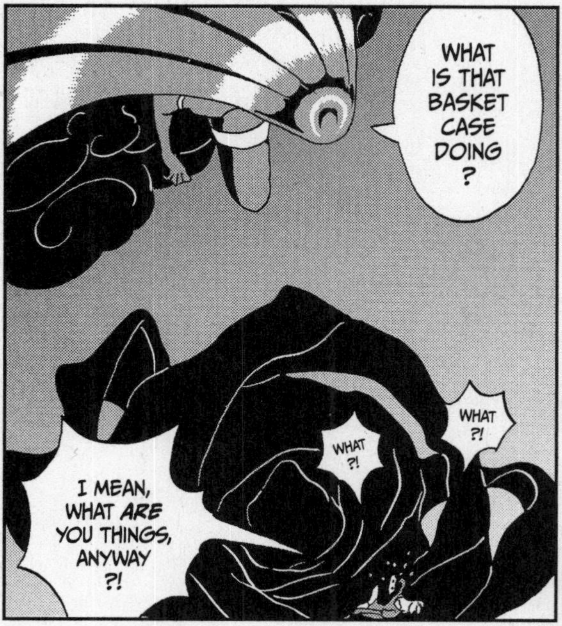
WHAT IS THAT BASKET CASE DOING?
WHAT?!
WHAT?!
I MEAN, WHAT *ARE* YOU THINGS, ANYWAY?!

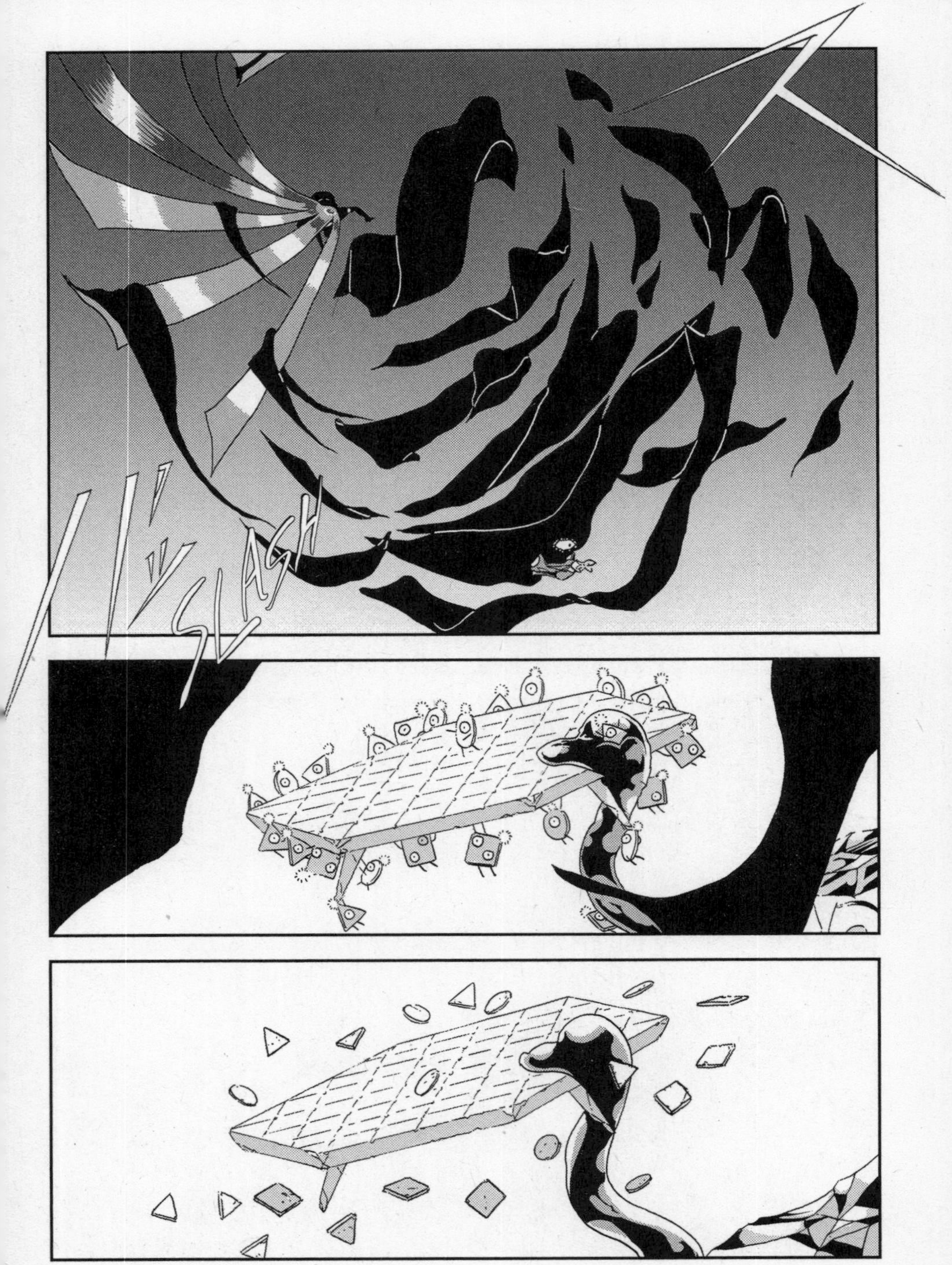
SLASH

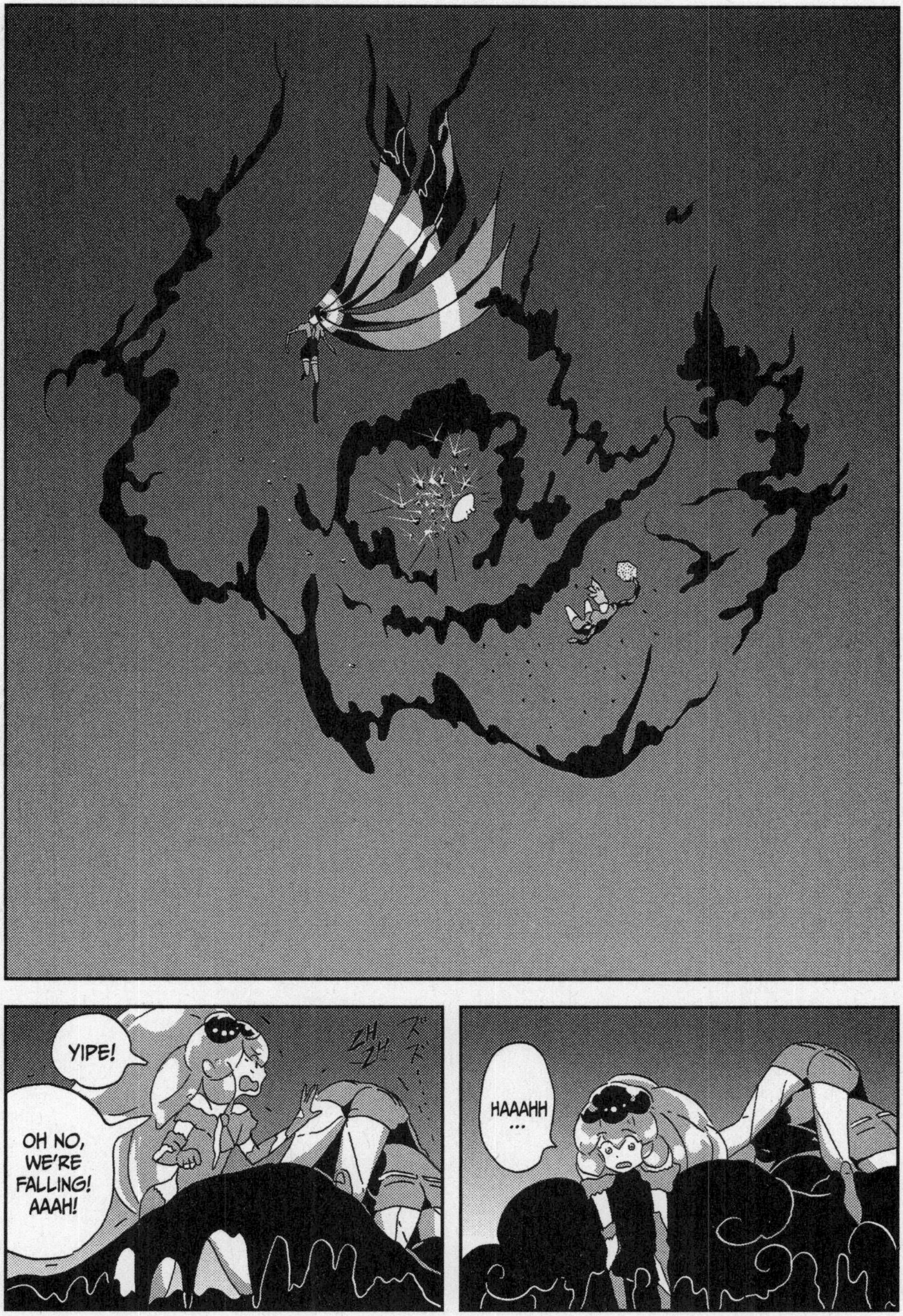
HAAAHH ...
ZH ZH
YIPE!
OH NO, WE'RE FALLING! AAAH!

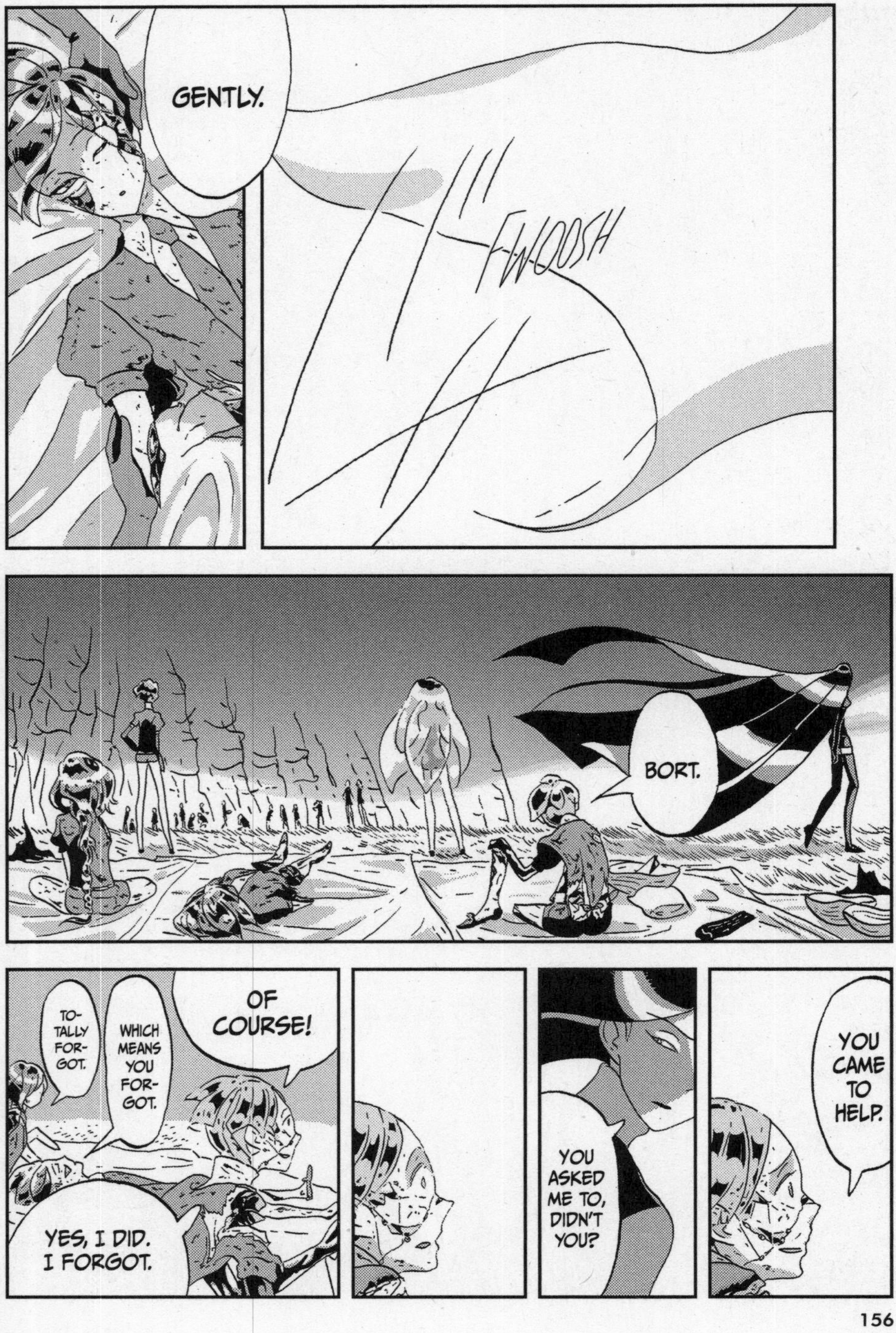
FWOOSH
GENTLY.
BORT.
YOU CAME TO HELP.
YOU ASKED ME TO, DIDN'T YOU?
OF COURSE!
WHICH MEANS YOU FOR-GOT.
TO-TALLY FOR-GOT.
YES, I DID. I FORGOT.

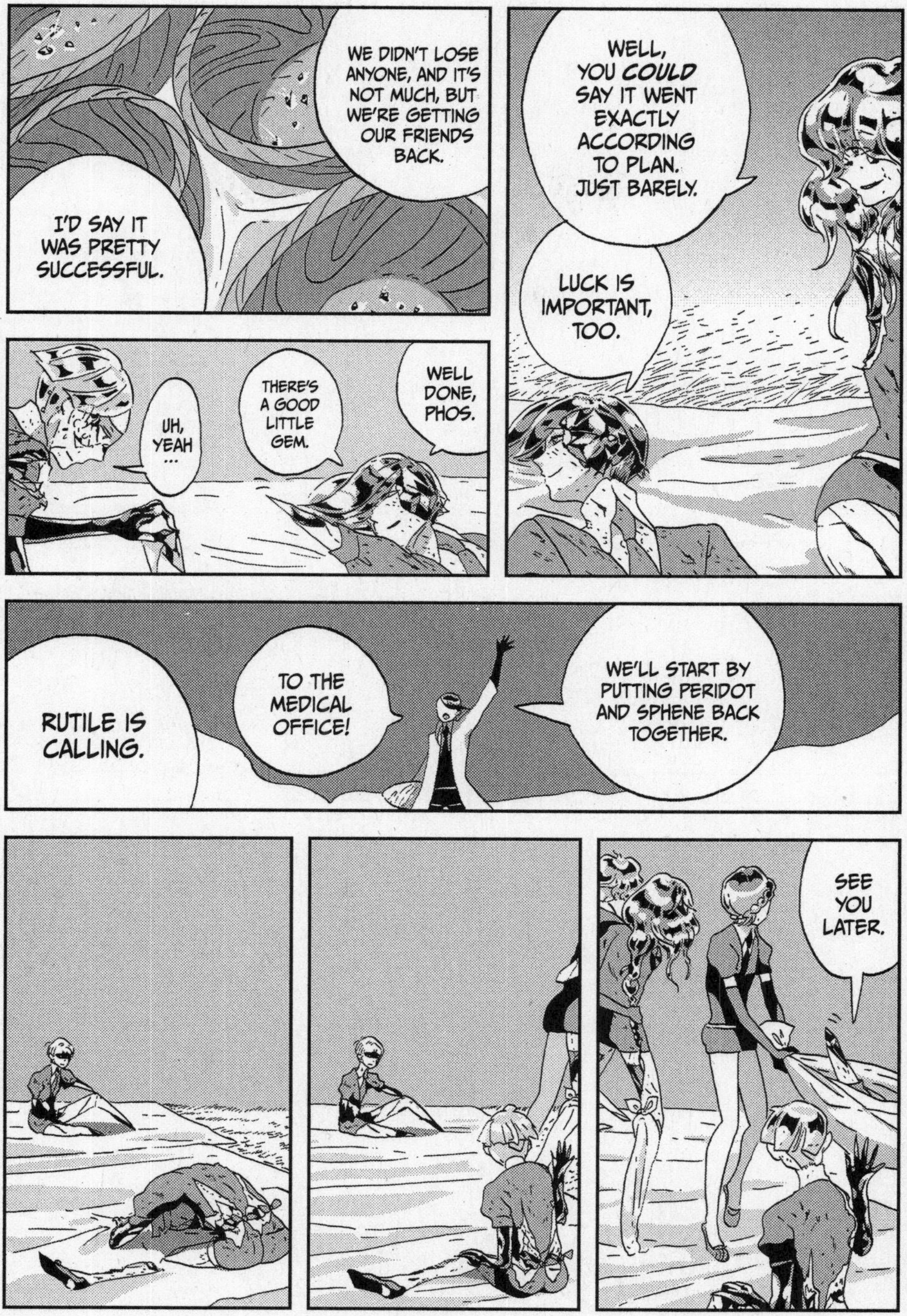
WELL, YOU COULD SAY IT WENT EXACTLY ACCORDING TO PLAN. JUST BARELY.
LUCK IS IMPORTANT, TOO.
WE DIDN'T LOSE ANYONE, AND IT'S NOT MUCH, BUT WE'RE GETTING OUR FRIENDS BACK.
I'D SAY IT WAS PRETTY SUCCESSFUL.
WELL DONE, PHOS.
THERE'S A GOOD LITTLE GEM.
UH, YEAH ...
WE'LL START BY PUTTING PERIDOT AND SPHENE BACK TOGETHER.
TO THE MEDICAL OFFICE!
RUTILE IS CALLING.
SEE YOU LATER.

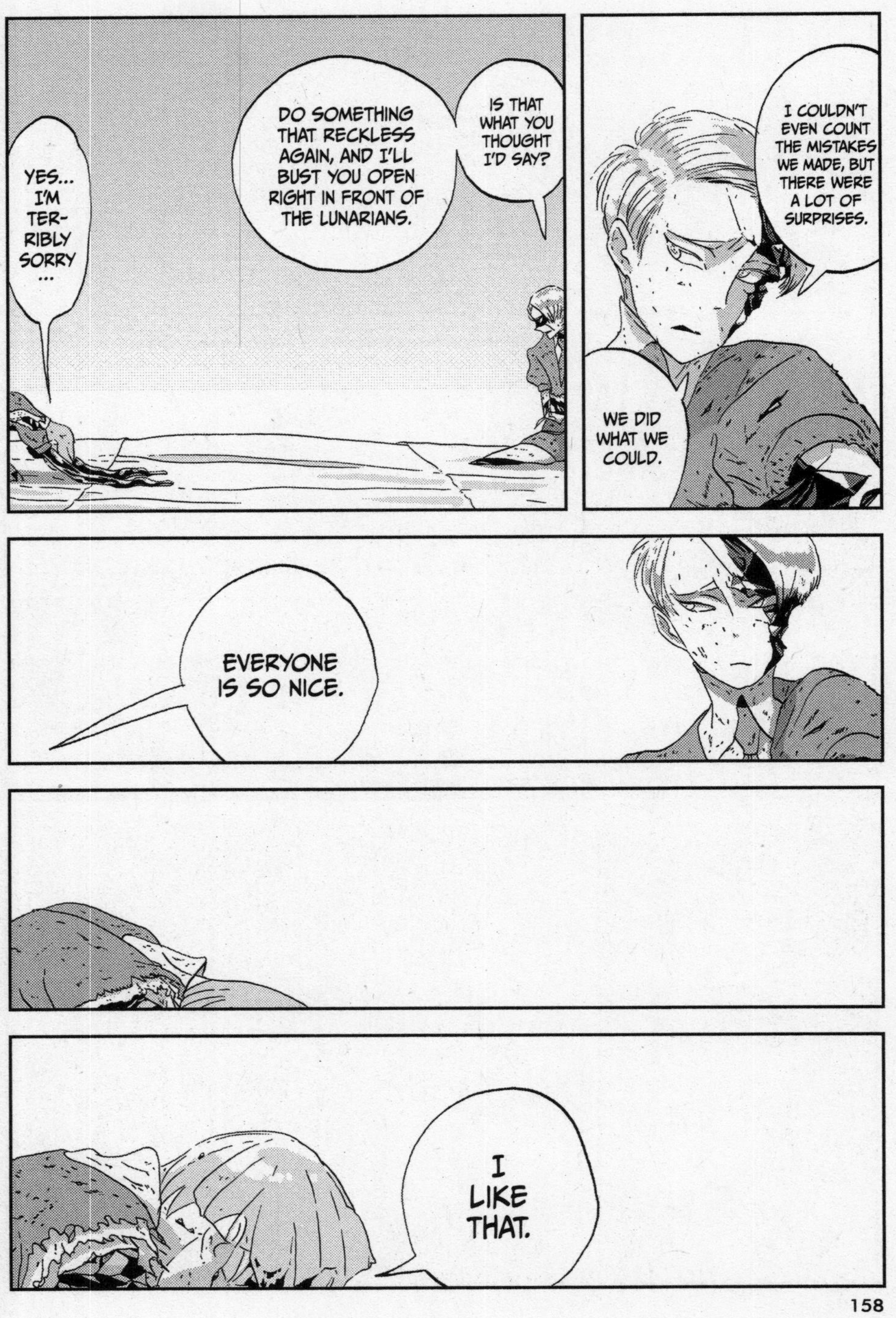
I COULDN'T EVEN COUNT THE MISTAKES WE MADE, BUT THERE WERE A LOT OF SURPRISES.
WE DID WHAT WE COULD.
IS THAT WHAT YOU THOUGHT I'D SAY?
DO SOMETHING THAT RECKLESS AGAIN, AND I'LL BUST YOU OPEN RIGHT IN FRONT OF THE LUNARIANS.
YES... I'M TER-RIBLY SORRY...
EVERYONE IS SO NICE.
I LIKE THAT.

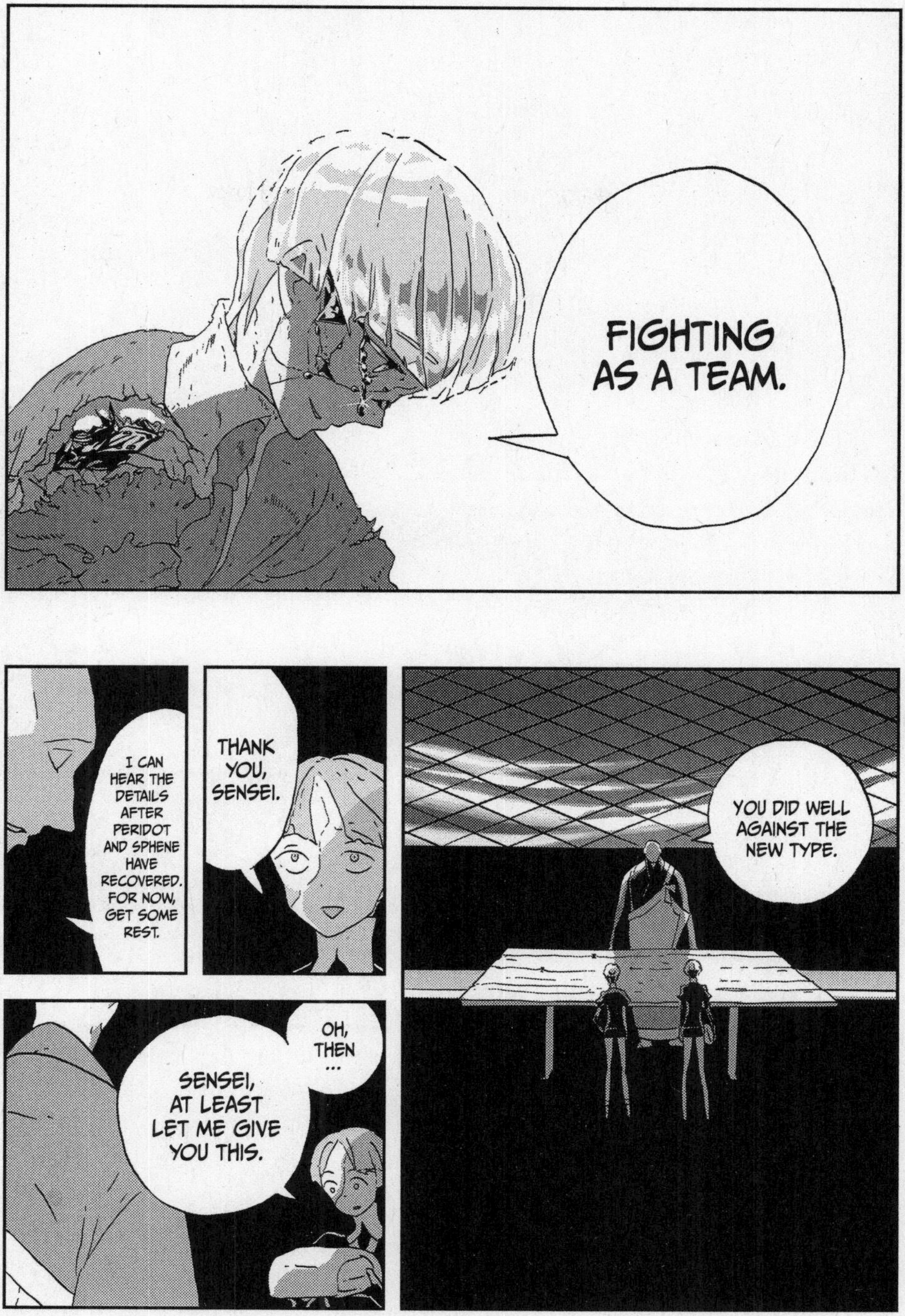
FIGHTING AS A TEAM.
YOU DID WELL AGAINST THE NEW TYPE.
THANK YOU, SENSEI.
I CAN HEAR THE DETAILS AFTER PERIDOT AND SPHENE HAVE RECOVERED. FOR NOW, GET SOME REST.
OH, THEN...
SENSEI, AT LEAST LET ME GIVE YOU THIS.

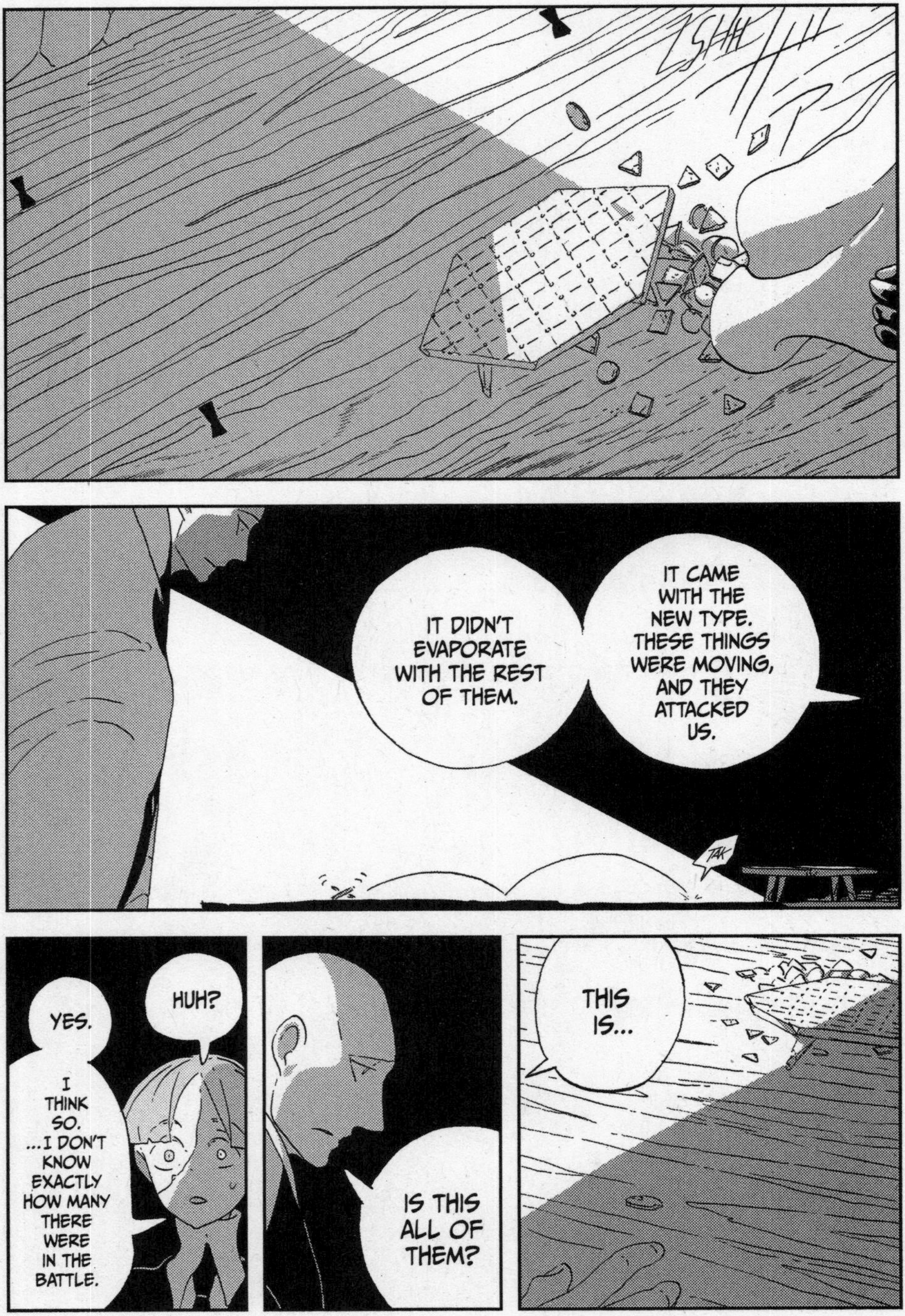
IT CAME WITH THE NEW TYPE. THESE THINGS WERE MOVING, AND THEY ATTACKED US.
IT DIDN'T EVAPORATE WITH THE REST OF THEM.
TAK
THIS IS...
IS THIS ALL OF THEM?
HUH?
YES.
I THINK SO. ...I DON'T KNOW EXACTLY HOW MANY THERE WERE IN THE BATTLE.

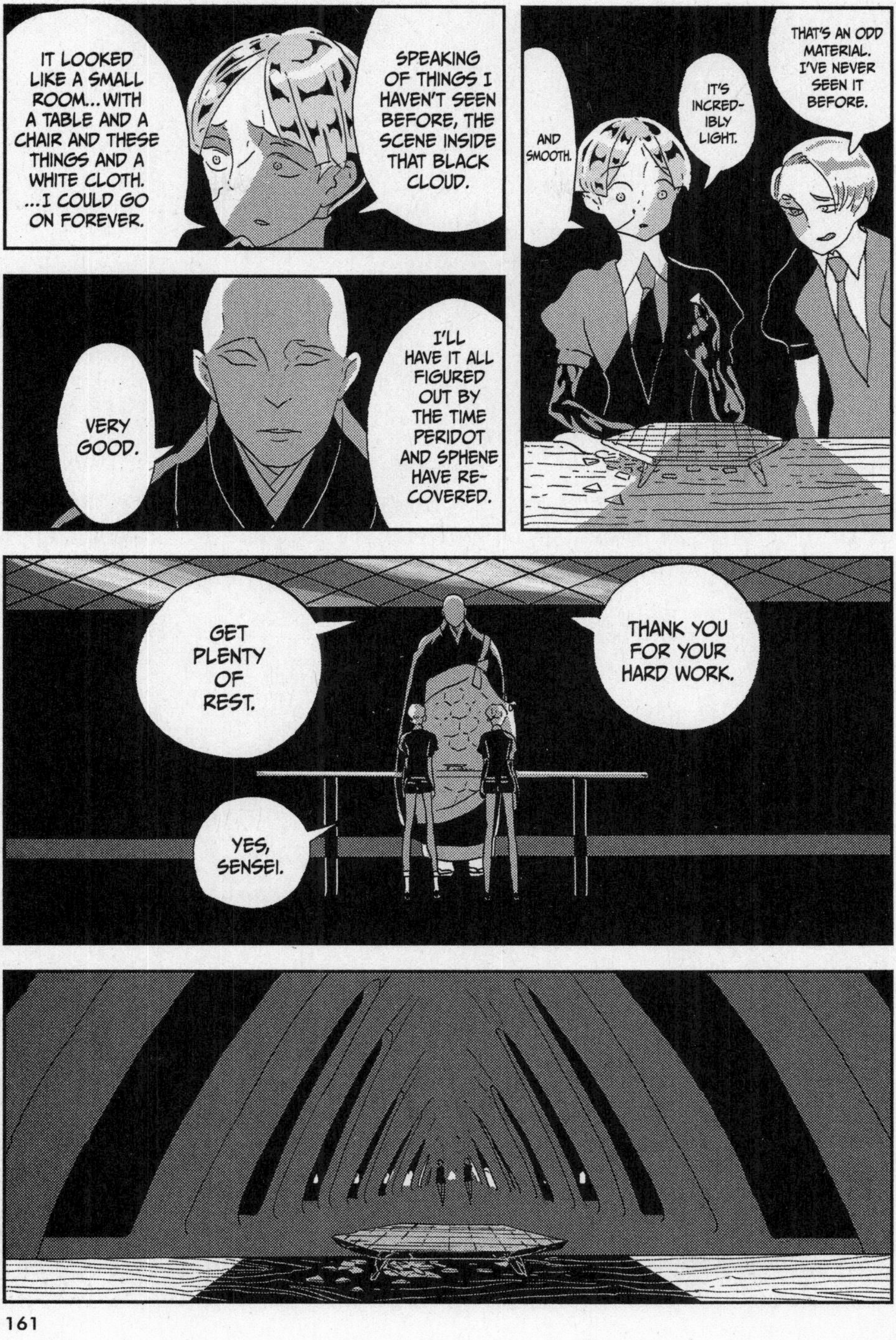
THAT'S AN ODD MATERIAL. I'VE NEVER SEEN IT BEFORE.
IT'S INCRED-IBLY LIGHT.
AND SMOOTH.
SPEAKING OF THINGS I HAVEN'T SEEN BEFORE, THE SCENE INSIDE THAT BLACK CLOUD.
IT LOOKED LIKE A SMALL ROOM...WITH A TABLE AND A CHAIR AND THESE THINGS AND A WHITE CLOTH. ...I COULD GO ON FOREVER.
I'LL HAVE IT ALL FIGURED OUT BY THE TIME PERIDOT AND SPHENE HAVE RE-COVERED.
VERY GOOD.
THANK YOU FOR YOUR HARD WORK.
GET PLENTY OF REST.
YES, SENSEI.

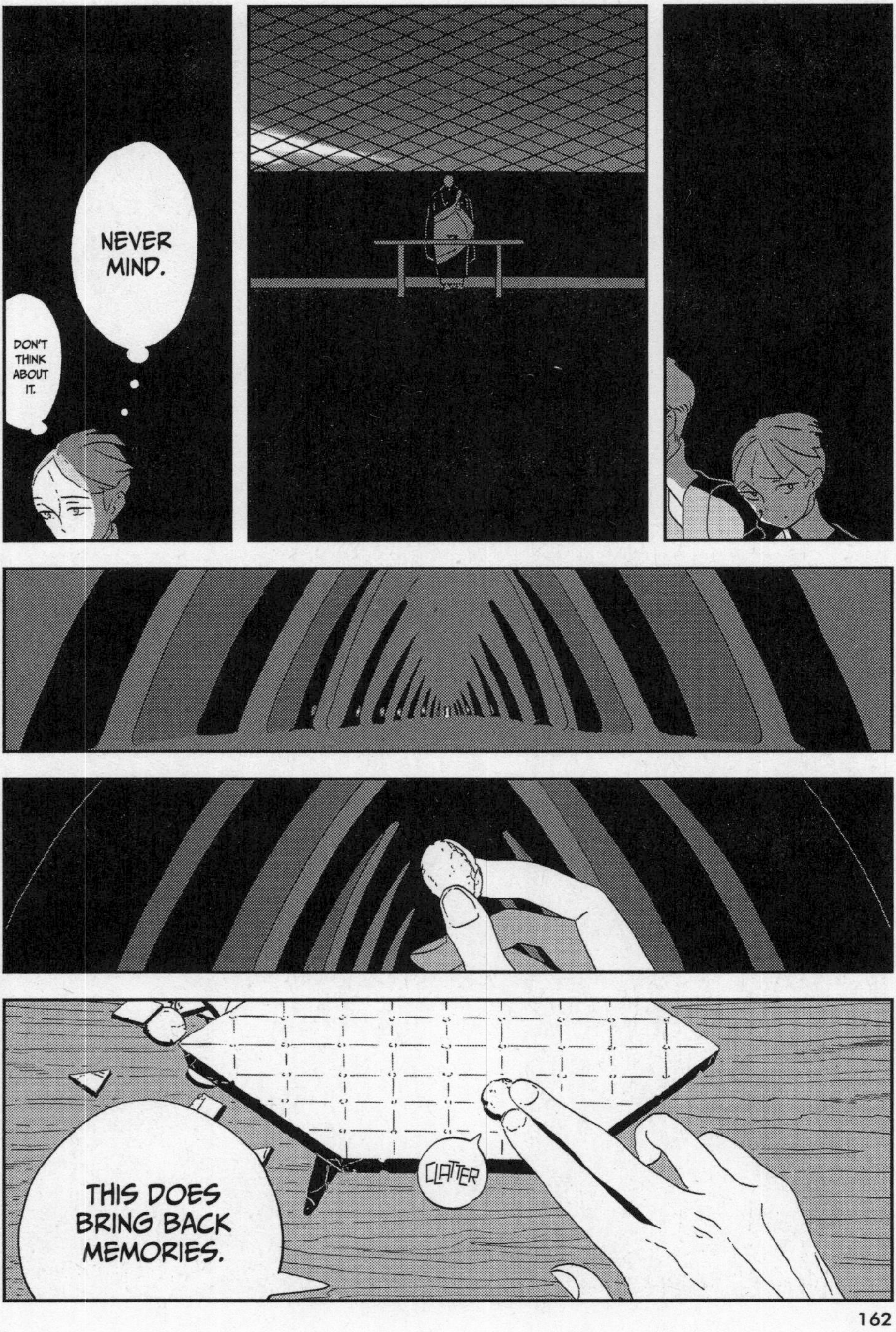
NEVER MIND.
DON'T THINK ABOUT IT.
CLATTER
THIS DOES BRING BACK MEMORIES.

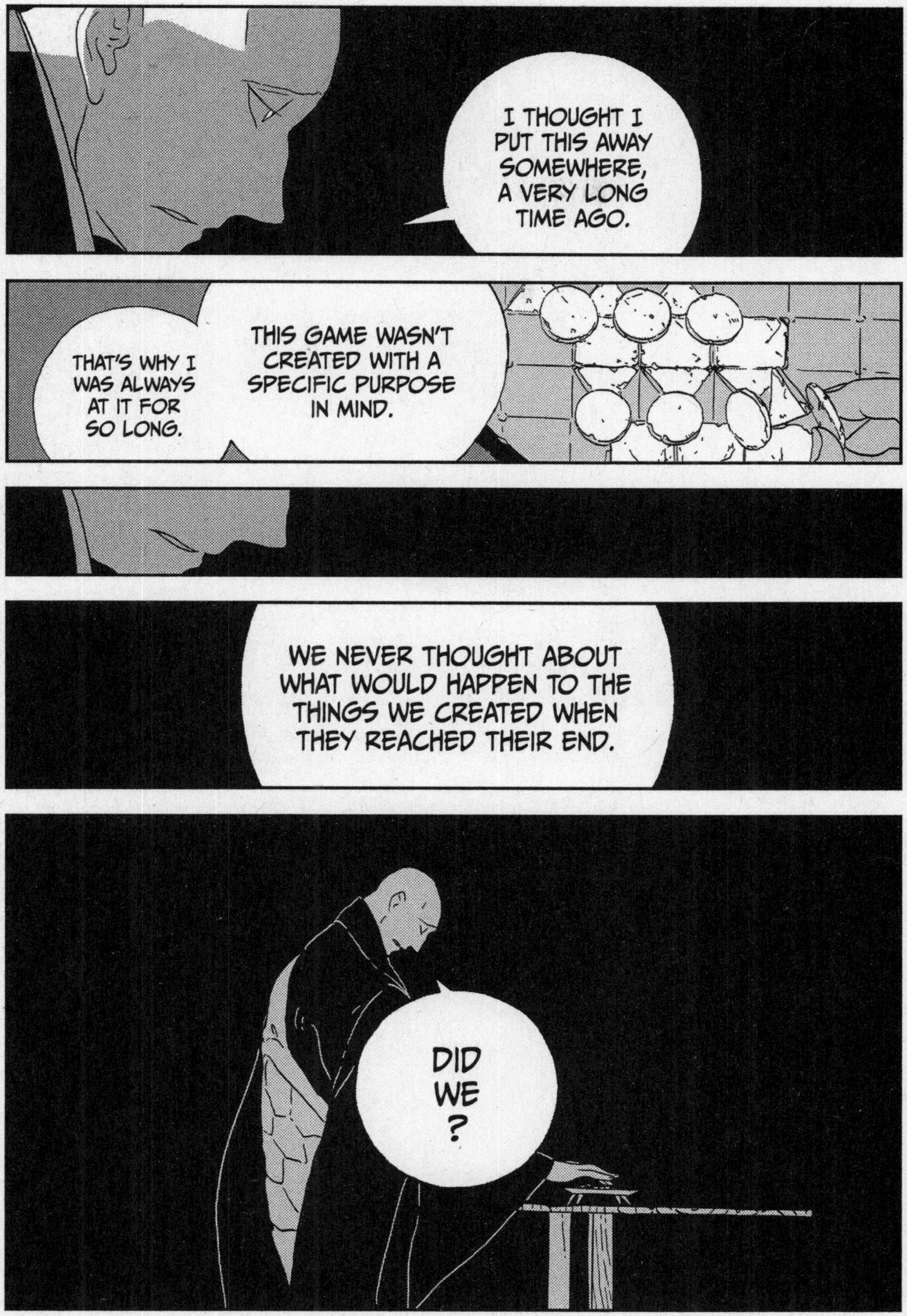
I THOUGHT I PUT THIS AWAY SOMEWHERE, A VERY LONG TIME AGO.
THIS GAME WASN'T CREATED WITH A SPECIFIC PURPOSE IN MIND.
THAT'S WHY I WAS ALWAYS AT IT FOR SO LONG.
WE NEVER THOUGHT ABOUT WHAT WOULD HAPPEN TO THE THINGS WE CREATED WHEN THEY REACHED THEIR END.
DID WE ?

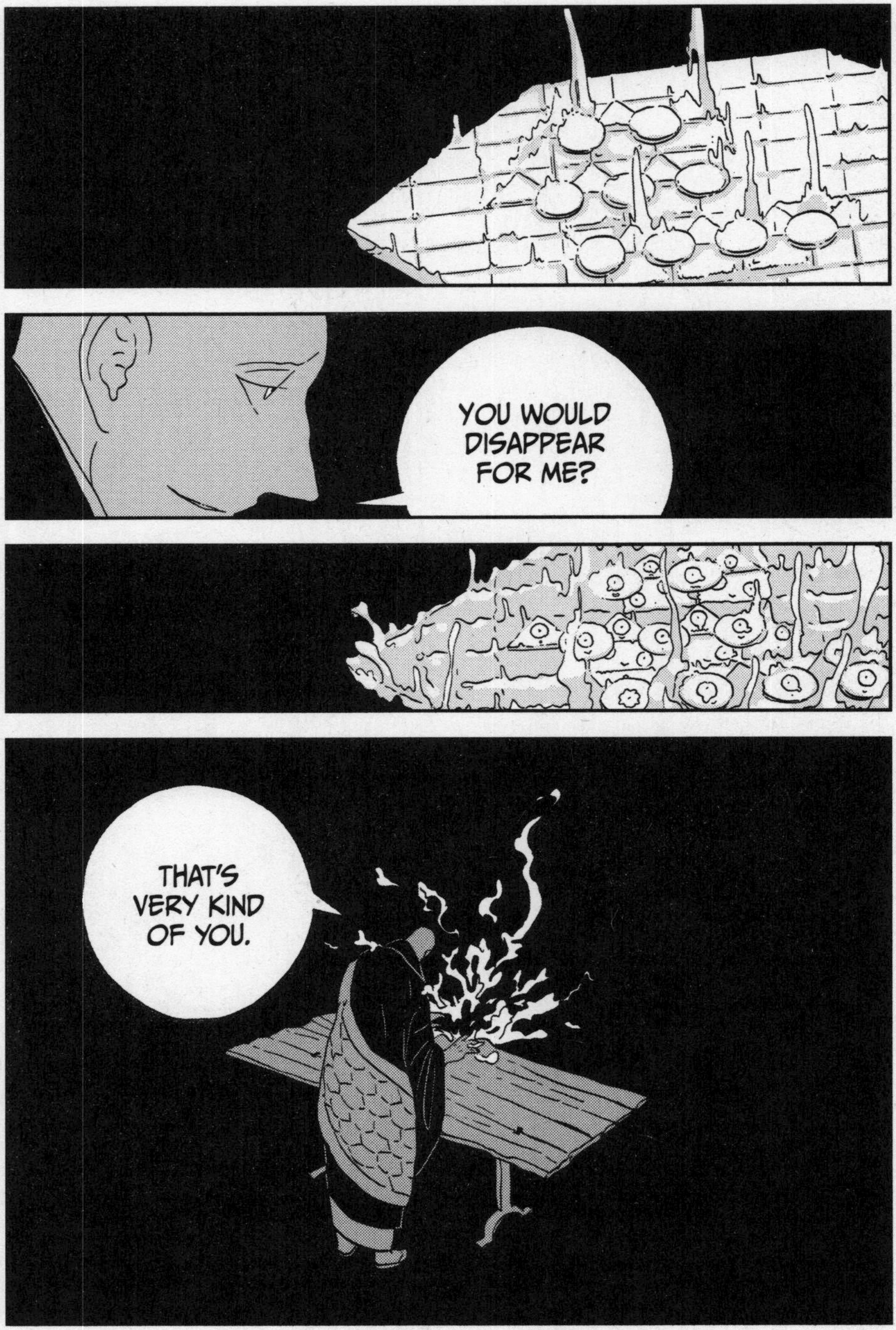
YOU WOULD DISAPPEAR FOR ME?
THAT'S VERY KIND OF YOU.

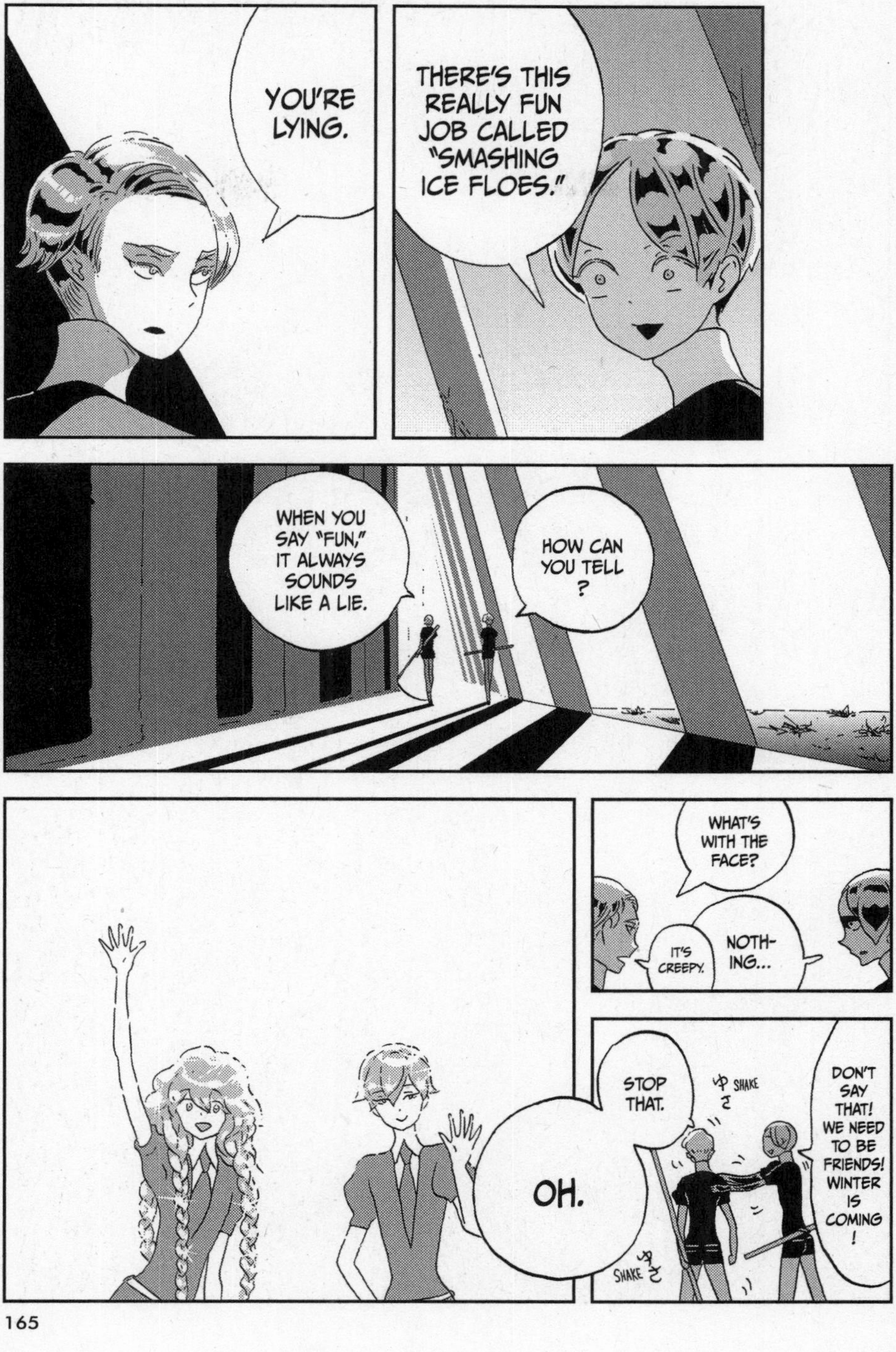
THERE'S THIS REALLY FUN JOB CALLED "SMASHING ICE FLOES."
YOU'RE LYING.
HOW CAN YOU TELL?
WHEN YOU SAY "FUN," IT ALWAYS SOUNDS LIKE A LIE.
WHAT'S WITH THE FACE?
NOTHING...
IT'S CREEPY.
DON'T SAY THAT! WE NEED TO BE FRIENDS! WINTER IS COMING!
SHAKE
STOP THAT.
SHAKE
OH.

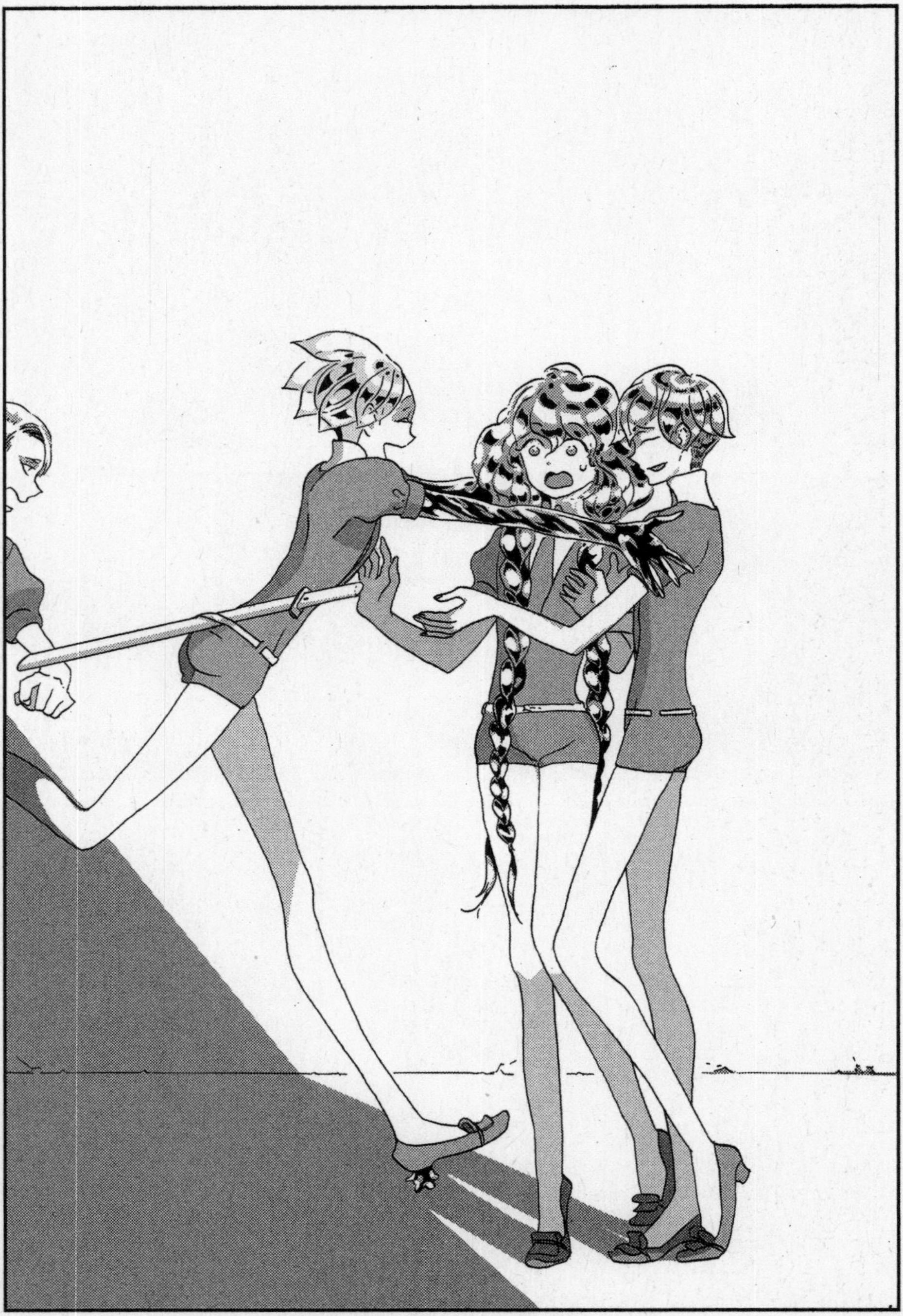

CHAPTER 43: The Game Board END

CHAPTER 44:

Shortcut

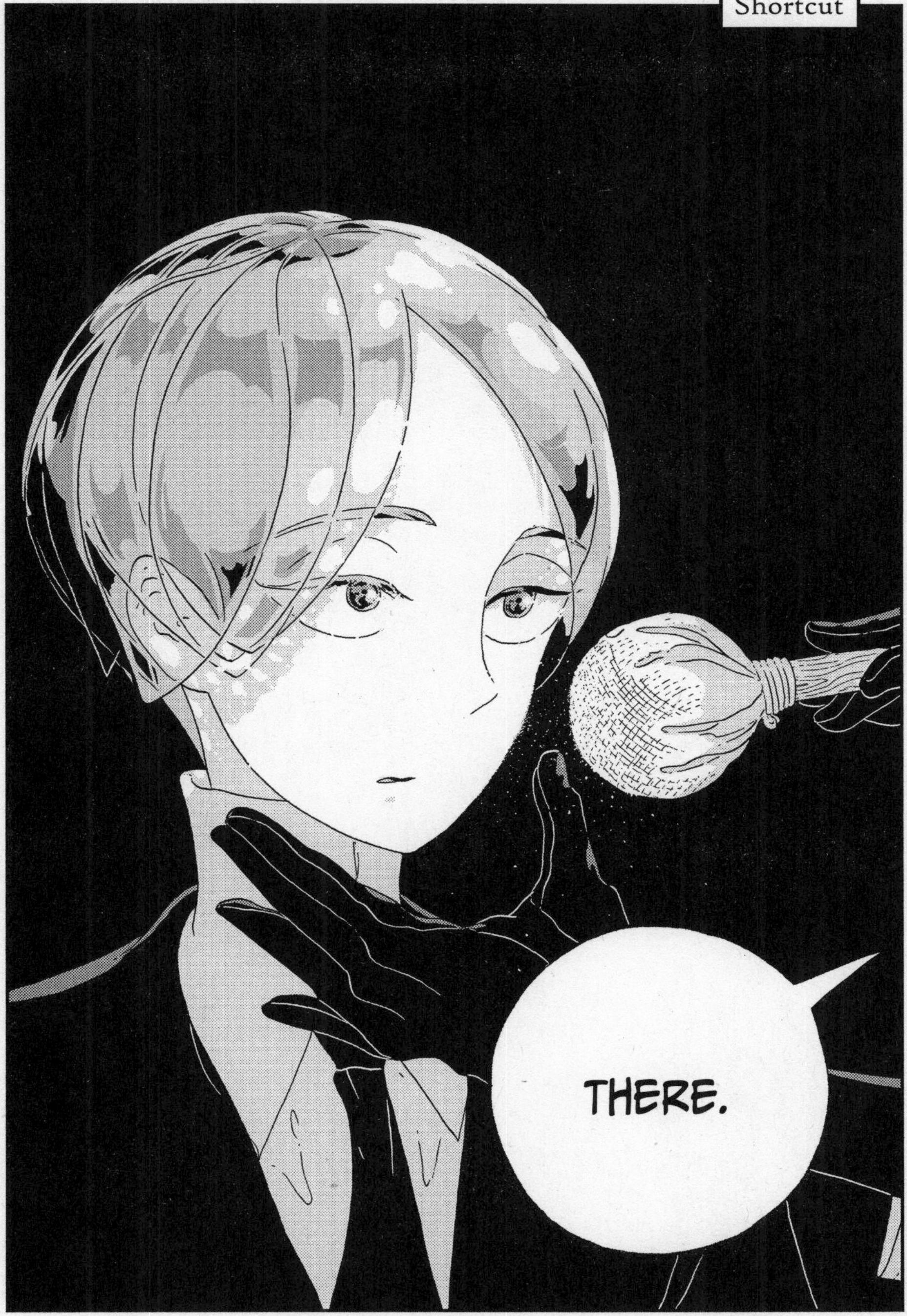
THERE.

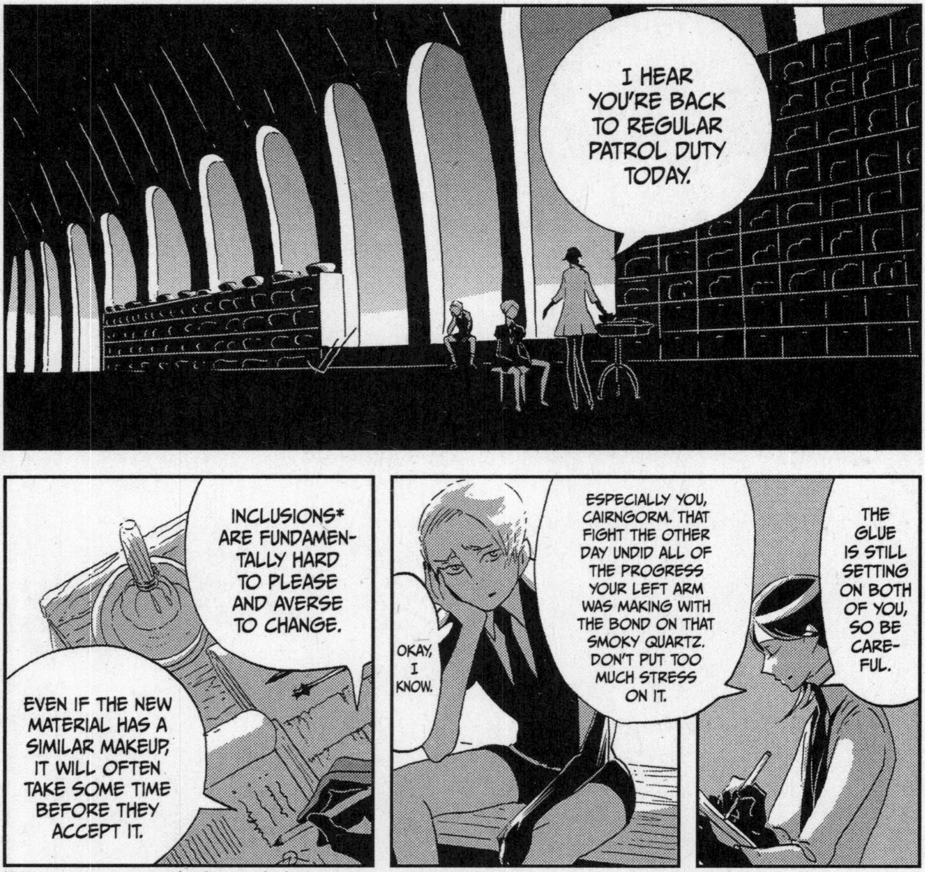
I HEAR YOU'RE BACK TO REGULAR PATROL DUTY TODAY.
THE GLUE IS STILL SETTING ON BOTH OF YOU, SO BE CARE-FUL.
ESPECIALLY YOU, CAIRNGORM. THAT FIGHT THE OTHER DAY UNDID ALL OF THE PROGRESS YOUR LEFT ARM WAS MAKING WITH THE BOND ON THAT SMOKY QUARTZ. DON'T PUT TOO MUCH STRESS ON IT.
OKAY, I KNOW.
INCLUSIONS* ARE FUNDAMEN-TALLY HARD TO PLEASE AND AVERSE TO CHANGE.
EVEN IF THE NEW MATERIAL HAS A SIMILAR MAKEUP, IT WILL OFTEN TAKE SOME TIME BEFORE THEY ACCEPT IT.

*Microscopic organisms that live inside the Lustrous.

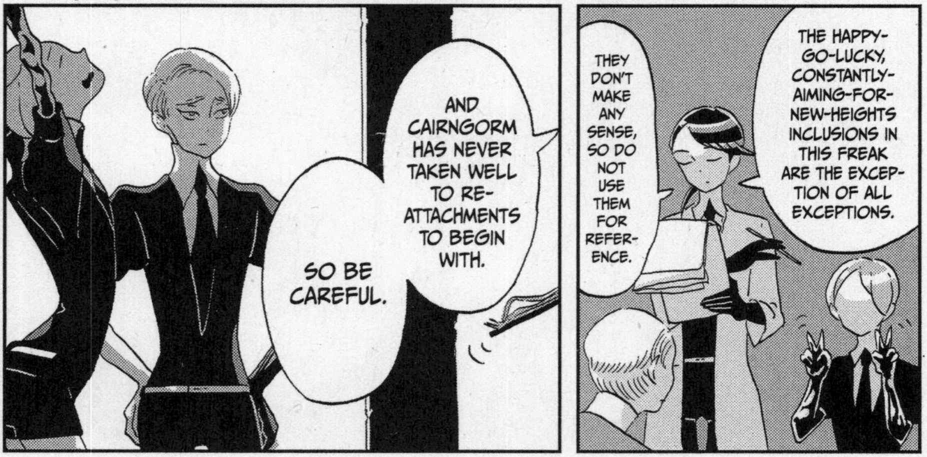
THE HAPPY-GO-LUCKY, CONSTANTLY-AIMING-FOR-NEW-HEIGHTS INCLUSIONS IN THIS FREAK ARE THE EXCEP-TION OF ALL EXCEPTIONS.
THEY DON'T MAKE ANY SENSE, SO DO NOT USE THEM FOR REFER-ENCE.
AND CAIRNGORM HAS NEVER TAKEN WELL TO RE-ATTACHMENTS TO BEGIN WITH.
SO BE CAREFUL.

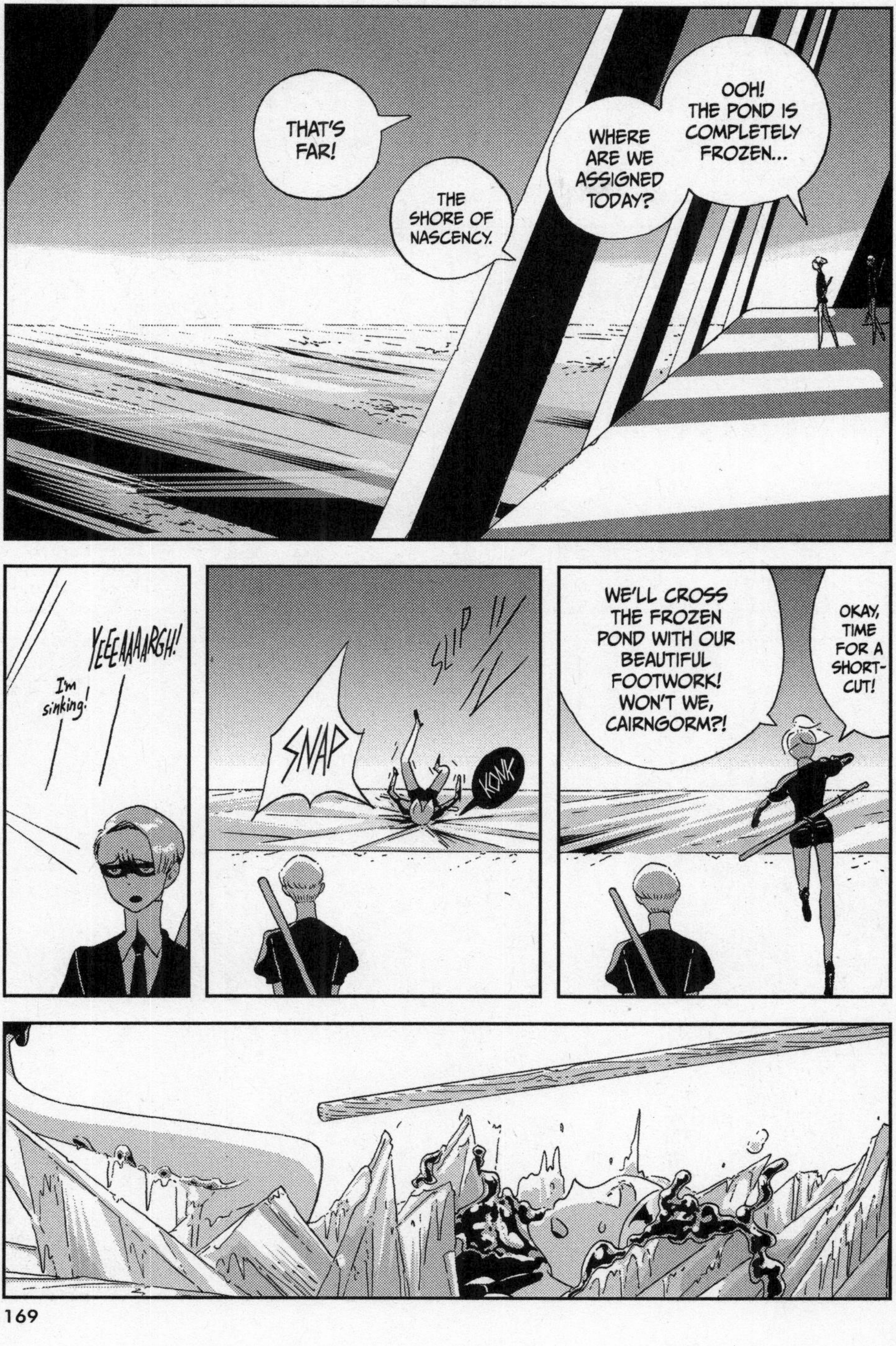
OOH! THE POND IS COMPLETELY FROZEN...
WHERE ARE WE ASSIGNED TODAY?
THE SHORE OF NASCENCY.
THAT'S FAR!
OKAY, TIME FOR A SHORT-CUT!
WE'LL CROSS THE FROZEN POND WITH OUR BEAUTIFUL FOOTWORK! WON'T WE, CAIRNGORM?!
SLIP
SNAP
KONK
YEEEAAAARGH!
I'm sinking!

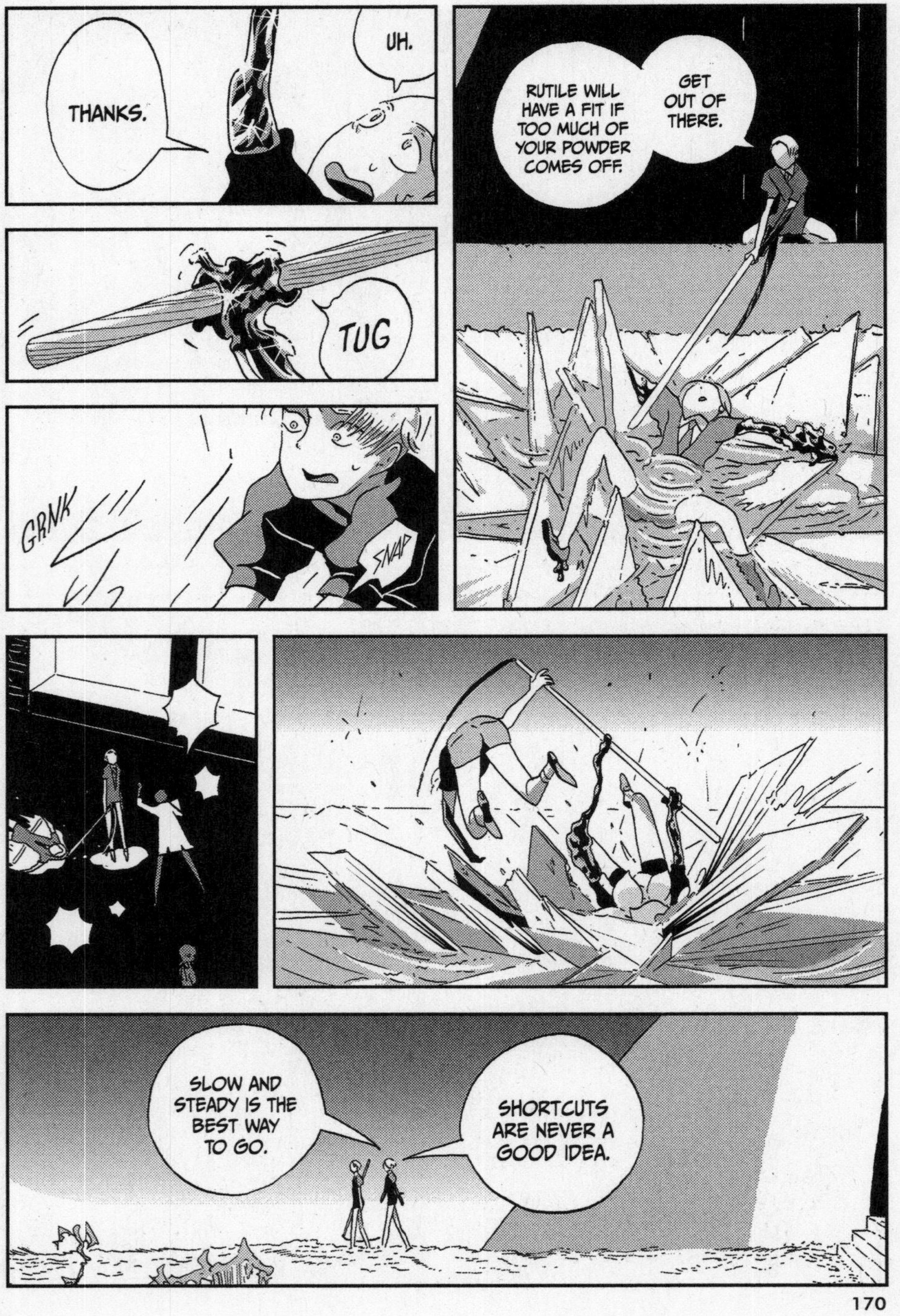
GET OUT OF THERE.
RUTILE WILL HAVE A FIT IF TOO MUCH OF YOUR POWDER COMES OFF.
UH.
THANKS.
TUG
SNAP
GRNK
SHORTCUTS ARE NEVER A GOOD IDEA.
SLOW AND STEADY IS THE BEST WAY TO GO.

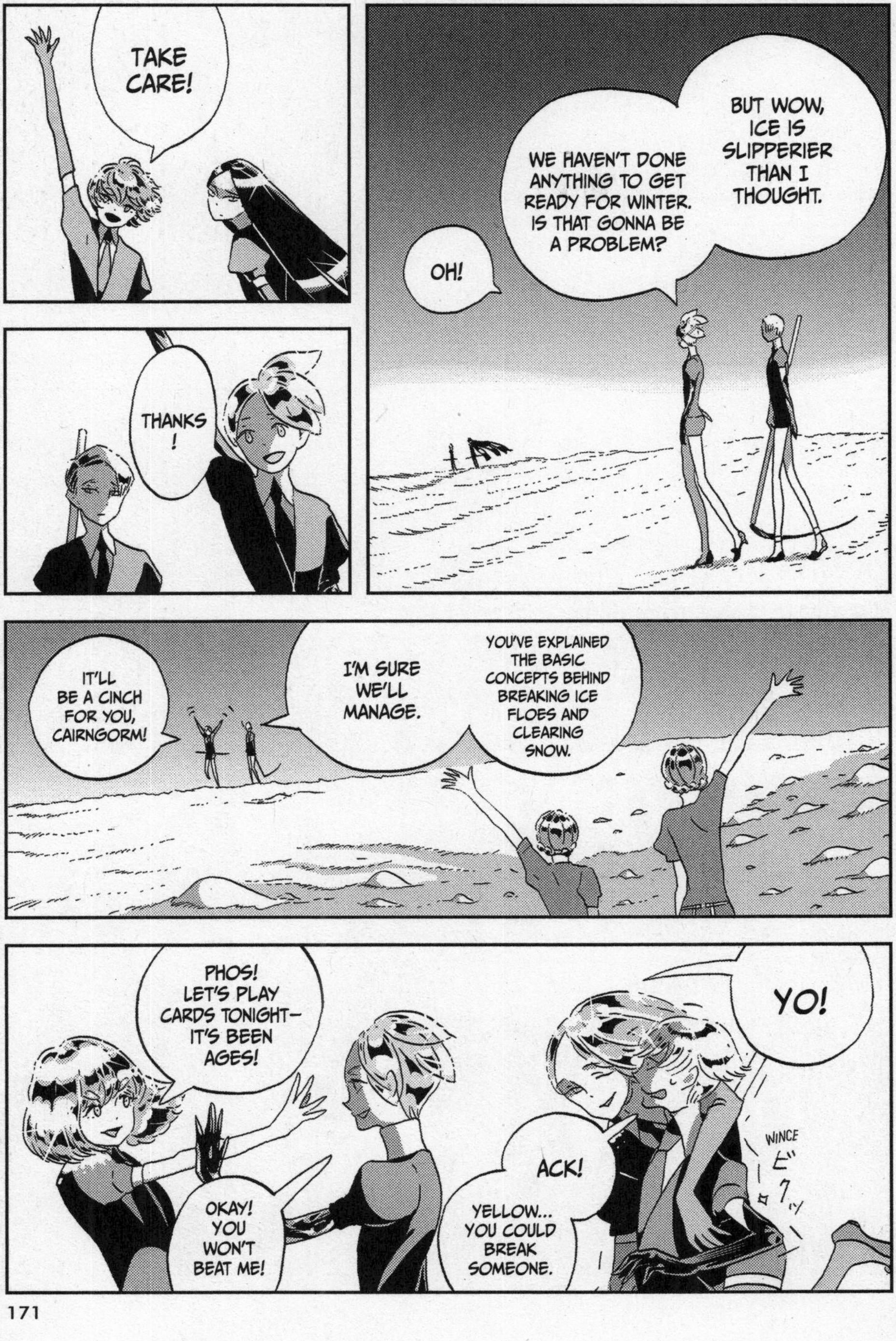
BUT WOW, ICE IS SLIPPERIER THAN I THOUGHT.
WE HAVEN'T DONE ANYTHING TO GET READY FOR WINTER. IS THAT GONNA BE A PROBLEM?
OH!
TAKE CARE!
THANKS!
YOU'VE EXPLAINED THE BASIC CONCEPTS BEHIND BREAKING ICE FLOES AND CLEARING SNOW.
I'M SURE WE'LL MANAGE.
IT'LL BE A CINCH FOR YOU, CAIRNGORM!
YO!
WINCE
ビクッ
ACK!
YELLOW... YOU COULD BREAK SOMEONE.
PHOS! LET'S PLAY CARDS TONIGHT—IT'S BEEN AGES!
OKAY! YOU WON'T BEAT ME!

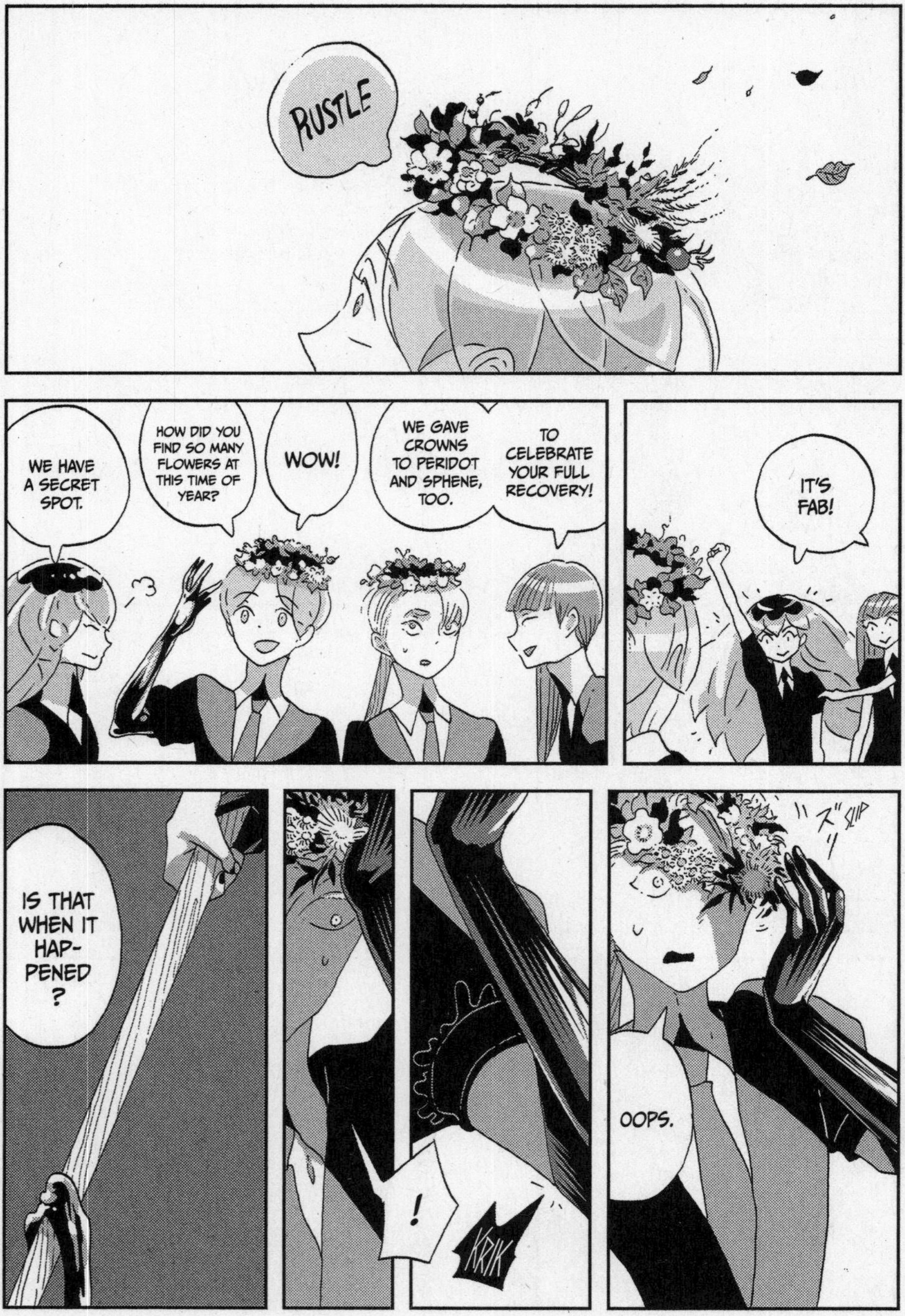
RUSTLE
IT'S FAB!
TO CELEBRATE YOUR FULL RECOVERY!
WE GAVE CROWNS TO PERIDOT AND SPHENE, TOO.
WOW!
HOW DID YOU FIND SO MANY FLOWERS AT THIS TIME OF YEAR?
WE HAVE A SECRET SPOT.
SLIP
OOPS.
KRIK
!
IS THAT WHEN IT HAP-PENED?

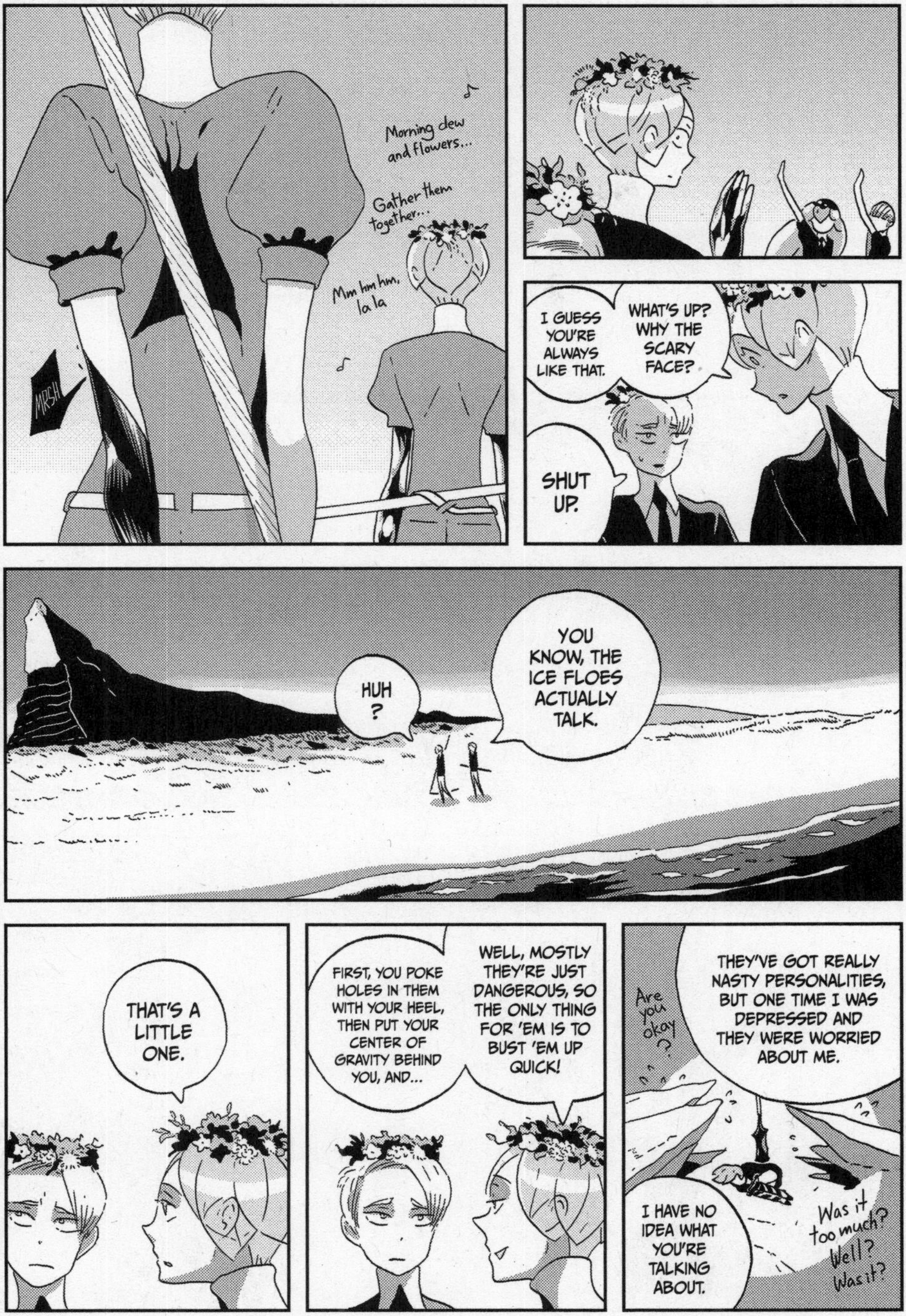
WHAT'S UP? WHY THE SCARY FACE?
I GUESS YOU'RE ALWAYS LIKE THAT.
SHUT UP.
Morning dew and flowers...
Gather them together...
Mm hm hm, la la
MRSH
YOU KNOW, THE ICE FLOES ACTUALLY TALK.
HUH?
THEY'VE GOT REALLY NASTY PERSONALITIES, BUT ONE TIME I WAS DEPRESSED AND THEY WERE WORRIED ABOUT ME.
Are you okay?
Was it too much? Well? Was it?
I HAVE NO IDEA WHAT YOU'RE TALKING ABOUT.
WELL, MOSTLY THEY'RE JUST DANGEROUS, SO THE ONLY THING FOR 'EM IS TO BUST 'EM UP QUICK!
FIRST, YOU POKE HOLES IN THEM WITH YOUR HEEL, THEN PUT YOUR CENTER OF GRAVITY BEHIND YOU, AND...
THAT'S A LITTLE ONE.

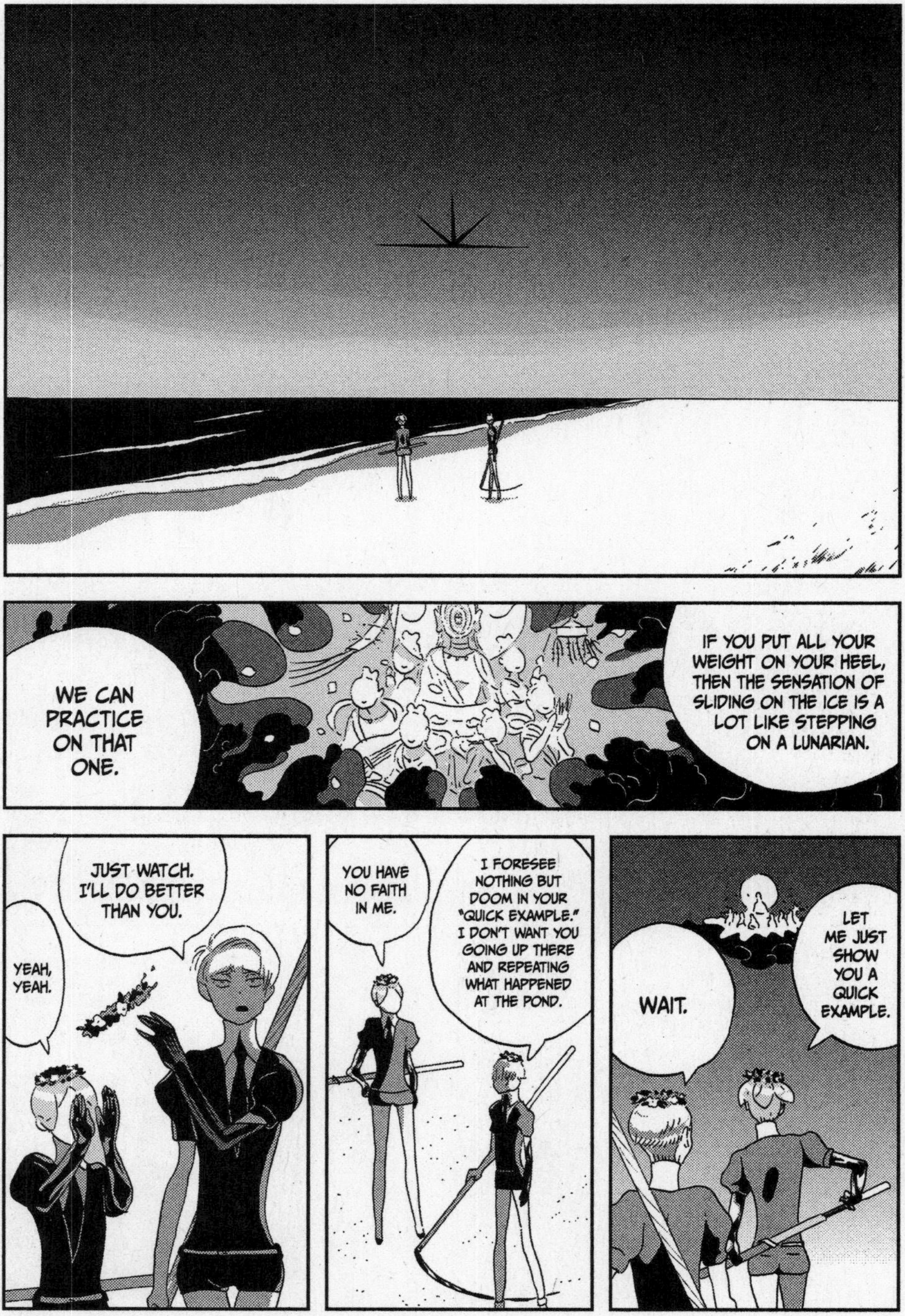
IF YOU PUT ALL YOUR WEIGHT ON YOUR HEEL, THEN THE SENSATION OF SLIDING ON THE ICE IS A LOT LIKE STEPPING ON A LUNARIAN.
WE CAN PRACTICE ON THAT ONE.
LET ME JUST SHOW YOU A QUICK EXAMPLE.
WAIT.
I FORESEE NOTHING BUT DOOM IN YOUR "QUICK EXAMPLE." I DON'T WANT YOU GOING UP THERE AND REPEATING WHAT HAPPENED AT THE POND.
YOU HAVE NO FAITH IN ME.
JUST WATCH. I'LL DO BETTER THAN YOU.
YEAH, YEAH.

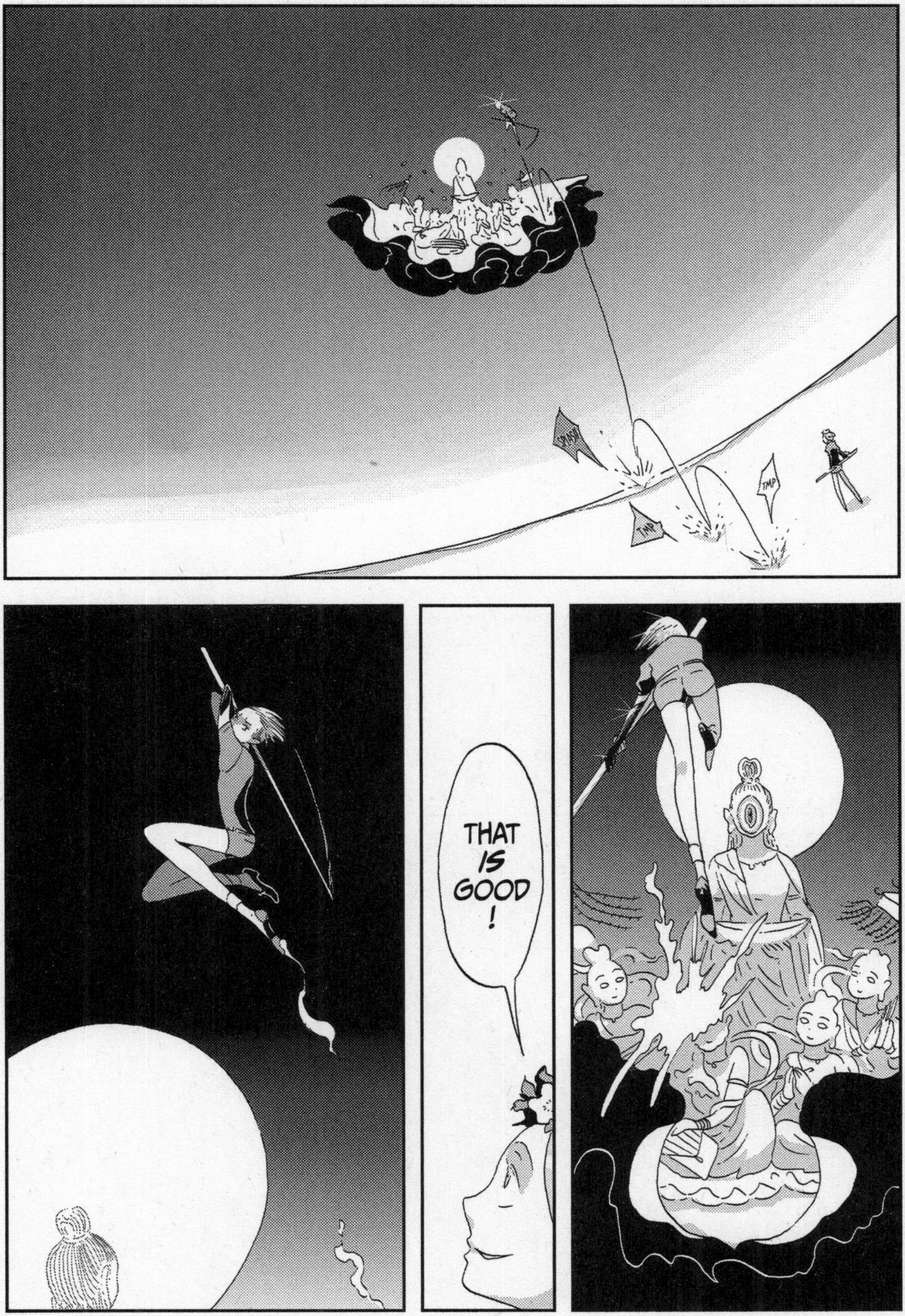
SPLASH
TMP
TMP
THAT IS GOOD !

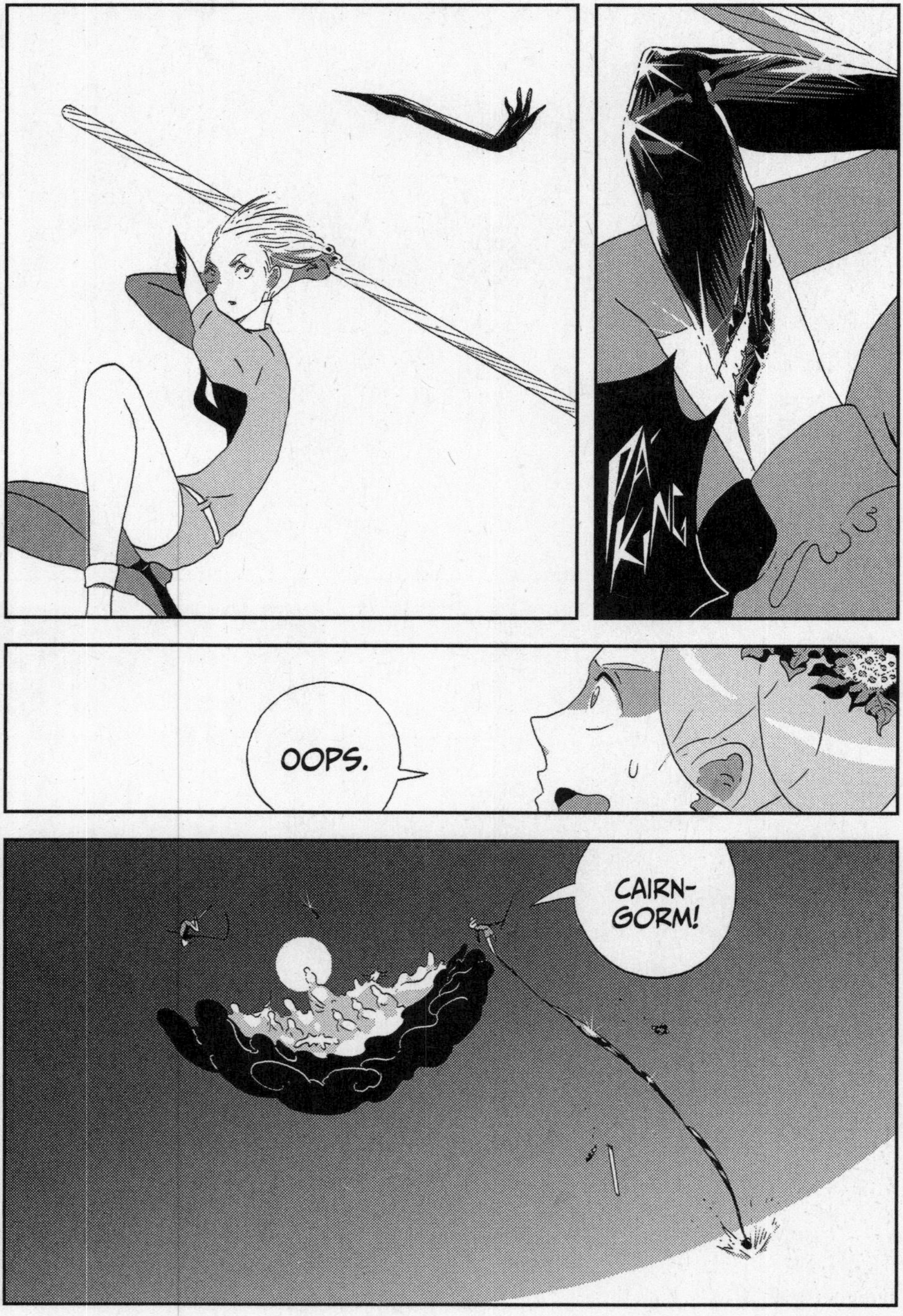
PAKING
OOPS.
CAIRN-GORM!

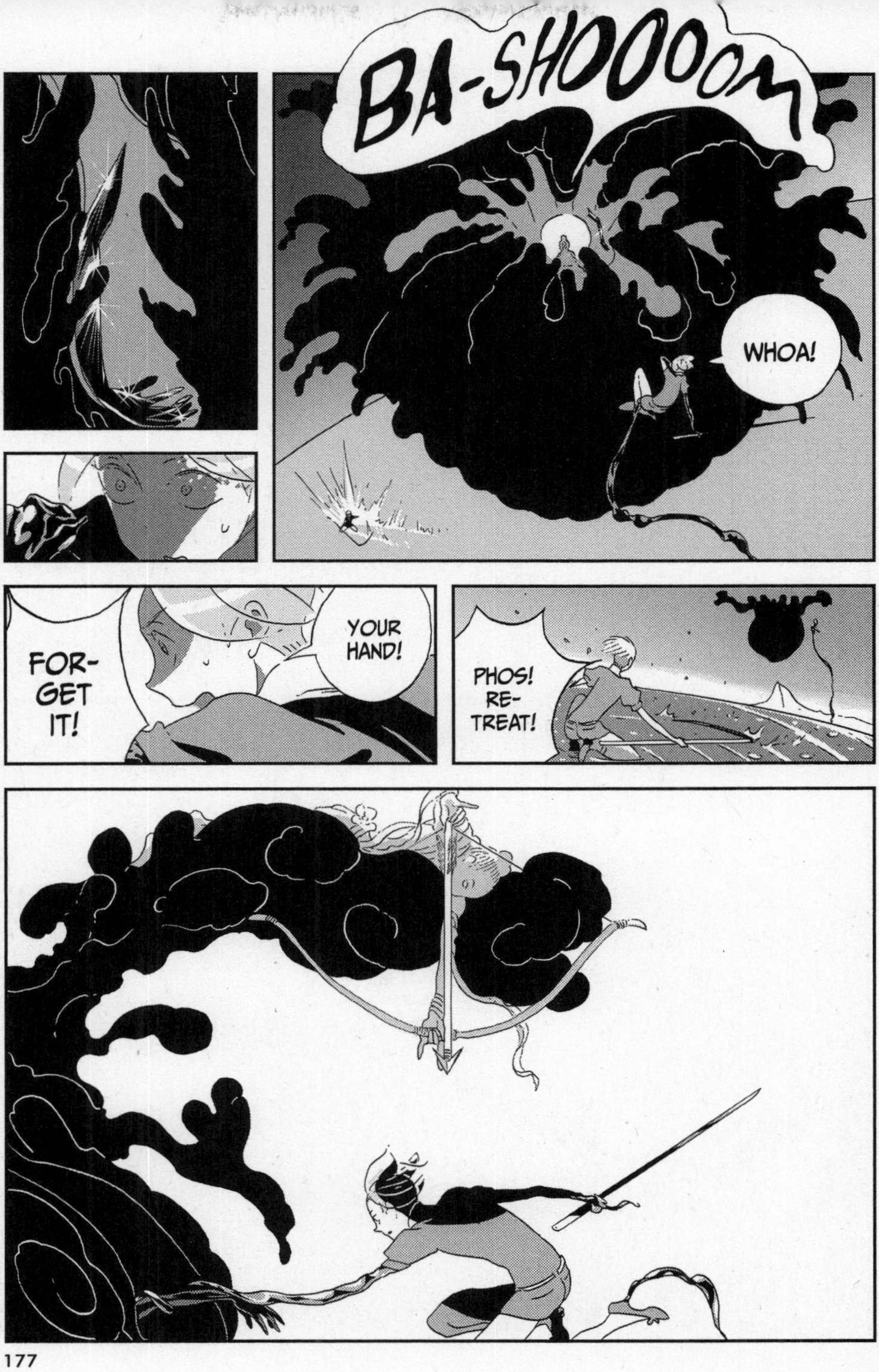
BA-SHOOOOM
WHOA!
PHOS! RE-TREAT!
YOUR HAND!
FOR-GET IT!

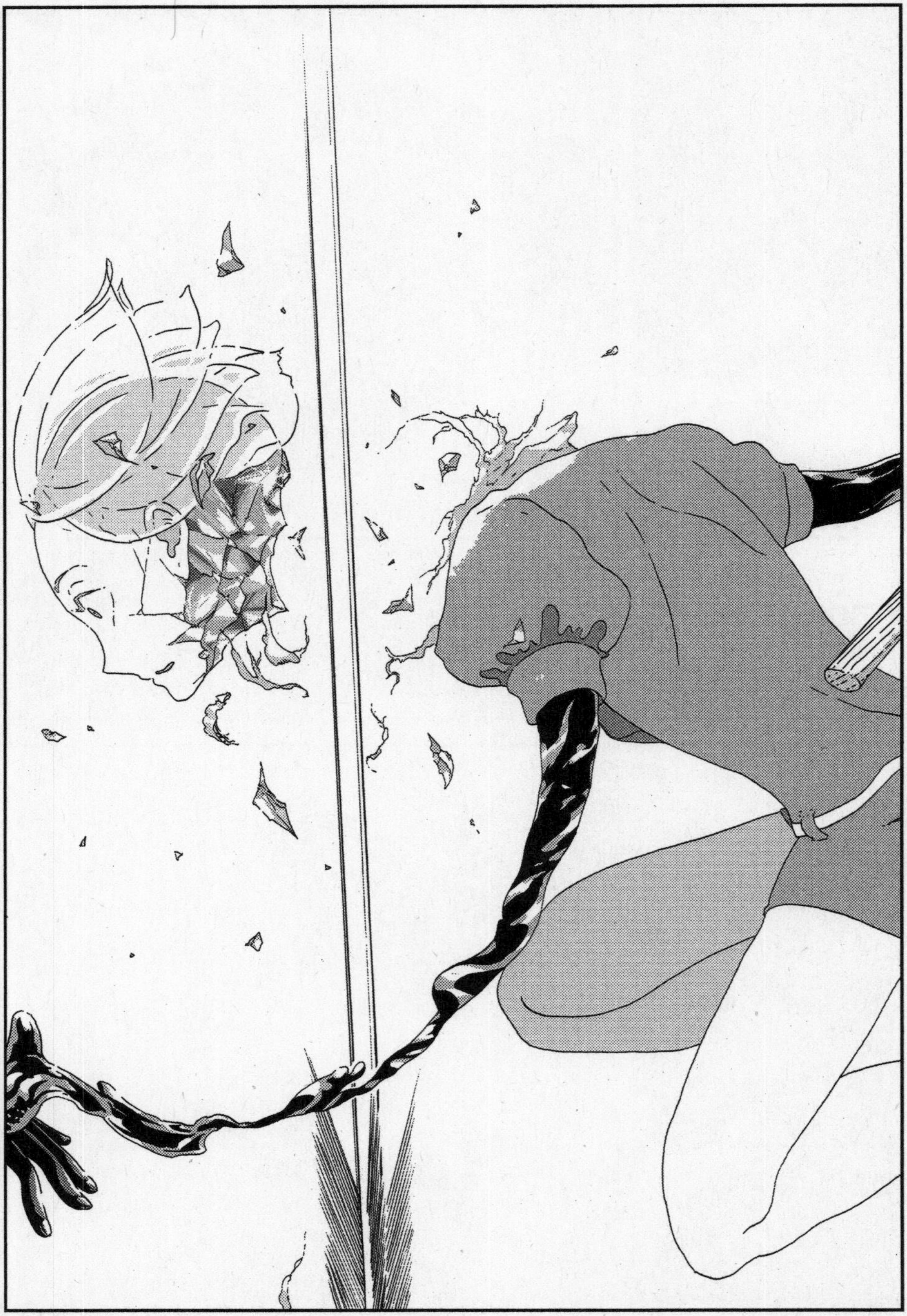

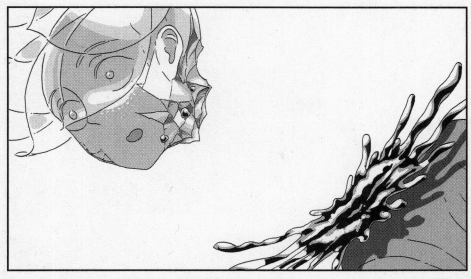

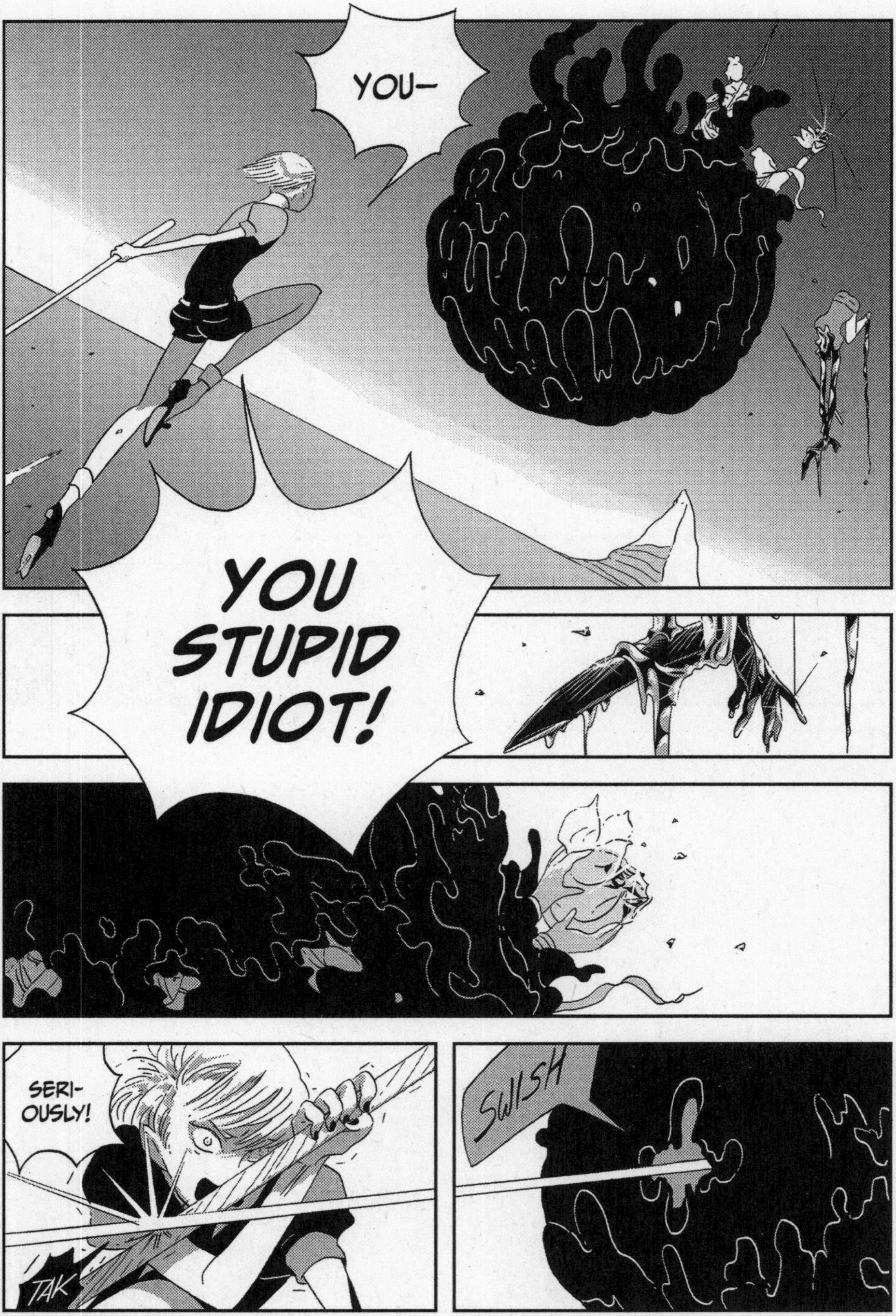
YOU–
YOU STUPID IDIOT!
SWISH
SERI-OUSLY!
TAK

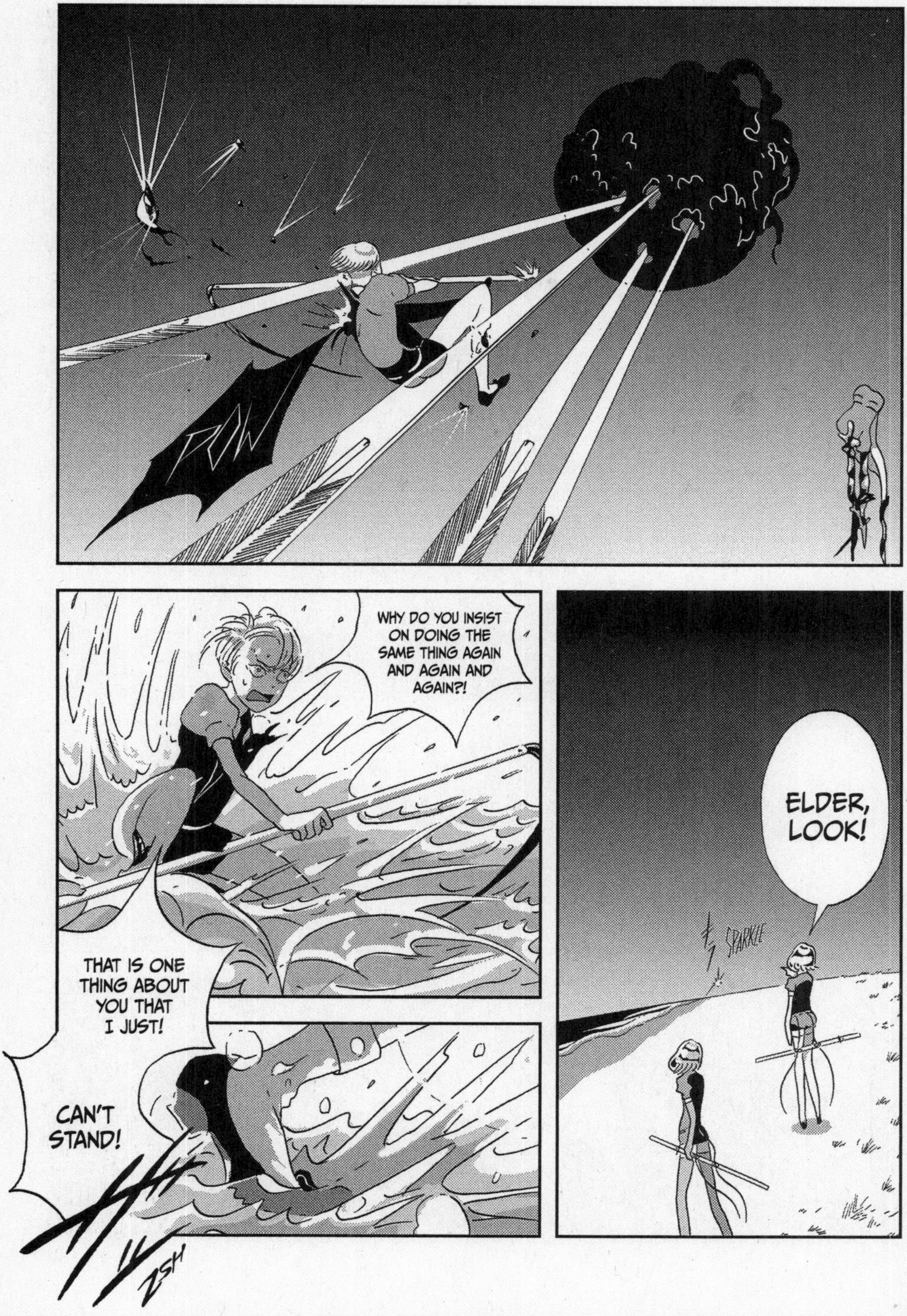
POW
ELDER, LOOK!
SPARKLE
WHY DO YOU INSIST ON DOING THE SAME THING AGAIN AND AGAIN AND AGAIN?!
THAT IS ONE THING ABOUT YOU THAT I JUST!
CAN'T STAND!
ZSH

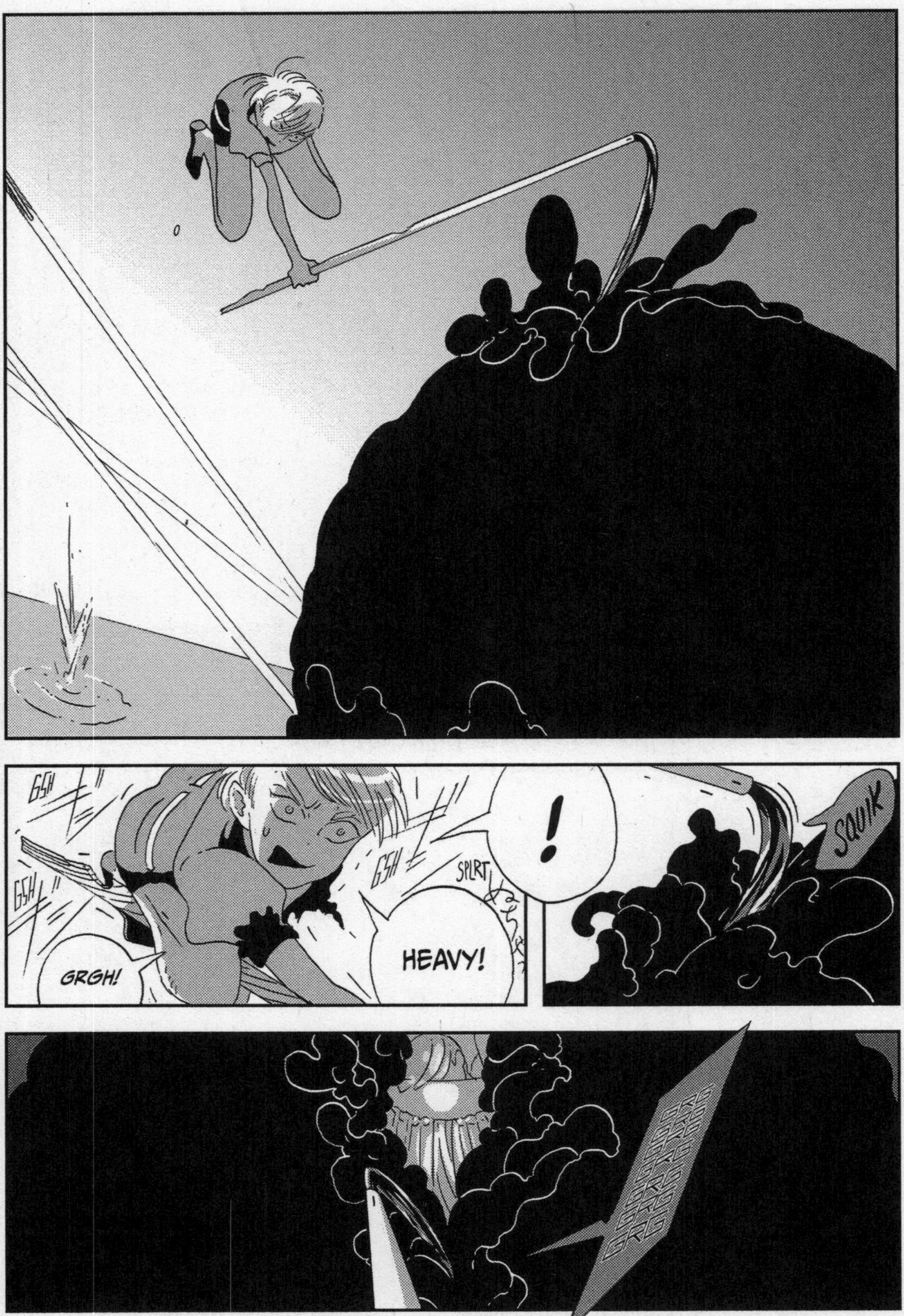
SQUIK
!
SPLRT
GSH
HEAVY!
GSH
GSH
GRGH!

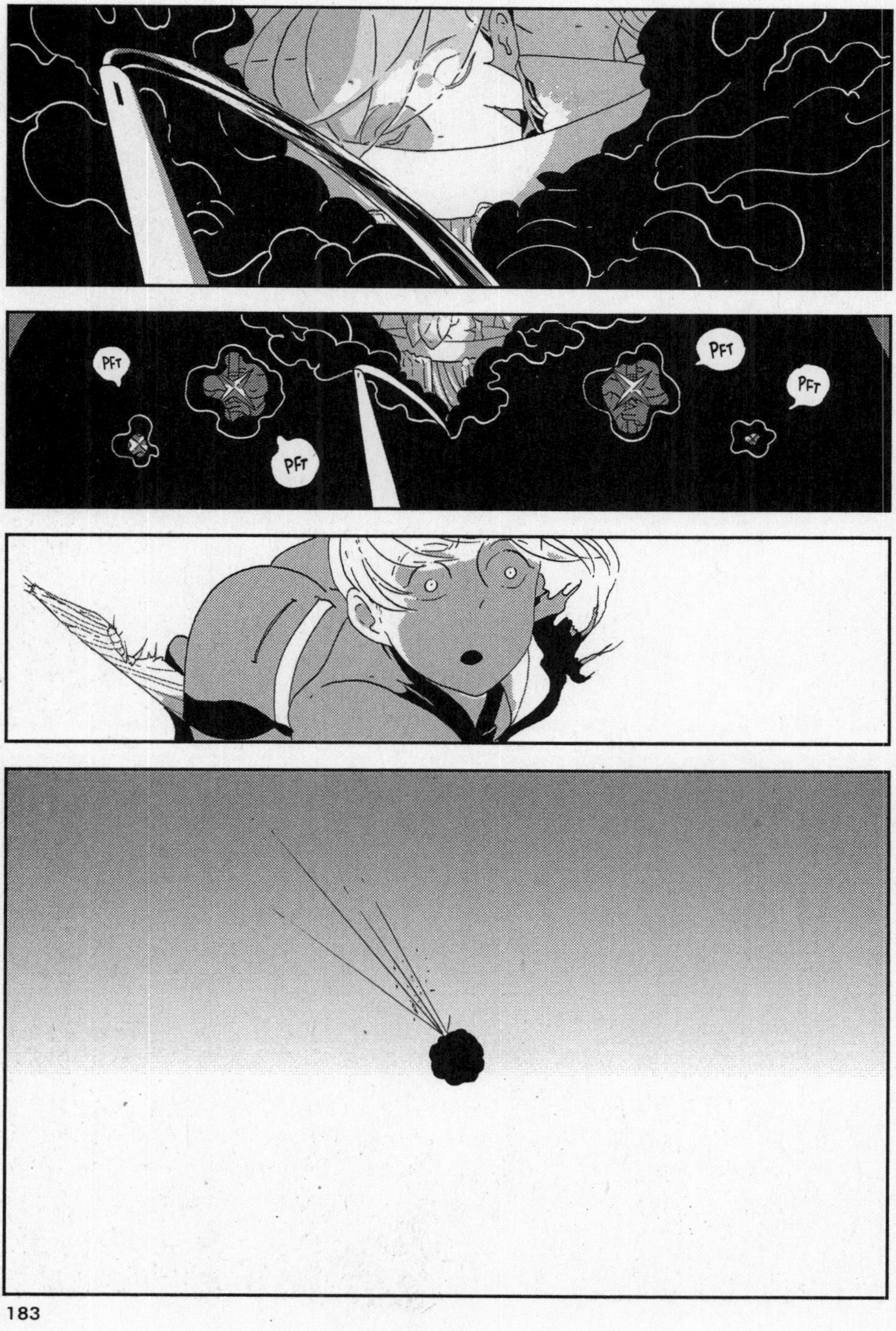
PFT
PFT
PFT
PFT
PFT

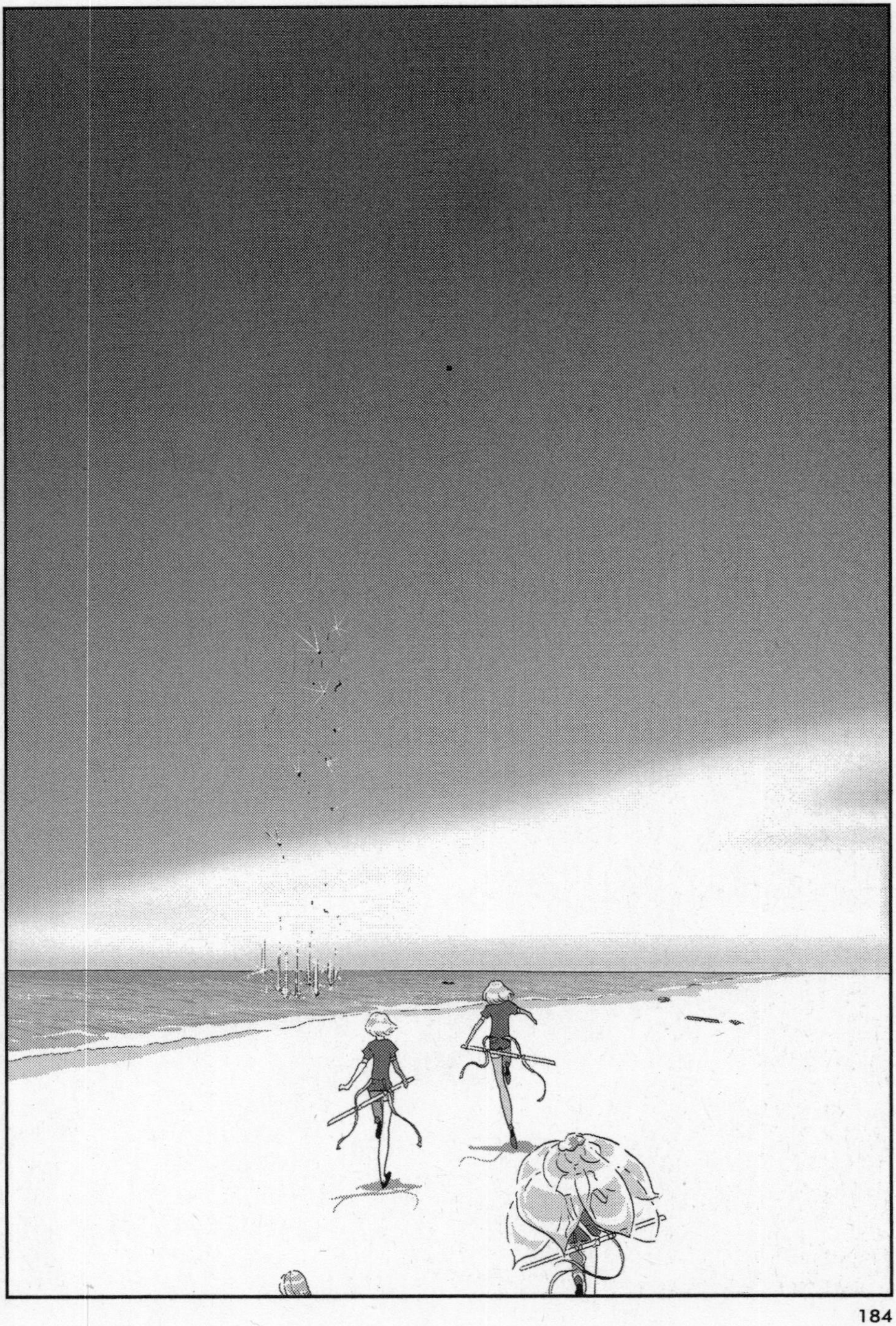

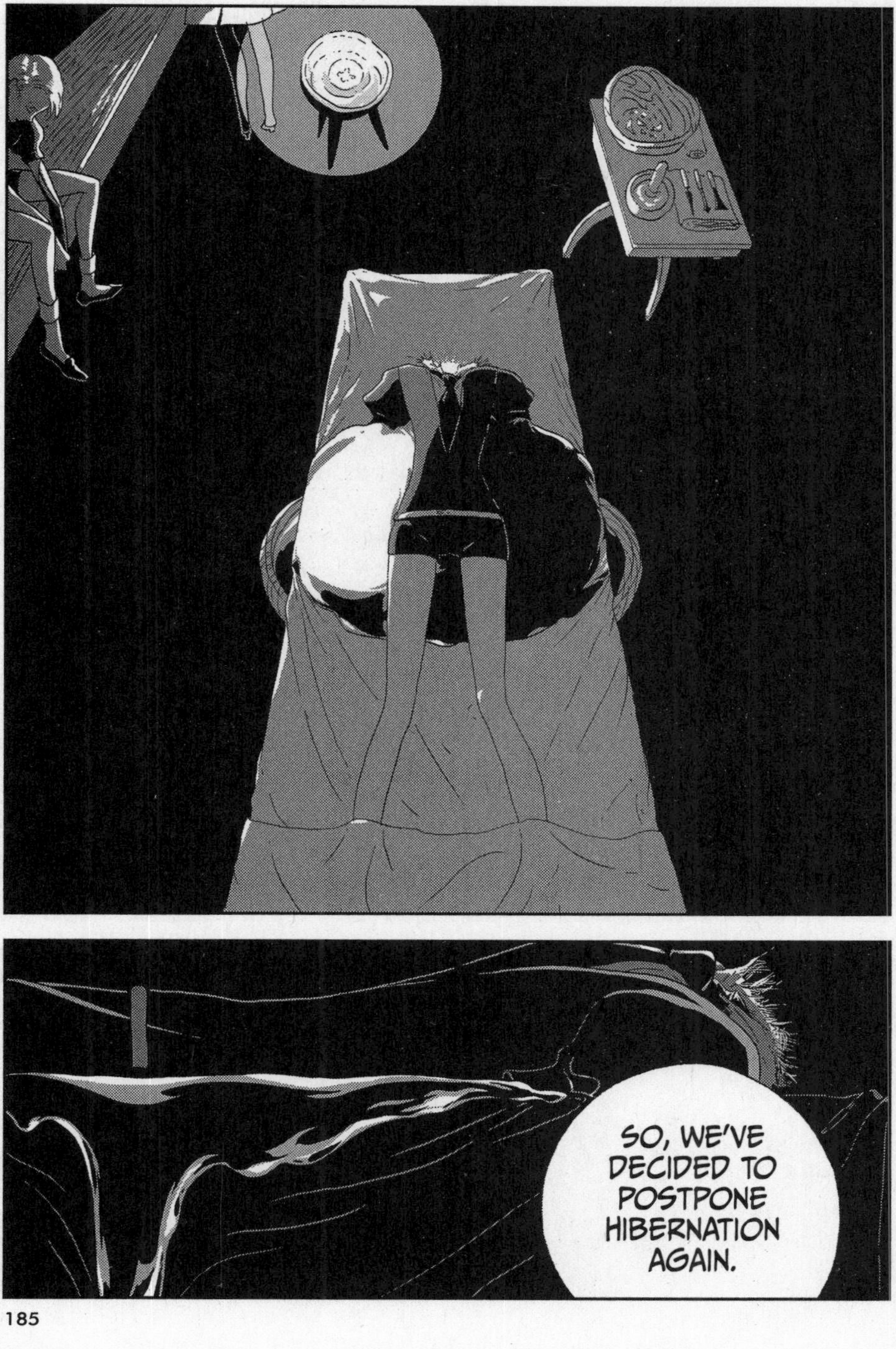
SO, WE'VE DECIDED TO POSTPONE HIBERNATION AGAIN.

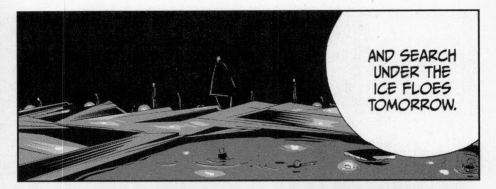

AND SEARCH UNDER THE ICE FLOES TOMORROW.
I HOPE WE CAN FIND SOME PART OF THE HEAD, EVEN A FEW SLIVERS.
I THINK WE'RE WASTING OUR TIME.
I SAW THE LUNARIANS GET A TIGHT GRIP ON IT.
I GUESS
WE'LL NEED A NEW HEAD.

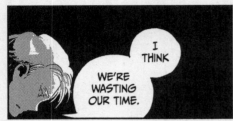

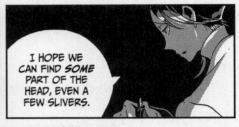

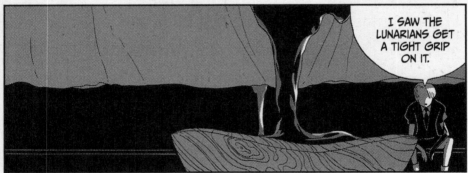

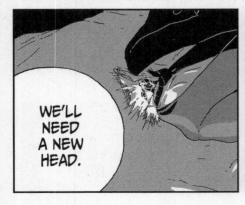

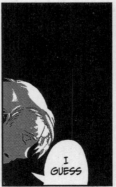

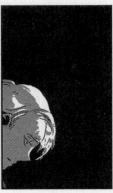

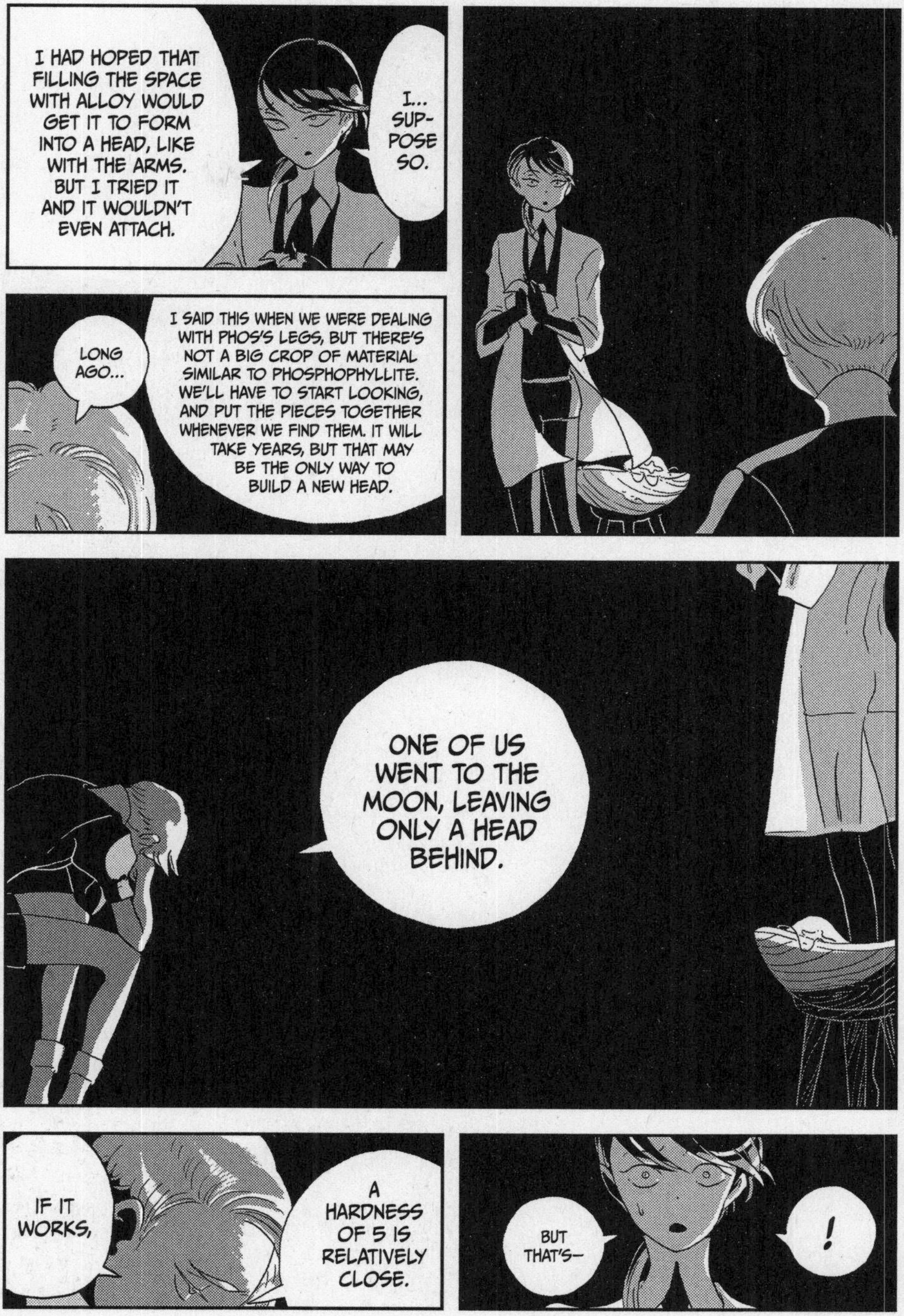

I... SUP-POSE SO.
I HAD HOPED THAT FILLING THE SPACE WITH ALLOY WOULD GET IT TO FORM INTO A HEAD, LIKE WITH THE ARMS. BUT I TRIED IT AND IT WOULDN'T EVEN ATTACH.
I SAID THIS WHEN WE WERE DEALING WITH PHOS'S LEGS, BUT THERE'S NOT A BIG CROP OF MATERIAL SIMILAR TO PHOSPHOPHYLLITE. WE'LL HAVE TO START LOOKING, AND PUT THE PIECES TOGETHER WHENEVER WE FIND THEM. IT WILL TAKE YEARS, BUT THAT MAY BE THE ONLY WAY TO BUILD A NEW HEAD.
LONG AGO...
ONE OF US WENT TO THE MOON, LEAVING ONLY A HEAD BEHIND.
!
BUT THAT'S—
A HARDNESS OF 5 IS RELATIVELY CLOSE.
IF IT WORKS,

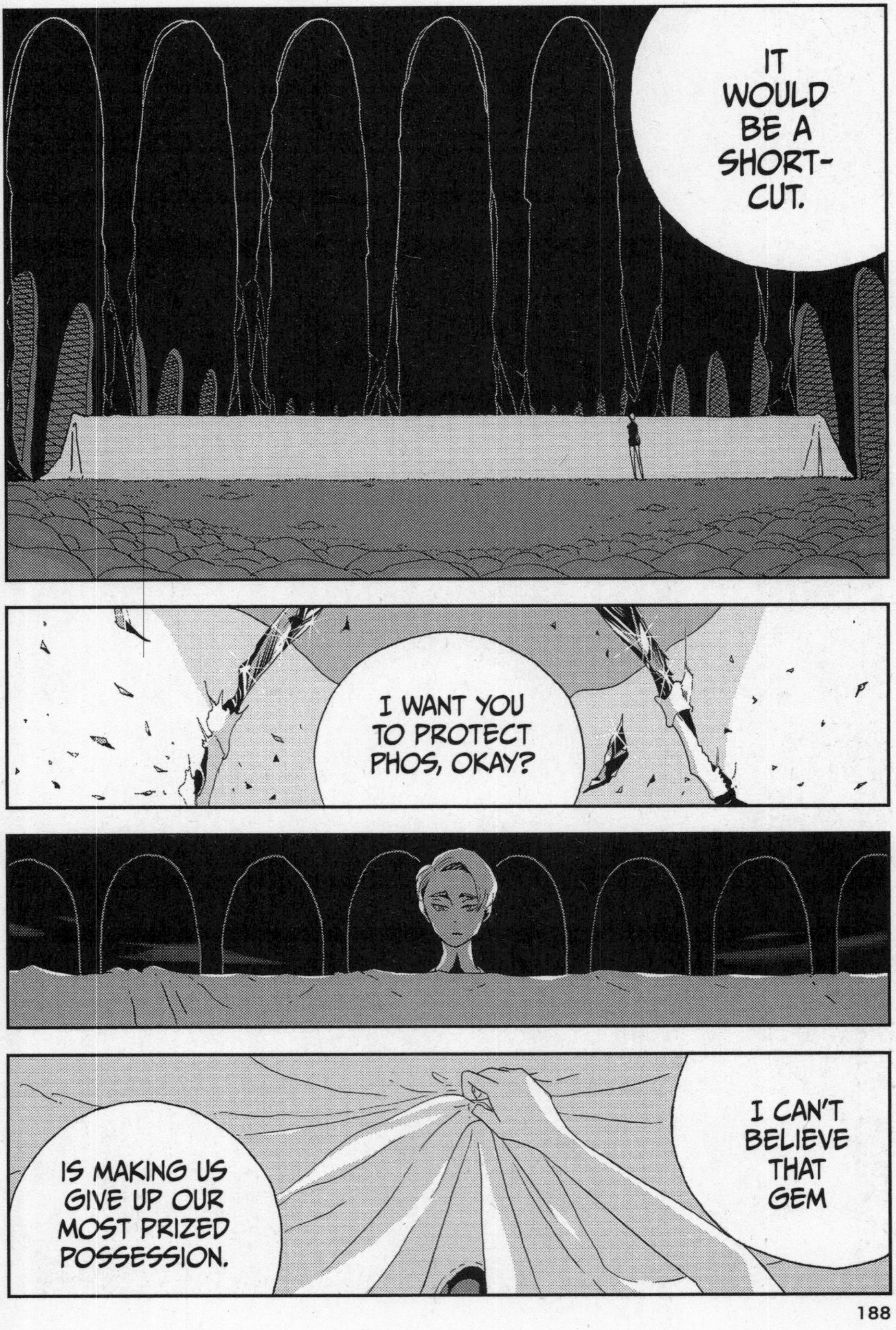
IT WOULD BE A SHORT-CUT.
I WANT YOU TO PROTECT PHOS, OKAY?
I CAN'T BELIEVE THAT GEM
IS MAKING US GIVE UP OUR MOST PRIZED POSSESSION.

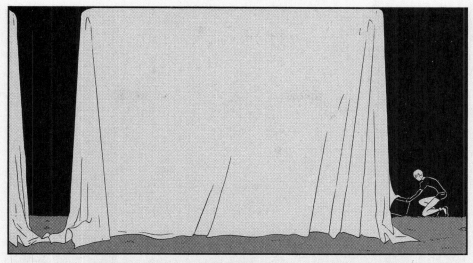

I'M
SORRY.

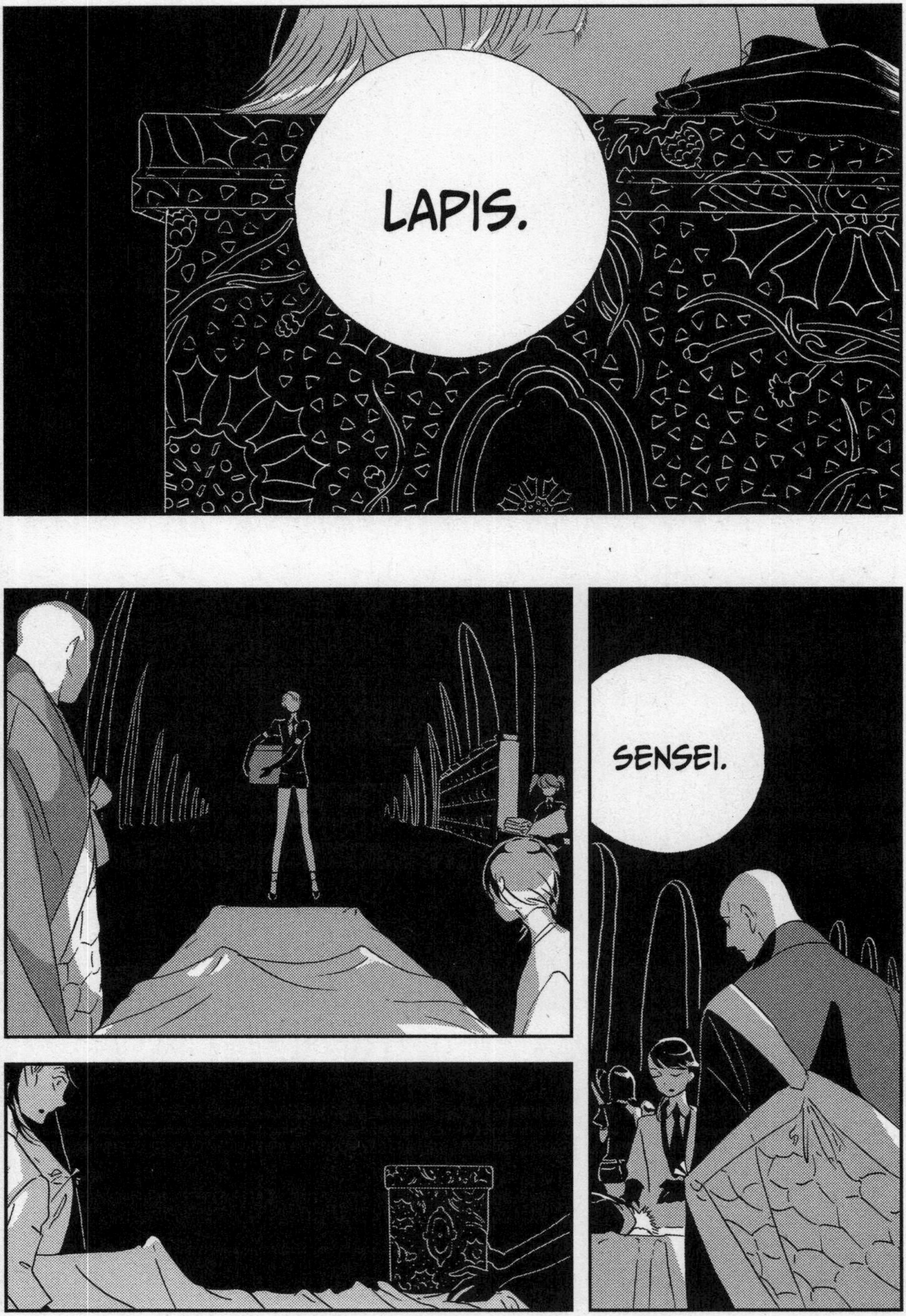
LAPIS.
SENSEI.

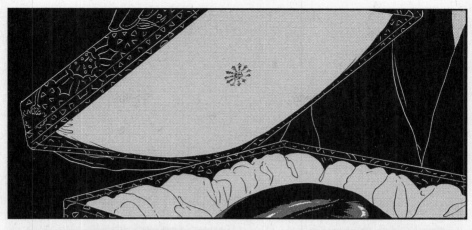

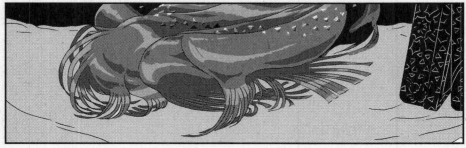

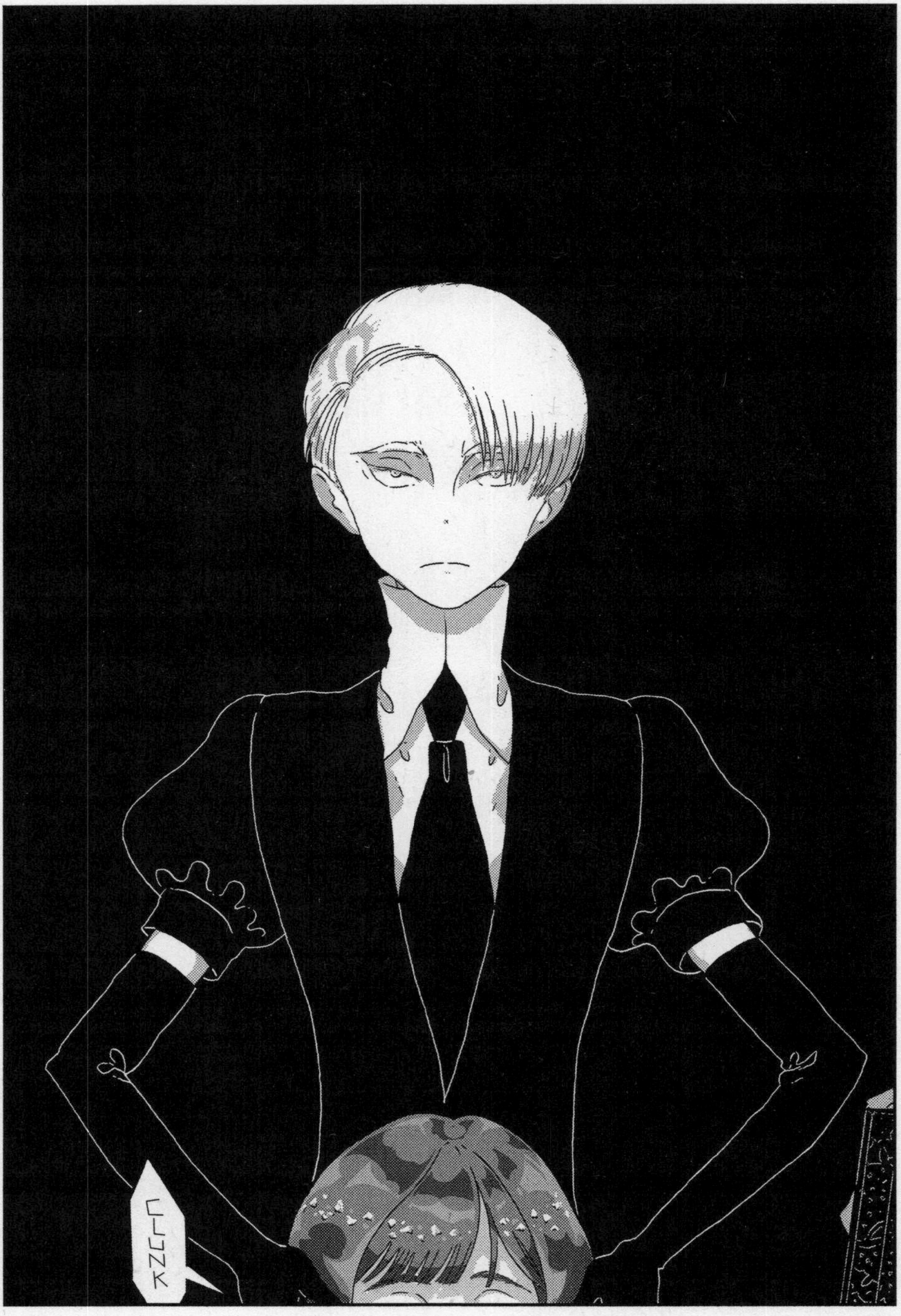
CLUNK

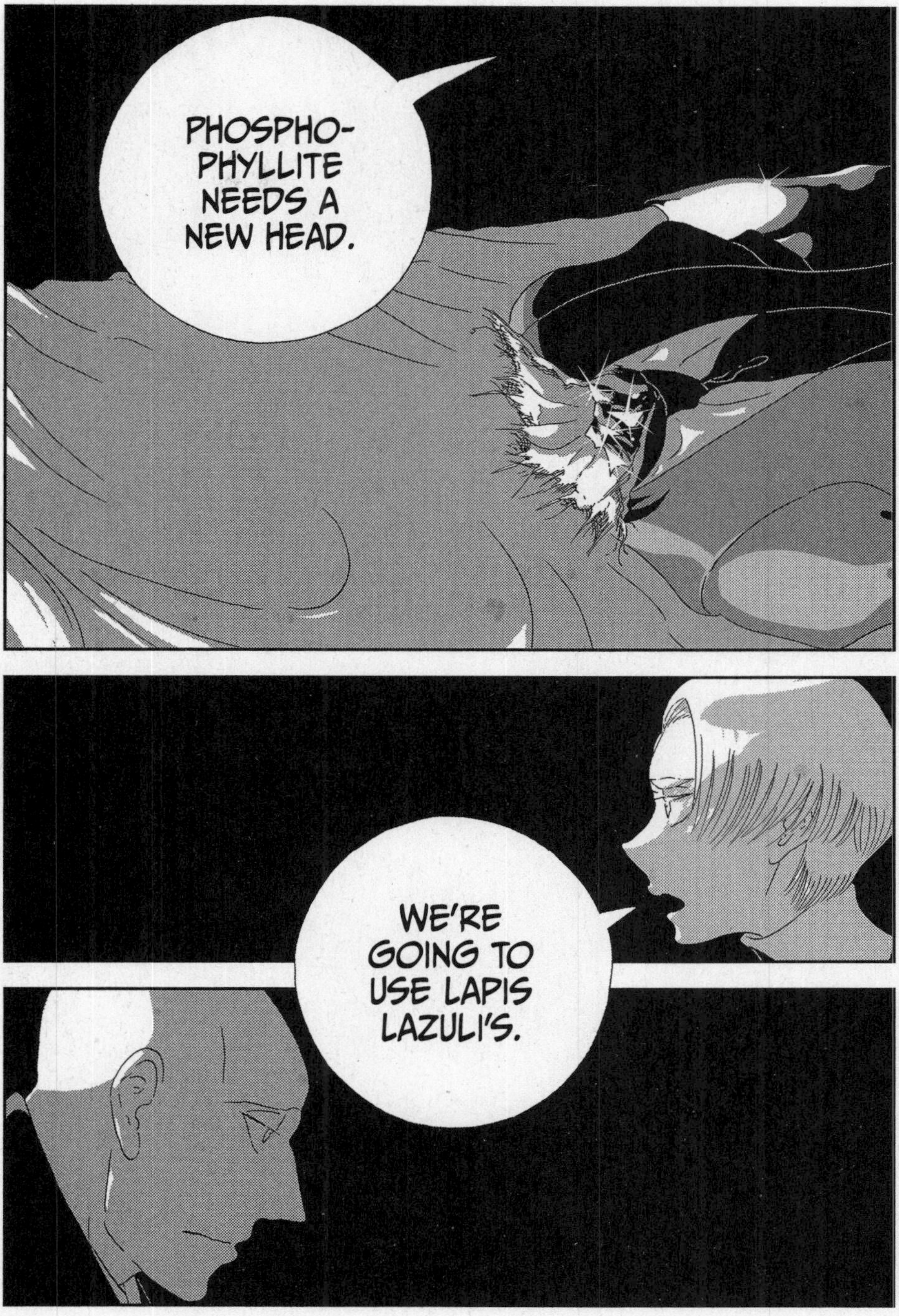
PHOSPHO-PHYLLITE NEEDS A NEW HEAD.
WE'RE GOING TO USE LAPIS LAZULI'S.

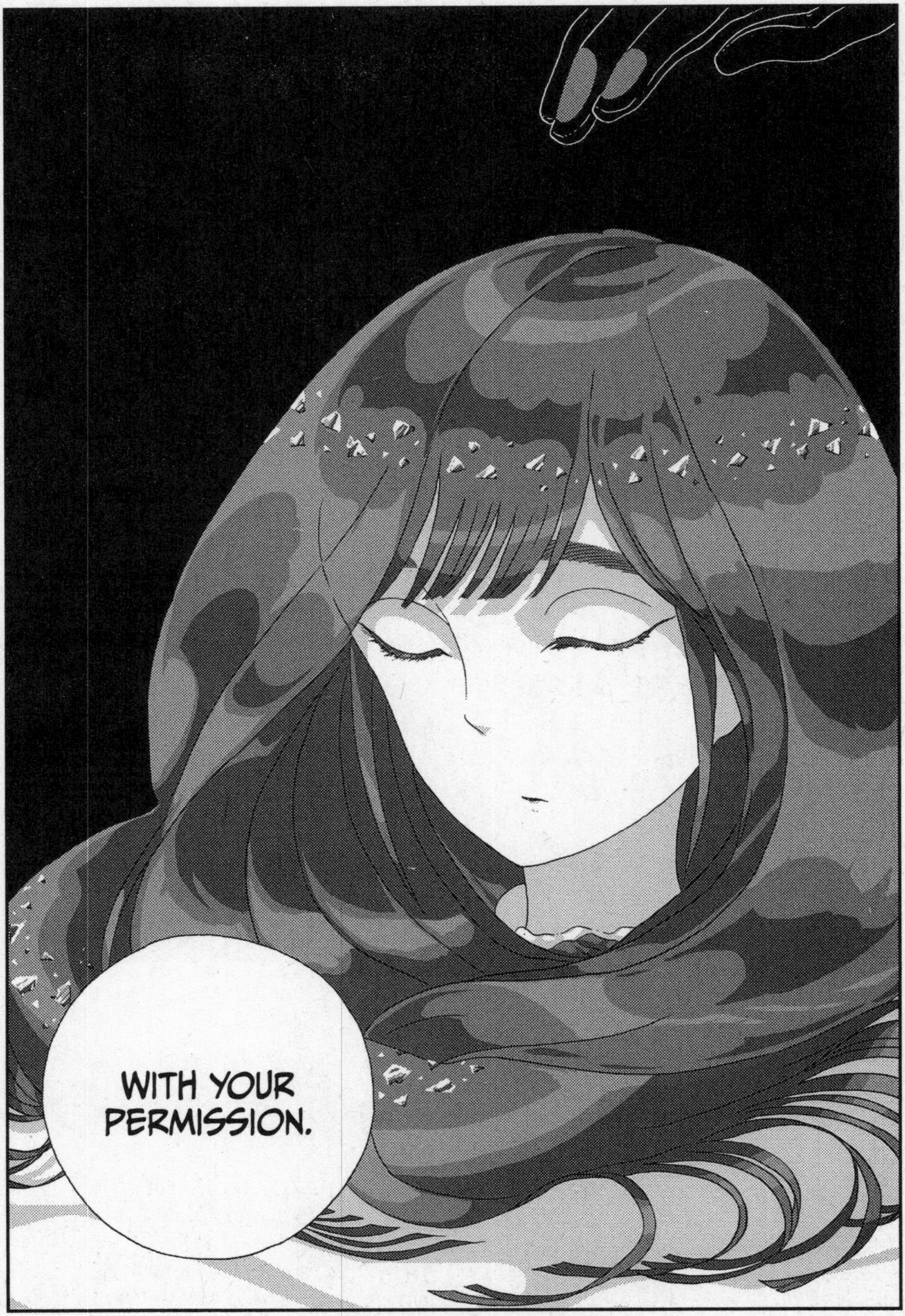
WITH YOUR PERMISSION.

CHAPTER 44: Shortcut END

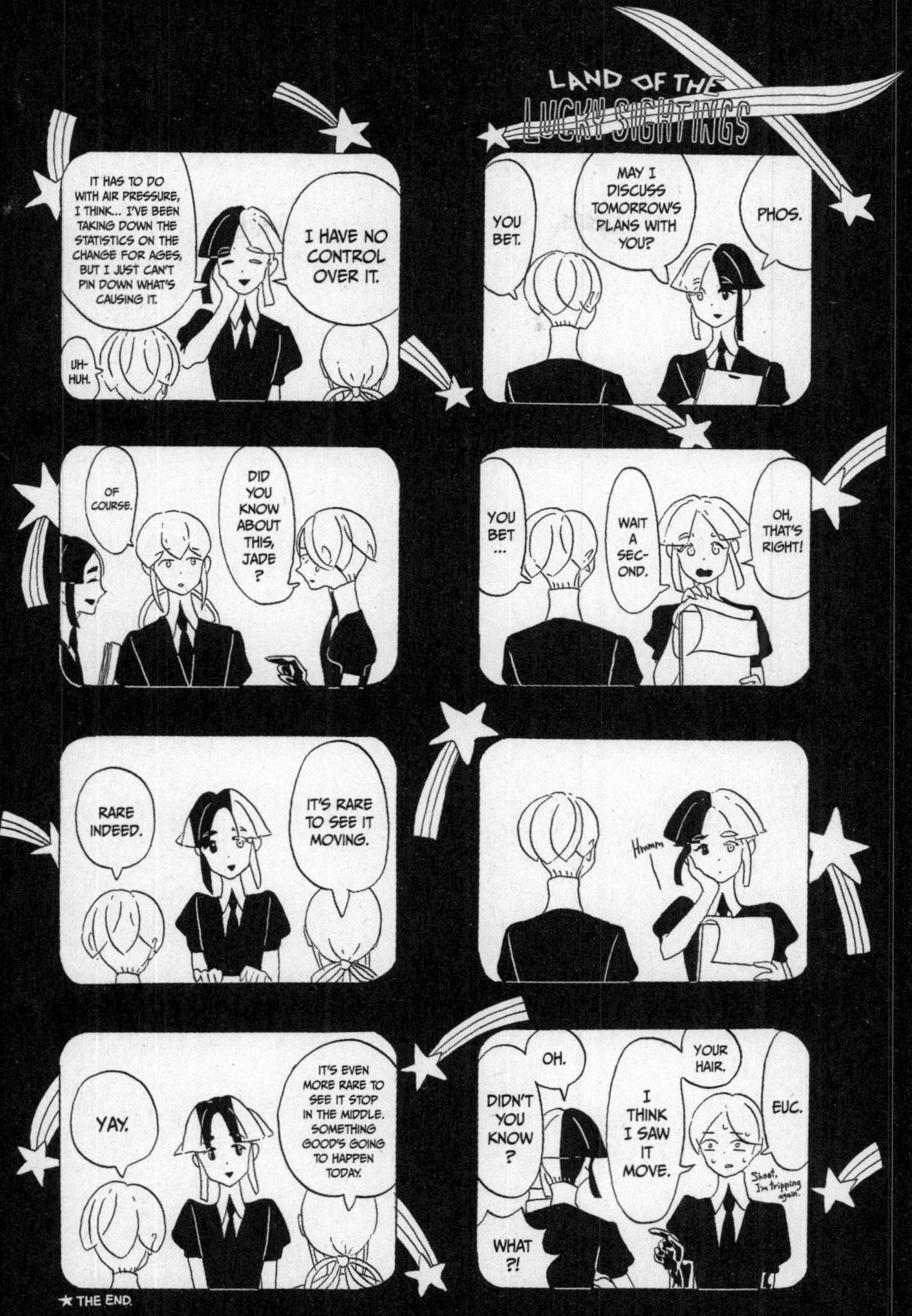
LAND OF THE LUCKY SIGHTINGS
PHOS.
MAY I DISCUSS TOMORROW'S PLANS WITH YOU?
YOU BET.
OH, THAT'S RIGHT!
WAIT A SEC- OND.
YOU BET ...
Hmmm
EUC.
YOUR HAIR.
I THINK I SAW IT MOVE.
OH.
DIDN'T YOU KNOW ?
Shoot, I'm tripping again.
WHAT ?!
I HAVE NO CONTROL OVER IT.
IT HAS TO DO WITH AIR PRESSURE, I THINK... I'VE BEEN TAKING DOWN THE STATISTICS ON THE CHANGE FOR AGES, BUT I JUST CAN'T PIN DOWN WHAT'S CAUSING IT.
UH-HUH.
DID YOU KNOW ABOUT THIS, JADE ?
OF COURSE.
IT'S RARE TO SEE IT MOVING.
RARE INDEED.
IT'S EVEN MORE RARE TO SEE IT STOP IN THE MIDDLE. SOMETHING GOOD'S GOING TO HAPPEN TODAY.
YAY.
★ THE END.

TRANSLATION NOTES

UNWELL-CUTE *page 97*

Phos is probably unaware that this is a reference to a real fashion
trend in Japan, known as *yami kawaii*. *Kawaii* means "cute," and
yami means "ill" or "unhealthy," often in a mental context. Now
that Phos's emotional issues have been partially resolved, the gem
is back to somewhat normal health, physically and mentally. The
fashion style tends to include eye patches, bandages, syringes, and
pastel colors.

CAIRNGORM'S SMOKY QUARTZ ARM *page 168*

As Rutile explains, when gems are missing large pieces,
those limbs can be replaced with materials similar to the
gem's mineral makeup. In the case of Cairngorm, smoky
quartz would be especially effective, because cairngorm is
itself the gemstone quality variety of smoky quartz. Inci-
dentally, the name "cairngorm" comes from the mountains
in Scotland where the gem can be found.

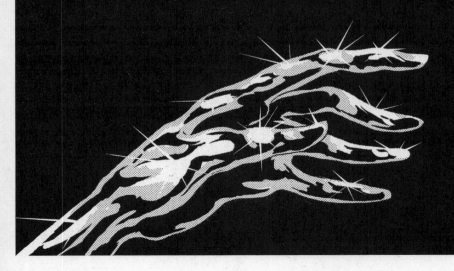

LAND OF THE LUSTROUS

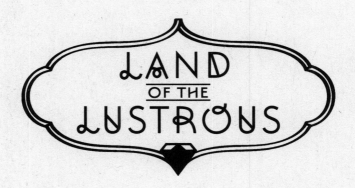

JAPANESE EDITION INSIDE COVER GALLERY
Volume 3

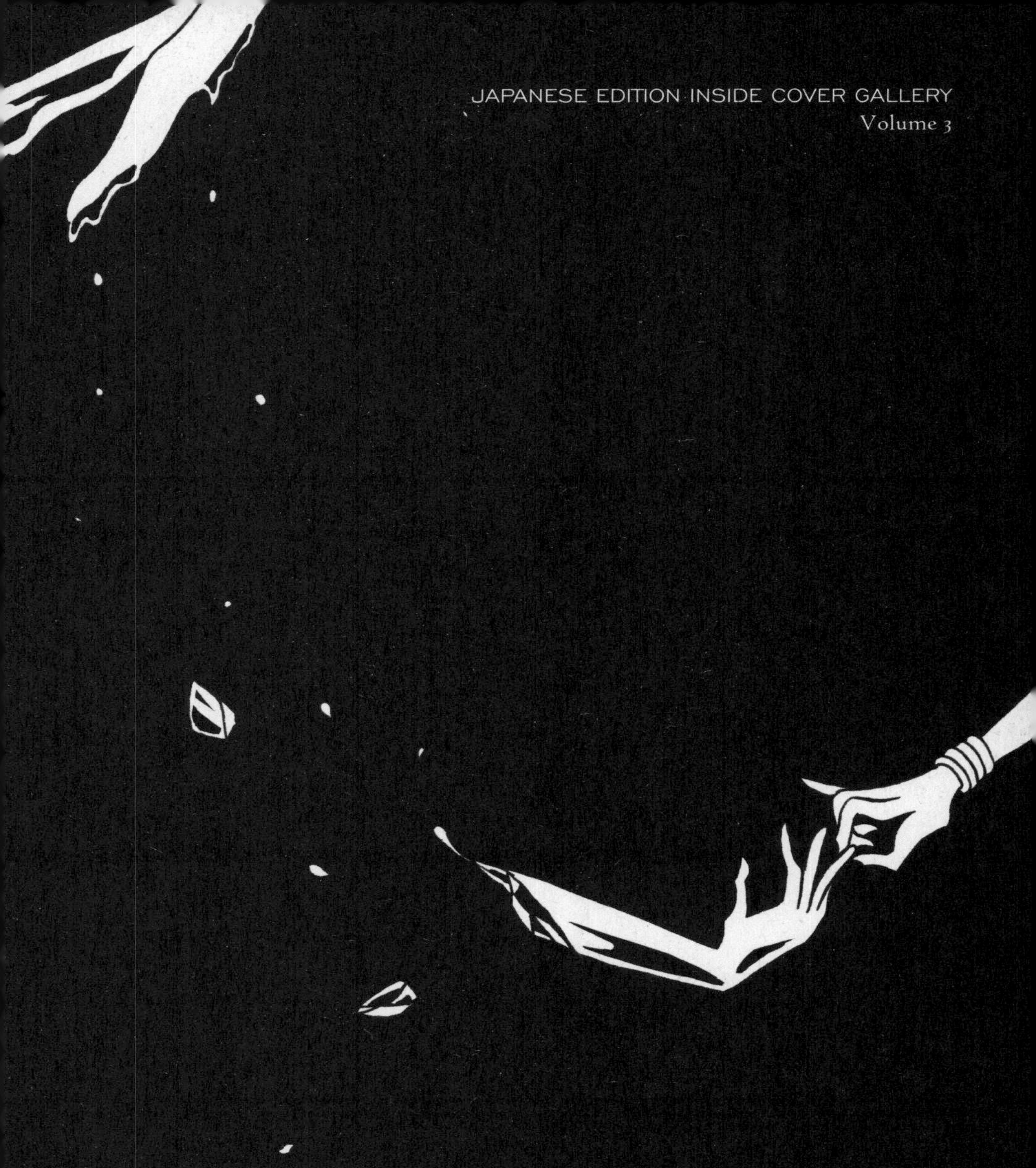

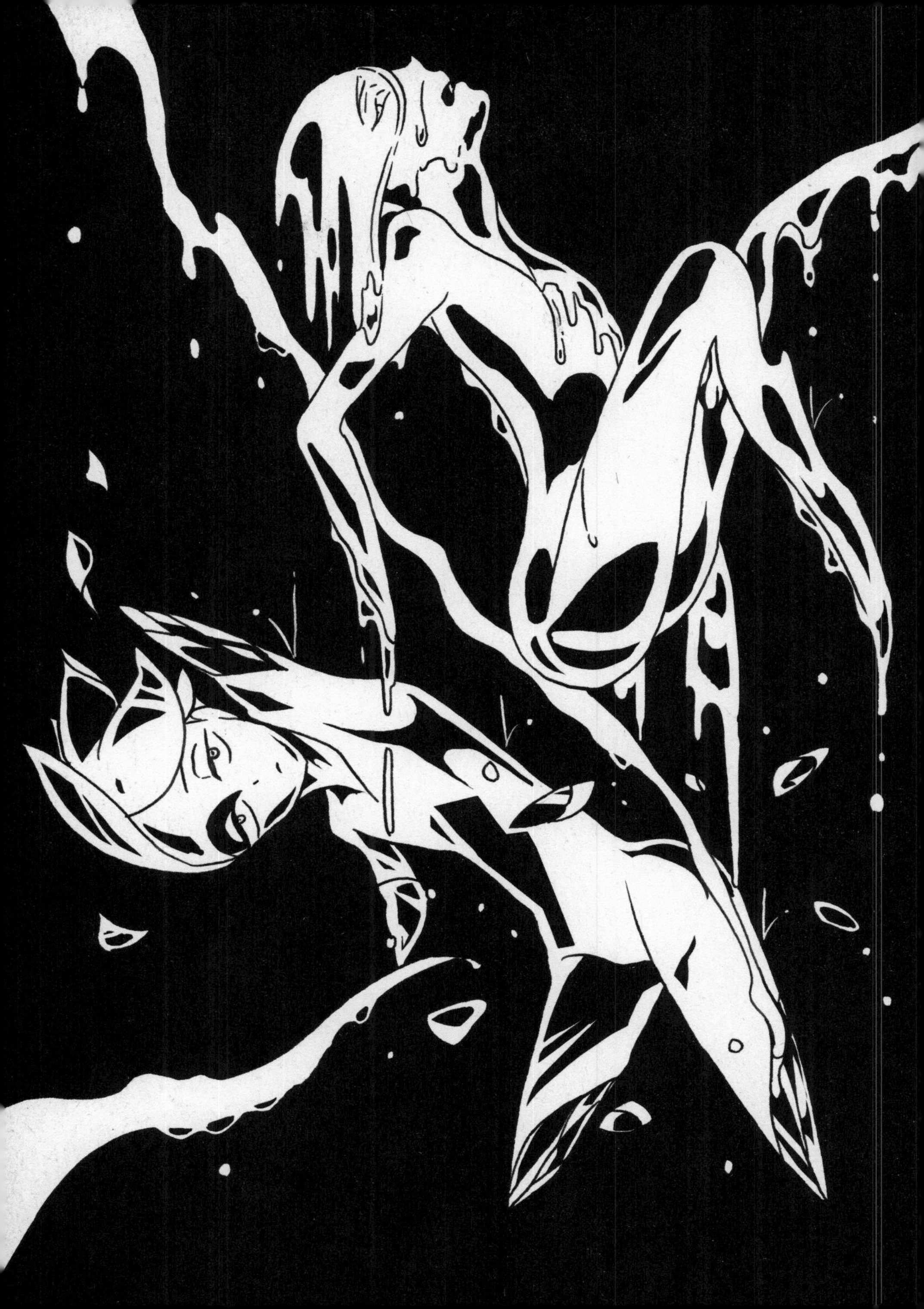

Volume 4

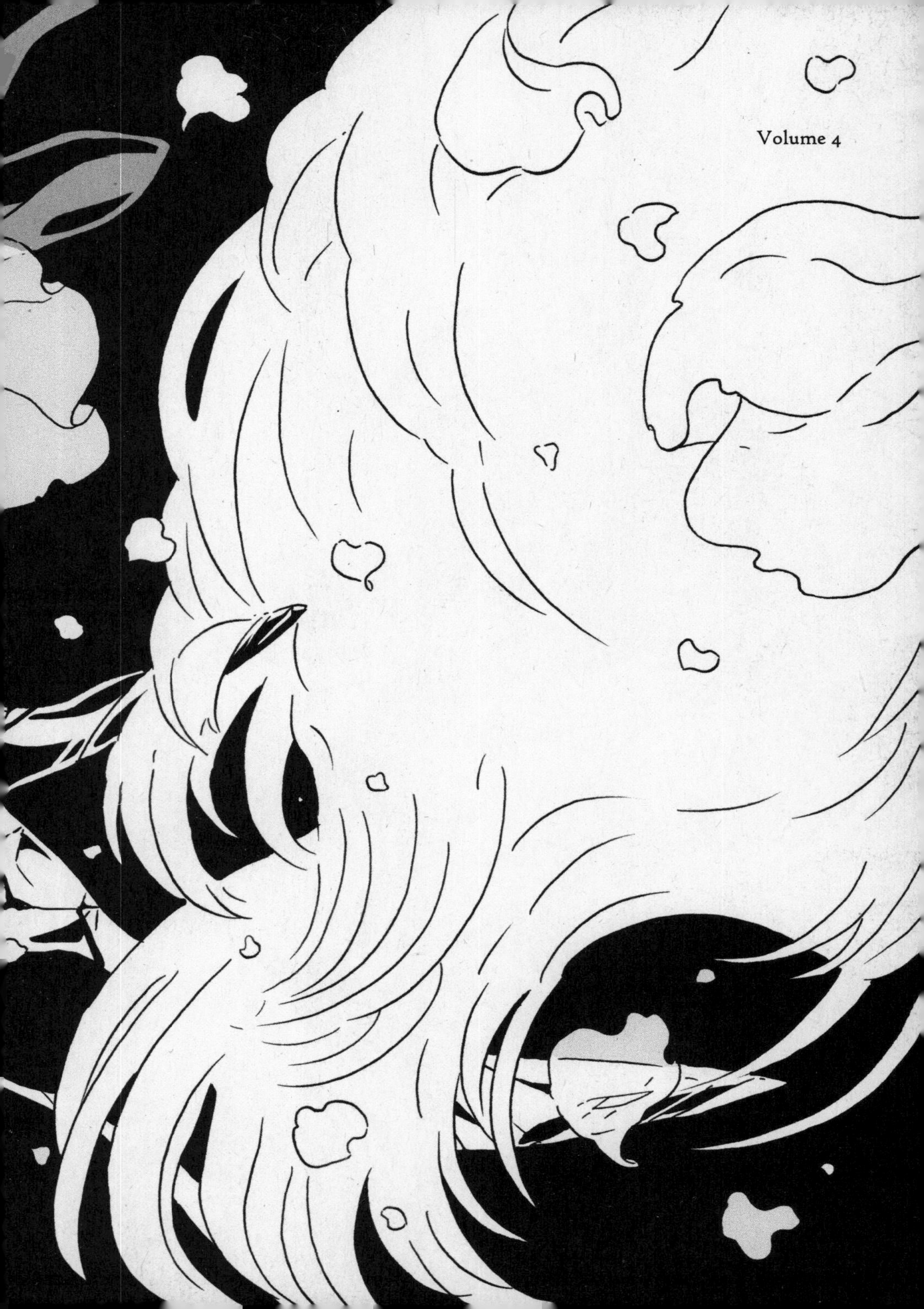

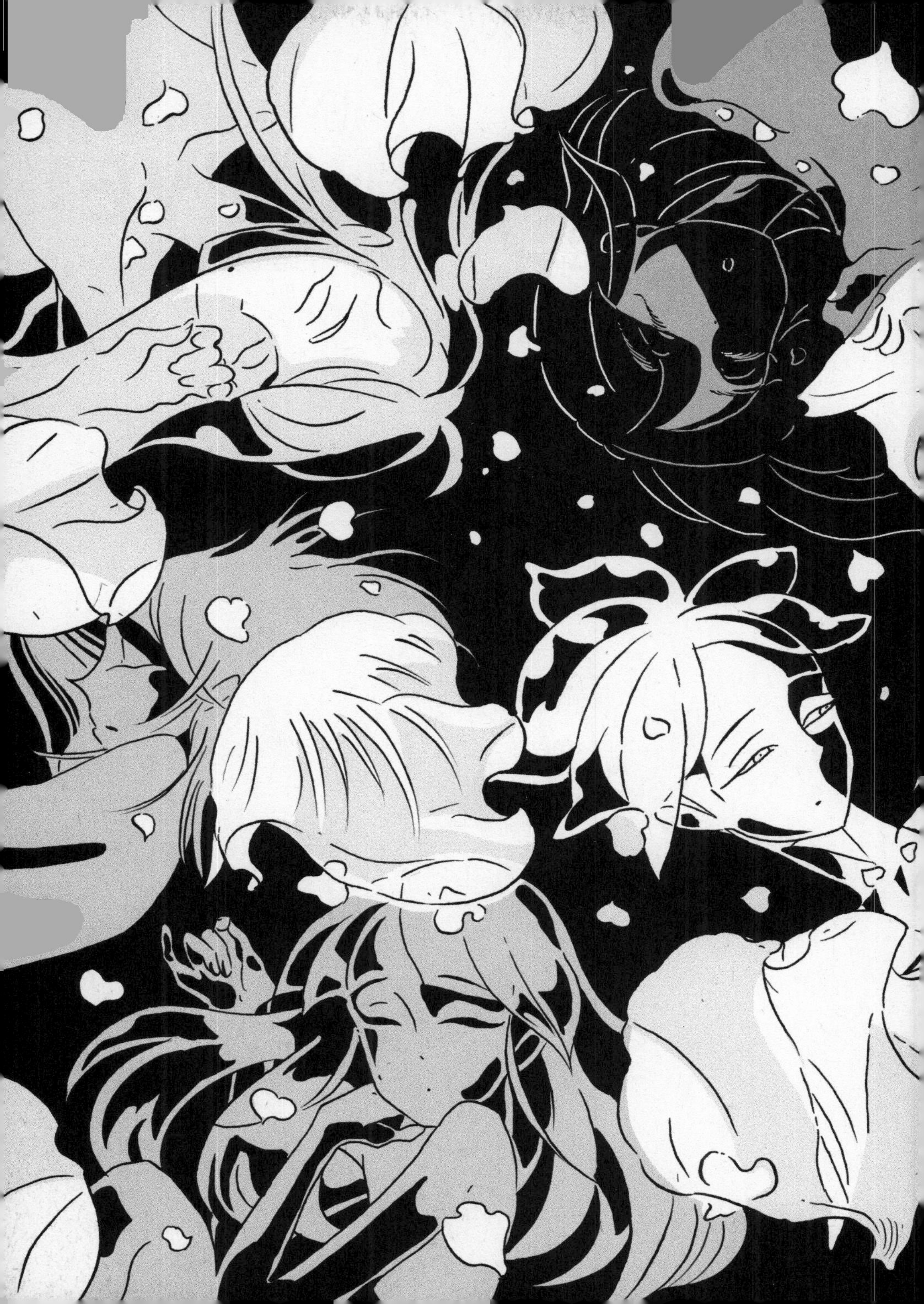

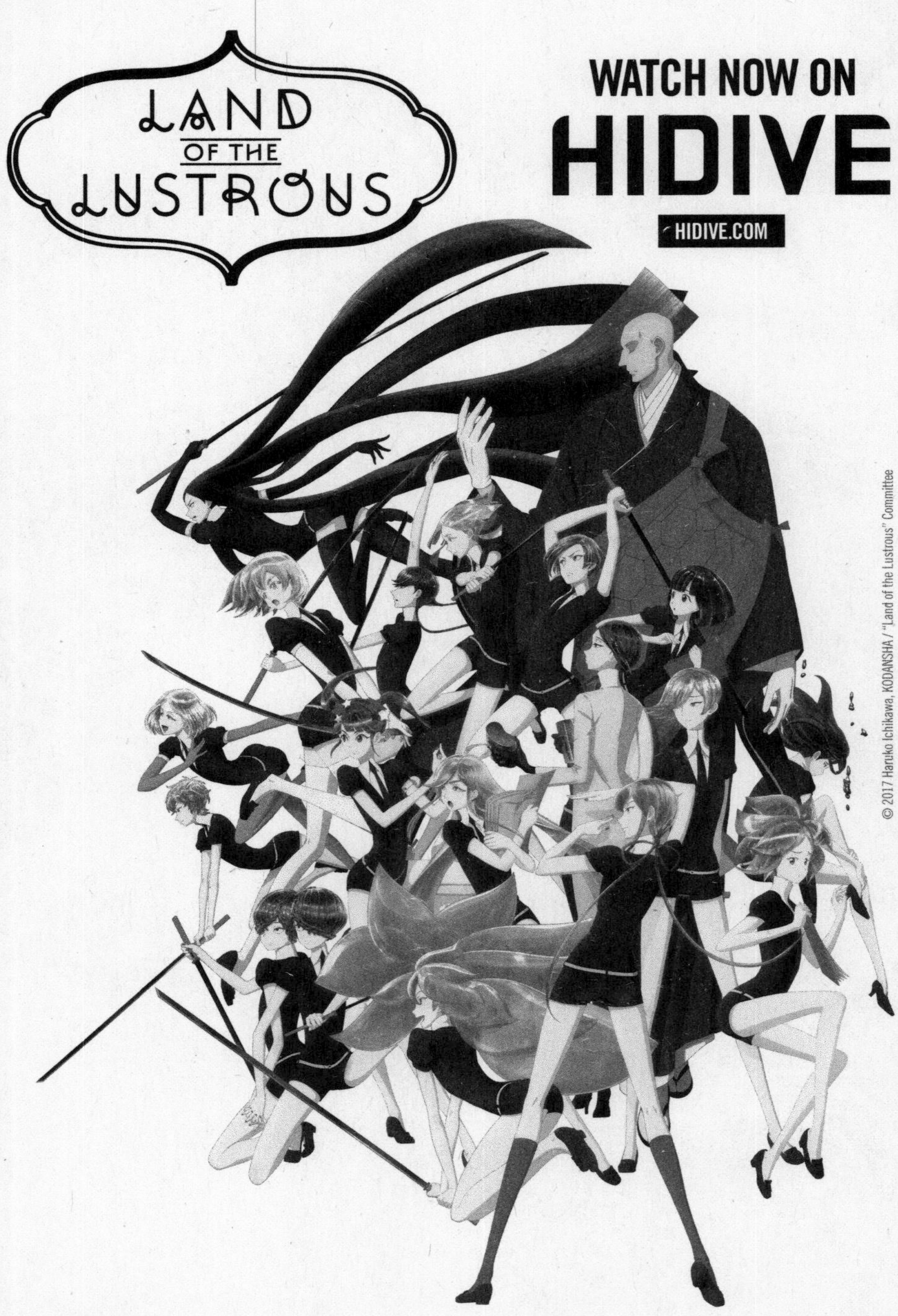

LAND OF THE LUSTROUS

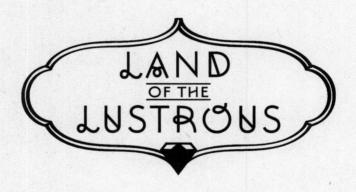

DELUXE EDITION

BATTLE ANGEL ALITA

After more than a decade out of print, the original cyberpunk action classic returns in glorious 400-page hardcover deluxe editions, featuring an all-new translation, color pages, and new cover designs!

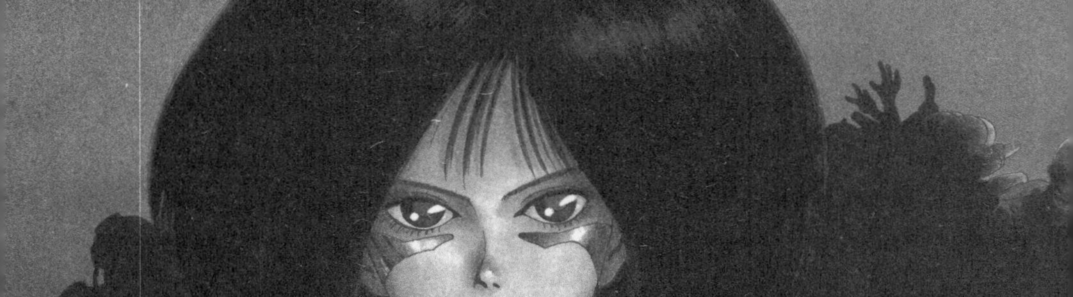
KC
KODANSHA COMICS

Far beneath the shimmering space-city of Zalem lie the trash-heaps of The Scrapyard... Here, cyber-doctor and bounty hunter Daisuke Ido finds the head and torso of an amnesiac cyborg girl. He names her Alita and vows to fill her life with beauty, but in a moment of desperation, a fragment of Alita's mysterious past awakens in her. She discovers that she possesses uncanny prowess in the legendary martial art known as panzerkunst. With her newfound skills, Alita decides to become a hunter-warrior - tracking down and taking out those who prey on the weak. But can she hold onto her humanity in the dark and gritty world of The Scrapyard?

KC

KODANSHA
COMICS

A new
series
from the
creator
of *Soul
Eater*, the
megahit
manga and
anime seen
on Toonami!

"Fun and lively...
a great start!"
-Adventures in
Poor Taste

FIRE FORCE

By Atsushi Ohkubo

The city of Tokyo is plagued by a deadly phenomenon: spontaneous human combustion! Luckily, a special team is there to quench the inferno: The Fire Force! The fire soldiers at Special Fire Cathedral 8 are about to get a unique addition. Enter Shinra, a boy who possesses the power to run at the speed of a rocket, leaving behind the famous "devil's footprints" (and destroying his shoes in the process). Can Shinra and his colleagues discover the source of this strange epidemic before the city burns to ashes?

Japan's most powerful spirit medium delves into the ghost world's greatest mysteries!

Story by Kyo Shirodaira, famed author of mystery fiction and creator of *Spiral*, *Blast of Tempest*, and *The Record of a Fallen Vampire*.

Both touched by spirits called yôkai, Kotoko and Kurô have gained unique superhuman powers. But to gain her powers Kotoko has given up an eye and a leg, and Kurô's personal life is in shambles. So when Kotoko suggests they team up to deal with renegades from the spirit world, Kurô doesn't have many other choices, but Kotoko might just have a few ulterior motives...

IN/SPECTRE

STORY BY **KYO SHIRODAIRA**
ART BY **CHASHIBA KATASE**

"I'm pleasantly surprised to find modern shojo using cross-dressing as a dramatic device to deliver social commentary... Recommended."

-Otaku USA Magazine

The prince in his dark days

By Hico Yamanaka

A drunkard for a father, a household of poverty... For 17-year-old Atsuko, misfortune is all she knows and believes in. Until one day, a chance encounter with Itaru–the wealthy heir of a huge corporation–changes everything. The two look identical, uncannily so. When Itaru curiously goes missing, Atsuko is roped into being his stand-in. There, in his shoes, Atsuko must parade like a prince in a palace. She encounters many new experiences, but at what cost…?

New action series from Hiroyuki Takei, creator of the classic shonen franchise Shaman King!

In medieval Japan, a bell hanging on the collar is a sign that a cat has a master. Norachiyo's bell hangs from his katana sheath, but he is nonetheless a stray — a ronin. This one-eyed cat samurai travels across a dishonest world, cutting through pretense and deception with his blade.

By
Hiroyuki Takei

Based on the critically acclaimed classic horror manga

The first new *Parasyte* manga in over 20 years!

NEO
ParaSyte f

BY ASUMIKO NAKAMURA, EMA TOYAMA, MIKI RINNO, LALAKO KOJIMA, KAORI YUKI, BANKO KUZE, YUUKI OBATA, KASHIO, YUI KUROE, ASIA WATANABE, MIKIMAKI, HIKARU SURUGA, HAJIME SHINJO, RENJURO KINDAICHI, AND YURI NARUSHIMA

A collection of chilling new *Parasyte* stories from Japan's top shojo artists!

Parasites: shape-shifting aliens whose only purpose is to assimilate with and consume the human race... but do these monsters have a different side? A parasite becomes a prince to save his romance-obsessed female host from a dangerous stalker. Another hosts a cooking show, in which the real monsters are revealed. These and 13 more stories, from some of the greatest shojo manga artists alive today, together make up a chilling, funny, and entertaining tribute to one of manga's horror classics!

KC
KODANSHA
COMICS

Again!!
アゲイン!!

Kinichiro Imamura isn't a bad guy, really, but on the first day of high school his narrow eyes and bleached blonde hair made him look so shifty that his classmates assumed the worst. Three years later, without any friends or fond memories, he isn't exactly feeling bittersweet about graduation. But after an accidental fall down a flight of stairs, Kinichiro wakes up three years in the past... on the first day of high school! School's starting again—but it's gonna be different this time around!

Vol. 1-3 now available in **PRINT** and **DIGITAL**!
Vol. 4 coming August 2018!
Find out **MORE** by visiting:
kodanshacomics.com/MitsurouKubo

ABOUT MITSUROU KUBO

Mitsurou Kubo is a manga artist born in Nagasaki prefecture. Her series *3.3.7 Byoshi!!* (2001-2003), *Tokkyu!!* (2004-2008), and *Again!!* (2011-2014) were published in *Weekly Shonen Magazine*, and *Moteki* (2008-2010) was published in the seinen comics magazine *Evening*. After the publication of *Again!!* concluded, she met Sayo Yamamoto, director of the global smash-hit anime *Yuri!!! on ICE*. Working with Yamamoto, Kubo contributed the original concept, original character designs, and initial script for *Yuri!!! on ICE*. *Again!!* is her first manga to be published in English.

KC KODANSHA COMICS

ANIME COMING SUMMER 2018

The award-winning manga about what happens inside you!

“Far more entertaining than it ought to be... What kid doesn’t want to think that every time they sneeze, a torpedo shoots out their nose?”

—Anime News Network

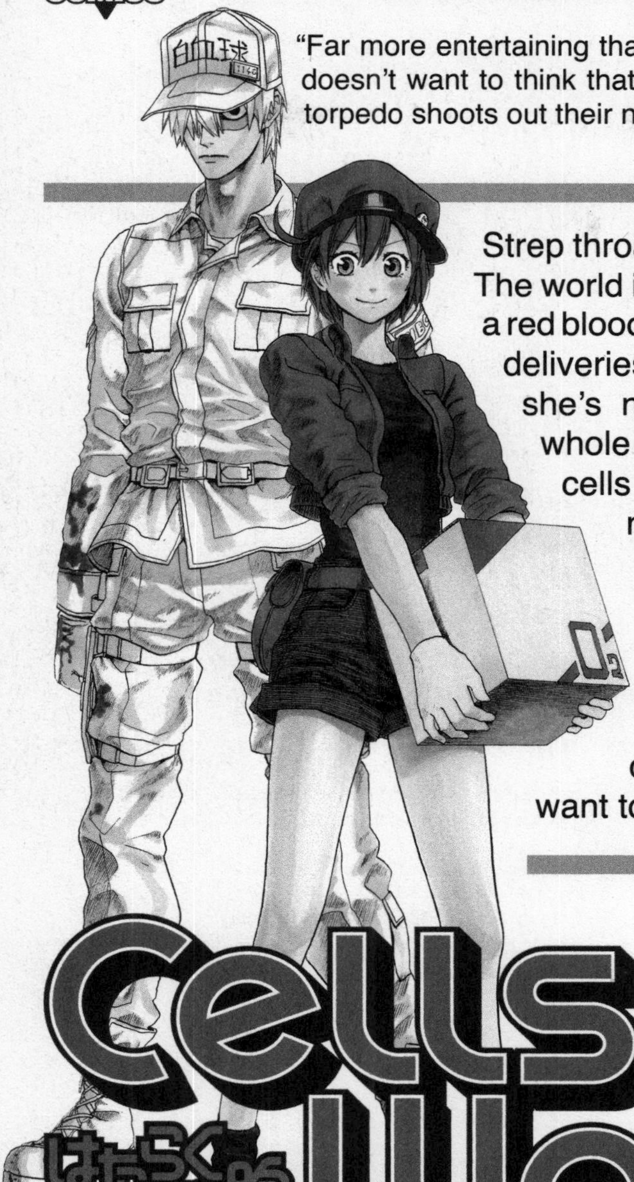

Strep throat! Hay fever! Influenza! The world is a dangerous place for a red blood cell just trying to get her deliveries finished. Fortunately, she’s not alone. She’s got a whole human body’s worth of cells ready to help out! The mysterious white blood cell, the buff and brash killer T cell, the nerdy neuron, even the cute little platelets—everyone’s got to come together if they want to keep you healthy!

Cells at Work!

はたらく細胞

By **Akane Shimizu**

A Kodansha Comics Trade Paperback Original.

Land of the Lustrous volume 6 copyright © 2016 Haruko Ichikawa
English translation copyright © 2018 Haruko Ichikawa

Published in the United States by Kodansha Comics, an imprint of Kodansha USA Publishing, LLC, New York.

Publication rights for this English edition arranged through Kodansha Ltd., Tokyo.

First published in Japan in 2016 by Kodansha Ltd., Tokyo.

ISBN 978-1-63236-636-8

Printed in the United States of America.

www.kodanshacomics.com

9 8 7 6 5 4 3 2 1

Translator: Alethea Nibley & Athena Nibley
Lettering: Evan Hayden
Editing: Lauren Scanlan